ANTHROPOLOGY AND ART

Texas Press Sourcebooks in Anthropology
were originally published by the Natural History Press, a division of Doubleday and Company, Inc. Responsibility for the series now resides with the University of Texas Press, Box 7819, Austin, Texas 78713-7819. Whereas the series has been a joint effort between the American Museum of Natural History and the Natural History Press, future volumes in the series will be selected through the auspices of the editorial offices of the University of Texas Press.

The purpose of the series will remain unchanged in its efforts to make available inexpensive, up-to-date, and authoritative volumes for the student and the general reader in the field of anthropology.

Charlotte M. Otten
received her M.A. from the University of Chicago and her Ph.D. from the University of Michigan. She has taught at the University of Minnesota and the University of Wisconsin and at present is professor of anthropology at Northern Illinois University.

Dr. Otten has participated in archaeological field work in Iraq, has conducted research in blood-group serology, and has taught courses in physical anthropology and primitive art. She is the editor of *Aggression and Evolution*.

Anthropology and Art

Readings in Cross-Cultural Aesthetics

Edited by Charlotte M. Otten

University of Texas Press
Austin

Copyright ©1971 by Charlotte M. Otten
All rights reserved
Printed in the United States of America

Third University of Texas Press Printing, 1990

Requests for permission to reproduce material from this work should be sent to Permissions, University of Texas Press, Box 7819, Austin, Texas 78713-7819.

∞ The paper used in this publication meets the minimum requirements of American National Standard for Information Sciences—Permanence of Paper for Printed Library Materials ANSI Z39.48-1984.

Previously published by the Natural History Press in cooperation with Doubleday & Co., Inc., and the American Museum of Natural History.

Library of Congress Cataloging-in-Publication Data

Otten, Charlotte M   1915– comp.

   Anthropology and art.
   (Texas Press sourcebooks in anthropology; 10)
   Reprint of the ed. published for the American Museum of Natural History by the Natural History Press, Garden City, N.Y., in series: American Museum sourcebooks in anthropology.
Bibliography: p.
Includes index.
1. Art, Primitive—Addresses, essays, lectures. I. Title. II. Series. III. Series: American Museum sourcebooks in anthropology.
[N5311.075   1976]   709'.01'1   75-43853
ISBN 0-292-70313-9

ACKNOWLEDGMENTS

I should like to thank Charles Wicke and Louise E. Sweet for helpfully criticizing the first draft of my introduction, and Paul Bohannan for editing the final version. I thank Catharine McClellan for suggesting articles to include. I am grateful to the authors and publishers whose co-operation has made this book possible, especially Peter J. Ucko and Andrée Rosenfeld, who kindly assisted with the abridgment of their text. I would also like to express my appreciation to Richard A. Waterman and Douglas Fraser for preparing adaptations of their articles for this volume. Lastly, I thank my colleagues on the Anthropology staff at Northern Illinois University for their moral support, and my cheerful typist, Arnette Hintz.

CONTENTS

Acknowledgments	vii
CHARLOTTE M. OTTEN Introduction	xi

PART I BACKGROUND

PAUL H. SCHILLER Figural Preferences in the Drawings of a Chimpanzee	3
DOUGLAS FRASER The Discovery of Primitive Art	20

PART II THEORY AND METHOD

ROBERT REDFIELD Art and Icon	39
GEORGE MILLS Art: An Introduction to Qualitative Anthropology	66
ALAN P. MERRIAM The Arts and Anthropology	93
WARNER MUENSTERBERGER Roots of Primitive Art	106
TATIANA PROSKOURIAKOFF Studies on Middle American Art	129
ROBERT L. RANDS Discussion of Proskouriakoff's Paper	137
JOHN L. FISCHER Art Styles as Cultural Cognitive Maps	141

PART III THE PRIMITIVE ARTIST

EDMUND CARPENTER The Eskimo Artist	163
PAUL BOHANNAN Artist and Critic in an African Society	172
JANE C. GOODALE and JOAN D. KOSS The Cultural Context of Creativity among Tiwi	182

PART IV ACCULTURATION

ROY SIEBER The Arts and Their Changing Social Function	203

GEORGE KUBLER On the Colonial Extinction of the Motifs of Pre-Columbian Art ... 212

RICHARD A. WATERMAN African Influence on the Music of the Americas ... 227

PART V ART AREAS

PETER J. UCKO and ANDRÉE ROSENFELD Critical Analysis of Interpretations, and Conclusions and Problems from *Palaeolithic Cave Art* ... 247

GORDON R. WILLEY The Early Great Styles and the Rise of the Pre-Columbian Civilization ... 282

DUDLEY T. EASBY, JR. Ancient American Goldsmiths ... 298

LUIS A. A. DE ANDA and GORDON F. ECKHOLM Clay Sculpture from Jaina ... 311

ERNA GUNTHER Northwest Coast Indian Art ... 318

FROELICH RAINEY The Vanishing Art of the Arctic ... 341

FRANK WILLETT Ife in Nigerian Art ... 354

ADRIAN A. GERBRANDS Art as an Element of Culture in Africa ... 366

RALPH LINTON and PAUL S. WINGERT Introduction, New Zealand, Sepik River, and New Ireland from *Arts of the South Seas* ... 383

Bibliography ... 405

Index ... 428

INTRODUCTION

WHAT CAN be said about primitive ("ethnographic") art which has not already been said by art critics and historians writing of the arts of the great civilizations? Do we, as anthropologists, find the arts of non-literate peoples really different in character, in content, and in function from our own?

A number of answers to this question have been offered since the first ethnographic expeditions of almost a century ago, each generation treating that aspect which reflected its own current emphases and interests. Accordingly, technical influences upon primitive style were explored in considerable detail, and the transformation of motifs from a supposed primal naturalism to conventionalization and abstraction. Thereafter attention to art lagged, a neglect characteristic of an era in which anthropology was proving itself a "science." Current interest in the nature and evolution of human communication and in the study of cultures as human value-systems has had the effect of bringing the subject back to the foci of our concerns.

The question of a functional relationship between art and culture was first introduced by Ernest Grosse in 1894. In a remarkably "modern" book, he recognized the indispensable social element in artistic behavior among non-literate peoples, and called for a scientific rather than an aesthetic approach to its study.

Further searches for a correlation of social and economic structure with art style were delayed for decades. In 1928, Honigsheim suggested a relationship between matrilineal kin groups and achievement in plastic arts. Thirty years later, in a highly original study, John L. Fischer (8) related stylistic categories to social stratification, residence pattern, and form of marriage.

Most recently, Alvin W. Wolfe (1969) inquires why some societies produce more and better art than others; he appears to find an answer in male "cleavages," that, is, in the alienation of males from local lineage centers, brought about by matriliny. This social situation appears to Wolfe to generate an emotional climate predisposing the men to aesthetic expression. This sort of attempt to discover and define the nature of correlations between artistic and social/economic phenomena may well provide inroads to some very basic understandings, and offers tremendous research potential.

Few anthropologists have been concerned with the problem of the relation of style to cultural function of the art object. The several exceptions include Adrian A. Gerbrands (22) who, by his account of Vandenhoute's investigation of Dan masks, demonstrates that since masks may radically change their cultural usage and significance, any such relationship clearly cannot persist. Among the Mende, however, Roy Sieber (1965) reported a correlation observable in secret society masks, which fall into stylistic categories coinciding with their cultural functions. Probably the clearest example has been presented by Joan M. Vastokas (1967) and Dorothy Ray (1967) in their respective writings on Eskimo masks. Both find mythological beings represented by excessively distorted and abstracted features ("spirit masks") in contrast to the more realistic features of many shaman animal masks and "face masks" placed on graves. Vastokas explicitly notes that an increasing degree of formal abstraction and fantasy reflect the degree of functional power and sacredness. (1967:30.)

In attempting to utilize form-function relationships as tools in the interpretation of paleolithic art (working from known form to unknown function by the use of ethnographic parallels), Peter Ucko and Andrée Rosenfeld (15) detail the limitations and difficulties encountered in a half-century of attempts to reconstruct cultural significance of Franco-Cantabrian cave painting.

An exciting recent contribution to an anthropological approach to art derives from the researches of Paul Schiller (1) and Desmond Morris (1961) on the aesthetics of non-human primates. Certainly Schiller's observations on his chimpanzee Alpha, who deliberately placed her scribbling so as to balance and complete eccentric figures, are revolutionary in the light of previous beliefs that aesthetic sensibility constitutes a qualitative distinction between man and other animals. Equally epochal are the astonishing "abstract" paintings produced by Morris' chimp Congo of the London Zoo, whose fan-pattern trade-mark evolved through a long series of variations: plain fans, split fans, superimposed fans, fans with contrasting central dots or blobs of color filling interstices or gaps in split-fan patterns, lopsided fans, and even, ultimately, reversed fans. Any uniquely human function, it now appears, must relate not to a kinesthetic sense of balance, rhythm, or symmetry, as demonstrated by Alpha and Congo as well as by other chimpanzees "dancing" or stamping in unison, but rather to the investment of markings (at first arbitrary, and then intentional) with "meaning," in other words, with symbolic significance. I write, of course, with a certainty which time may challenge, assuming here that no particular meaning attaches to, say, the fan pattern in the mind of Congo.

In any event, these considerations lead to that aspect which has been central to the interests of many of us. Concern for the symbolic nature of human thought, language, and art stems largely from the works of Charles Peirce (1931), Ernst Cassirer (1923, 1946), Susanne Langer (1942), C. K. Ogden and I. A. Richards (1923) and Charles Morris (1938) on the nature and function of symbolic phenomena. By "symbolic" I refer here not only to the direct denotative meaning or representation, but, as Alan P. Merriam (5) points out, also to emotional import and to cultural assignments (symbols designating or connotating class, clan, sex, age, political or religious affiliations, and economic status, as well as ritual, magical, or domestic usage, and so on) all functioning simultaneously. On a deeper level, art symbols are thought covertly or unconsciously to express forbidden and repressed sexual wishes and fantasies, according to the psychoanalytic hypotheses of Sigmund Freud (1922:314–15), as interpreted by Warner Muensterberger (10), George Devereux (1961), and Géza Róheim (1941).

Perhaps the most sensitive single work analyzing symbolic activities (arts, religion, ideology) in terms of specific Javanese culture is offered by Clifford Geertz (1957). Conceiving of man as a symboling, meaning-seeking, and meaning-assigning creature, he stresses man's primary need to make coherent sense out of experience, fully as pressing as the need for biological survival. This symbol-stressing approach is basic to the study of values and, accordingly, to an understanding of the forces resulting in the internal consistency of specific cultural idioms, styles, and processes; centripetal energy which holds them to their unique cultural configurations. "Their [sacred symbols'] peculiar power comes from their presumed ability to identify fact with value at the most fundamental level" (1957:422).

Here, I think, lies the heart of the matter, and a crucial reason why we *cannot* validly equate the arts of non-literate peoples with those of late civilizations in which writing has permeated the culture as the ordinary medium of communication and information storage, an equation which a host of well-meaning teachers and art critics are ever striving to enforce ("Their art is just like ours; it uses the same aesthetic bases, and seems strange only because of unfamiliarity, etc. etc."). In pre-literate or proto-literate culture, the art symbol *becomes* the fact; that is it simultaneously represents, defines, and manifests its referent. In such cultures, art objects and events serve as media for information storage, rather than books. In Western culture, conversely, we ordinarily define a fact in writing, or in the form of writing. Accordingly, in asking the "meaning" of an art event, we are asking for a translation into discursive mode, embalmed in a tradition of literacy, a translation which (as all artists are acutely aware) cannot be achieved, especially with regard to ethnographic and archaeologic expressions. The work of art remains essentially untranslatable (Langer 1942).

Our Western (increasingly "non-objective") art only partially and sporadically carries this freight of prescribed symbolic

Introduction xv

meaning functioning simultaneously on many levels, reinforcing cultural values and at once enlarging, sensitizing, and unifying our perceptions. Accordingly, we are experiencing along with the fragmentation of our value system, the disintegration of symbolic unity and coherence in art. This is, of course, why art invariably deteriorates and becomes peripheral when internal cultural integrity is disturbed and dislocated by new elements in acculturation and the breakdown of a former system of values.

The almost total neglect accorded the process of acculturation in art is difficult to explain. Almost any ethnographer will comment verbally upon the deterioration and rapid change in art style and function in his area associated with tourism and the almost limitless demand for cheap souvenir items or "pseudo-ethnographic" art objects. Yet systematic studies of the exact sources and nature of cultural pressures, the differential changes in various styles and functional categories, and the avenues and modes of transformation have been, as yet, hardly attempted. Meanwhile acculturation goes on apace. The writings of Roy Sieber (12) and George Kubler (13) are exceptions to this almost universal oversight and provide us with valuable first steps in analyzing the behavior of art symbols, styles, and functions under cultural duress.

The inclusion of only one work dealing with an art form other than visual is due both to the traditional emphasis in university curricula and to the limitations of the editor as well as available space. Students desiring further information on the anthropology of music are referred to Merriam's (1964) impressive work. A comprehensive introduction to literature on dance has been published by Gertrude Kurath (1960).

The areal studies included are, of course, in no way exhaustive, nor could they be, but represent rather a sampling of many excellent accounts. I regret that I have been unable to add selections from the Near East, Central Asia, the Far East, India, or Indonesia—but efforts to fill this gap were frustrated by the unavailability of articles, or failure to locate their authors, or elicit response.

Inevitably, in assembling such an anthology, one feels keenly the many oversights and omissions. Articles which rightfully belong among this company but which were too long and tightly woven for abridgment, or which were, for one reason or another, unavailable, were the necessary victims of a most difficult choice. So I offer this final collection with mixed feelings of satisfaction and apology, and the conviction that only in three volumes rather than one could a justly representative collection be assembled.

CHARLOTTE M. OTTEN

DeKalb, Illinois
1970

Part I ∥ BACKGROUND

FIGURAL PREFERENCES IN THE DRAWINGS OF A CHIMPANZEE

Paul H. Schiller[1]

THE STUDY of perceptual organization in animals has been hampered by the difficulty in finding clearly interpretable modes of testing other than by discriminative choice. The method of equivalent stimuli (Klüver 1933) has provided almost the only approach to analysis of visual organization. This method permits the study of selective figure formation and figural dominance, of similarities or common attributes of figures, and of some aspects of perceptual generalization, but it is very limited in the kinds of questions that it can present to the animal. The predilection of one of the chimpanzees at the Yerkes Laboratories for "drawing" has provided a unique method for analysis of structuring of the visual field. This animal, Alpha, an 18-year-old female,[2] has for many years shown a great interest in scribbling. Whenever she sees a member of the staff with pencil and notebook, she begs and, if given pencil and paper, retires with them to a corner

---

Reprinted from *The Journal of Comparative and Physiological Psychology* 44 (2) 1951:101–11, copyright by the American Psychological Association, by permission of Mrs. K. S. Lashley and the American Psychological Association.

[1] Among the effects of Dr. Schiller were more than two hundred "drawings" by the chimpanzee, Alpha. Except for a brief description prepared to accompany an exhibit of some drawings at the XII International Congress of Psychology, there were no notes on the experiments. I had frequently discussed the study with him and observed the experiments, and had myself made some earlier tests of Alpha's reactions to patterns. I have therefore undertaken to report the work with such of Dr. Schiller's interpretations as I recall. (K. S. Lashley)

[2] Her early development was studied by Jacobsen, Jacobsen, and Yoshioka (1932).

of her cage. She grasps the pencil with four fingers across the palm and with her thumb extended along it almost to the point. This clumsy grasp makes it necessary for her to keep her forearm almost vertical in order to bring the pencil point on the paper. She places the paper on the floor, makes a few marks on it, usually turns it over repeatedly, and continues to make marks until the pencil point breaks. She uses either hand with equal facility, but more frequently the right. Her "drawings" are formless scribbling, much like those produced by Klüver's Cebus, but it was noted that she tended to mark in the corners of the paper, often folding it, apparently to get new corners. This fact suggested a study of her reactions to figures already present on the drawing paper.

METHOD

Although Alpha will occasionally return the paper after making her drawing, she usually tears it up. To avoid such destruction of the records, the paper was fastened to a 12×15 in. board having a short handle, which could be inserted through the space below the cage door and held by the experimenter. A gray cardboard frame, 2 in. wide, was attached to the drawing board and sheets of paper slipped under the frame, which thus exposed a surface 8×11 in. As test objects, various figures were cut from colored paper and pasted to sheets of contrasting color, or openings were cut in the sheets and contrasting paper pasted behind.

Alpha was given one or sometimes two pencils of different colors and allowed to draw for from 10 to 180 sec. before the board was withdrawn. Only rarely did she attempt to snatch the board or to tear off the paper. Throughout the test periods she usually squatted before the drawing board, intent on her scribbling. The date, time spent in drawing, and unusual distractions such as screaming by other animals, were noted on each drawing.

The test objects were devised for a variety of purposes: study of color preference, of figure formation, of the influence of the form, position, and size of figure or groups of figures, and of tendencies to figure-completion and to production of symmetrical, balanced masses. More than two hundred drawings were secured. A few of these have been selected for reproduction.

Many of the drawings are in colored crayon on paper of the same color and do not photograph well. Because of this and to save cost of half tones, the drawings have been copied with India ink at reduced size. The figures presented by the experimenter are indicated by dotted outlines or, in a few cases where outlines might be ambiguous, by stippled surfaces. Alpha's scribblings were copied free-hand, with the aid of projection apparatus and proportional dividers. All short dashes and distinct lines are reproduced with reasonable accuracy; in dense scribbling the direction of the lines was copied but not their number, which often could not be made out. In each case the top of the text figure is the edge next to the side of the cage. Alpha usually sat facing the bottom of the figure but sometimes worked from the side.

RESULTS

General conditions

The materials which elicit Alpha's drawings are limited. Only pencils or wood-covered crayons are used. Colored chalk or paper-wrapped wax crayons are chewed up without attempts to mark with them. Alpha never draws on the gray cement walls or floor of her cage. Paper and cardboard are used, but plywood and heavier materials are rejected.[3]

Types of markings

Alpha uses chiefly two strokes: (1) Short dashes made by flexing the wrist, with little arm movement. The direction is usually in the line from thumb to elbow, with greatest pressure at the start. Unsteadiness in bringing pencil to paper often produces a sort

---

[3] Dr. Nissen reports that once when no paper was provided, she found and tried to draw on a dead leaf.

of check mark. These dashes are most frequent when the drawing field is restricted or when she is following contours. (2) Broad, nearly parallel, zigzag strokes made from the elbow, extending from lower left to upper right, if made with the right hand, or with opposite slope, if with the left. Curved lines and flourishes are rare. There is some preference for short strokes with a sharp pencil and for broader scribbling with a soft crayon, making wider marks.

Drawing on blank paper

Given an unmarked sheet, Alpha usually makes short strokes in each corner, then along the margins, and finally fills in the middle with coarser scribblings (Figure 1). This pattern is much the same, whether she is drawing with black on white, with white on black, or with black on black. The presence of scattered dashes and lines made by the experimenter and similar to those which she herself makes does not seem to influence her drawing. She marked on the gray frame only two or three times during the entire series of tests.

During the 6 months when she had almost daily tests her drawings on blank paper changed considerably. Some of the later ones consist entirely of broad, heavy strokes centered on the paper (Figure 2).

Influence of a single figure

If a square or irregular polygon more than an inch in diameter is placed on the paper, Alpha marks almost exclusively within the figure (Figures 3 and 4). This is true, whether the figure is in black on white ground, in white on black ground, or in any combination of colors. The degree of visibility of her marks seems of no consequence. Of 25 large, single figures presented, only three show a significant number of marks outside of the figure.

If the single figure is less than an inch in diameter, Alpha rarely marks within it as she does with larger figures. Nevertheless, the presence of the single figure distinctly modified her reaction to the background. In 21 such tests she only once produced a

Figural Preferences in Drawings of a Chimpanzee

 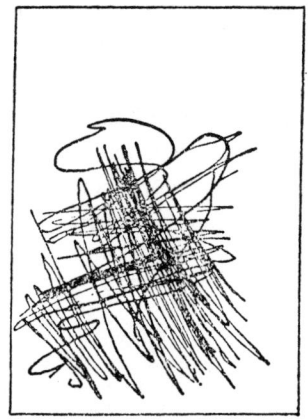

FIG. 1. Aug. 13. White Ground, Blue and Red Crayons, 3 Min.
FIG. 2. Dec. 18. White Ground, Black and Blue Crayons, 40 Sec.

 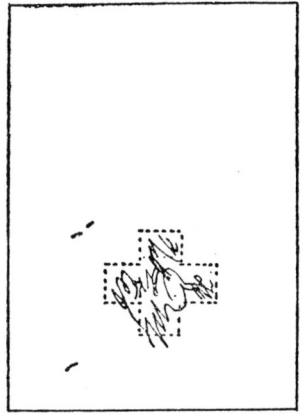

FIG. 3. Sept. 15. Black Circle, White Ground, Yellow Crayon, 1 Min.
FIG. 4. Aug. 18. White Cross, Black Ground, Yellow Crayon, 1 Min.

pattern like her typical response to the blank sheet, marking in the corners and along the margins. The remaining examples fall definitely into two types: If the figure is near the middle of the sheet, it becomes a starting point or focal point for broad scribbling (Figure 5). If it is off center, she tends to focus her scribbling in the largest open space (Figure 6), producing a sort of balance between her markings and the presented figure. There is some reason to believe that this is a genuine tendency to balance masses in the total configuration, since the very strong tendency to draw at the corners and margins of a blank sheet is completely inhibited by the small figure, and the position of her drawing therefore cannot be interpreted merely as a tendency to fill the blank spaces.

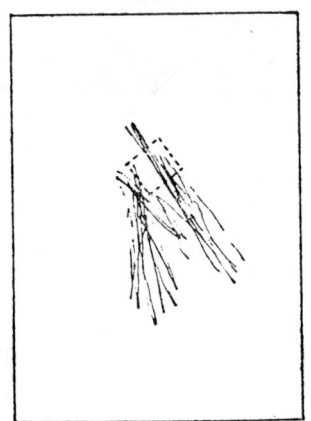 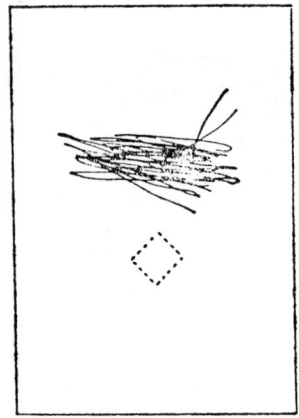

Fig. 5. Dec. 12. Green Square, White Ground, Green and Blue Crayons, 10 Sec.
Fig. 6. Dec. 6. Green Square, Black Ground, Green and Blue Crayons, 10 Sec.

Heavy, single bars across the page induce sweeping marks more or less at right angles to them. In four tests, each with a single black bar, horizontal, vertical, and at 45 degrees from right and from left, all are crossed by scores of scribbled lines. In three of the four there is not a single line crossing the bar at less than 45 degrees. In two instances a bar of gray paper, one-half inch wide, of the same shade as the framing cardboard was pasted across the sheet. The reaction to this was entirely different from that to black bars. No marks were made on it, and each half of the sheet was treated as a separate blank sheet, as in Figure 1.

Outlined figures

If instead of solid figures outlines are presented, scribbling is largely or wholly restricted to the space within the outline (Figure 7). This is true in 22 of 24 examples. The value of the outline is readily modified, however. When the width of the lines is greater than one-fourth of the enclosed space, the space and enclosing lines are treated as separate figures, the space being filled with scribbling and the outline with short dashes (Figure 8) (three of four examples). When a large solid figure is placed within the outline, it and the outline are treated as figures and the space between usually left blank (four of five examples).

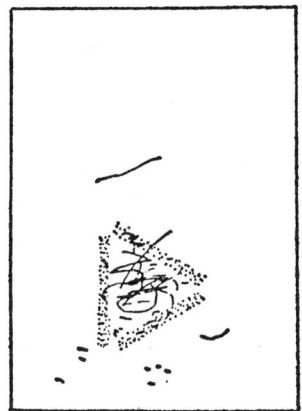 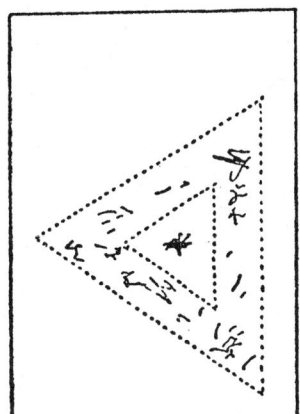

FIG. 7. Aug. 28. White Outlines, Black Ground, Green Crayon, 90 Sec.
FIG. 8. Aug. 27. Red Triangle, Green Center, Green Ground, Black Crayon, 2 Min.

Structuring of multiple spots

Spots scattered at random on a sheet do not define a field for Alpha. If large, each is treated as a separate figure within which her scribblings are confined. If small, she fills in the spaces between them or, if they form a close group, she scribbles over them

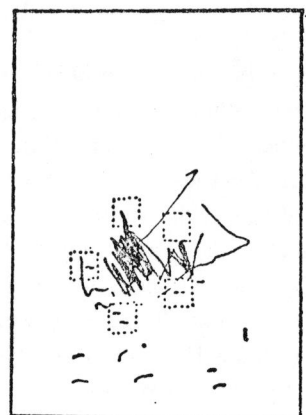 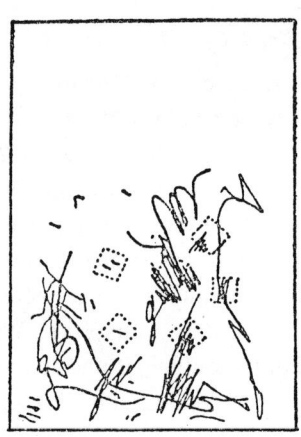

FIG. 9. Aug. 27. White Squares, Black Ground, Green Crayon, 90 Sec.
FIG. 10. Sept. 26. White Squares, Violet Ground, Yellow Crayon, 3 Min.

as if they were a single large figure. Although she never marks upon a single small figure, she frequently puts check marks on each when there are several on the sheet (Figures 9 and 10).

When the small spots enclose a fairly regular polygon, this becomes an in-field within which almost all of the scribbling is confined (Figure 9). Three spots, defining a triangle, and four spots, defining a square, do not regularly elicit this response. There is a greater tendency to mark in the space which they surround than at the sides or corners of the sheet, but the large spaces between the spots invite excursions outside. Where five or more spots define a regular figure, practically all scribblings are within that figure (eight of eight examples).

The addition of a large central spot destroys the effectiveness of the in-field, and the sheet is then covered with random scribblings (Figure 10). This is in contrast to the effect of a figure within a continuous outline, as in Figure 21, where the central spot and outline are treated as separate units, or the space between the central object and the outline becomes the effective field, as in Figure 18.

Figural Preferences in Drawings of a Chimpanzee 11

Figure-completion

For study of completion of figures three types of test objects were used: solid geometrical figures from which a segment had

 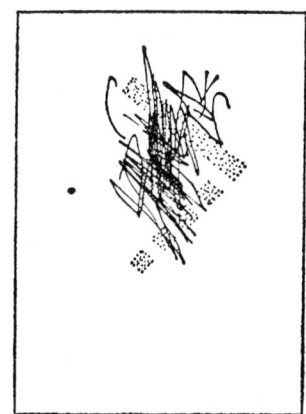

FIG. 11. Oct. 3. Green Lines, White Ground, Green Crayon, 90 Sec.
FIG. 12. Sept. 1. Blue Circle, White Ground, Blue Crayon, 60 Sec.

been cut, continuous but incomplete outlines, and symmetrical arrangements of dots with one or more omitted. Results differ for these types.

The solid figure with a segment cut out is generally marked upon and the open space left blank. However, in two of six cases the open space is rather carefully filled in, with few marks on the rest of the figure (Figure 12).

Lines forming two sides of a triangle are never completed. The space between them is filled by dashes and lines, generally crowded toward the apex (Figure 11). The same is true of lines forming three sides of a square or less regular polygon (13 examples) and of incomplete circles formed by a continuous line.

Tests with omitted dots gave consistent completion. A space left in a circle of six or more dots is in every case filled in, as in Figure 13, with few or no lines on the remainder of the sheet (six examples). A square, 3×3, with one element missing has the blank space filled in, in eight of eight examples (Figure 14). The few other combinations tried, such as five spots in an incomplete rectangle, are not completed.

Ambiguous figures

A number of figures after Rubin's ambiguous type, in which either part may be taken by man as ground, were used as test

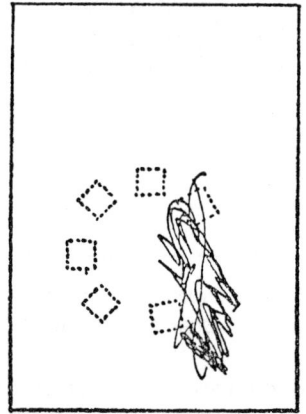 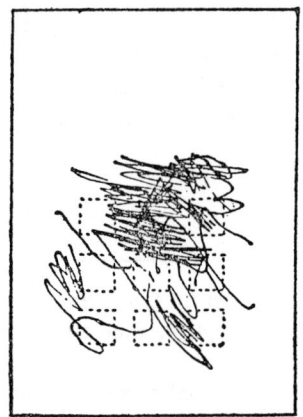

FIG. 13. Sept. 20. Blue Squares, White Ground, Blue Crayon, 60 Sec.
FIG. 14. Nov. 19. Green Squares, White Ground, Purple Crayon, 20 Sec.

objects. In the majority of such cases Alpha drew on both parts of the figure, with little indication that either part was dominant. There is, however, a tendency to draw more upon the lighter part of the configuration (Figures 15 and 16).

Symmetry

In reporting the influence of single small figures, it was pointed out that there is a tendency to produce a symmetry or balance of masses on the page. To seek more definite evidence on this point, a number of asymmetrical test figures were used. Alpha's response to about half of these figures involves major scribblings

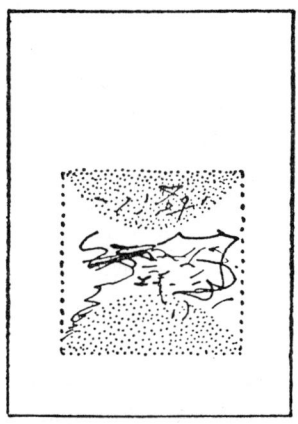 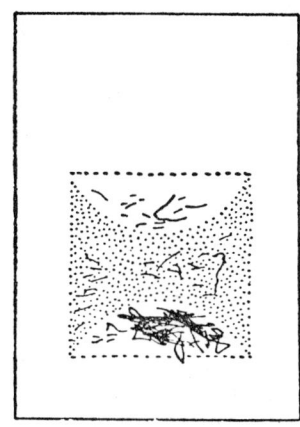

FIG. 15. Aug. 20. White Hourglass on Black Square, Green Ground, Red Crayon, 90 Sec.
FIG. 16. Aug. 20. Black Hourglass on White Square, Green Ground, Red Crayon, 2 Min.

 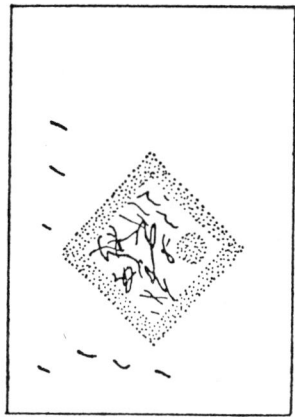

FIG. 17. Nov. 7. Black Triangle on Green Square (Stippled), Black Ground, Green and Yellow Crayons, 40 Sec.
FIG. 18. Sept. 1. Blue Circle, Blue Outline, White Ground, Blue Crayon, 90 Sec.

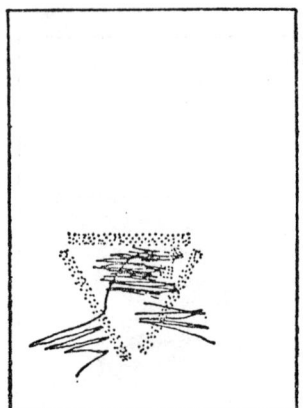 

FIG. 19. Oct. 31. Violet Squares and Outline, Black Ground, Red Crayon, 15 Sec.
FIG. 20. Nov. 19. Green Circle, Green Outline, White Ground, Blue Crayon, 30 Sec.

in an area roughly symmetrical with the unbalanced portion of the figure (Figures 17 and 18), but in an equal number the entire blank portion of the figure is filled in or the entire figure scribbled over.

The most impressive indication of a tendency to symmetrical arrangement is her response to triangular figures. Five of seven triangular outlines show scribbling symmetrically centered along the sides as in Figures 19 and 20. Square and circular outlines do not call out such a response and, in fact, show few lines outside of the enclosed space (Figure 18). Of two circles with enclosed triangles, however, each has three groups of scribbles outside of the circle and opposite the sides of the triangles. Five circular outlines enclosing irregular groups of small spots show no such marks in the out-field.

Such symmetries might be explained by a tendency to fill in blank spaces and to scribble across bars, but the spacing of the marks is significantly different from that filling-in around unorganized figures, of which Figure 10 is typical, and from the scribbling across bars. The proportion of symmetrically spaced scribbles in the total collection is so great as to argue strongly that Alpha has some feeling for a balance of masses on the page.

Contrast and color

Many of the tests were interrupted after 5 to 30 sec., and Alpha was given a second crayon of a different color. In no case did the change in color of her crayon affect the location of the scribbling. Thus Figure 17 contains about equal portions of green (first) and yellow (second) lines with almost exactly the same distribution. Only when the two crayons were used with different hands is there a difference in the direction of lines, but even in such cases the location is the same. There is no indication that the degree of color contrast between crayon and paper in any way influences Alpha's drawings. She uses yellow crayon on yellow figures, black on black as readily as more contrasting colors. Thus Figure 4 is in pale yellow crayon, almost invisible on the white cross, conspicuous on the black ground, yet almost entirely restricted to the figure.

A number of test fields made up of two colors were used; e.g., a sheet half orange, half blue; a black and a white circle on gray ground. In all such cases Alpha marked on both colors. As with the ambiguous figures, however, there are more marks on the lighter shades, even when crayons of the same hue were used. There seems to be some preference for red, orange, and yellow over shorter wave lengths, but the range of shades used is not great enough to rule out brightness as the determining factor in such cases.

Satiation

In all of the drawings collected the paper was withdrawn after from 10 to 180 sec. The drawings represent Alpha's first reaction to the configurations presented. If the paper is left for a longer time, her concentration on the figure diminishes and the whole sheet is eventually covered with scribblings. The time of attention to the figure does not seem to be a function of the amount of scribbling on it, for it may be abandoned when only a few strokes have been made or not until it is almost obliterated with heavy lines.

Changes in style

Drawings made during the first month of the experiment (August) contain a large proportion of short dashes and fine wavy lines. This is illustrated in Figure 21, made 2 weeks after the beginning of the experiment, and by a majority of the test-figures dated in August. From the latter part of September through October a majority of the drawings are made up of open zigzags and rambling lines, as in Figures 10, 11, 12, and 13. Drawings obtained in the following January are mostly a scratching-out of the entire figure with dense, heavy lines, as in Figure 22, or a similar dense mass on the blank sheet, as in Figure 2. The reason for this change is not apparent. Twenty months later Alpha returned to the original style, like Figure 1.

Motor tendencies

Alpha is evidently not so much interested in the effects of her drawings as in the action itself. She is not influenced by the color of the figures or background or the visibility of her markings. Pencil lines drawn on or around the figures by the experimenter do not influence the position of her scribblings. She pokes toward the figure with the crayon, exploring its outlines and interior. If she gets an edge loose, she tries to peel the figure off of the sheet. The pencil is used as is the finger in grooming, in an attempt to scratch beneath the figure or to scrape it off.

Yet there is certainly another factor at work. She does not draw with a pointed stick and discards or chews up the crayon when the point breaks and it no longer marks. Given paper and pencil with broken point, she retires to a corner, examines the point, makes a few tentative strokes, then returns to the front of the cage to beg. The fact of marking is thus an essential part of the activity. The earlier drawings indicate a sort of emphasizing of the structure of the figure; the later might almost

Figural Preferences in Drawings of a Chimpanzee

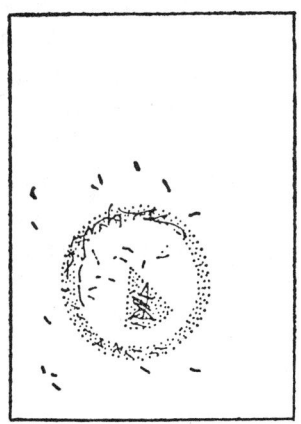 

FIG. 21. Sept. 1. White Figures on Blue Ground, Yellow Crayon, 2 Min.

FIG. 22. Jan. 30. Black Outline on White Ground, Red Crayon, 15 Sec.

be interpreted as an attempt to obliterate the figure, as a child "writes out" a part of a picture.

Motivation

The tests extended over a period of about 6 months. During the last 2 months it became increasingly difficult to get Alpha to draw, and tests were finally terminated because of her loss of interest. When tested again, 20 months after the end of the experiment, she was again very eager to draw.

There is no record of when Alpha first started to draw. During her infancy she was given Gesell tests, but the last record of these, made at the age of 40 weeks, states that she did not scribble when given crayon and paper (Jacobsen, Jacobsen, and Yoshioka 1932). For at least the past 10 years her behavior with pencil and paper has been essentially as at present. During this time she has never been directly rewarded for drawing, and it is quite evident that the activity does not involve social rewards. If possible, she retires with her paper to a far side of the cage, turns her back to the observer, works for a time with complete preoccupation, and eventually tears up the paper. If caged with another animal that watches her drawing, she shoulders the other aside or turns away to work in a corner. The motivation is intense. She will disregard food when she sees someone with pencil and paper and will beg for these. The diary records contain frequent notations concerning her interest in mechanical devices and she continually begs for opportunity to untie shoelaces or unbutton cuffs. The drive to manipulation is apparently autonomous. A few other of the 60 animals in the colony show similar mechanical interests but in no other adult is it so strongly developed.

DISCUSSION

The chief interest in the collection of Alpha's drawings is in their exposition of her perceptual reactions to a situation with which she had little or no prior experience; that is, to objects of varying degrees of physical relatedness within a constant and restricted field. Her identifications of figure or in-field could, in general, have been predicted from human perceptual organization, and no significant differences are indicated. However, the drawings emphasize a fact that is often disregarded in studies of discriminative learning in animals. The location of the scribblings indicates the dominant aspect of the total configuration presented, and this dominance is quite evidently determined by the physical proportions and arrangement of the elements of the situation and not by a selective conditioning.

The drawings are in no case representations. In this respect they are at the level of the scribbling of the human infant of 12 to 18 months (Gesell 1925). There is no sign of imitative drawing, even in making single strokes. Studies of the development of children's drawings have been chiefly concerned with the beginning of representation, and there seems to be no systematic analysis of early scribbling or of reactions to presented figures. The later ones of Alpha's drawings (Figure 22) resemble the scribbling-over or "writing-out" of parts of pictures which frequently appear in the drawing books of young children. Scribbling has been interpreted as a stage in the development of representative drawing. The character and limitations of Alpha's drawings suggest, on the contrary, that scribbling is primarily a motor expression and that imitative and reproductive drawing derive from a quite different "category of perception" (Koffka 1925) or of conceptual organization.

THE DISCOVERY OF PRIMITIVE ART

Douglas Fraser

IN THE SUMMER of 1888, an inquisitive marine biologist landed on one of the islands of the Torres Straits, the narrow water-area between New Guinea and Australia. His purpose, as he had previously described it in an application for financial support, was "to investigate the fauna, structure and mode of formation of the coral reefs in the Torres Straits" and "with the information thus obtained to study the raised coral formation on the various islands so as to be able to approximately determine the exact conditions under which the various formations were formed." The biologist never published the results of his calcareous researches. Instead, in 1894 he wrote what was perhaps the first book in history that proposed an all-inclusive esthetic of primitive art, *The Decorative Art of British New Guinea*.

There is practically no evidence in the official record of Alfred Cort Haddon, marine biologist, that might have led an inquiring Board of Trustees to suspect that he was to be part of an artistic revolution. Graduated from Cambridge in 1879 with honors in Zoology and Comparative Anatomy, he spent the next twenty years of his life as Professor of Zoology at the Royal College of Science in Dublin. Besides his zoological work, however, Haddon managed to measure the heads of the Irish of Aran Island, County Galway, and to develop his childhood hobby of inventing new type faces for his family's printing business. What made Haddon different from any other similarly situated

---

Reprinted from Arts Yearbook I: *The Turn of the Century,* Hilton Kramer, editor, 1957, pp. 119–33, by permission of the author and *Arts Magazine* (*The Art Digest*).

professor was not any single characteristic or attribute he might have possessed. Rather it seems to have been the result of a combination of broad historical processes and private personal events which, by their interaction and effect on his thinking, allowed Haddon to envision new modes of classifying experience.

In the second half of the nineteenth century, the age of triumphant Darwinism, it was "natural" for a scholar to apply the theory of natural selection to the field of art, as did such men as Stolpe, Balfour, March and Charles Read. For Haddon, who conceived the idea independently in 1892, there were, as there must have been for each of the others, special stimuli that prompted his imagination. Perhaps the simplest was the fact that he frequently identified himself with Charles Darwin!

Haddon and Darwin had much in common. Both had nonconformist religious attitudes and a typically nineteenth-century faith in "science," the philosophical basis for accepting evolutionary views. Both men had gone out to the Torres Straits as marine biologists, Darwin in the 1830's, Haddon a half-century later. And both had thereupon been converted to the science of man. The transposition of Darwinism to the esthetic field which Haddon effected in the 1890's and which now seems so inadequate was a logical development of his situation at the time. Restless, obstinate, but a man of keen visual sensibilities, Haddon strove to find the key to human variation in its form and expression. That the need to master diversity was for him a deeply personal problem may be seen in his dual definition of the word "savage." As a noun, for Haddon, "savage" meant "a dweller in the woods, i.e. backward people driven into out-of-the-way places"; as an adjective, "containing all those bad qualities which have been produced by contact with stronger peoples." It is fascinating to compare these statements with the photographs of Haddon, alone and in groups, made between the years 1865 and 1900: he always turns away from the camera. Haddon found it difficult to face himself for the very reasons that made him great, the anxiety about being backward or marginal and, at the same time, his fear of the brutal outcome of contact with more self-assured people. A shy child, shifted from school to school because of his family's precarious financial position, Haddon grew to dread weakness in himself, so that he early developed the defense of self-isolation—and of attacking others. When he finally achieved mastery of his field after 1900, he faced himself—and the camera.

Although Haddon first collected primitive art as "curios" to help pay for his expedition, there is a remarkable similarity between his taste in art and the saggital and frontal sections of zoology he drew so well. The art of British New Guinea in which he was particularly interested is predominantly linear, with a high degree of legibility of parts, the whole being, however, like a scientific drawing, rather confusing to the uninformed eye. There is even a similarity in the iconographic, preferences of the Papuans—birds, fish, sea mammals and human heads—to Haddon's chief preoccupations!

Haddon's evolutionary theory paid less attention to particular forms of art than to their relative positions in a biological scheme of development. To ascertain the status of a single art style, the investigator, Haddon explained, must first acquire a large number of objects and classify them according to their degree of naturalism. The genetic descent of works of art, which for Haddon may be direct imitations of nature, more complex formulations, or "degenerations," i.e., simplifications due to hackneyed repetition, can then be observed. Haddon's own conclusions —that art can be studied biologically, that its sources lie in nature and that "it is inconceivable that a savage should copy or adapt a certain design because it promises to develop into a more pleasing pattern"—seem rather appallingly unesthetic. But it must be remembered that Nature at this time was both a religious and scientific shibboleth and that all "art" was, in a sense, "realistic." Yet in the 1890's a new wave of stylized forms— Art Nouveau, Jugendstil, English illustration—raised new questions about geometric design as opposed to natural form.

Haddon's attitude also reflected the whole of the nineteenth century in its preoccupation with style; like Coleridge and Flaubert, he considered style as a manifestation of something of a higher order. Haddon's approach was nevertheless important because his system disengaged the idea of style from the particular object (where style had always been analyzed). He then inserted all styles into a common family of formal statements. This meant that all styles (and all arts), because of their genetic relationships to one another, became accessible to the artist on the level of their forms. Admittedly, Haddon himself did not intend to arrive at this end. He was impelled to it by the combination of his scientific passion for completeness, his commitment to the naturalistic esthetic, and, ironically, by his own artistic sensitivity.

Haddon was not the only man of his time to express an ambivalent attitude toward primitive art. One need only glance at *Noa Noa,* the book which Gauguin, who was only seven years older than Haddon, wrote and illustrated in the South Seas in 1892. He too describes native sculptures in nonesthetic terms (while wondering if the Polynesians really have a sense of the beautiful). The majestic form of a native queen may remind Gauguin of his beloved Virgin, but that he never completely releases himself into full association with the primitive world may be seen in his *Self-Portrait.* The coloristic differences between himself and the Polynesians are considerably heightened. Gauguin imagined himself a sort of Christ, backed up but never replaced by a series of shadowy figures. His containment and conscious self-isolation contribute to his detachment. Only in describing the massive stone figures of Easter Island does Gauguin express any appreciation for primitive art: "They bear witness to a special conception of beauty and a genuine skill in the art of working stones and architecture constructed of superimposed blocks with original and ingenious combinations of color." But, it must be noted sadly, he is actually paraphrasing an early nineteenth-century Dutch writer, since of course Gauguin never visited Easter Island at all.

The ease with which the great painter resorted to standard literary expressions of value in art (a common enough error, to be sure) is paralleled by his well-known tendency to combine synthetically the images of widely different cultures. His famous conversions of a Marquesan club into a kind of Epinal crucifix is the best example of Gauguin's eclecticism. But he is not so wide-ranging in his choices as it first appears. Obsessed with ideas about human freedom, destiny and authority, Gauguin extracts from context the Buddhist and Polynesian figures that accord with his vision of the world. In so doing, he is indeed expressing some sense of esteem for the primitive, but in a way that always circumvents mutuality or a general accessibility on the level of form. Yet Gauguin grants that the subject matter of Polynesian art is valid for its own sake—an allowance that Haddon probably would have hesitated to make. How is it that two men of so widely differing interests as Gauguin and Haddon came to converge on an art form essentially alien to both of them? The answer lies in what may be called the history of the appreciation of primitive art.

Admiration of the art of another culture is neither a recent nor exclusively a Western phenomenon. The world's first historian, Herodotus, who lived before the Periclean age in Greece and had traveled widely, made numerous references to the art of primitive peoples. He described Caspian, Ethiopian and Thracian clothing, decoration and body painting and mentioned how the Carthaginians traded goods for gold with the Africans beyond the Pillars of Hercules. He remained always, however, "a gatherer and disposer of other men's stuff," interested in, but expressing little understanding of or sympathy for alien art forms. Plato, on the other hand, with his idea of the priority of mind, art and law over material elements, said in the *Laws* that "the great and primitive works and actions will be works of art." Of course he is speaking of the cosmos rather than about art and would have shunned a truly primitive object; but the imagery employed by Plato demonstrates how easily a man may become esthetically involved with an art style or the outlook it expresses without actually being willing to espouse the art as a whole. . . .

It was not until the Renaissance and Albrecht Duerer that

there is a demonstrably appreciative utterance on the subject of primitive art. During his visit to Brussels in 1520, Duerer wrote: "I saw the things which have been brought to the King from the new land of Gold [Mexico]—a sun all of gold a whole fathom broad and a moon all of silver of the same size, also two rooms full of the armor of the people there and all manner of wondrous weapons of theirs, harness and darts, very strange clothing, beds and all kinds of wonderful objects of human use, much better worth seeing than prodigies [events of extraordinary or prophetic significance]. These things were all so precious that they are valued at 100,000 florins . . . All the days of my life I have seen nothing that rejoiced my heart so much as these things, for I saw amongst them wonderful works of art and I marveled at the subtle ingenuity of men in foreign lands. Indeed I cannot express all that I thought there."

Although Duerer was obviously in a receptive mood and went on to discourse on fish bones, stones and other objects, there can be little doubt that a large part of his interest was due to his visual susceptibility as an artist. Brought up in the Gothic North, Duerer was in contact with the Venetian, North Italian and Florentine traditions as well as that of the Franco-Flemish Renaissance. His broad experience and interest in the particular appearance of things may have permitted him to see what others merely glanced at.

Another widening of esthetic horizons which occurred in the mid-eighteenth century was Captain Cook's expedition to the South Seas, originally intended to permit the observation of the transit of the planet Venus. Instead he opened up a new world. Cook visited the Northwest Coast of America, Hawaii, Tahiti, Samoa, Tonga, New Zealand, Australia and many other areas. He collected hundreds of examples of native arts, some of which were packed off by King George III to his beloved Göttingen University and through a miracle were not opened until 1927. Imagine the delight of the museum director who found himself suddenly in the possession of ancient Hawaiian feather cloaks, helmets and capes—all retaining, long after such art had ceased to be produced, the unfaded glory of tropical plumage! The most remarkable thing about Cook's material, though, was the mixture of contempt and excitement with which it was received. (A large book was issued to shed light on native textiles—illustrated with real tapa! Apparently no one in those days worried about the preservation of material so long as it was widely distributed.) Such an attitude must be seen in the context of the Enlightenment and the notion of progress, for it implies that whatever supersedes something else is automatically of greater value. In such a climate there can be little use for primitive art. Yet Cook's collections and other similar ones survived, even though there were in that period no true museums.

The early nineteenth century was hardly more receptive to primitive art; there was practically no trade or contact with primitive peoples other than by missionaries and sailors, scarcely the most appreciative students of primitive art. Yet some of the missionaries, like William Ellis, who served in Tahiti and Hawaii, were of two minds. They exhorted the people to destroy their "false gods" and at the same time sent examples of "heathen idols" home for safekeeping. The sailors were less interested in souls, but they often delighted in curios, weird objects to remind themselves of distant worlds. There were also voyages of discovery which provided a fair record of exotic lands, sometimes even including, as did the report of De Freycinet, drawings made by primitive peoples. The besetting obstacle to appreciation of these art forms was the universal inability or disinclination of the voyagers to see native customs and objects in native terms. Everything was reckoned according to the degree it approached Judeo-Christian and Classical-Western concepts. Thus, art (meaning idealized nature) was beyond the achievements of primitive man; Ruskin's remark that "there is no art in the whole of Africa, Asia or America" stems from this ill-nourished root. In a broad sense, though, the picture was not that of any previous era. Europe had experienced the influence of Chinese and Etruscan arts, indirectly it is true, but important as a *relievo* for the norms of Neo-Classicism, Egyptian, Mesopotamian, Indian and Moslem arts of North Africa were being invoked in the name of Romanticism. Things, it seemed, would never be the same.

Between 1850 and 1890, new interests led to still other ways of looking at primitive art. Imperialism raised questions about the character and productivity of overseas possessions, and exhibitions helped to explain these countries to prospective investors. Among the many marvels of the London Exhibition of 1851 was a Maori fortified village brought all the way from New Zealand by ship. The beautiful reed-woven panels of the Maori houses impressed many visitors, especially Gottfried Semper, a German architect and student of ornament (and independent discoverer of evolution) who incorporated some of his impressions in an important book on the origins of decoration. Semper was one of the first writers to analyze ornament (from all over the world) as a structure independent of meaning or natural connotation. By attributing the origins of decoration to material, technique and purpose, Semper inaugurated functionalism and signalized the beginning of materialistic theories of art. The consequences for the appreciation of primitive art were mainly negative—the replacement of romantic notions of the primitive by a bourgeois esthetic of technical achievement.

Opportunities for the artist to experience aboriginal work in the great expositions at London in 1887 and at Paris in 1854 and 1878 culminated in the Universal Exposition of 1889, which formed Gauguin's and Van Gogh's introduction to primitive art. With his extraordinary responsiveness to human works, Van Gogh immediately admired a sketch of an ancient Mexican dwelling: "primitive and very beautiful."

Aside from such emotional *rapport* as the susceptible artist might have felt momentarily with a work of primitive art, the style was still virtually inaccessible as art in any self-sustaining sense. The ethnological museums were only just being formed, and their exhibition techniques were extremely crude. The crowding together of objects, characteristic of these museums, was not necessarily detrimental to the viewing of art objects since this was pretty much the way the second half of the nineteenth century saw everything (including life itself). The difficulty from the viewpoint of the artist was the extraordinary stability of the conditions under which primitive art was viewed. Art, after all, as it was understood by the West, was either monumental and assimilated to an extra-esthetic system of values, or personal and characterized by intimacy. Finally, around 1900, Ensor "discovered" Congo art in the Belgian museum at Tervuren, and in 1904 Vlaminck had his famous encounter in the Paris *bistro* with the Negro figurines. Excited by their remarkable visual qualities, Vlaminck immediately purchased the statuettes and eagerly displayed them to his artist friends.

To look for a single cause for these discoveries either in contemporary art or in the attitudes toward the primitive would be futile. Yet, in 1897, the British had sent an expedition to Benin, Nigeria, to avenge the execution of some Englishmen who had tried to enter the forbidden city. Expecting to find a barbarian culture, the punitive army was amazed to discover instead a rich, aristocratic society, well ornamented with technically proficient bronze castings, ivory carvings and coral decorations. The majority of these objects soon turned up in Europe with expensive price tags (probably because of the materials used, since esthetically they are not particularly impressive). This event served, however, to draw attention to the continent of Africa, which, although it had been visited since the fifteenth century, was only just beginning, under the banner of imperialism, to open out to European eyes. Luckily, from these early days an extraordinary amount of precious ethnographical data has been preserved—primarily by civil servants and medical missionaries, men who had the leisure time and the intellectual cultivation to make the best use of their intimacy with the natives.

The discovery of primitive art actually was not so much a discovery as a gradual development of awareness. Just as the imagery of Columbus' description of the New World is based on Provençal romances, so the enlarging view of primitive art in the early years of the twentieth century retained many of the features of earlier interpretations. Picasso, on being shown a Negro sculpture by Derain, is reported to have said, "It is more beautiful than the Venus de Milo." The statement is significant. Not only does Picasso resort automatically to classical imagery, but he expresses himself in terms of an extreme contrast; for him the two objects are similar in their absolutism.

In 1909, Guillaume Apollinaire, the poet and philosopher of the Cubist movement, described Matisse as a "shrewd Fauve, surrounding himself with old and new objects, precious materials and those sculptures in which the Negroes of Guinea, Senegal or Gabun have demonstrated with unique purity their frightening emotions." Apollinaire was an idealist, believing as he did that "to insist on purity is to baptize instinct, to humanize art and to deify personality." And because he believed art to be a more or less intellectual function of mankind, not necessarily expressed from the intimate and personal nature of the artist, a view perhaps encouraged by an aristocratic classical education, Apollinaire could take a relatively anachronistic and uninvolved attitude toward primitive art. He doesn't even mention Negro sculpture in his book on the Cubists. That it was nevertheless in his mind can be seen in a poem of 1912:

> Tu marches vers Auteuil
> tu veux aller chez toi à pied
> dormir parmi tes fétiches d'Océanie et de Guinée.

A similar *"avant-garde-retardataire"* approach in a very different esthetic setting came from Wilhelm Worringer, a German Expressionist writer on art. Drawing his conclusions largely from the examination of German Bronze and Iron Age remains, he contended that the self-destructiveness of the primitive had provided a mystical energy for all forms of Germanic (Northern) art (including the cool Gothic of the Ile de France). Although Worringer's interpretation of primitive peoples is unsupported, his concept of spiritualized violence nonetheless betrays a certain synthesis of the oldest views of primitive man—that of the lurking cannibal with that of the noble savage. Another artist-writer of this time, a certain C. Praetorius (probably Charles Praetorius, producer of several facsimiles of sixteenth-century books) similarly envisioned the magic-haunted headhunter finding solace in his pipe, his untutored hand still capable of works of "a quaint imaginative power and sense of beauty." The firm amalgamation of the "hard" and the "soft" concepts of primitivism made by artists and critics at this time, while it perpetuated a long line of confusion in philosophical attitudes toward the primitive world, was now newly established in the viewing of primitive art. It stands forth in clear contrast with, say, Andrew Lang's "The Art of Savages," an article written in 1882, with its Semperian rationalisms: "the savage has sense enough to confine himself to the sort of work for which his materials are fitted." The new concept of the primitive combines the old criticisms of savage art—that it is demonic or incompetent—with new romantic notions about its purity, vigor, reasonableness or technical efficiency.

How adequate to the actual African sculptures seen by modern artists were these interpretations? One may consider, for example, a Baoulé figure from the Ivory Coast of West Africa. Does this object demonstrate Apollinaire's "unique purity and frightening emotions," Worringer's "exaggerations of guilt" or Praetorius' "grotesque imagination"? Such figures are commemorative containers for the spirits of dead relatives and have, in their naturalism, an ancestor-portrait character. The body posture with its sophisticated modeling characterizes the deceased but still-effective elder as responsive both to inner drives and external suggestions. Fastidious in technique and expression, the Baoulé figure also conveys in the placement and treatment of the hands the idea of a self-caress. Indeed, a knowledge of Baoulé culture seems to support this notion—the Baoulé being extremely sensitive to cleanliness (they refuse to sit on the ground because it would make them dirty). The sense of containment of the forms does not prevent relief in the projection of beard, scarification, nipples, etc.; these however are the decorative and hypersensitive extensions of the body. Their freedom to experience the world is inhibited by the closure of the eyes and the withholding of the hands, normally the two most perceptive forms for the artist. There is a high degree of estheticism and self-contemplation in Baoulé figures.

This type of Ivory Coast art was among the African styles best known to the French artists of the early twentieth century. (See Plates 1 and 2.) Closer in spirit to their interpretations of primitive art is Bambara sculpture from the French Sudan. The reproduced figure is constructed in a series of geometric shapes aligned architecturally in horizontals and verticals. The summary treatment of details and surfaces and the abrupt angular transitions in the forms create a sense of anxiety in their arbitrariness and unexpectedness of direction. Rising majestically on its axis, the Bambara figure seems sovereign and self-sufficient in a manner well adjusted to its function in the culture. This is a fertility goddess, an omnipotent deity that demands sacrifice of and bestows blessings indiscriminately on her people. The complete authority of this figure is perhaps best evidenced in the hands, where her ambiguous relationship to the people is expressed by their open yet withholding forms.

Another entirely different set of attitudes is implied in the art of Benin which represents rulers and court retainers. The bodies are frontal, compact and highly legible, and despite the many levels of relief, are completely insensitive to spatial voids. Ceremonial self-presentation with ritual concentration on an external object results in loss of the inwardness of the figures. There is great interest in costume, equipage and cosmetic practices. The hands hold or touch objects, implying a world oriented toward manipulation, extension, release and contraction. Each form, thus relativized and significant only in relation to something other than itself, expresses an ideal of social hierarchy based on predictable public behavior.

A fourth interpretation of primitive life may be seen in the Lower Congo commemorative carvings. Allegorical or memorial in character and without grandiose religious or social sentiments, these works have personal, secular, even intimate themes. The manner of presentation, moreover, tends to avoid the problematical and to make the subject self-evident. Usually the head, the center of individuality and sensitivity, is the culmination. The inclination of the axis of the body is the bearer of consciousness and suggests a certain fragility and human responsiveness. With quiet drama conveyed by gesture and body pantomime, such figures invite the observer to sympathetic participation in the continuity of experience.

Can one say that the modern affinity for primitive art is due to a particular attitude which it symbolizes? Is simplicity, forcefulness, rationality or directness sufficiently expressed in each figure to be the sole reason for the esteem suddenly showered on primitive art? It hardly seems appropriate to so complex a problem to explain this phenomenon by referring to some quality assumed to be inherent in native arts. The alternative is to find in the art of the early twentieth century values or attributes that entail a direct *rapport* with primitive art. . . .

Of all modern artists, Picasso is most frequently identified with the discovery of primitive art, but the precise relationship of the great Spaniard to aboriginal art has never been clearly established. Max Jacob, who was with him in the early part of the century, insisted that Cubism was born of Negro sculpture. More recently, Picasso, asserting that his inspiration stemmed from Iberian sculpture, has denied that he knew Negro art until after the completion of the *Demoiselles d'Avignon*. (See Plate 3.) Whatever the truth may be (and Picasso makes little effort to disguise his contempt for the autopsy treatment of his art), his self-portrait of 1906 establishes the character of his attitudes. As though to isolate himself from the world, Picasso circumscribes himself with a line. He exposes himself through his technique, however, especially in the treatment of the hand—the instrument of his creativity. In other words, he dramatizes himself as a performer, as an esthetic spectacle, but shuts off all other contact with the observer. Picasso's *rapport* with objects of primitive art is primarily on the level of their formal statement. When he encounters an object of interest for him, the fact is not automatically intimated in his art; he tends rather to savor the idea, slowly evolving it into a system which is itself in constant process of re-examination. But the assimilation of style is so complete that even in an apparent parallel, as with an Itumba mask from French Equatorial Africa, the element of certainty is lacking. The mask in question is usually photographed in a "cubistic" fashion and on closer examination shows a lack of that degree of concentration and assertiveness so characteristic of Picasso's art.

The *Demoiselles d'Avignon* holds a key position in Picasso's development of primitive art. Started in 1906 and partially repainted in 1907, it seems to mark the beginning of abstractionism, a trait which has been linked to primitive art. The familiar notion that the primitive artist abstracts from reality the elements that are meaningful for him cannot in fact be proved. The primitive carver works in a traditional style with relatively rigid conventions; hence his contribution is in the realm of nuance, stress and general expressive tone. That Picasso would accept such restrictions on his own art is of course highly improbable. Rather, he appears to have been impressed by the achievement of the artist, the mastery of art within a constrained situation—and this appreciation seems to have reinforced and sustained his initial esthetic acceptance of primitive art. Despite the fact that he rarely quoted from it, Picasso, simply by virtue of his all-encompassing eye, was in his day probably as intimately involved with primitive art and as keenly attuned to it as any person could be. . . .

Oceanic art, for a variety of reasons, played a role somewhat different from that of African sculpture in relation to modern art. The contacts of the West with South Pacific art were not particularly sustained until colonial museums sprang into existence in the 1880's and 90's, and even then the character of the art was still obscured by an idyllic vision of life in the South Seas. But with the development of copra, sugar and pineapple plantations in the area, a new demand for cheap native labor created the difficulties of slavery and indentured service among peoples known for their resistance to authority. The attendant contacts with primitive peoples in Polynesia and Melanesia were far from peaceable; yet the numerous trading stations and outposts set up to protect colonial interests helped in the acquisition of primitive objects.

As in Africa, the styles of Oceania are by no means homogeneous. Consider for a moment the *korvars* or ancestor figures from West Irian. (See Plate 36.) Such figures can be traced back across Indonesia to southeast Asia. They serve as resting places for souls of deceased relatives, who are believed to be entirely present in the society. The placement of the figure behind a shield made up of protective curves symbolizes the power of the ancestor to shelter his descendants from harm. In its vigorous curves and pose, the *korvar* ideally expresses stability and protection through symmetry and restraint.

There is little restraint in works like the lime containers produced by the Mundugumor of the Sepik River. Often decorated with fiber, shells, beads, fur, grass or hair, the containers are elaborately painted in white, rose and tan. The attention lavished on these objects and the excellence of their purely sculptural statement serve to enhance the feeling of wholeness and give them a sort of barbaric splendor. The Mundugumor by all accounts are an extremely vigorous, assertive group, even in an area where aggressiveness is expected behavior. They measure an individual's worth by prowess in headhunting and the possession of goods, and art functions in their culture as a symbol of acquired prestige. Hence the dazzling splendor and intricacy of lime containers help to advance the standing of the individual according to a culturally recognized scale of values. That a bizarre and gorgeous art should be a means of advancement sheds light on the instinctive responsiveness to art which is in all men.

The dance masks of the Papuan Gulf in South New Guinea are made by covering a cane and palm-wood frame with painted bark cloth. Comprising several large elements, these masks attain a truly impressive size (up to thirty feet high) with a minimum of weight. Since the masks are employed in ceremonies as embodiments of friendly spirits, they are highly ritualistic in feeling. Yet the comic aspect of these forms is not lost on the natives, the type illustrated being worn by ceremonial clowns. Working with the most perishable materials, the Papuan artist has nonetheless evolved, through the employment of scale, forms that possess considerable monumentality.

The slit gong from New Hebrides, despite the cleverness of the eye treatment, is basically of the rough-and-ready school of primitive art. The "spookiness" of such art is proverbial and is wonderfully manifested in the dualism of the eyes. Such figures are, however, full of interestingly balanced asymmetries, a feature that redeems their otherwise relatively crude esthetic form.

In Polynesia, an entirely different culture and art style prevailed. The carving from Mangareva, Central Polynesia, has the technical facility and particularization of form that are associated with a specialized society and an aristocratic patronage. The naturalistic smooth surfaces are modeled in curves, while the body rotates on its axis in an elegant manner. There is an intense selfhood to the figure expressed in the tenseness of the features and their sharpness in comparison with the soft, indolent shapes of the body.

The changing appreciation of primitive art (in itself an extremely varied and complex style) depends primarily upon the particular programs and problems of the artists involved. In later years, Léger, Modigliani, the Surrealists and Paul Klee utilized African and Oceanic art with special purposes and under unique conditions of vision. Meanwhile anthropologists were not only adding to the stock of objects and knowledge but also confusing matters with their sallies into the field of art interpretation. Haddon's contemporary, Franz Boas, who also came to anthropology from the physical sciences, collected quantities of Northwest Coast Indian art in the 1890's and 1900's. When it came to analysis, Boas limited himself to a discussion of technical influences on art and to a theory of representational art based on recognition of the familiar as the key emotion-producing element.

He attributed esthetic pleasure to the enjoyment of technical control. The subsequent efforts of Frobenius to refer African art to a Germanic vitalist theory in which the artist must always conquer to survive is equally unconvincing. More recently, psychoanalytic theory has been applied, perhaps too loosely, to the field.

The discovery of primitive art, as has been seen, was of great importance not only for its direct influence on modern art, but also for its own sake and the as yet unexhausted ideas it could supply modern artists. This revolution in taste, initiated by anthropological curiosity in man's work, reached a new public through the advanced vision of the artist. The process of diffusion depended not only on new notions of the nature of art, but also on a new concept of humanity—that all men are, in spirit, brothers. Primitive art both stems from and confirms this assertion.

Part II ∥ THEORY AND METHOD

ART AND ICON

Robert Redfield

WE HAVE come together to consider some questions about primitive art. The very existence of The Museum of Primitive Art implies these questions. Why should there be a museum of primitive art? To an anthropologist it seems natural that these African sculptures and Melanesian masks be presented to the public in ethnographical museums with some account of the use and meaning of the objects in the lives of the people who made them. What, then, are they doing here in collections arranged as are Renaissance paintings or the sculptures of Henry Moore? Why are objects from different tribes or peoples placed together, and why are we shown these objects with little more explanation of their origins and settings in custom and belief than that this head and bust came from the Baga of French Guinea and that that Liberian mask, composed of wood, tin, cord, fibre, cloth, nails and cartridge cases, is a "Poro Society mask"? Looking at the mask and the label in a museum of primitive art you find out little about the Poro Society; and if the mask is art, it can be looked upon in the ethnographical collection in which it is more customary to place it. So may the anthropologist think. This evening I shall try to think about what he thinks, and I shall try to think too, as far as I am able, about the interests and ideas that bring about the exhibition of these primitive artifacts also in collections offered as art.

Of course we should have some of these primitive objects right here before us to look at while we put our minds to these matters.

Reprinted from *Aspects of Primitive Art,* published by The Museum of Primitive Art, 1959, pp. 12–40, by permission of Mrs. Margaret Park Redfield and The Museum of Primitive Art.

Failing that, let us examine photographs of them, and restrict our immediate attention to three objects from a single people, the Dogon, who live in the Sudan at the great bend of the Niger River.

The first two (see Plate 4) recall to your mind the long narrow lines of the Dogon figures, the straight arms almost without elbows, the general impression of balanced verticality. These two figures suggest that we are in the presence of a style. This suggestion is strengthened, I think, by a third Dogon woodcarving which I now show. (See Plate 5.) This object is not from the collections of our museum; it is in the Barnes collection. The photograph is reproduced in the book *Primitive Negro Sculpture* (Guillaume and Munro 1926). A photograph of this same object is also reproduced in Andre Malraux's book *The Voices of Silence*. The identification there reads: "Sudan. Dogon: The Male and Female Principals (Funerary Figures)" (Malraux 1953: 571). I propose that this double figure remain through the evening the principal work of primitive art to which in recollection our minds may return.

I will read two comments that have been made relative to it. The first is by Guillaume and Munro and appears in their book on Negro sculpture, opposite to the plate that shows the object. It is as follows:

> Less monumental, but more complex and delicate, is the network of slender rods into which the seated male and female figures are bound together. The trunks, stiff and solid, are entwined with smaller rods, some long and some shortened into mere protuberances, all jointed in an angular and staccato rhythm, and flowing down with increasing unison to the springy and intricate framework of the base. The constantly varying direction of the rods gives the design three-dimensionality, in spite of the slenderness of the parts. The spaces between the rods, especially around the shoulders and hips, function as do those about the flying buttresses of a Gothic cathedral, to give a sense of airy dispersion and delicately articulated structure (Guillaume and Munro 1926:82).

Art and Icon

The second comment needs a somewhat longer introduction. The Dogon were studied for about twenty years by Professor Marcel Griaule and his associates. They have published many articles and monographs about this Sudanese people. Most of the publications tell of the ideas and feelings that the Dogon have about the universe and about man's place in it: their cosmogony, their ritual and religion, their ordered knowledge of all things. The publications about them include a book for the general reader entitled *Dieu d'Eau* ("God of Water"). It consists of a record of thirty-three interviews had with one Dogon man named Ogotemmêli. This man, by nature a thinker, by profession a diviner, by misfortune blind, sat in his darkness and told Griaule what the world and man meant to him and how it all came to be. His account begins with the creation of the heavenly bodies and of the earth, and then tells of the divine genealogy of mankind that began with intercourse of the creator-God with the female earth. The first attempt to create beings failed. Then come the words I shall quote containing reference to the beings who are presented in the double figure. Ogotemmêli does not call them "Male and Female Principals," nor would we expect him to. I make the identification from the correspondence of the form of the two joined figures with what the old diviner said. If the identification is wrong, this example of two-fold significance in a work of primitive art falls. But I do not think it is wrong. We shall understand that the old blind Dogon does not have before his mind's eye this particular representation of the beings he talks about, or any representation of them. He is thinking of the beings, as we may suppose that the carver of the image before us may have thought of them or as some other Dogon may have thought of them in a moment of religious feeling and action. Here are the words of Ogotemmêli as Professor Griaule put them into French from the Dogon language and as my wife and I put them from French into English:

> Water, the divine semen, then entered the womb of earth and generation followed its regular cycle in the birth of twins. Two beings took form.

God created them out of water. They were green in color, having the shape of human and of serpent. From head to loins they were human; below, serpent.

Their red eyes were shaped as those of men, their tongues forked as those of serpents. Their flexible arms had no joints. Their bodies, all green and smooth like the surface of water, bore short green hair, sign of vegetation and germination.

These spirits, called Nommo, alike in nature, begotten by God, like himself of divine essence, were conceived without mischance and developed as they should in the womb of earth. Their destiny led them to the heavens where they received their father's teaching. None but God could instruct them in the Word, that which is to all beings indispensable, as it is to the order of the universe. The two were born complete and perfect in their eight limbs; their sign was eight, the symbol of the Word.

They possessed also the essence of God, for they were made of his semen which is at once the support, the form and the matter of the vital force of the world, the source of movement and persistence in every being. And this force is water. The couple is present in all water, that of the sea, of water confined, of streams, of rainstorms, and of every spoonful one drinks (Griaule 1948:25).

It is, of course, the contrast between these two comments that concerns us now. To the two critics this woodcarving is one thing; to such a Dogon as Ogotemmêli it would be quite another thing. Guillaume and Munro, coming to the object very much from outside of the Dogon world, see it as a work of art. The Dogon sees it as a representation of a sacred being. For the people within whose world it was made, it stands for, it evokes, ordered ideas as to the origins and the right nature of the universe. As such, we on the outside say that for them it is representative and symbolic. In the aspect it shows to the Dogon, it is an icon. An icon is a sign standing for its subject. An icon is not always a representation, a likeness, as are the ikons (in a narrower sense) of the Greek Orthodox Church. An icon may be not a likeness but an analogy, as the dove may stand for Christ, or as the blood smeared on the bodies of certain Australian aborigines stands for the Creative Mother of their mythology.

The wooden object that is our central text may be seen as art or as icon according to the kind of meaning that is attributed to or connected with it. This difference in kind of meaning may be stated more generally by taking a word from Eliseo Vivas, a philosopher who has written about art. For him who experiences an object only as art its meanings are immanent in the object (Vivas 1955:95). In contrast, we may add, to him for whom the object is a stimulus for associations it has with something other than the object, its meanings are transcendent: they go beyond or outside of it. The icon is only one kind of object with both immanent and transcendent meanings. Among other works of primitive art a decorated pot has for its maker and its user meanings of usefulness, perhaps of ritual context for which it is reserved. It is no icon. The totem pole, iconic in part, refers the mind of the Haida Indian also to the genealogy and social position of the man who sets it up. All these meanings are of a kind that carries the mind of him who so understands them outside of the object itself into knowledge and experience that is somewhere else—in custom and society, in personal life.

Tonight we need not be concerned with a general theory of aesthetics. Indeed, our immediate attention, restricted as it is to one carved object that is both art and icon, is too narrow for general theories. Of course aesthetic experiences, however they may be distinguished from other experiences, occur in connection with many other objects and activities—an unrolling fern frond or a charming child, a well-formed speech, music or expressive ritual. Tonight it is only the products of art that result from the creative composition of elements of form, and of these, only those that have been created by people very alien to us, and again out of all primitive art, a few African wooden figures. We are considering carved or sculptured art that appears in museums of two contrasting kinds, with predilections respectively aesthetic and iconic. We are trying to help the inexperienced viewer of such objects to the enjoyment and understanding of both kinds of corresponding experiences.

To see and experience a work of art only as such, free from all associations that transcend it, is probably neither easy nor frequent. One may very abstractly define what such an aesthetic experience would be. Vivas defines it when he writes that a purely aesthetic experience is one of "rapt attention which involves the intransitive apprehension of the object's immanent meanings in their full presentational immediacy" (Vivas 1955: 95). By saying "intransitive" he is again telling us that the attention does not move away from the object to that for which, in its local life, it stands. In contrast, the iconic experience of the object is described by the earlier American philosopher, C. S. Peirce, who writes: "So, in contemplating a painting"—and obviously he is thinking of representational painting—"there is a moment when we lose consciousness that it is not the thing, the distinction of the real and the copy vanishes, and it is for a moment a pure dream—not any particular existence and yet not general. At that moment we are contemplating an icon" (Peirce 1885:181).

I say again that neither of these pure experiences can be common. An occasional person of aesthetic sensibility may fix his rapt attention upon a work of art so that all of its depictive and evocative meanings disappear and only its aesthetic qualities are immediately and intensely felt. An occasional mystic, gazing upon the icon, may experience its complete identification with the spiritual being that it stands for. But as most of us look at what we see in museums of art, we have neither of these experiences in absolute purity.

Indeed, about the pure experiencing of art or of icon there is not much to be said. Like other intense and intimate experiences, it is ineffable. And as soon as one begins to talk about the experience one begins to import into the ideas and feelings about it elements drawn from outside of the figure, from some body of associations with which it comes almost at once to be connected. You will have noticed that neither Guillaume and Munro, nor yet Ogotemmêli, was talking about an experience, either aesthetic or iconic. Each was talking about some considered order he found, or might have found, in or connected with the object. Both were giving reasons why on the one hand the object is a work of art, or on the other a representation of and stimulus for religious and cosmogonic ideas. We just don't know how intensely the Dogon experience the iconic qualities of such an object. As for the words of Guillaume and Munro, in telling us about the ordered form in which they find its aesthetic appeal, they are driven to compare certain elements in the design with the airy spaces between the flying buttresses of Gothic cathedrals. They may have had a pure aesthetic experience in looking at the figure of the sacred twins, but when they talk to us about it as art, they bring with them comparisons and analogies that they have learned about elsewhere, that transcend the object.

What has this distinction between art and icon to do with the experiences in art museums of those of us who are neither pure aestheticians nor yet religious mystics? What kind of experience is had by the ordinary viewer of a work of art? I think it is almost always mixed, an experience composed of both immanent and transcendent meanings and values. The object holds the attention and its forms and colors create, out of themselves, at least an impression. But these impressions are mixed with others derived from the viewer's experience with life as he knows it. In looking at representational art of our own tradition, it is the iconic and associated meanings that usually predominate. Ortega y Gasset puts this fact simply; he says that by art the majority of people "understand a means through which they are brought into contact with interesting human affairs" (Ortega y Gasset 1956:9). Art is a way of access to people and passions, differing from common experience in only accidental qualities, being perhaps less utilitarian, more intense and free from painful consequences. So Ortega y Gasset on the experience of the common viewer. In short, for most people who look on painting or sculpture that presents familiar life, it is a way, intensified and liberated, of having the usual content of human experience. Insofar as the immanent aesthetic values are appreciated also, they support this experiencing of the human and add their special pleasurable quality. This element of pleasure, together with whatever unusual treatment of the subject has been given to it by the artist, may further increase the experience, in totality, by moving the viewer's imagination to conceive aspects of reality or of possibility which otherwise he would not encounter. Art pushes our experience just a little farther.

On the other hand, there is a question as to how well we can pursue at the same time both the immanent and the transcendent meanings. Art, says this Spanish thinker, is like a window with a garden behind it. One may focus on either the garden or the window. The common viewer of a Constable landscape or a statue by St. Gaudens focuses on the garden. Not many people, says Ortega, "are capable of adjusting their perceptive apparatus to the windowpane and the transparency that is the work of art" (Ortega y Gasset 1956:10).

But what if there is no garden behind the windowpane? What if there are only patches of color or unrecognizable three-dimensional forms that show nothing of the familiar life of human experience? This is, of course, the case with modern non-objective art. Then what happens to the ordinary viewer is less predictable. Having no garden to look at, he may reject the object entirely, put off by the emptiness of human content, or by its very strangeness, or by the chance associations that the object just happens to suggest to him. Or, possibly, forced to look at the window because the object is all window, he may begin to find aesthetic meanings and values in it.

In much the same way one who looks at a work of primitive art may reject it because it is strange in form and strange or apparently empty in content. Looking at the seated twins of the Dogon, one does not feel cozily at home as in looking at a painting by Vermeer. Peering beyond the exotic frame of this exotic window to see the garden beyond, the visitor to the African collection sees no garden. The clues given by the forms are enigmatic. So modern art and primitive art are difficult, and it would seem that the causes of difficulty are the same in the two cases.

Let us examine further the undeniable connections that these two kinds of art show with one another. Similarities of form are often noted; all of us have seen the two reproduced side by side, the early Sumerian carving and the modern head and bust, the Melanesian mask and the semi-abstraction. In many objects of the one kind or the other we soon come to recognize a distortion of reality that goes far beyond the distortions effected by Michelangelo or El Greco. Also, the two kinds of art are similar in that both tend to draw the same kind of appreciators—young people and people not conservative in their general tastes. The effort required to look at either very modern art or primitive art and find something meaningful in it is hard for many older people to make.

Nevertheless modern art and primitive art differ in two respects. The first of these is important to our problem tonight, the problem arising from the rival claims of art and icon, of art museums and ethnographical collections. If, as Ortega says, every work of art, or at least every iconic work of art, is a windowframe—the aesthetic form—, with behind it a garden—the content of human experience to which the form refers us—, then the non-objective painting or the sculpture of the extreme modernist is all window. There is no garden. If the work is a symbol, an icon of sorts, it is one private to the artist. We have nothing to attend to but the window.

In contrast, the work of primitive art, as exemplified by the Dogon carving, does have behind it a garden, a wonderfully and complexly designed garden. Only, we cannot see it. We cannot see it because it is a garden we have never visited, a work of reshaping the natural world into a system of ideas and feelings that is unknown to us. So slight are the indications given by the object as to this garden that we may not even suspect that it is there. We catch a glimpse of it when Ogotemmêli talks to us of the twin beings made of the very essence of God, human down to the loins, serpent below. Now we begin to see in the form of the image clues to the transcendent meanings that were hidden from us before. The jointlessness of the arms, the fluidity of the legs, mean water, the divine substance.

This is the first respect in which primitive and abstract modern art are unlike: one lies within and may stand for a complex world of traditional meaning; the other does not. Such modern art is a departure from, even a revolt against, the incorporation of these traditional meanings into a work conceived as a work of aesthetic appeal in and for itself, for its newly discovered arrangements of form and color.

Modern art differs in a second respect from primitive art in its relation to traditional style. Now we are thinking not of the transcendent meanings, but of the system of forms in which the immanent aesthetic meanings find their expression. The very modern artist creates or invents his own style, one peculiar to himself, or characteristic of his small group, his "movement." He is self-conscious about this; he knows he is departing from the familiar systems of forms to find fresh ones; he and his fellows are creating styles. A Picasso may keep on creating them. But the primitive artist is, of course, making works of art within a highly formalized, intensely local and very long established style. If the primitive artist works in true primitive isolation, he is probably largely unaware of the qualities of the style he follows; he uses it as he does his language, rightly, and without self-consciousness. He is disciplined, but does not have to struggle for the discipline. We, in our civilization, refer to certain of our artists as "primitives," meaning, I suppose, that they paint without the benefit of formal instruction and without the discipline of a traditional style. They are spontaneous and "natural." In this sense primitive art is not primitive at all; it is not naive but sophisticated in that it expresses the controls and follows the directions of, in many cases, ancient and highly developed styles. There is no art more sophisticated, in this meaning of the word, than such as is represented by the African woodcarver.

But it is difficult for him who looks at such a work for the first time to see the style it represents. The system of forms within which this creation lies is strange to him; it takes time to see the style and to appreciate it. And this fact is the other half of the difficulty of the common viewer of primitive art. Neglecting the garden, because it is hidden from him, and trying to attend to the interest and beauty of the window, he is, at least at first, insensitive to the traditional forms within which this particular artist worked to produce this particular work of art. So the common viewer is blocked when he tries to see the work as icon, and he is at least much hindered when he tries to understand and appreciate it as a work of art.

It seems that I have arrived at a point of frustration, at an impasse in the road of developing understanding. Almost I seem to be telling the common viewer to leave the museum and go home. When I visited the African loan collection I overheard a lady say of those woodcarvings, "I think they are horrid." I suppose she did soon go home. Is there nothing we can tell her that might induce her to stay at The Museum of Primitive Art, or perhaps to go over to the Museum of Natural History?

This lady is perhaps a hard case. But all that I know about her is that she thought those wooden figures horrid. Let us endow her with other qualities that will make her our common viewer: the audience to whom we may direct any advice or suggestions that may be generated from this point on in our thinking.

She tells us, let us suppose, that the Dogon figures repelled her because the latticed backbone of the figure I showed in the second slide reminded her of an anatomical dissection—as, she adds, do also some of Picasso's separated women. But, although repelled, she is still interested; will we please tell her how she may develop an understanding and appreciation of these figures? What should she now look at, what read, what think about?

Her questions make us again confront the opposing claims of art and icon. Are we to tell her to look at the figures as art only and to listen to the analysis of aesthetic form offered by Guillaume and Munro? Or are we to tell her to devote herself to reading about the customs and religion of the Dogon? Or do we recommend some combination of the two approaches? And if we do recommend a combination, will the result be to hasten her progress along both paths or will it confuse and delay her progress by either? In other words, can one effectively see and appreciate both the window and the garden in the case of a work of primitive art? Ortega y Gasset almost says that one cannot, in these words: "Preoccupation with the human content of the work is in principle incompatible with aesthetic enjoyment proper." Shall we then tell our troubled lady that in practice too one must make a choice—do the one thing or the other, but not both?

As anthropologist, I turn first to the understanding of the content, those meanings that lie in Dogon life. Having read not only the reported words of Ogotemmêli, but also other writings about this people, I have some impression of the depth and complexities of the system of ideas associated with the figure of the seated twins. The words we heard from the old diviner barely begin to unfold these complexities. The twin figures at which we looked are not, in Dogon thought, one male and the other female. You probably noticed that the artist had provided both of them with beards and both of them with breasts. Each being, reports Griaule, was "equipped with two spiritual principles of opposite sex" (Griaule and Dieterlen 1953:86), each of them, therefore, was himself a pair. "Both," said Ogotemmêli, "were of the same kind." Moreover, we learn that after a series of intricately symbolic acts of incomplete creation, the primordial twins reappear in an eight-fold avatar: there are now twice four of these beings. Certain of them then begin the symbolic correspondences to one another of all things in Dogon life into eight and then twenty-two categories of related entities, heavenly or mundane. An extraordinarily elaborate cosmological and metaphysical system is implicit in and connected with the twin figures carved in wood. The French ethnologists studied the Dogon for about twenty years and feel that they by no means reached complete understanding.

This is a prospect to discourage the lady who asks our advice. Plainly she cannot expect really to know Dogon world view. Moreover, she is interested in art from other primitive peoples. In one museum she finds works from dozens of tribes and archaic states. Some of these objects stand, of course, for ideas simpler than those connected with our object, but clearly she may not

Art and Icon

hope to learn very much of the meanings transcendent in the native life of any of them. She is no ethnologist; she is a common viewer. And still further, for some works of early primitive art there are and can never be any authorities to consult as to the transcendent meanings. None of us shall ever know the world view that may be implied by the painted bisons on the walls of Magdalenian caves.

Yet we do not have to tell her that she can learn nothing about the meanings and values which the native connects with his art. If she will take the trouble, she too may read Griaule's writings. There are many primitive peoples, producers of art, about whom ethnological accounts exist: the ivory-carving Eskimo, the Haida and the Tsimshian wood-carvers and painters, the potters and effigy-makers of our Indian Southwest, the ancient Aztec and Zapotec goldworkers, terrible in their religious imagination. There is more than enough ethnology for our lady to read and think about.

We might offer her more particular guidance, some principle of selection in pursuing her study of the iconic aspects. I would tell her that she will learn most about all primitive peoples, as it is relevant to their art, if she learns as much as she can about some one of them. The central and more or less common fact about them is that each group, in its aboriginal condition, lives in terms of a coherent vision of the universe and of man's place within it. One may come to understand this general truth about them as well by reading about the Hopi Indians as by reading about the Sudanese Dogon. If one wants to develop some apprehension of the setting of a Hopi *kachina* figure or of a Dogon effigy, or of any work of primitive art, it seems to me more enlightening to acquire understanding of the integrity of Hopi or Dogon traditional life, of its consistent assertion of the right meaning of all things, than to get some miscellaneous information about this ceremony in one tribe and that technical process in another. The explanatory labels in the anthropological museums and the excellent dioramic presentations of Indians or Africans doing this or that, are well prepared and fascinating;

but they are fragmentary and tantalizing. They are separated glimpses of one after another exotic garden, each very different from the others, and no one of which may there be viewed broadly, as a garden with a design.

The position, or general attitude, taken by primitive peoples with reference to their place in the universe has always a positive character. In every case it is an assertion that things are in some comprehensible order and a declaration as to how man should accordingly act. It is never an abandonment to chaos. André Malraux puts it in one of his comprehensive, vague, essentially correct intuitions when he writes: "Implicit in these creations is an awareness of the universe, an awareness quite different from ours and unconcerned with history, involving a union with the cosmos and not a surrender to chaos: a conquest, not an abdication. From Benin to Polynesia, by way of thousands of tentative or triumphant images, we respond to the significance with which this compelling presence invests an effigy in straw" (Malraux 1953:570–71).

I do not know if Malraux came to understand this general truth about the world views of the isolated primitive peoples by reading ethnology or by just looking at objects made by primitive artists. I do not think I could come to understand it from the objects alone. I should advise our troubled lady to read about one or more exotic peoples that have been well and intimately reported if she wishes to enrich her compound experience when she comes to The Museum of Primitive Art: in, for example, *African Worlds,* recently published for the International Institute of Africanists. In this book a reader may vicariously experience, however dimly, nine of these intellectual and emotional interpretations of the universe and of man which primitive or barbaric peoples have achieved. That one book alone is something of an introduction to Malraux's truth as to the triumphant union with the cosmos which has been man's finest achievement, an achievement made so variously and so slowly, through many generations, by hundreds and hundreds of human groups. If the common viewer wants to enlarge her understanding of primitive life, as manifest in art, she may both read and read and also look and look, and perhaps come to see that the style of the art and the style of the whole life of that people are parallel systems of form and of meaning.

So I say that in spite of the difficulties, it is possible for the lady we have imagined to come to understand something of the uses and functions of the object at which she is looking and also about the kind of world that the African's mind inhabits. Looking at some of the pieces in the loan collection, she may then respond to them not only as they are works of art but also as they are signs and symbols of an exotic way of life. It seems to me that then her total experience will be enriched. She has now two kinds of experience to enjoy and to pursue. The object may disclose to her both its aesthetic and its transcendent meanings and values. If she comes to see the art style and also to apprehend something of the whole style of life within which that art lies, she will be having such a mixed experience as is had by many in the enjoyment of Dutch interiors or Renoir's paintings. I am now saying no more than that in the case of primitive art and a mixed experience is possible, though difficult, and I am also recognizing that two kinds of experience are more widely rewarding than is one alone.

But the lady is not satisfied with this. She says she would indeed like to enjoy such a mixed experience, but please will we tell her how to achieve it. She says she quite understands that there is more to these figures than appears to one who does no more than see them in The Museum of Primitive Art, and she says she will call upon the anthropologists and get their advice as to books about primitive peoples. But she wonders if in going into ethnological investigation she may not be somewhat distracted from pursuing her equal ambition to appreciate and understand these works as art. In particular will we make it clear to her if understanding the objects as related to local customs and religion will help her to understand them as art. She makes me ask myself if, in accepting the possibility and value of a mixed experience, I have denied that assertion made by Ortega y Gasset that "preoccupation with the human content of the work is in principle incompatible with aesthetic enjoyment proper"? This common viewer is a useful gadfly in her simple way. She makes me come directly to the questions that arise when one tries to appreciate and understand these objects as art. How does one do so? What helps? What hinders?

I would begin by assuring her that in the remarks so far made I have not denied Ortega's assertion. I was talking about the enrichment of the appreciative understanding of a work of art that comes *after* one knows the world it lies in and stands for and *after* one has come understandingly to appreciate its aesthetic qualities. Ortega's dictum, on the other hand, refers to the process of learning and appreciating. He thinks of the concentrated activity in which we either look at and appreciate our twin-figure, or learn about the beliefs of the Dogon people. It is not, according to him, enjoyment of the one experience that is incompatible with the other, but preoccupation by the one with preoccupation by the other. One cannot at the same moment focus on two diverging objects, window frame and garden. To look fully and intently at the wooden carving, to invite it to disclose the immanent values of its arrangement of form, we need freedom from distraction. And then ethnology *is* a distraction: it draws one away, along another path of thought and feeling. Fascinating and rewarding as is the exploration of these exotic words, they are, in the moment and effort of appreciation of art as controlled form, a hindrance.

So I do not favor the abolition of The Museum of Primitive Art and the transfer of its collections to the care of anthropologists. I admit that as long as it and its kind exist, there will appear some conflict of interest, both between the man of art and the man of science, and also within the experience of the common viewer. Set there on its well-lighted pedestal, the object is both a temptation to mistaken speculation about primitive peoples and an invitation to forget, for the time, those peoples and look at the thing as art. The viewer may succumb to the temptation; he will, perhaps, follow whatever the object as representation or symbol suggests to him, and form ideas as to the mind of primitive man or as to the element of terror in primitive religion, or as to the originality of the primitive artist, or conceive I don't know what other fancies (Leach 1954:25–38). Then he will risk the scorn of the anthropologist and hear the voice of that specialist inviting him to come over to his kind of museum and learn the truth.

But if this invitation is politely refused, but for the time being only, and if the viewer instead accepts that other invitation implicit in the object on its pedestal, he begins to see the work as art. It is the object itself that is the first teacher. There is no beginning here other than to look at the thing and let it affect one. Aesthetic experience—I state what you all know—is direct and personal. The thing speaks; one hears and is moved. "Art is like the vision of Saul; there is a voice, a presence, an impact" (Mills 1957:6). If the twin-figure does not speak to you, even in a whisper, one can always look again; maybe then it will. When it speaks, you answer. You say, with the lady I overheard, "It is horrid," or you say, "this is good." You may of course say, "This is bad," and if you mean bad as art, you are on your way too, by the chosen path. For art, in its public product, is controlled experience with personal qualities for both artist and appreciator. It is the management of some medium so as to achieve forms that present and suggest such qualities (Mills 1957:6). If the Dogon carving is art, it is these qualities, in their structure of forms, that will speak and make you respond. It is *your* feeling and judgment about them that begins to establish appreciation and understanding.

But also it is true that every established art is an expression of a style, which is a language, traditional like other natural languages, in which the forms are found, the qualities are set forth. In coming to see the style, the persisting structure of available forms, we are helped to see the work as art. We are helped also to begin to make the discrimination of better and worse, or of more or less successful achievement. In the arts of the West, we have already some ability in these languages of form. For the exotic arts we have to learn them. It follows, I think, that that exhibition of primitive art which presents together several objects in the same stylistic tradition gets us along faster in our appreciation and understanding than that exhibition which shows us one object beside one other object of another tradition. Even within West Africa the tribal styles differ as widely as do styles of civilized peoples thousands of miles apart. It is good, then, to look first at one Dogon carving and then at another. One begins to say to one's self, "The fellow who made that one really pulled it off." Now the object speaks with the accent of its style. One begins to sense what system of forms propelled and also limited the artist. One glimpses his hand working obedient to its mandates. One begins to see that here he realized and perhaps surpassed these instructions from tradition, and there he weakly imitated.

This is appreciation. It is not quite understanding, if we mean by understanding the formulation of defensible reasons why the object is good or bad. Appreciation is aesthetic experience; understanding, or thoughtful justification, is cognitive in mode. As I am no aesthetician nor any kind of philosopher, I am free to admit that I am not quite sure what is the relationship between appreciation and this kind of understanding. I am ready to believe that appreciation is strengthened and kept going by understanding, and I am pretty sure that considered understanding, like other activities of the intellect, is a good in itself. But I also feel a strong sympathy for the viewer who just enjoys, condemns or praises, and lets it go at that.

In our course of thinking tonight it was Guillaume and Munro, with their comment on the Dogon carving, who began the analysis of forms that may contribute to understanding the work. I hear what they say about angular and staccato rhythms and the way the spaces around the shoulders and hips function like the buttresses of Gothic cathedrals. I am interested, but I do not accept these assertions as the one necessary key to understanding of the figure. I want to look again at the figure for myself: Do I see or hear those rhythms, do I think of Gothic cathedrals?

Maybe I see and think of something else. I want to talk the matter over with Guillaume and Munro, with the seated twins right there before us. I foresee conversations, in the cognitive mode, about the figure, with probable repercussions upon my appreciation of it. With primitive as with other art one may begin to state to one's self and to propose to others elements that compose the standard of excellence which the artist has at first only suggested to you, the viewer, as implicit in his work. I am by no means sure that such elements are discoverable that apply to all styles and kinds of art. I do not imagine that our understanding appraisal may ever be reduced to a check list whereon we mark off, *seriatim,* failures and successes. The considered understanding of aesthetic worth is more probably an interminable dialogue. In the case of primitive art the dialogue has hardly begun.

As I say the word "dialogue" I seem to hear objections raised in quarters where the primitive person and his way of life are prime matters of concern. Your dialogue, these voices say, seems to be a somewhat private affair. Are you and those two art critics to carry it on without inviting to take part him whose ideas about this work of art may be most relevant and persuasive— the primitive artist himself? Yes, and the primitive critic, or, as there are no professional critics in primitive groups, the other people of that tribe or state who did not make the work but who judge it as done well or ill. You outsiders to the native life, by what right do you take it upon yourself to judge this work, by your own insights and standards, without even moving to hear what its maker and receiver think and feel about it? Perhaps the values they see in the work, the aesthetic values, are quite different from what you outsiders see.

These objections seem to be important and weighty. But, as I think about them, they grow lighter and lighter, less and less to be seriously considered. How are we to listen to the native artist's views? He is so far away; in many cases his art is no longer carried on; it is represented in works of his production which the descendants of the artist, if they still exist, no longer carry on. Moreover, in those cases where the artists still produce the art, we are not likely to find, should we go to them and their people, that he has very much to tell us as to standards of artistic excellence. Our ethnological friends, to whose thunder on the left we are now attending, have not made many studies of aesthetic judgments in primitive societies. The few such studies that I have read suggest that while judgments of better and worse are made by Indians or Africans with regard to their artistic productions, the reasons they give for justifying their judgments hardly constitute an aesthetic. The African responds to the ethnologist's request that he range twenty-four decorated calabashes in the order in which the African likes them, and does so. When asked why he likes the first one best, he says that on this one the black spots are in the right place. Pushed further by questioning, he declares that in one calabash there is too much black, and he begins to use some word translated as "balance" in reference to the placing of the elements of design. I am sure that more could be learned about these aesthetic judgments, but I do not think that any much discussed or much considered formulation of aesthetic taste is likely to appear in an isolated primitive group where style is traditional and learned without awareness of other possibilities.

Ruth Bunzel's study of Pueblo Indian potters (Bunzel 1929) leads to the same conclusion. She found that within a single small linguistic and cultural community potters stated much the same very general principles of design. For simple designs, the best choice is to use four elements; three is also very good; six is permissible; but five is not good. The Zuñi potters usually confined their critical comment about Zuñi pots to such a remark as "I don't like that," but one potter ventured to say that the deer on a certain pot "looked like pigs," and condemned another as "uneven"; several jars were called "funny." Other potters characterized pots that bore, in their judgment, too much pigment, as "dirty." On the whole, with a small exception in the case of Zuñi where Bunzel found some potters able to state such simple principles as the number of elements to be used, she concluded

Art and Icon

that Pueblo potters were "entirely unconscious" of the principles of design their own pots exemplified. And their unawareness is further evidenced by the fact that in not a few cases the actual pots made and praised did not obey these simple principles. For example, in spite of the stated preference for four elements, many pots showed only three. Apparently the ritual importance of four in Southwest Indian thought shaped the explicit principle which, then, did not really derive from the potter's practice. A considered aesthetic is not to be found among primitive peoples. Like many of us, they don't know much about art but they know what they like.

I imagine our common viewer not quite satisfied. She is ready to take part in discussions about why she and other people praise or dispraise works of primitive art, but this exclusion of the artist and his own audience from the discussions seems to her somehow not quite right—a great-power decision on the aesthetic affairs of little peoples. And indeed in this thunder from the left about the point there is another argument, a more theoretical argument, to be met. I have said that it is difficult to bring the primitive person to the aesthetic dialogue and that if one got him there he would not have much to say. The argument I have not met questions the full worth of the judgments made by the critic of Western tradition and training upon works of exotic art. I have heard it said that the Western critic brings to the primitive work aesthetic judgments that are "ethnocentric," or "culture-bound," that is, that are conditioned by his experience with and judgments of the arts of his own tradition. This is said with the implication that his judgment on the exotic work is correspondingly vitiated, or at least rendered erroneous.

To this argument I think the reply is in the form of a lawyer's demurrer, expressible in layman's language as "So what?" The allegation is admitted, but not its purported consequences. Yes, the judgment of the Western is culture-bound. Yes, he brings to the primitive work conceptions and comparisons that come from his experience, not from the experience of the primitive artist (those Gothic cathedrals again!). No, he is in no position to speak for the exotic artist and his community, and indeed it is quite possible that the implicit standards of taste that found expression in a carving we outsiders judge in terms of staccato rhythms and flying buttresses were different from those brought to the work by men familiar with Western art and perhaps also with some of the arts of the civilized Asian peoples. This we admit. But we reply that nevertheless there is no one in any better position to attempt to find reasons for the artistic success of the primitive artist than we modern Western outsiders for the reason that no one else has as much experience with many kinds of art. Certainly the modern critic has more such experience than the artist who carved the figure; he knew only his own artistic tradition. He is at a loss when confronting other arts. Ruth Bunzel found that Pueblo potters usually found the pots made in other pueblos, not far away from their own, baffling or uninteresting. The isolated primitive person has learned from one source only: his own ancestors. The Post-Impressionists learned something from the primitive artists. The primitive artists learned nothing from the Post-Impressionists. It is the nature of civilization, as contrasted with primitive life, that its carriers and beneficiaries come to know, to think and to judge in terms of forms and ideas that come from peoples other than their own. Civilized life, anywhere, differs from primitive life in that some men and women have the time and develop the will and capacity to reflect and to judge with respect to some aspect of the common life. In certain civilizations—medieval Japan is such a case—it is the aesthetic discriminations which are so cultivated and refined. Moreover, the great civilizations of wide influence represent a coming together of various traditions. They are a mixing, a stimulating, a comparing of one traditional way with another. In these the habit develops of putting one meaning or value beside another. Western civilization is such a civilization. It is here in the West that some people have gone farthest in developing an interest in and appreciation of art derived from some knowledge of the arts of many traditions. We have today a far from universal view of art, but it is a view wider than others have. And surely

Art and Icon

in this regard primitive life and civilized life are not equal. In judging art the civilized person has advantages denied to the primitive: a more inclusive field of comparisons, and some practice in thinking about aesthetic judgments.

It seems to me that we have almost concluded our reply to the troubled lady. She is to be encouraged to pursue, if she cares to, both the aesthetic and the iconic meanings and values of primitive art. She will find The Museum of Primitive Art a good place to develop her appreciation and understanding of the one, and she will find the anthropologists and the ethnological book collections ready to help her with the other. She will find that insofar as she concentrates on art she will not be getting much ahead with ethnology. But, as one can arrange one's life in more than one way, she may go in for the one endeavor without much attention to the other, or find the time and strength to cultivate both interests. We have warned her that in looking at these primitive works she is not likely to learn much that is trustworthy about the thoughts and beliefs of primitive peoples. On the other hand, in the anthropological museum she is not placed in the best possible position for the appreciation of the works as art. The anthropological presentation is so very inviting with respect to the meanings and uses of the artifacts, and not always do we find in such presentations the most favorable circumstances for the undistracted contemplation of a few artistic works arranged so that the control of form, by their makers, is readily apparent and unconfused by other references carried by the objects.

But I think we have not quite answered that question of hers as to whether the acquisition of knowledge of the meanings and values in the native life will be helpful to her when she turns to consider the aesthetic meanings. This is the part of her uncertainty which I share; I find that I cannot fully solve it. Perhaps you can do better with it than I can. I think I do see that if she comes to African carvings with some knowledge of native life, and if that knowledge aroused an interest, not unfavorable, in Africans, she may be, as the psychologists say, "motivated" to look upon the works without initial disfavor or resentment; she is less likely to dismiss them as horrid. She may at least look again.

Beyond this easy assertion is, however, a much more difficult question. To what extent, if at all, does the art communicate something about the special nature, the characteristic world view of the people who made the art? You understand that we are not here considering how the subject matter of an art tells us something of the people. This is obvious: if we had no information about the Paleolithic Europeans except what appears in their wall paintings, we should know they were much interested in hunting certain animals. But even as to subject matter there are obvious limitations on the trustworthiness of such inferences. Meyer Schapiro remarks that the absence of human form in Muslim art is no basis for an inference that the Muslims were or are disinterested in the human body (Schapiro 1953:309).

No, we take her question to be: Wishing to understand the people through the art, can she look at the pieces just as art and derive from what she sees some true conclusions as to what kind of a people they are? It is so often said that the art of a people expresses that people that I hesitate to deny it. Oswald Spengler, who did not hesitate much, asserted that Greek character or ethos is expressed in Greek art, and modern character or ethos in modern art and architecture. Among both historians of art and anthropologists there have been a few who have seen art styles as expressions in concrete form of the thought and feeling that pervades and characterizes the whole culture. I hope our common viewer finds these interpretations interesting, but I should not advise her to expect to derive much valid understanding of a primitive world view from the art style of that people. True, one might argue that such a correspondence is more likely to appear in a primitive than in a civilized art because in simple isolated groups there is less variation within the style and because the art there is produced, usually, for no special group or class but for everybody. On the other hand, the common viewer will not have that knowledge of the history of the people and of the art which aids the modern art historian when he discovers these correspondences. Schapiro reminds us that it is after the work of nearly two centuries of scholars that a sensitive mind "can respond directly to the 'Greek mind' in those ancient buildings and sculptures" (Schapiro 1953:307). No one can provide the common viewer with similar historical knowledge of a Melanesian tribal culture and of its art. Moreover, a little experience with some primitive arts suggests caution in deriving art styles from world view. It is true that if I know something of the restraint and harmony in Zuñi life generally I am not surprised when I find restraint and harmony in the decoration applied to Zuñi pottery. But the formal geometric decorations on the skin bags made by Plains Indians are very misleading indications of the view of life of those tribes, with their emphasis on individual military exploit and intense private religious experience. Art somehow, in some large sense, does tend to be a consistent part of the very general emotional and intellectual dispositions of peoples, but the connections are not close enough or clear enough to be of much use to the common viewer.

The aesthetic and the iconic are two worlds of thought. In the case of works of art they are bound one to the other by the physical object, the artifact, which is, as it were, a body in which two souls dwell. Unlike the two beings represented by the twin-figure that has served us this evening as a concrete text, these two creatures of the mind are not identical twins, "of the same kind"; they are of different kinds. Between the two, as systems of thought and feeling, of meaning and value, there are only slight direct connections; like the twin figures of the Dogon they are united, but only by slender rods of interconnection, rods that will not bear much weight of reasoned inference.

Although I have here spoken of the difference and degree of separateness of the appreciation and understanding of the two kinds of meanings and values in primitive works of art, I would not leave with you the impression that the two endeavors are opposed to each other. The artifact as art and the artifact as icon are abstractions from the total body of meanings that attach to the physical object. The rivalry between the two kinds of museums for presentation of the object and for explanation of the meanings arises as much from the different interests and trainings of the two kinds of potential custodians as from the fact, which I have stressed, that to look hard at the object one must focus either on window frame or on garden. I have wanted to acknowledge the justice of the claims of both kinds of museums and of specialists to these objects.

In a context of learning and appreciation wider than either a concentration upon art or a concentration upon ethnological use and meaning, the two efforts, toward art and toward understanding of icon, are not divergent, are not at all opposed, are, indeed, parallel. Better said, the two kinds of effort are of the same kind; the understanding of the work as art is enclosed within, is a special case of, the understanding of an exotic culture. For both are aspects of the widening of our comprehension of the human. Whether we come to see the artifact as a creative mastery of form, or see it as a sign or symbol of a traditional way of life, we are discovering, for ourselves, new territory of our common humanity. We are enlarging the range of our recognition of human sameness as it appears in human difference. At first the figure or the mask looks, perhaps, wholly alien and incomprehensible. It may seem to represent nothing of art and nothing human. But the path toward aesthetic appreciation leads to a recognition that, after all, it is art; it is another expression of a creative power, an aesthetic sensibility, and a control of a system of forms applied to a medium which, in these general powers and effects, are the same human qualities that we have taken for granted in the art we know best. The system of forms is different, but the human impulses and productions are the same kind of thing. And this is but one aspect of the exploration of human universality in difference which is, for a wider territory of human life, carried on by those who come to understand that alien cultures are again expressions of human universality in difference. He who goes to live with an exotic people often begins, as does many a common viewer of primitive art, with a first impression that these people are opaque, not to be understood, somehow not me at all but something quite different. The usual outcome of persisting effort to understand is so to alter this first impression as to make the exotic people seem almost like the outsider's friends back home. One of the best of the ethnological students of West African peoples has confessed that when he began to study a certain people there, about whom he is now the leading authority, he thought of them as hardly human. They have become human to him, quite human. In coming to understand an alien way of life, as in coming to understand an alien art, the course of personal experience is essentially the same: one looks first at an incomprehensible other; one comes to see that other as one's self in another guise. This widening of our comprehension of the human has been going on, I suppose, since the day thousands of years ago, when some primitive hunter relaxed his suspicion of or hostility to the people over the hill long enough to think to himself, "Well, I guess those fellows have something there after all." It goes on today, in spite of all the hatreds and conflicts between peoples. Slowly, for one or another of us, the vision and comprehension of humanity, both in its extraordinary variety of expressions and its fundamental sameness, is widened. Both take part in this widening, ethnologist and student of exotic art. Both the study of art and the study of cultures as whole ways of life, contribute. The two paths of endeavor that we have pointed out to the common viewer lead in the same direction after all.

ART: AN INTRODUCTION
TO QUALITATIVE ANTHROPOLOGY

George Mills

TWO INDEPENDENT lines of development are converging in anthropology.[1] The first is concerned with the study of art. The limitations of our treatment of art can be shown by reference to four of its aspects: technique and materials, social function, style, and its nature as a medium of expression. Anthropologists have been interested in the following questions: Is there an evolution of styles from representative to geometric forms or vice versa (Stolpe, Boas), what is the effect of technique upon style (Holmes), how may regional styles be defined (Stolpe, Haddon, Wingert), how do art objects function within the religious, social, and economic life of a culture (any good ethnography), what is the nature of the processes by which arts are created (Teit, Bunzel), and how does the definition of the artistic role affect these processes (Himmelheber)? Of the four aspects of art mentioned above, that which has been consistently ignored is the most obvious: art as a medium of expression. One of the basic assumptions of social science is that we can abstract stable, central tendencies—call them patterns, configurations, values, or what you will—from patterns of behavior, regularities of per-

---

Reprinted from *The Journal of Aesthetics and Art Criticism,* 16 (1) 1957: 1–17, by permission of the author and The American Society for Aesthetics.

[1] I am grateful to Prof. J. Glenn Gray for permission to take part in his course on aesthetics and to Prof. E. Darnell Rucker for the opportunity of attending his course on the philosophy of science. I have drawn on discussions that took place in both of these courses for ideas expressed in this paper. I wish to thank Prof. Gray and Mr. Richard Grove for reading and criticizing my manuscript.

sonality, and language usages. None of these sources of data reflects only these central and enduring tendencies; personality, for instance, is shaped in part by the physical characteristics of the human beings who live according to the way of life studied. None of these sources of data fully reflects these central tendencies which can be thoroughly understood only by comparing all sources of information. Much attention, from this point of view, has been given behavior, personality expressions, and language, but art has been ignored—at least by social scientists. It is not surprising that the chapter in *Anthropology Today* which deals with this problem was written by an art historian and that most of the people whose work he discusses are also art historians.

The second line of development has to do with the understanding of a way of life from within. It is recognized that by arranging ethnological facts according to our own habits of thought —under such headings as religion, social organization, economics, life cycle—we make it difficult to determine how a people articulate their own thoughts, feelings, and activities. This realization has led to a new interest in largely affective states, such as the fears of the Eskimos, the anxieties of the Navahos, and the "awayness" of the Balinese; to new methods, such as analysis of personal histories, for examining the inner articulation of cultures; and to new conceptual tools like value, value-orientation, and symbolic act for considering the role of affects in behavior.

David McAllester's *Enemy Way Music* (1954) is a recent exemplification of the convergence of aesthetic and anthropological interests, a development which promises to broaden our insight into problems of culture as well as improve our methods for dealing with these problems. The purpose of this paper is to sketch some ideas about art that will make this important human undertaking more intelligible to the social scientist.

THE ARTISTIC PROCESS

It is easy to oversimplify the artistic process. We may base conclusions on a single medium of expression or raid the arts for those features which fit our preconceptions and, by ignoring other facts, give cogency to superficial conclusions. Freud's treatment of Leonardo de Vinci is a classic example, as Abell has shown. Of all the features of style and iconography that appear in Leonardo's work, how few are recognized and used, and yet what large results are achieved. The following diagram, intended to mark off the major turning points in the artistic process, will be used as a basis for discussing various concepts and matters of aesthetic fact.

SUMMARY OF THE ARTISTIC PROCESS

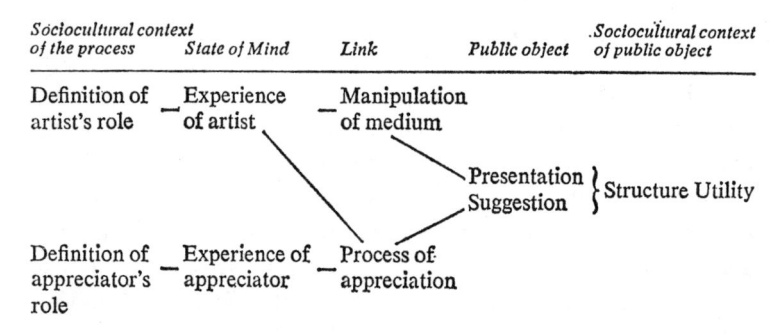

Sociocultural context of the process	State of Mind	Link	Public object	Sociocultural context of public object
Definition of artist's role	Experience of artist	Manipulation of medium		
			Presentation Suggestion	Structure Utility
Definition of appreciator's role	Experience of appreciator	Process of appreciation		

Artistic roles

In constituting part of the role structure of society, the role of the artist is no different from that of general, policeman, or teacher. Like the rest of us, the artist must live up to expectations or suffer. The individual responsible for the making of drypaintings in Navaho culture has religious and medical functions because art for the Navahos is intimately bound up with the maintenance of health and cosmic organization. Memory for the traditional, carefully specified designs is more important in this Navaho art than originality. American culture offers a variety of roles for artistic skills. The responsibilities assumed by non-objective painter, commercial artist, and architect are quite different.

In many cultures, the role of art lover lacks definition because art is not viewed as a separate activity. This does not prevent individuals from attending to and being moved by objects and events in a way which we may call aesthetic. Our own society does provide a fairly well-defined role for the connoisseur and collector, as well as a special sanctuary, the museum, into which they may occasionally retreat with their refined tastes.

Experience of the artist

What is the relation of the quality of the artist's experience to his final product? Does it pre-exist the manipulation of the medium, or are the quality of the experience and the style of the art so interwoven with the manipulation of the medium as to emerge simultaneously from it? The experience of the artist is the most covert and elusive phase of the entire process. One cannot rely upon even the artist's description of his inner states, for his understanding of these states is unwittingly influenced by the expectations which his role establishes. In a culture which demands originality, the artist will honestly overlook many borrowings. To use a sacramental analogy, the artist's state of mind is the invisible grace of which the work of art is the visible form. Nevertheless, by studying the artist's choice of medium, his products, the definition of his role, and what he says about his work—by studying each of these in the light of all the others, we shall learn a good deal about the artist's inner workings.

Skill

Skillful manipulation of a medium in order to achieve certain effects is the most common criterion of art, implicit even in such a phrase as "the black arts." Skills of perception, memory, tool handling, bodily movement, and organizational ability are part of the makeup of the artist on which the nature of his experience and of his work depends.

Materiality

One can discuss at length what a medium comprises. Materials? The use to which materials are put (oil paint may be applied slickly or crustily)? The complex of images and experiences which the artist selects for expression? One can even argue whether or not the material embodiment is essential to the existence of art. As for the first question, all three types of fact are important; what is not so important is deciding where the medium ends and analysis of the object begins. As for the second question, since the social scientist cannot deal with unexpressed intuitions, we shall say that art does not exist until the artist has set his hand to a medium and has produced a painting, musical score, dance notation, or other public object. If it is true that the intuition of the artist is formed only through struggles with his medium, then the process of having intuitions is inseparable from the process of making them public.

The idea of embodying an intuition in a medium applies to painting, sculpture, and architecture. In the dance, the artist's body is his medium, and it would be more correct to say that he manipulates this medium in such a way as to make his intuition known. Music presents a different problem. The public object of the musician is not always his own creation. He provides clues, in the form of a score, to the nature of the public object, but the completion of this object may depend upon the skill of a performer. Musical instruments have a similar effect; a composition intended for the harpsichord is qualitatively different when played upon the piano.

These are important differences, for by overlooking them we oversimplify our aesthetics. What mediums are included under the rubric of art? The answer to this question must wait upon a more precise answer to the question, What is art? We may be sure in advance that we shall encounter fuzzy edges, and that some activities may or may not be considered art depending upon the expansiveness of one's sympathies. What are the limitations of each medium? This problem cannot be solved until that

Judgment Day when the work of all artists in all mediums can be perused. Before that time, however, we may be able to form opinions about the expressive bias of each medium, and these opinions will help us to understand the more elusive parts of the creative process, for in so far as a choice exists, the selection of a medium means the selection of opportunities to experience in a particular fashion.

The public object

The insistence upon materiality provides us with a public object or event in which all relevant experiences of all possible observers remain potential.

Thomas Munro (1949:354) distinguishes three aspects of the public object: the presented, the suggested, and the structural. The first includes all that is present to the senses of the individual: shapes, colors, tones, textures, and the like. Suggestion achieves effects that are not immediately sensuous through the presentation of sensuous materials. Through its arrangement of shapes and colors a two-dimensional painting may suggest a three-dimensional object. Suggestion, according to Munro, takes several forms. It may be mimetic, as in *trompe l'oeil* painting; symbolic, as when a cross brings to mind the essentials of Christianity; or it may operate through common and often unconscious associations, as when a zigzag line conveys a sense of motion.

The presented and suggested aspects of the public object are structured or organized. One might define art as a portion of experience small enough to be organized as man would have his whole experience organized. By reducing organization to such principles as repetition, contrast, balance, etc., valuable analytic tools though these may be, or even to dichotomies like romantic and classic types of structure, we misunderstand the chief point about organization: that one element must be considered in relation to all of the others that make up the work. The effect may be chaotic, as in the anti-art products of Dadaism, but it remains deliberate chaos which is a special type of chaos, meaningful only in relation to the artistic cosmos which it denies.

Structure is as significant expressively as the presented and suggested aspects of the object.

Style

A style is a recurrent way of structuring and presenting. It is a regularity, an aesthetic pattern, that is abstracted from a number of works of art. The number of works may range from those executed by a single artist during a period of his life to styles characteristic of whole nations or ages. Although styles differ markedly—and defining the nature of these differences is not easy—one fact is common to all styles: they are not a reproduction or literal copy of nature. Commonly a distinction is made between naturalistic and abstract art. This is misleading. First, because it obscures the fact that all art is abstract in the sense that style implies selection of elements from human experience and their reordering in new structures. "Naturalistic" simply means less abstract than "abstract" art. Second, the use of such dichotomies leads you to label an art as either abstract or naturalistic, although it may be naturalistic in some respects, but abstract in others, as when a Spanish-American attaches a portrait-like head to a body that stylizes the human physique, or a Navaho sand-painter places naturalistic animals beside the geometric representations of Holy People from his mythology. As a result, the term psychical distance, coined by Bullough, is gaining currency. This concept indicates, not two or three possible relations between style and reality, but an infinity of ways and degrees in which style may depart from reality as it is known in everyday life.

Because it requires a medium, and because of its distance from daily life, art has developmental tendencies that may trace, as Kroeber (1944b) has shown, a trajectory different from those of associated cultural patterns. Little is known about the immanent directioning of aesthetic patterns, but they are of obvious importance for the study of art-in-culture. If they exist, fluctuations of style may be determined by previous states of the art as well as by contemporaneous cultural values.

Utility

Just as the experience of the artist is related to sociocultural demands through the definition of role, so the public object is related to sociocultural demands through its utility. It is important to keep in mind the distinction between the object's utility and its function. Utility is a matter of entering into action, function of entering into awareness. The design of a piece of cloth has utility when the cloth is made into curtains, but it does not function until we take time to contemplate the curtain. Function is essential to art, utility not. In keeping with this thought, devotees of the fine arts have insisted on cutting away the utilitarian aspect of art. However, from the fact that utility is not essential to art, it does not follow that lack of utility makes an object art. In other quarters, the confusion of utility and function is so thoroughgoing that the elimination of utility seems to do away with all of the uses of art which comes to be defined as an indulgence for the idle. A further result is to lower the quality of the products of utilitarian skill; a great mistake, for utilitarian objects, providing numerous opportunities for aesthetic contemplation, ought to be fashioned with the greatest care. At the same time it is difficult to appreciate arts that have utility, for familiar and useful objects are precisely those we are least apt to see except as they serve practical ends.

The purist says that art is divorced from daily life while the relationist says, with the dogmatism of some theologians, that divorce is a sin. It is possible that both purist and relationist are reasonable and that the important question is not, "Which view gives us the essence of art?" but, "How are these two facts of art related to one another?" Art is fraternal, yea-saying, delighted with commonplace sensuous resources, overjoyed to be the tool worn smooth by a man's hand, the clothing warmed by his body, the cockleshell that bobs between him and the ocean floor. Art has room for criminality and sin as well as cognition and sanctity. No situation or subject matter is alien: religious dogma, ceremonial, eating and sleeping, cities and hermits, saints and storms at sea. Using without being used, it remains embracive but elusive. Our conception of art must cover fishhooks and window shades as well as nonobjective painting and fugues.

Appreciation

This concept is necessary because it makes clear that those who are not artists may profit from art; when we do so, we receive impacts of color, sound, form, movement, perceive relations among these, and entertain suggestions similar to those the artist experiences in the course of his work.

The President, while attending the theater, is assassinated, and the assassin jumps onto the stage and shouts, "Sic semper tyrannis." If the play which the President was attending happened to be a performance of *Julius Caesar* in modern dress, the reality of the murder and the reality of the play would be confused, and the audience would do nothing to pursue the criminal. This inhibition of practical action before the work of art, so different from the response accorded similar events in daily life, is brought about by another aspect of psychical distance.

Aesthetic experience

If this conclusion about appreciation be true, the experience of the art lover is similar to that of the artist. Is this experience so distinctive that it warrants the use of such terms as aesthetic experience, aesthetic contemplation, and the like? Many have distinguished aesthetic experience by saying that it is intrinsically valuable, whereas other experiences are instrumentally valuable. However, every choice we make is decided in part by anticipating that the chosen course will be more interesting, more valuable for its own sake, than the rejected one. This is not the only standard of choice, and often this one is overborne by more urgent considerations. We come closer to an important feature of aesthetic experience when we recall the distinction between two kinds of knowing made in French, Spanish, and German: knowing by acquaintance and knowing by understanding. Many sceptics have studied the life of Christ without altering their scepticism, but one moment of knowledge by acquaintance, such as that which came to Saul, may do what years of knowledge by understanding have not accomplished. Art is like the vision of Saul: there is a voice, a presence, an impact. We recall that a basic aspect of the public object is presentational. Suggestion and structure come to us vividly, immediately, sensuously. At first this does not seem to hold true of literature that is not read aloud. However, Joseph Conrad (1947:707, 708) is not describing his methods alone when he says that all "art . . . appeals primarily to the senses, and the artistic aim when expressing itself in written words must also make its appeal through the senses, if its high desire is to reach the secret spring of responsive emotions."

> . . . My task which I am trying to achieve is, by the power of the written word, to make you hear, to make you feel—it is, before all, to make you *see*. That—and no more, and it is everything. If I succeed, you shall find there, according to your deserts, encouragement, consolation, fear, charm, all you demand —and, perhaps, also that glimpse of truth for which you have forgotten to ask.

The importance of art's function can be studied in terms of the trouble individuals will take to alter their surroundings. Navaho blankets would be just as useful if they lacked the meticulous outlining, found in some styles, which costs much time and labor. The same is true of carved fish floats, painted pots, elaborate eating utensils, projectile points, masks, shields, and countless other objects of daily use. We say that these objects have been embellished, have had decoration added to them. When one considers the cost of the decoration, it appears that what is added is as important as the original object, so that the separation of creation and decoration is arbitrary. It would be more correct to say that a function, which we do not wholly understand, has been added to utility.

Universality

Art appears in all cultures that we know about. A conception that does not prove useful in dealing with arts from cultures other than our own will not be adequate.

BASES FOR DEFINING ART

If we take another look at the diagram, we find that the artistic process has four major aspects: sociocultural context, state of mind, public object, and the link between state of mind and object. Each of these aspects of the process has become the center for theories of art. Marxist views, as in the writing of Plekhanov, tend to make art a passive reflection of conditions of production, thus emphasizing the sociocultural context of creation. Croce's treatment of "intuition" lays stress upon the artist's state of mind, and Dewey's (1934) use of "quality" embraces the state of mind of art lovers. The public object becomes the center of iconological definitions of art, as well as of theories of significant form in so far as these are concerned with form. In so far as they are concerned with significance, and most of them remain obscure about this, they seem to point to the next aspect, the linkage between public object and state of mind. Here we have a variety of definitions: art as the exercise of skills, expressive theories according to which states of mind are given appropriate embodiment, including the psychoanalytic theory of art as a disguised expression of socially unacceptable impulses. Semiotic theories, like theories of significant form, are undecided as to whether the locus of art is in the public object or in some state of mind with which the object corresponds. There are also notions which distribute their definitional emphasis among more than one aspect of the process. Talcott Parsons gives equal attention to role, expression, symbol, and affect. Thomas Munro, having given most thought to the problems of a combined definition, offers a way of differentiating particular arts on the basis of process, medium, and product.

If we agree that definitions vary with the purposes of the definers we are not surprised to see so much contention over the nature of art; what is surprising is that each scholar should treat his own view of the essence of art as the last word that need be said. We must keep all phases of the process in mind, but in order not to be embarrassed by our riches, we must select one phase of this process as the primary differentia of art and allow the other phases to fall in place alongside. Such a definition should enable us to distinguish artistic activity from other activities, but it should also help with the specifically anthropological problems mentioned at the start of the paper: relating art to the rest of culture, and making available the methods and conclusions of art historians, aestheticians, and psychologists of art.

The idea of art offered here is not a new one. Emphasizing that aspect of the process summed up in "state of mind," it employs "qualities of experience" as its genus. Recognizing that non-aesthetic as well as aesthetic experiences have a qualitative side, we are obliged to specify that which distinguishes artistic qualities from non-artistic. Qualitative experiences are of two sorts. First, there are those qualities which occur in the course of, and are controlled by, experiences forced upon us by non-aesthetic requirements. Man has to eat to live, so he works to acquire food. He may hunt, gather, farm, or labor for wages, exchanging money for food. Each of these economic activities is qualitatively different from the others. Economic behavior falls within narrow limits set by ability, situational requirements, and cultural patterns, so that preferences based upon taste in qualities of experience had small room in which to operate. Second, there are those experiences which are controlled by qualitative considerations, and we here approximate aesthetic experience. The factor of qualitativeness refers to the immediacy of art—its presence, impact, sensuousness. The factor of control further restricts the qualitative experiences that are covered by the definition of art. These two factors—quality and control—are not sufficient, for we can all think of controlled qualitative experiences that we would hardly consider art. But before proceeding to refine this idea, I must consider the view of John Dewey, who also uses quality as the primary criterion of artistic experience, clarify the meaning of qualitative, and show why the definition offered here is a useful one.

Dewey defines "an experience" as an interactive sequence between creature and environment that runs its course to fulfillment and which is a whole, marked off from other experiences, because it has a dominant quality. The roots of art are found in an experience which has aesthetic character even though it is not dominantly an aesthetic experience. But how can quality which is a passive concomitant of action in daily life attain independent status in the world of art? I say passive because while for Dewey quality gives unity to an experience by dyeing disparate materials with its color, it does not give shape to an experience. This shape is the result of interaction between creature and environment. The length of the experience, the placing of its climax, the nature of its trajectory are determined by the ease or difficulty which the creature encounters in attaining its end, and the quality of that action is a creaturely reflection of the shape of the experience. If these are the roots of art, it is difficult to see how the roots can ever put forth a flower. Dewey's answer is that art is a prototype of successful action. It can be a prototype because (a) artistic efforts are worthwhile in themselves, as all action should be, and (b) the artist, through his choice of techniques, controls the environment of his action as well as its aim. The first argument is not convincing because, as we have seen, art is not alone in being intrinsically worthwhile. Other pursuits, including philosophy, might be taken as the prototype of successful action because—we must assume—the philosopher finds it qualitatively worthwhile and intrinsically satisfying. The second argument adds the virtue of controlling the environment of action as well as its aim. But this is also true of the mathematician who is able to raise a world upon the basis of whatever axioms he chooses. Since mathematics may also have cognitive uses which art appears to lack, it is not clear why art should persist as the prototype of successful action. I believe art has value, not merely as a prototype, but also as a type of successful action, and the problem, not solved by Dewey, is to find wherein this value lies.

Quality is a good word in anyone's lexicon, but we cannot allow eulogistic auras to substitute for clear meanings. Since any art object may prompt long reveries having nothing to do with art, we must insist on limiting ourselves to qualitative experiences that are relevant to the public object. Presentation, suggestion, and structure may all prompt qualitative experiences. Materials arouse sensations—the paint is shiny or dull, the tone sharp or mellow, the color red or blue, the movement fast or slow, the texture rough or smooth, the shape slim or dumpy. Structures have effects comparable to sensations: tight, swirling, monumental, or chaotic. Some of these structural associations may not be as constant as, say, the association of redness with that patch of material, but where a structure-quality pattern *is* established, the suggestion operates as immediately as does sensation. Structure and presentation conspire to suggest all sorts of things, so that we must add to the qualitative experience of sensuous materials and structures the qualities associated with suggested entities or events. This is how the mistaken conception of art-as-an-imitation-of-reality arises. If the depicted mountain arouses the same qualitative experience as a real mountain, then the real and depicted mountains may be identified with one another; forms productive of the same quality are experientially equal to one another. Since it is easier to believe that art imitates nature than the reverse, the real mountain may be seen as a whole, while the depicted mountain is excised from the context of the painting and treated as if it were a lesser version of a real mountain. The depicted mountain should be treated as the prompter of a qualitative experience which, in so far as it is isolable, *may* be compared with the qualitative experience aroused by real mountains but which, given the obvious intention of the artist, is better related to the qualitative experience prompted by the materials and structure of the work. Out of this whole arises a whole experience, and not until this act of aesthetic relating is completed should the idea of real mountains enter our minds. Considerations associated with utility of the object are also appropriate matters for suggestion. The effect of a work of art radiates outward in all directions; each suggestion arouses novel emotions, desires, and ideas, the mind moving as rapidly over these as a train climbs its horizontal ladder. In theory we could move in unbroken career from Sassetta's "Journey of the Magi" to the squaring of the circle. In doing so we would cross the boundary of art. A single painting cannot bear the freight of all human experience. This is why, to learn whether or not the promptings of the mind are relevant to the art, we must constantly return to the public object, to the primary, sensuous, structural vehicle, because it is there that the qualitative experience is framed as truly as is the painting.

Why does this treatment of art as controlled qualitative experience serve us better than the notions of art as skill, as expression, or as significant form? First, to fix attention upon other points of the process before the qualitative culmination is reached leaves the artistic process incomplete, inexplicable. Art involves skill, but precisely why do we lavish skill upon these objects? If, in talking about art as expression, we mean the expression of moods and emotions encountered in experience, we have to ask, "Why trouble to express these in art when they have been expressed in experience?" If art is formal and stylistic, a similar question arises, "Why this particular style and not some other?" Since the answer to these questions lies in the nature of the qualitative experiences which art controls, I take qualitative experience to be the crux of our study of the artistic process.

Second, qualitative experience is the point at which the artistic process relates most profitably to non-aesthetic experiences of interest to the social scientist. Symbols are encountered throughout human experience; why isn't this as good a place to start? Chiefly because we know too little about the nature of artistic symbols. And we will never understand such symbols until we know something of the experiences underlying them. If art is a sacrament, an objectification of qualitative states which are critical in human behavior, then we may understand the significance of styles only by studying qualities. Since I previously said that qualities can be understood only by studying, among other things, styles, it now appears that the argument has come full circle. No doubt the early stages of art-in-culture research will require some arbitrary assumptions for the control of this circularity.[2] The equality of qualitative experience and style, and therefore the circularity that obtains between them, is methodological, not vital. Art objects are no more valuable in themselves than barometers; they are exceedingly delicate instruments for recording changes in the qualitative atmosphere.

ART AND THE QUALITATIVE MODE

Experience is largely controlled in ways summed up by two types of statement. The formula for cognitive experience is: "it" (pointing to some entity in the world around us) "is" (or equals) "x" (whatever, as a result of cognition, may be predicated of "it"). The second type of statement gives us the results of a qualitative experience. Though it has the same form as the first (subject, verb, and predicate) it expresses a totally different relation. The predicate is not a qualification of subject but an object which, arousing, attracting, or repelling the subject, is a kind of emotional *agent provocateur*.

Cognitive statements purport to give information about the world regardless of the individual's interest in or proximity to

---

[2] The necessity for arbitrary assumptions may be illustrated by a problem I encountered in my Navaho work. I had to find a way of relating cultural values to facts of style. The psychology of art contains many assertions of the sort, "These constricted forms express these kinds of anxiety." Such material promised the link I sought but had the drawback of being based on research within our own culture. I made the arbitrary assumption that these form-quality linkages are universal and proceeded to apply them to the Navaho situation. The results, arbitrarily founded though they are, offer new viewpoints on Navaho life and confirm the usefulness of further art-in-culture studies.

the facts he describes. The observation, "Indians are dirty and lazy" is of the same sort as "The pencil is six inches long." That the first statement may disguise a personal view does not alter the fact that it is phrased so as to offer unexceptionable information about all Indians. Cognitive statements require a symbolic microcosm in terms of which the macrocosm of entities and their relations may be described and understood. The typical cognitive symbol must point to an entity or relation as if it existed independently of the world of discourse. So cognitive structures docilely assume the shape of reality. Yet they are also capable of breaking away and, being more manipulable than brute reality, of assuming independent and novel forms. Though you cannot add apples and oranges, if you replace apples and oranges by numbers, you find that addition and other mathematical operations are feasible. The mind can outrun even the world of numbers so that generalization to the level of symbols like "n" becomes necessary. Heisenberg says that atomic physics has gone beyond the possibilities of its mathematics. Similarly, it has been said that Einstein was able to think without symbols, requiring them only to make his findings public. We are always looking for more complex and flexible symbol systems with which to try out all of the transformations that the mind invents.

Cognition is extremely useful as compared with animal gropings. A dog is bound to immediate sensing of a fresh spoor, and this knowledge of the nose is small in amount and unreliable. Unlike the dog, a man can report that there are deer or apple trees behind that hill. This capacity for unsensed truths has made possible the development of culture and the importance of learning in human societies. Symbolic systems also facilitate the discovery of totally new relations before it is guessed that they may have significance outside the universe of discourse. Non-Euclidean geometries are pure symbolic structures that seem to contradict all we know about reality. Yet it was such a free-wheeling system that Einstein found necessary for propounding his discoveries about the physical world.

Symbolic manipulability is practical because it enables us vicariously to live through situations and reap the fruits of action without incurring its dangers. Because symbol "i" is more hardheaded than I am, it takes more chances in its ideal world than I, surrounded by the angular furniture of this world, can afford to. Death and accident are locked out of the house of animal understanding, yet they enter man's awareness as easily as invited guests. By pushing the limits of space and time infinitely beyond the periphery of our senses, we recall that once we were not as we are now and infer that soon we will not be either as we are now or as we were then. A strange cocktail party this, the self being locked in a house with death and accident as well as joy. It is no wonder that the host finds it difficult to commune with some of the guests and feels trepidation and sorrow as well as delight in the house of its inheritance.

In so far as cognition deals with objectivities it has little to do with the self. Or if it does, as in an autobiography, it transforms the self into an object as much there as a piano is. We talk about the objectivity of a dispassionate mind, and it is worth speculating whether a mind that was freed of its passionate concomitants would retain a sense of self in the face of its tendency to be diffused among the objects of its attention. The scientist makes a career of disinterest and the saint a life, but for the rest of us the emotions and the sense of self which nucleates them are standard accessories.

In calling them accessories I seem to echo Santayana's remark that emotions are about nothing. It is truer to say that we are here introduced to a qualitative counterpart of cognition that is hardly exhausted by the usual terms emotion and feeling. We have left the realm of "it is x" and are now in the realm of "I x it." Comparison of these two statements makes clear the difference between cognition and qualitative experience. Since the x'ing of the second statement is attached to an ego, the world has drawn in its boundaries again and only those entities and relations are significant which are experienced immediately by the individual. This, as we saw, is one of the outstanding characteristics of art which may therefore be considered a kind of qualitative experience.

How may cognition and qualitative experience be related to one another? Although generally both are distinguishably present in the same experience, there may be experiences in which they merge and lose their identities. Mystic experience is obviously qualitative (the equanimity of the Buddhist, the Christian's peace that passes understanding) but it also purports to be cognitive, providing knowledge of transcendent reality. If the reality is immanent as well as transcendent, this fusion of quality and knowledge is understandable.

When cognition and qualitative experience agree upon an end of action, both may be submerged in the resulting action. If a friend swallows poison and we decide, because of our knowledge of these matters and our anxiety at this turn of events, to run to the corner for an antidote, while running we neither count over our stock of assumptions, concepts, and facts, nor savor the anxiety and sense of speed that constitute our qualitative state at the moment.

It can be argued that qualitative experience is the matrix of cognitive efforts. The foundations of science are aesthetic, and not merely in the sense that observation is a necessary phase and that hunches and feelings are often decisive in scientific choices. The belief that the world is organized, especially the atomic theory that the diversity of its phenomena is reducible to a single substance, is an article of faith; one that has borne fruit, but an article of faith none the less. Coordinating concepts like that of causation are useful inferences from much human experience but also belong with matters of faith. The scientist lives by a calculus of probability, that the world tomorrow will be sufficiently like what it is today for him to complete his experiments. This faith in natural order, a faith that precedes, parallels, and rounds out the work of science, is of the qualitative sort, akin to the structuring of art, because it is grounded in little more than the feeling that the world has to be like this.

It is often said that action is motivated by imbalance in the organism or between the organism and its environment. Cognitively, this imbalance manifests itself in a sense of problem aroused by the failure of a prediction, a conflict of principles, or other contradiction in experience. This sense of contradiction is as qualitative as the clash of colors in a painting or the clash of hunger and anticipated satiety, so that what initiates the most complex chains of thought is not an abstract interest in thought but an immediate experience. The scientist indulges in these chains of thought because they please him; once initiated qualitatively, thought is sustained qualitatively. The sequence completes itself when contradiction disappears and harmony rules the surrogate world of the mind. So compelling is this quality of harmony, that men as eminent as Darwin and Poincaré have said the job of the scientist is not to prove his theory (indeed proof is impossible) but to disprove it and pass on to a larger synthesis.

The two kinds of experience are also related to one another in complex ways throughout human exchanges. Ideas may conform with qualitative states, as when a boy accepts a conventional teaching, say, that all Negroes are dirty and stupid, and reacts with aversion to his Negro classmate. If a class project forces the boy to cooperate with the Negro, he may find that this individual is not dirty and stupid. In time, the disconformity between his qualitative reaction to this Negro and his generalization about Negroes may bring about alterations in his cognitive structure.

Qualitative experience is not epiphenomenal, a bright streamer attached to the juggernaut of intellect. As there are times when only intellect can cope with perplexities, so there are times when qualitative experiences make all of the difference. Even when the intellectual *yin* grows thinnest beside the bulk of the qualitative *yang,* cognition is there latent perhaps, yet ready to assert itself. Experience is like a river, one bank of which is cognitive, the other qualitative. It is as incorrect to speak of a cognitive experience or a qualitative experience as it is to speak of a river with one bank. We may speak, however, of experience in the cognitive mode, as when a chess problem is being solved, or in the qualitative mode, as when an epicure is enjoying his first taste of mango.

Experiences in the cognitive mode range from customary ideas, deposits of past discoveries which may no longer be true, to conventional structures like philosophy and science designed for the revision of conventional beliefs. Cognition becomes specialized partly to improve upon the practical results of thinking, partly to advance the careers of those who find this occupation more delightful than any other, and partly to satisfy the qualitative yearning to know how the universe is ordered. If it is true that experience in the qualitative mode may be as decisive as experience in the cognitive mode, it would be surprising if there were no qualitative undertakings analogous to those which science and philosophy represent for cognition, no provision in the human scheme for approaching the mode of qualitative experience in the fullness of wonder. I believe that art is the activity we are looking for, an activity that allows us to experiment with the qualitative mode of experience as the traditions of science and philosophy allow us to experiment with the mode of cognition.

The mode of cognition frees itself from the demands of practical action to take up a position from which nothing escapes scrutiny and criticism. Art shows similar "stages" which we shall follow in the visual arts. There is, first, the qualitative aspect of practical action. When the mother feeds the crying child, the child is gratified not merely because its hunger is appeased but also because the response of the mother assures him that he has well-wishers in his strange environment. We go further when we use blankets, curtains, wall paper, etc., designed and decorated for a function beyond the utilitarian one. Such objects represent a second stage, for they are concerned, not with qualities *of* action, but with qualities *in* action. By means of the decorative arts we make daily life an opportunity to experience qualities as we make a garden an opportunity to see flowers.

In the third stage, art ceases to be an incident of daily life and the conditions of daily life become an incident in art. This is shown in landscape painting, most photography, portraiture, program music, certain kinds of poetry, drama, and the novel. If the second stage, that of the "decorative arts," constitutes a qualitative alarm clock reminding us that it is never too late to attend to the qualitative aspect of experience, the arts of the third stage constitute an inquiry into the kind of experiences in the qualitative mode which are possible under the conditions of daily life specified in the art itself. Art does not imitate reality; it uses portions of reality to demonstrate experience in the qualitative mode.

This third stage is comparable to Euclidean geometry. The items of common experience found in such art have a pleasant cogency as do the axioms of Euclid which long convinced everyone that space must be exactly like this. The fourth phase of art is non-Euclidean. The artist makes no attempt to introduce conditions from daily life. Elements of the work of art prompt experiences of qualities, but experience of secondary qualities, those associated with suggested situations and events, is minimized. This type of art is represented by non-objective painting, most architecture, some kinds of poetry, and non-programmatic music.

Can the design of an alarm clock be as significant aesthetically as a quartet or symphony? The question is false because the symphony is designed as a separate experience whereas the alarm clock is thought of as part of a larger whole, as one of a number of well-designed house furnishings. But, you say, no single artist, no man of talent, designs these larger wholes that contain clocks, Hollywood beds, highboys, and now and then an epergne. This art is in the hands of interior decorators and newlyweds who imagine that they are guided by prevailing canons of taste. They are artists in their fashion even though their raw materials are not raw, being objects designed apart from one another as occasions for qualitative experiences. The frequent casualness of these practical wholes, perhaps mixing modern with Victorian, is itself important. Beethoven's Ninth is more rarified than interior decoration but it is not with you day in and day out. Though we have affairs with masterpieces and marriages with utilitarian objects, both relations, being based on love, have lasting effects.

In some such manner we may follow the transition from the qualitative mode of practical action to the role of the artist who experiments with the qualitative mode of experience freed from utilitarian demands. Qualitative experiences in art are more manipulable than the qualitative mode of daily experiences and less risky. Yet art, an experiment with the raw stuff of life, promises the greatest danger of all: that we may discover or create in art qualitative modes of experience which daily life cannot admit, cannot tolerate, and that there may become fixed in our minds that dream, at once the culmination of sanity and the beginning of madness, of remaking life according to harmonies found only in art. What Sapir (1949:347) said of religion applies also to artistic experiences:

> There can be neither fear nor humiliation for deeply religious natures, for they have intuitively experienced both of these emotions in advance of the declared hostility of an overwhelming world, coldly indifferent to human desires.

The cognitive problem is to build a symbolic structure that matches but is more manipulable than the objective world. The problem of aesthetic structures is different. Qualitative experience is immediate. When it occurs in the flux of life it is too intimately bound up with practical objectives to be more than a clue to the successfulness of action. Our understanding of experience in the qualitative mode cannot advance if the experience remains dissolved in activity. Yet we cannot adopt the procedure of cognition and step back into a symbolic microcosm, for this filters out the qualitativeness we wish to understand. Qualities must be made objective in the sense of being rescued from the stream of utilitarian doings and undergoings, but not objective in the cognitive sense. It is this kind of objectivity which art achieves, and it does so not symbolically but conditionally. By controlling or creating the conditions of experience, the artist examines the nature and intensity of the qualitative mode in which he is primarily interested.

Before defining art more closely, let me, by referring to the "lower sense arts," bring out additional points. Are cooking and sexuality arts? Cooking provides a recipe, as much a public object as a piano score which might be considered a recipe for music. That a recipe may have many associations is seen in the link between commensality and friendship or in the symbolism of the Eucharist. Although the consumption of the blood and body of Christ has important qualitative implications, it would seem a little odd if one exclaimed over the savor of the host and asked how it was prepared. The qualities of cuisine are specific. One does not seek to repeat the experience of eating apple pie in other forms of activity, as the Buddhist seeks serenity in all that overtakes him. This is why during the last war the patriotic posters which tried to convince our boys that they were fighting for a fifth freedom, the freedom to eat chocolate sundaes, seemed ridiculous. Such qualities are not sufficiently general to be significant except as they become symbols of experiences, like coming home, which prompt more powerful qualitative responses.

Since sexual indulgence is clearly a qualitative experience, why isn't the master amorist who arranges the conditions for this qualitative experience an artist? No permanent object—not even a score, in the form of a *Kama Sutra*—results, yet this is no different from the dance. Love-making might be regarded as a kind of choreography, and one with philosophic implications, as in Tibetan representations of copulation between a god and his consort. Treatments of the Bridegroom theme also suggest that sexuality is the closest common equivalent to the qualitative experiences of the mystic. What distinguishes the dance from love-making is that the first is performed publicly, the latter not, so that shareability is another essential aspect of art. An idea of an audience—even if it be an imaginary audience—capable of entering into the conditions of the experience provided by the public object or event, and joining in this communal act of appreciation, is part of every definition of the artist's role.

Art then is the creation, by manipulating a medium, of public objects or events which serve as deliberately organized sets of conditions for experience in the qualitative mode. Since the artist is unable to control the suggestions that arise from the presented and structural aspects of his work, as the user of concepts is able to restrict the meaning of his terms, and since the nature of these suggestions varies with the experience and sensitivity of each individual, I can never be sure that my qualitative experience is the same as that which this object furnishes you or the man who made it. At the same time, if the audience—ideal or not—is as important to the artist as I believe it is, the artist does not leave the effect of his work to chance. In so far as he uses established form-quality linkages (and this has nothing to do with the originality of his work), the experience of his audience will be in harmony with his own. We may even call art communication if we remember that what is communicated is a *range* of qualities rather than *a* quality. This is to be expected, for the discrimination of qualities does not encourage the military discipline and precision one encounters in the kingdom of ideas.[3]

We may now return to the purist-relationist paradox. The moment the artist loses sight of qualitative experience and makes his art a soapbox or debating society, he adds cognitive—polemic and expository—tasks to his job as an artist. This is possible because cognitive and qualitative are banks of one stream of experience; it is natural because art can make ideas as well as objects the conditions of experience in the qualitative mode. True, works of art from Dante to Dana have enunciated a message and have helped to bring about social changes while losing none of their integrity. The artist may intend or hope for

---

[3] This matter of art and communication is important and complex, especially as it relates to the influence arts may have beyond the boundaries of the culture that produces them. Does the artist work for the universal audience of the scientist?

such a result, because to assume that artists are not moved by injustice and do not desire to use their skills in remedying it is foolishness. But he succeeds by remaining an artist, by treating the situation as a condition of the qualitative effect he is creating. If this is what is meant by purism, the purist argument is sound.

The purist does not say that art has no effect upon life. He says merely that the artist cannot treat art, a matter of immediate qualities, as a mediate venture. The relationist position is not ruled out, it is just not clear how it can be true. Mathematics lies between referential symbolism and art. Like symbolism, it does not rely upon qualities, but like non-objective art, it dispenses with references to the real world. The mathematician works with pure structures, as the artist works with vivid structures, and the physicist with referential structures. Physics looks for that mathematical system which best fits the arrangement of the physical world. What would happen if a high school student, aping the physicist, consciously compared the structure of Hamlet's experience with his own? Either the two structures would match or they would not. If they matched, the individual would accept the aesthetic structure. However, the fact of their matching means that the art, as a tasteful elaboration of already familiar experience, would be supererogatory. If the two structures did not match, it is difficult to see what could be done with the aesthetic structure but reject it as irrelevant. This hypothetical, conscious approach to relationism in the arts seems absurd, yet it underlies the popular attitude toward contemporary painting, an attitude summed up in the recurring question, "What does the painting represent?" That is, into what pigeonhole of my past experience does it fit? If the painting is found to be too large for any of these pigeonholes, it will be crammed in by means of joking descriptions like that attributed to Mark Twain—this is a picture of a cat having a fit in a plate of tomatoes.

Art is such that the relating of these two structures cannot be undertaken deliberately, it just happens. The qualitative experience which is art slips into the rich earth of personality like a seed. If the seed falls upon stoney ground or is eaten up by birds of distraction, the sowing is fruitless. No conscious effort but that of giving oneself to the experience offered by the work can cause the seeds to break open, put out roots, and flower. Insistence upon a particular kind of relatedness makes impossible the transformation of our nature which art brings about.

SUMMARY

Though many cultures do not have a concept of art, all cultures produce art objects. Art, sometimes significant linguistically, is always significant experientially. Because it occurs in all cultures we know anything about, it has its origins in profoundly human experience. Our problem is to understand the nature of this experience, bearing in mind three possibilities: that, without sacrificing any of its "purity," art may be related to other life processes; that understanding of qualitative experience through analysis of at least the more general aesthetic patterns called styles may shed light upon the interior articulation of cultures; that through this definition of art the methods and insights of art history, aesthetics, and the psychology of art may prove useful to the social sciences.

The more important phases of the artistic process were discussed and reasons given for selecting quality of experience as the nucleus of our definition. Comparison with cognition brought out the nature and importance of those experiences in the qualitative mode with which art is concerned.

THE ARTS AND ANTHROPOLOGY

Alan P. Merriam

THE RELATIONSHIP between the arts and anthropology is a problem which has been discussed from time to time, but unfortunately usually without much result. While anthropologists have long been interested in the arts, particularly among nonliterate peoples, it is only recently that significant studies have begun to appear. Herta Haselberger (1961:342) tells us that "specimens of ethnological art had been included in European collections as early as the fifteenth century," and references to African music extend well back into the seventeenth century (Dapper 1676). In dance, the study of European forms received impetus from the research of Cecil Sharp in England early in the twentieth century, but a survey of studies made in the Soviet Union shows materials dating back to 1848 (cf., Kurath 1960). Concentrated studies of oral literature were begun in Germany by the Grimm brothers early in the nineteenth century, and the word "folklore" was coined by William John Thoms in 1846 (Emrich 1946). The earliest publications in ethnomusicology as such, date from 1882 with Theodore Baker's doctoral dissertation at the University of Leipzig, *On the Music of the North American Savages;* and the study of the visual arts among peoples other than ourselves began to receive significant impetus in the decades surrounding the advent of the twentieth century.

We can thus look back on the study of the arts in cultures other than our own and see a slow development over a rather

Reprinted by permission of the author and publisher from *Horizons of Anthropology,* Sol Tax, editor, pp. 224–36. (Chicago, Aldine Publishing Company, 1964): copyright © 1964 by Aldine Publishing Company.

extended period of time: at least four hundred years ago we find interest being shown, though it is not until the turn of this century that extensive and serious studies begin to appear. And it is not until very recent times that a major attempt has been made to deal with anthropology and the arts in more than descriptive terms.

Interest in specific arts as aspects of anthropology has also varied enormously. The study of drama, for example, has hardly been touched upon in anthropology, though a very few studies such as F. E. Williams' *Drama of Orokolo* (1940), and Melville J. Herskovits' "Dramatic Expression Among Primitive Peoples" (1944) are to be found. Similarly, architectural studies have played a very small part in anthropology, although descriptions of house types are found in almost every ethnography; and even dance has not received the attention it deserves. On the other hand, the anthropological literature is full of references to the graphic and plastic, or visual arts, to music, and to oral literature; and so it is that the study of the arts remains unbalanced, with much emphasis on some forms and very little upon others. It seems reasonable to say that, with the possible exception of oral literature, the study of the arts in anthropology generally has been seriously neglected and undervalued when viewed in broad perspective. The average text in anthropology, for example, devotes a single chapter or a portion of a single chapter to all of the arts taken together, and the contrast between this allotment and the space given to problems of social structure or political organization is indeed striking.

This relative neglect of the humanistic aspects of culture derives in part at least from two major misunderstandings about the arts and how they should be handled in the investigation of the patterns of human behavior. The first of these stems from the failure to understand the essential nature of the content of the social sciences, on the one hand, and the humanities, on the other, and the basic relationship between them. I have argued this point at some length elsewhere (Merriam 1962), but essentially the content of the social sciences—that is, the subject matter which is of concern to them—derives from the institutionalizing behavior of man through which he solves the problems which arise from his own biosocial existence. That is, man must regulate his economic, social, political, and enculturative behavior with his fellow men, and these are problems which arise, on the one hand, from the needs of the biological organism, and on the other, from the group life to which man is so irretrievably committed. The essential nature of the content of the humanities, however, seems to arise from man's need to supply himself with what A. I. Hallowell (1947:550–51) has referred to as ". . . mediative factors in man's cultural mode of adaptation . . . whereby a world of common meanings has been created in human societies." In other words:

> Through the humanistic elements of his culture, man seems to be making pointed commentary on how he lives; he seems in the humanities to sum up what he thinks of life. In short, man lives as a social animal, but he does not live as a social animal alone. For his social life in itself seems to bring about conditions under which he is unable to restrain himself from commenting upon himself and enunciating and interpreting his actions, his aspirations, and his values. (Merriam 1962:14)

The social sciences, then, deal with man as a social animal and the ways in which he solves his social and biological problems in daily living, while the humanities take man beyond his biosocial living into his own distillations of his life experiences which he uses, in turn, as an expression of his basic sanctions and values.

It may conceivably be argued that the social sciences are necessarily prior to the humanities because they deal with absolute fundamentals of existence. I think this is a proper conclusion only in the sense that man as a social animal *is* basic; that is, men do live together. But at the same time, both the social and the humanistic aspects of man's life are universals in his culture and experience, and thus the question is not at all one of priority, but rather one of unity. If man cannot live, as apparently he cannot, without either his social institutions or his humanistic responses, then the two become merely two sides of the same coin and neither can be examined without involving the other (cf., Merriam 1962).

The second major misunderstanding about the arts and their anthropological context derives from the nature of the arts themselves, and from the ways in which they have previously been studied. The arts are perhaps peculiar among man's cultural creations simply because the behavior involved in their creation produces a product which, as an object of study, can be treated quite divorced from cultural context. The same, of course, is true of tools and house types, for example, but there is some argument as to whether these may not most logically be treated as arts as well. Herein, of course, lies the difficulty in the treatment by anthropologists of what are commonly known as the "arts and crafts," or simply as "crafts." In reality, these seem to me to be of such a nature as to be classed with the fine arts, and it is but a convention of our own culture that prevents us from doing so, and leads us, instead, to set them apart. In any case, what is important here is that the art product is conceptually, and in certain ways practically separable from its cultural context. Thus musicians, no matter in what culture they are found, produce a product, musical sound, which can be recorded, transcribed to paper, and analyzed as a structural entity. Dance is objectified by a system of graphic shorthand; oral literature is reduced to writing; the visual arts cannot exist without a tangible product; architecture results in buildings; and drama, reduced to writing after observation, shows structural characteristics of sequence in time, plot, climax, and the like.

This peculiar characteristic of the arts seems to set them apart from those organizations of society which we call its institutions, for in the case of institutions what is important is the organization itself which is directed toward shaping the behavior of the individuals concerned. With the arts, on the other hand, the importance lies in the product, and artistic behavior is directed toward it; without musical sound, music does not exist, but society is behaving.

At the same time, what draws the two broad fields of inquiry together is not only the fact that they are inseparable, but also the fact that both must inevitably deal wih human behavior. That is, the artist produces a product, and this is his ultimate and direct aim, but in doing so he behaves in certain ways.

This distinction between the product, on the one hand, and the behavior which produces it, on the other, is one which has not often been made in studies of the arts. On the contrary, most investigations have tended to concentrate exclusively or almost exclusively upon the product which is visualized as a structure or system, the parts of which interact with each other to form a cohesive whole. Our studies of the visual arts are primarily concerned with the painting or sculpture itself, not with the artist; our studies of oral literature concentrate upon the tale or proverb or myth, not with the teller; our investigations into music deal almost exclusively with the musical sound and not with the musician.

Behavior, then, is separable from the product conceptually; in fact, of course, it is inseparable because no product can exist without the behavior of some individual or individuals. And this behavior is exemplified in two major ways: first, because the producer of music, for example, conceptualizes his product in certain ways; and second, because the producer of music is a musician and thus shapes his behavior to accord with what the society at large conceives to be musicianly behavior. Thus, the behavior of any artist is underlain by his conceptualization of the product he wishes to produce as well as his concept of himself as an artist.

Finally, the product as such has a feedback effect upon the artist's conceptualization. If the musical sound produced is pleasing to the performer and to his audience, then the particular concept is reinforced; if it is not pleasing, the artist is forced to change his concept, which in turn means a change in behavior, resulting finally in a changed product.

There is, then, a fourfold organizational pattern involved in the arts: concept, leading to behavior, resulting in product, which in turn feeds back upon the concept. Of these four aspects of the art process, only the product has been studied in anything approaching detail; concept, behavior, and feedback upon concept, have been almost totally neglected. In these terms, it is perhaps not surprising that the study of the arts has not been of central concern to anthropology, for studies of product are essentially descriptive in nature. And any descriptive study must develop a technical terminology which quickly surpasses the competence of individuals who are not primarily concerned with the object of the study at hand. Thus in dealing with the music product, ethnomusicologists speak of "melodic level," "modal analyses," or "triadic split fifths," and use a large number of further terms incomprehensible to those not directly involved in this sort of analysis. Artists have their own technical vocabulary to describe visual products; students of dance deal in special ways with dance forms, and so forth. The study of artistic product is a highly technical field of inquiry, and it is also a restricted one.

But if we look at art as behavior in the kinds of terms I have just suggested, then it becomes apparent that the product is but one part of art, and that our frame of reference falls very sharply into the kinds of inquiry which are of primary interest to anthropology. Anthropology seeks descriptive facts, it is true, but of much more importance are the reasons that lie behind those facts. The straight description of a kinship system is not our ultimate aim; what we want to know is how this system works, and particularly, why it works in the ways it does. I submit, then, that in the study of the arts, the major emphasis has been placed upon the product, with the result that such systemic, structural, or synchronic descriptions dominate the literature, leaving little room for behavioral studies which will help us toward an understanding of the how and why of human behavior. If we look past the product as a product, and consider some of the deeper manifestations which it and the behavior

The Arts and Anthropology

which underlies it represent, we arrive at an understanding of the kinds of questions which are beginning to preoccupy more and more students of the arts and human behavior.

Perhaps these various levels of analysis can best be illustrated by one or two examples from the music system of the Basongye people of the Kasai Province in the Republic of the Congo (formerly the Belgian Congo), with whom I spent a year in 1959–60.

The Basongye conceptualize music as a uniquely human phenomenon through distinctions made between noise on the one hand and music on the other. These distinctions are summarized in a series of aphorismic statements made by individuals as they discuss the problem:

When you are content you sing; when you are angry, you make noise.

When one shouts, he is not thinking; when he sings, he is thinking.

A song is tranquil; a noise is not.

When one shouts, his voice is forced; when he sings, it is not.

On bases such as these, the Basongye separate noise from music, or more precisely, non-music from music. Thus non-music includes such sounds as those made by birds or animals, wind blowing through the trees, a single pulse upon a drum or xylophone, whistling, or blowing into cupped hands when these are used for signalling. Music, on the other hand, includes the sound of the drums when played together and over a period of time, the human voice when it is not "shouting" or speaking, whistling when it is co-ordinated and used as accompaniment to the dance, and other like productions. The Basongye "theory" of music, then, seems to involve three essential features in the distinction between music and non-music: first, the fact that music always involves human beings, and that those sounds emanating from non-human sources are not music. Second, the musical sounds that humans produce are organized; thus a single tap on the drum is not music, but the drums playing together in the patterned forms which the drummers use, do make music. And third, there must be continuity in time; even all the drums struck but once simultaneously do not make music; they must continue over time.

This conception of music as distinct from non-music is, of course, an abstraction of principles expressed in a variety of ways by a number of informants; yet the statements of the Basongye point to a conception of music which underlies all musical production. Music is a non-mechanistic, humanly-produced phenomenon, and this conception colors the entire attitude of the Basongye toward their music. (Merriam 1962:27-8)

On a somewhat different level it is clear that the conceptualization of his instrument by the musician clearly affects the music he produces upon it. For example, the Basongye think of every known bass xylophone pattern as having definite starting and ending points, and these points are not those at which the Western-oriented musician would place them. Without a knowledge, then, of the Basongye distinction between music and non-music, of their concept of music and musical instruments, and of a large number of further points, we cannot hope to understand clearly the sound product.

Similarly, concept is translated into behavior, and here our wider approach to the study of the arts leads us, for example, into investigation of the creative person, both as an individual and as a member of his society. Ruth Benedict's remarkable study of Zuni mythology, for example, at one point discusses the individual narrator of myths, and how the personalities of the tellers affect the eventual product. One of her informants was a social deviant, a man of considerable self-reliance, individualism, and ability, and a person with a deep-seated need for achieving personal eminence; the myths he told differed markedly from those given by other informants (1935:xxxviii-xl). And similarly, the artist in society plays certain roles, thinks of himself in certain ways *vis à vis* the society of which he is a member, and is thought of in special ways by persons who are not artists; inevitably this particular social role shapes the product he produces.

If we look at the arts, then, as human behavior, we stretch our concepts considerably, for our studies are no longer only descriptive and thus synchronic, but become instead processual. And this applies to studies of the product as well. For example, most contemporary philosophers are agreed that the arts perform an essentially symbolic function in human society. Thus Ernst Cassirer (1944:168), for example, says flatly: "Art may be defined as a symbolic language"; and speaking of music, Susanne Langer (1953:32) comments: ". . . music is 'significant form,' and its significance is that of a symbol, a highly articulated, sensuous object, which by virtue of its dynamic structure can express the forms of vital experience which language is peculiarly unfit to convey. Feeling, life, motion and emotion constitute its import." While I have no doubt that the arts are symbolic, the problem here is precisely what is meant by the term, for it seems clear that the arts are symbolic in at least four different ways. Let us discuss these briefly.

In the first place, art can be symbolic in its conveyance of direct meanings. Thus, for example, some dance is mimetic, some visual art is representational, and song texts express through the symbolism of language certain attitudes and emotions as well as direct statements of fact. In one sense, perhaps, such behavior is "signing" rather than symboling, for the nature of the product directly represents human action; thus erotic movements in the dance are the same movements used in actual behavior, or a sculptured bust is a direct representation of the person involved. In any case, this kind of representation is symbolic, though perhaps not technically so, on the most direct level (see White 1949: 22–39; Morris 1955).

On a second level, the arts are symbolic in that they are reflective of emotion and meaning; we can refer to this as "affective" or "cultural" meaning. In this case, the symbolism is distinct and culturally defined. In our own Western music, for example, we assign the emotion of sadness to what we call a minor scale; certain combinations of musical instruments playing together suggest certain physical or emotional phenomena, and selections of particular combinations of notes can and do symbolize particular states of being. Edward Lowinsky (1946:79) has noted that:

> Chromaticism always represents the extraordinary . . . Again and again we find chromatic treatment given to such highly

emotional concepts as crying, lamenting, mourning, moaning, inconsolability, shrouding one's head, breaking down, and so forth.

In the Italian madrigal the same concepts find expression through the medium of chromaticism. There they represent man as entangled in his earthly passions, while in the music of the Netherlands they symbolize the devout believer struggling with the burden of sorrow which God has laid upon him to test his faith.

Or again, in oral literature, Lowie (1956:118) reports a number of linguistic usages which function among the Crow Indians as part of story telling but to which are assigned culturally defined meanings: "returning with blackened face" means "triumph," "having one's moccasins made" means "getting ready for a raid," "carrying the pipe" is equivalent to being captain of a party. Similar examples could be quoted at considerable length for all of the arts, but the point is clear; the arts are symbolic in the sense that they indicate affective or cultural meanings through the use of devices that are inherent in their own structures.

A third symbolic level is found in the principle that the arts reflect certain social behavior, political institutions, economic organization, and the like. In the dance, for example, Gertrude Kurath (1960:236–37; Fenton and Kurath 1953:233) has pointed out how dancing reflects male-female roles and even the clan and moiety organization of the Iroquois. One of the outstanding examples of this kind of study is to be found in David P. McAllester's *Enemy Way Music* (1954:86–88), a study of the Navaho. Working through the framework of existential and normative values, McAllester concluded that Navaho music reflects Navaho culture in three major ways. First, a characteristic of Navaho cultural values is expressed in individualism: in respect to music, "what one does with one's property, knowledge, songs, is one's own affair." Second is the fact that the Navaho are essentially provincial and conservative: in music, "foreign music is dangerous and not for Navahos." Finally, the Navaho, McAllester says, sustain a formal culture, and in music the same formalism is expressed in the summatory statement that "there is a right way to sing every kind of song." In a study somewhat similar to McAllester's, Alan Lomax (1959:950) has written that "the basic color of a music symbolizes fundamental social-psychological patterns, common to a given culture," and suggests that music sound reflects the sexual code, the position of women, and the treatment of children in a culture. All these studies, then, are looking at the arts as reflective of other aspects and principles of culture; in this sense too, the arts are symbolic.

Finally, the fourth level on which the arts can be regarded as symbolic is in respect to deeper processes of human thought and behavior on a world-wide basis and not on the level of any particular culture. We have very little information concerning this aspect of artistic symbolism, but Curt Sachs (1937:127–38), for example, has postulated an elaborate scheme in which three major types of musical material are correlated with femininity or masculinity, physical type, size of dance steps, and even such general cultural traits as "warlike" or "peace-loving" peoples. Further, in connection with the symbolism of musical instruments, the same writer has made some speculations using a primarily Freudian conception. He notes, for example:

> Tubular wind instruments, straight and elongated like a man's organ, belong to man, and a mixture of symbols arises when a flute is globular instead of tubular, or when a trumpet is made out of a conch shell which is connected with water. . . .
> Sound, also, is a factor as well as form in these connotations. Most of the instruments reserved for men have a harsh, aggressive, indeed ugly tone; most instruments preferred by women have a muffled timbre (Sachs 1940:52).

The quarrel we may have with formulations such as these is not so much with the exploratory nature of the ideas, but rather with the categories of correlation selected; thus the definition of what is to be considered a "warlike" or "peace-loving" people is extremely difficult, if not impossible to reach, and a strictly Freudian interpretation is not convincing to some. However, this approach, which seeks to correlate sound on a human level and a world basis, rather than to specific behavior in specific cultures, is clearly the broadest attack that can be made on the arts as symbolism. What I am trying to stress, however, is that in looking at art as a symbol we are doing more than a descripton, although the product is our focus. The result of such analysis is an approach to an understanding of the arts as they reflect and as they influence behavior.

In a somewhat different vein it has sometimes been stressed that the function of the arts is their integrative role in society; this point of view has perhaps been best expressed by A. R. Radcliffe-Brown (1948:330–41) in his study of the Andaman Islanders. Radcliffe-Brown cites a legend of the Andamanese which explains the origin of night and correlates the social life of the individual with the alternation of dark and light and with the dependence of the individual on society. Social life, he says, gives a sense of security, and thus when night falls, the individual is less secure because social life ceases. He reports that the particular legend tells of a time when there was no night and thus when social life went on without interruption; this was followed by the disruption of the pattern into day and night in which social life is, of course, interrupted. The tale points up the interpretation that night or darkness is a force hostile to society and thus stresses the individual's participation in and dependence upon the social group. The function of the tale, then, says Radcliffe-Brown, is to emphasize the importance of society, thus contributing to its integration by reinforcing the notion of the individual's dependence upon society.

This is, of course, but one interpretation of the function, in this case, of oral literature, but it stresses meaning and importance both of the product as a product, and of man's behavior in creating and using it.

In the past, then, the arts have been studied in anthropology, primarily as products, that is, on a descriptive level which stresses their own internal structure. What is argued here is that the product must inevitably be produced by human beings who behave in certain ways in so doing. Further, all human behavior arises out of peoples' thought and concepts of what proper behavior should be; and finally, the success or failure of the product itself causes changes in concept which accounts, in part at least, for internal change and stability. The approach argued here is essentially a broadening one which calls for the real combination of techniques of analysis from both the social sciences and humanities. It is the kind of study which is gradually emerging in the investigation of the arts and anthropology.

ROOTS OF PRIMITIVE ART

Warner Muensterberger

DURING the first decade of the twentieth century, a small group of young European painters and sculptors broke away from the schools of naturalism and impressionism. This development did not come unexpectedly. It had its forerunners, especially in such daring artists as Gauguin, Van Gogh and Toulouse-Lautrec. These men took a decisive step in a new direction. They initiated a different approach. They laid emphasis on subjective presentation and steered toward a more devious style which, considering all the substyles, may be called "anaturalism."

The masses were either shocked or they overlooked the new and unusual presentation of a landscape or a person or even an abstract composition. Accepted forms and values appeared distorted and unreal, and at the same time a new sense of artistic expression seems to have emerged out of a less reality-directed artistic experience.

It was during the same period that some artists and art critics "discovered" the strange sculptural art of the primitive peoples of West Africa, the South Seas and the Americas.

Both forms of artistic creativity, the anaturalism of the European artists as well as the masks and figures of the primitive craftsmen did not find acceptance for a good while. The subjects

---

Reprinted from *Psychoanalysis and Culture:* Essays in Honor of Géza Róheim; G. B. Wilber and W. Muensterberger, editors, International Universities Press, Inc., 1951, pp. 371–89, with permission of the author and publisher.

Read in part before the Committee on Creative Activity of the American Psychoanalytic Association, New York, November 1950.

were unfamiliar. We might say that the audience did not master this kind of art, in a large part, because of the anamorphosis expressed in these figures and paintings—it came too close to the unconscious infantile fear of destruction and object loss.

Acceptance by the mass of people is assured only when the audience is already more or less familiar with the statement of the subject. As a precondition for immediate, positive response, one could say that the art object must be acceptable in its presentation. The objects which we usually display to a child are simple, direct, and readily identified by him. A new picture shown to him is quickly recognized as "house," "daddy," "mother," "dog"—at any rate they are things or persons belonging to his known environment, and in a style more or less familiar to him. The young child feels at home with these pictures or objects. In play analysis we make use of this psychological condition and apply it therapeutically. A new and strange object would arouse uneasiness or even anxiety, and it would be difficult for the child to master the situation. A boy of twenty-nine months, who was shown the mask of an ugly old woman which looked dangerous to him, suffered from a severe trauma. For a while, he became obsessed with the delusion of being persecuted by elderly women. The boy was unable to cope with the conflict aroused by the threat of the dangerous-looking mask. The sight of an unfamiliar object, one that does not "click" with the spectator's perception of the external world, leads to confusion or terror, reactions springing from fear of destruction and castration.

This little boy represents the essence of the rejecting type of spectator. On the other hand we have the *avant* guard, those who are willing and able to accept a "new art" or a "new style." The limitation on the degree of acceptance or rejection seems to be dictated by the superego, although a number of causes are responsible for the specific reaction formation.

But on the whole, forms or compositions which are unfamiliar, and in which the suddenness of unexpected experience goes too far for comfort, can lead to confusion, disgust, explosion or repression of affect.[1]

This was the response which primitive art received from the large part of the Euro-American audiences. The art form went far beyond the extension of imagination which one could permit in a painting or a figure. It was too daring even for a fraction of that small minority which refers to itself as the art lovers. The unusual could be identified only with such a powerful attempt at aggression and destruction that merely a few were able to bear the effect of these objects. It was the *avant* guard which had the courage to accept this unknown form of artistic expression.

Under what conditions, then, will a new style be acceptable? As psychoanalysis has shown, the spectator is inclined to identify with the values and ideas of the artist who finds utterance for his unconscious desires. The artist's aggression, expressed in his work, causes the spectator pain or pleasure. Understanding a work of art, just as understanding a caricature or a joke, seems to be based on a momentary identification of the onlooker with the artist. The onlooker borrows, so to speak, the artist's id powers, indulging indirectly in aggression and partial restoration (Kris 1934). But just as a joke which we know and hear for a second time loses so much of its liberating effect, an artistic style or expression which has become familiar to the superego, no longer serves its original purpose. The temporary, surreptitiously obtained relief which was achieved by the new joke or artistic expression has to be replaced by another attempt. New channels are sought. The alleviation found by artistic expression urges the artists continuously to "discover" new and different styles, forms, compositions, color combinations, and techniques.

---

[1] Speaking of poetry, Hanns Sachs pointed out: (Some poets) "by neglecting the façade and the 'pre-pleasure' which they owe to their audience and to their own conscience, may produce almost undisguised presentations of repressed fantasies, and thus cause revulsion instead of attraction." (1951: 53).

Now the artist as well as the spectator (and the narrator as well as the listener) are elated and relieved of tension on account of the temporary removal of inhibitions.

The success of the innovation in style and form thus depends largely upon the time element and the degree of deviation. New styles must be introduced at a time when the older expressions have become the customary ones, i.e., when they can no longer liberate pleasure from the unconscious sources. Yet, the innovation must not go too far lest it cause irritation or disturbance because the aggressive tendency is poorly disguised. We can take Picasso's style development as a proper example: the body distortion presented in his later work would most probably have been rejected by his early admirers who were ready to accept the more naturalistic presentations of his blue and rose period.

The unknown or untraditional form of art makes identification by the spectator with the artist less possible. If we consider that the psychic process aroused by the art object is a kind of an echo of the artist's original hostility, it is evident that the liberating effect of the art object might go so far that, instead of serving to remove inhibitions of the spectator, a state of terror and anxiety is produced, which in turn prevents the discharge of repressed hostile tendencies.

An observation of the reaction to the art of the natives of West Africa and Oceania might help us exemplify this kind of "preventive terror" which to some extent is analogous to dream censorship (Freud 1938:442ff.). The majority of Western spectators experienced the entirely strange form as a threat. They unconsciously understood the close connection between destruction and restoration, put into form in these images. They reinforced their ego boundaries in order to prevent the emergence of confusion, explosion, and unconscious guilt feelings. It seems that they understood the inimical tendency re-enacted in these idols of a foreign world. Only a few were able to accept the emotional effect of the mysterious expression of African and Oceanic masks and figures. But step by step through more frequent presentations the tension was lessened and a larger audience was able to be deeply impressed by the psychic force which emanates from primitive art.

I

It is only with a certain reservation that we can speak of primitive art as "art." Among those peoples called "primitives," art and subjects which we label as "art"—according to the principle of "art for art's sake"—have a certain function in the social life of the group or in interpersonal affairs. A figure, a mask, a decorated skull, an amulet, a poem, or a dance have a specific meaning to the group, the tribe or the village. A mask, for example, is made under certain ceremonial conditions because of its religious significance. It is used in a dance or a ritual, and the dance, although quite often a source of pleasure, has its proper place in the social and religious activity of the group. Among many tribes, the objects have to be consecrated in order to become endowed with magic so that it can be used successfully for the purpose of its owner.

It was not too long ago that primitive images in European collections were described as "heathen figures" or "fetishes." But among primitive peoples even a simple ornament on a stick or a basket has its magic meaning and tradition and consequently its usefulness. Decoration has a purpose among these peoples. At least for one area, Indonesia, famous for ornamental design, it was shown that seemingly superficial and playful ornaments were part of magic proceedings. (Steinman 1939; Tillmann 1940:II, 7–15; Muensterberger 1939:I, 337–43.) The contact with Europe in recent decennia has led to a kind of mass production of sculpture in West Africa and elsewhere. Generally, however, it can be said that primitive art is integrated in its specific function, while Western art is largely, or became, just a by-product without immediate function in our daily life.

That profound links exist between magic, religion, social organization and creative activity can be observed among a number of primitive peoples. The life of the aboriginal Australians points up the interaction of mores, economic demands, religious ceremonials with artistic expression.

To trail the kangaroo is not enough; it is necessary so to influence it that it will stand within range. To aim at the fish will not of itself insure accuracy. It must be drawn to the spear of the fisherman. For such purposes, charms, rites, paintings and sacred objects are employed. So, too, man does not just wait for nature and its species to bring forth in due season. He performs rites, giving his own energy, pouring his blood on symbols of the species, and expressing his desire and need by action and chant, by decoration of his own body, and by painting or engraving sacred symbols or galleries. *For the time being he becomes the hero or the ancestor,* or he is in the presence of the 'god' who made tribal world what it is. *By re-enacting what that ancestor or great being did, he becomes a life-giver too;* therefore, nature will be productive and the food-species multiply (Elkin and Berndt 1950:2ff.).

Several Dayak groups of Borneo put effigies called *hampatong* or *tempatan* at the entrances of their villages. These statues differ from village to village but are similar in so far as they represent spirits, demons, or ancestors who are feared by the members of the tribe. They are made after a successful head-hunt or after the death of a tribesman. Among the Ngadju Dayak of the Katingan area, a *hampatong* is made for each head captured during such an expedition. The spot where the image is erected is sacred and during the ceremonial festivities offerings are made. On the occasion of the death ritual, *hampatongs* are made for each of the deceased (Schärer 1946:166ff.; Muensterberger 1940:50ff.). These figures are quite eccentric and bizarre. Many of them bear a rather strong resemblance to the gargoyles and chimeras of medieval cathedrals, those images which lived in the minds of men during the Middle Ages and which could be placed *on* the churches, but never inside. They were always projected into the outside world. As in the case of the Borneo figures, they are undoubtedly a threat to those not belonging to their own community, and at the same time serve as a protection to the villagers who consider themselves the legitimate owners of the land.

It is evident that the skulls and the *hampatongs* are used to protect one from, and to fight against, strangers and enemies, passively and actively. The skulls and images are substitutes for the man who has been killed, and who in dance and ceremony is converted into an honored and worshipped member of the tribe.

In some areas of Australia and Oceania instead of hunting the head of a member of another tribe, people preserve the skulls of their own ancestors. The sculptured, painted and decorated skulls of the Sepik region in New Guinea are famous for the special treatment accorded them. (See Plate 8.) About a year after the burial the skull is taken out of the grave and cleaned. The lower jaw is fixed. The skull then serves as a base for a layer of clay and resin, from which the face is remodeled. Apparently these people do not try to recapture the actual facial expression or features of the deceased, but instead decorate this skull with precisely the same pattern which he wore at feasts and ceremonies during his lifetime. This is a very special and individual ornament, the man's personal signature or his particular identification mark. People may forget a face, but they will remember for a considerable time the way in which his face was painted. And now, after his death, his skull is decorated with this individual stamp.

A closely related custom was recently discovered in Australia. Here too, skulls are painted and decorated and "are carried about by close relatives of the deceased, either thrown over one's back as a kind of necklet when traveling, or hung in the camp or an adjacent tree. . . . The top of the skull is painted with the deceased's clan design" (Elkin and Berndt 1950:98ff.).

A somewhat similar method is used among the Solomon Islanders, in the New Hebrides, in New Britain and New Ireland, and in a certain sense also among the Maori of New Zealand. The version of this custom which we find in New Britain is interesting enough to be mentioned. Here only the front part of the skull is used and prepared and then worn as a mask by the oldest son of the deceased, in ceremonial dances.

The interdependence of artistic creation and oedipal aggression becomes obvious. The image or the mask, molded on the ancestral skull, has the specific function of helping the individual or the entire group to overcome the conflict situation. In many cases the object is a means of warding off the threat of demons and evil spirits (Wirz 1950:411ff.; Muensterberger 1950:313ff.). Thus with the help of the parental image the owner can identify with the strong parent image and indulge in fertility and omnipotence. He and the "life-giving" ancestor are one.

This particular fact might explain the generally outstanding position of the artist in his tribe.

The Borneo figures may be half human and half animal, or often even creatures without immediate relationship to man or beast. In the wide area from India to Polynesia, we observe the importance of tusks or teeth. Dangerous or protective creatures are shown with large tusks. In Borneo, one of the most frequently represented figures is the immensely feared tiger, usually shown with a large protruding tongue, tusks and an erected penis. In this area, it is the tooth of the tiger that is considered to be of high magical value and the possessor of it is powerful, respected and feared. Chieftainship is sometimes connected with the possession of what in Malay is called *kabasaran,* i.e., the tiger tooth or magically potent ornaments which are its equivalents. In any case, these regalia are considered to be sacred, full of supernatural power and taboo, and no one would dare to touch them (Kruijt 1906:224ff.; Duyvendak 1940:134ff.).

In other areas of South East Asia and Oceania such as the Solomon Islands, the New Hebrides, in many parts of New Guinea, some islands of the Moluccas, etc., tusks and teeth have high value. In certain regions, teeth are used as currency. The owner of such objects is considered a man of high social status. In the central New Hebrides and the Banks Islands, especially, the ownership of a number of tusks and the social position and influence of a man are closely interrelated (Speiser 1924:74ff.).

There is another prevalent ritual which involves the teeth. Among many tribes, tooth filing and tooth evulsion belong to the essential part of the initiation ritual. Tooth evulsion is often a substitute for circumcision, which again shows the phallic significance of the tooth. Among the Wonghi of New South Wales, for instance, the elder during the initiation ceremony of the young man is obliged to knock out a tooth, "indicating the change from youth to manhood (Cameron 1885:XIV, 357; Uhle 1887; Jensen 1933). The evidence for the equation tooth-phallus is so often met in dreams and free associations, that there cannot be any doubt about its symbolic meaning (Freud 1938:388ff.; Reik 1919:66 ff.; Klein 1949:187).

Similarly, among many tribes the symbolic meaning of the nose is given expression in art objects. In New Guinea, to pierce the nasal septum is part of the initiation ritual. The purpose of the perforation is to permit the wearing of ornaments such as rings, sticks, etc. The importance of the nose is especially noticeable in the images and masks of the Sepik region. It is almost beak-shaped and often continues to and joins the penis, making them one and the same extension. (See Plate 7.) The figures themselves bear a strong resemblance to representations of anthropomorphized birds. In other areas of Oceania, the Solomon Islands and Easter Island, the mongrel representation of man and bird is well known. In the religious ideas of many peoples of the South Seas the "soul-bird" is of great importance. According to their belief, part of the soul or vital essence of life of the deceased does not disappear, but is retained in one or the other form and often taken over by birds. This belief, then, is characterized in these carvings.[2]

Certain masks of the BaYaka of the Belgian Congo also show, by comparison, a large nose which is turned up. The face of this mask is inscribed in a circle. These masks, we are told, were held in hand by an envoy negotiating with other tribes. Some an-

---

[2] A young artist, in his analysis, had the following dream: "I saw a man in transparent underwear. His penis was enormous. It was grey and big, like the trunk of an elephant."

thropologists believe that the strange nose represents the beak of a bird (Kochnitzky 1949:32; Olbrechts 1946:48ff.). The heavy "erected" nose seems a symbol for the strength and virility of the BaYaka envoys—as a warning for the opponent, as are the tusks of the Borneo images.

What we find here is the symbolic connection between the sacrifice of human beings and their representations in masks and images with oversized phallic symbols. In the object, the skull or the tusk or the figure with horns, one's sexual strength, is symbolically expressed. We have sufficient clinical data to believe in the universal unconscious meaning of the nose, horn, tusk and beak as phallic symbols. Hence, having the dead one's potency added to one's own, displays the procreative faculty of the owner of the object. By killing the object, his death is experienced as a castration which counteracts the castration anxiety of the murderer. It is then transformed into increased vital power for the slayer. It often occurs that the owner of the skull takes the name of the victim in order to perpetuate his strength. This carrying over is part of the castration phobia and an obvious form of identification with the enemy, i.e., originally with the father. Head and phallus represent an ideal condensation of his potency and enable the son or the owner to fight the dread of death and impotence.

Among many primitive tribes, people do not only preserve the tusk of the animal but the entire skull and, in addition, head-hunting used to belong to the daily order. The power accumulated in an animal's tooth and skull was originally the procreative power and potency accumulated in a man's head and penis. Among the Dayaks, it used to be necessary for a young man first to hunt a human head before a girl would consider marrying him. His social status in this more genital-centered culture and his success as a head-hunter were closely connected.

In the Lower Congo region in West Africa, to be exact among the BaFioti, we find a great number of the so-called nail fetishes. (See Plate 6.) These images are usually of humans and sometimes of animals. They are very naturalistic, rather typical for

West African stylization. Now the BaFioti believe that a spirit living in these fetishes can be influenced by hammering a nail into its "body." This nail causes pain and hurts the spirit as long as he has not fulfilled the owner's wish, voiced while putting the nail in it. We have a comparatively early account about these nail fetishes:

> When a party enters the wood of the nganga (or the doctor) attached to the service of the fetishes *zinkici mbowu,* into which nails are driven, for the purpose of cutting the 'Muamba' tree, with the intention of making a fetish, it is forbidden for anyone to call another by his name. If he does so, that man will die, and his *kulu* ('soul') will enter into the tree and become the presiding spirit of the fetish when made; and the caller will of course have to answer with his life to the relations of the man whose life has been thus wantonly thrown away. So, generally speaking, a palavar is held, and it is decided whose *kulu* it is that is to enter the Muamba tree and to preside over the fetish to be made. A boy of great spirit, or else, above all, a great and daring hunter, is chosen. Then they get into the bush and call his name. The Nganga cuts down the tree, and blood is said to gush forth. A fowl is killed and its blood mingled with the blood that they say comes from the tree. The named one then dies, certainly within ten days. His life has been sacrificed for what the Zinganga consider the welfare of the people. They say that the named one never fails to die—and they repudiate all idea of his being poisoned (Dennett 1906:93 ff.). Only after the ceremony can the image be made.

We owe a somewhat similar description to R. Visser who traveled extensively in the same area. Anyone who wishes to have such a fetish must first get a corpse. Then he goes into the wood and fells a tree which he has chosen for the image. It is actually the craftsman who makes the sculpture but under the supervision and according to the conception of the owner. While this work is being done, the corpse has to be smoked. A red-colored substance is constantly smeared over its body and the genitals which are covered with a piece of cloth. When the work is finished, the cloth is taken from the genitals of the corpse and put around the lower part of the figure (Visser 1906/7:52ff.).

In focusing on the matter of the connection between the creative activity of primitives and of killing we observe the Adouma in the French Congo. These people preserve the skulls of their dead chiefs and keep them in baskets which are decorated with an idol called *mbouéti*. This is an oddly shaped piece of wood, often in the form of a half moon. Two round or oval pieces of brass or copper represent the eyes; the nose is a protruding piece of the same metal, but the mouth is rarely shown. Again, the field reports differ slightly; while some describe the head in the basket as that of the chief of the tribe, others claim that it can be also that of a rich man or a famous hunter (Von Sydow 1930:I, 485).

In Melanesia we also find data which point to the affinity between aggression and artistic activity. In New Ireland, a successive number of ceremonial feasts are given in honor of the deceased head of a totem group. To be exact: thirteen feasts are necessary to honor the dead one properly. Since this is rather costly, several totem groups get together and join their forces.

After a first, provisional, burial they exhume the skull, clean it and cover it with bee's wax. During this ritual the men sit on the floor, each holding a long stick upright in front of him. The next feast follows shortly afterwards. They build a small hut for its preparation. In these huts as well as on their roofs they put ancestral figures which are carved out of soft wood and painted profusely with white, red and black and in more recent times also in blue and green paint. The next goal is to collect food, as much as possible, and to store it in these little huts. The ceremony itself consists of the destruction of the huts, but not before the images are taken away. After the destruction, the stored food is distributed among the men. A variety of ceremonies is repeated until the twelfth feast when the women get permission to participate. After having used small ancestral figures until now, for this ceremony, large ones are brought in. For each man present a pig has to be killed, and after a ritual dance the skull of the deceased person, honored in thirteen feasts, has to be burned. The ashes are thrown into the sea (Neverman 1933:127ff.).

In Lesu, a village on the northeast coast of New Ireland, large images (*malanggans*) are made for the dead by the clan members. In the case of an old, important man the *malanggan* is made at the time of his death. But usually there is an interval during which food is stored and collected in order to prepare for the occasion. It is noteworthy that these feasts are merged with the initiation ceremonies for the young boys (Powdermaker 1933:315ff., 116ff.).

The possession of an ancestral corpse or skull or its substitute seems, then, to be a prerequisite for making an image. The Orokaiva of northeast New Guinea carve the so-called *naterari,* a post which is set up in the center of the village, several months after a man's death. The carving itself may be anthropomorphic, zoomorphic or even nonobjective, but it is regarded as a true representative of the dead man. Such a taboo post was cut by a man, Bararipa, "pending a feast in honour of his deceased father Komona; and the figure, by Bararipa's word, was a picture of Komona himself" (Williams 1930:226ff.).

While in societies like these, the mask or the image is usually carved after a person's death so that he is represented in the object, we observe among other peoples murder or a death wish as a condition for the realization of creative activity. No doubt, there are many local variations—variations which stress always the passionate or the phobic side. The dance with the mask or a stick, i.e., the ancestral skull or phallus may cause anxiety, invite attraction, give a feeling of security or amuse dancer and audience—the fundamental mechanism remains the same; namely, the omnipotent control over and identification with the ancestor.

The underlying connection between ancestral cult, initiation ritual of the young men, fertility rites and creative activity, becomes evident in the sacred art of the aboriginals of the northern territory of Australia. The aim of their rituals is to increase their totems and to ensure fertility in general. In dance and ceremony they use sacred emblems, the *rangga*. These are "sacred lifegiving sticks," symbolizing an iguana tail. There is a myth concerning ancestral beings who brought with them a large mat and these sticks. The mat, as Elkin and Berndt found, symbolizes the womb, while the sticks, representing the male genital organ, were kept hidden in the mat. In the beginning the female ancestors "were the sole custodians of the religious objects. . . . The symbols they used and the actions of their dancing signified the sexual act, pregnancy and birth. As men today emphatically state: 'Then we had nothing, no sacred objects, no sacred ceremonies; the women had everything.' One day, however, while the women were out collecting mussels, the men stole the sacred paraphernalia, and taking them to their own camp held the sacred 'dancing' connected with them" (Elkin and Berndt 1950: 29ff.; Róheim 1951). Today, this ceremony is conducted by the initiated men on sacred ground where a hut has been constructed. "This hut also 'is' the womb; there the *rangga* are stored," Elkin and Berndt write.

Essentially these symbols are the first ancestor's genital organ, and it seems that the art of carving them is the oldest of all native arts in Arnhem Land. Through the centuries these *rangga* became highly stylized; they exhibit different designs and totemic patterns. There are simple straight sticks and comparatively elaborate anthropomorphic figures. But all of them are considered to be *rangga* and are used as such.

In their functional context it is clear that the *rangga* represents the paternal phallus, symbolizing the castration of and the identification (in the ritual) with the father.

The same is partially demonstrated in the creative achievements of the Batak of Sumatra. Here the *datu,* a priest or shaman, uses several objects for his performances, among them a magic horn, a magic book and a magic wand. It is the magic wand (*tunggal panaluan*) which is a symbol of supernatural power. Hostility against the paternal authority is expressed in a myth connected with the magic wand. It depicts the power over the father and the shaman's omnipotence. He is the medium of the gods and ancestors, a doctor, sorcerer, prophet, artist, although he is not the official head of the tribe. It is he who carves the object he uses, i.e., the stick, the impressive mask, the book, and the horn.

The magic wand has a dramatic origin of which every Batak knows: Many centuries ago twins were born. Twins are considered quite an unlucky sign. It is even worse when they are a boy and a girl. In the case of the Batak myth the brother and sister grew up together and were inseparable. Their parents were afraid of incest and sent the girl away. They told their son that his sister had died, but he did not believe them. He searched for his sister and found her in the jungle. There the two stayed together. One day the girl saw a tree with sweet and ripe fruit. She wanted to eat some and asked her brother to fetch some for her. But as soon as he climbed the tree, he turned into wood and the boy and the tree became one. After some time the girl also climbed the tree in order to look for her brother. But she met the same fate. Three shamans trying to save them, followed the couple. They also turned into wood, as did several animals, a buffalo, a crocodile and a serpent. Another shaman came and used this tree as a magic wand, called *tunggal panaluan,* which means "the one who overpowers (others)."

We will not consider the variations of this myth as we have to disregard interpretation in so far as it is not relevant to our subject. In order to assure the magic wand its potency, the *datu* has to fill a small opening in the wand with a rare substance made out of the corpse of a dead person killed especially for this purpose. Again we see death as a prerequisite to the creation of an "artistic" object. "It seems that it is an attempt to project the cruelty manifested in murdering their helpless victim as a weapon against the enemy," wrote Róheim with reference to the magic wand of the Batak (Róheim 1930:127ff.).

In the case of the BaFioti we found that it is either a successful hunter or a boy "of great spirit" who is murdered with the intention to make the image productive. The same holds true for the Batak. The Australian aborigines explain that the life-giving sticks were removed from the womb. This might be interpreted as father's penis being forcibly taken out of mother. It seems quite obvious that there is a repetition of a displacement from the father (ancestor) to the hunter, a member of another tribe or a courageous boy. The father, the hunter, the stranger, the daring boy have the same subliminal meaning. Emphasis is laid upon the destruction, the death of one of these human beings, and upon the following restitution which is carried out in the procedure of making an image. The artistic object, and particularly the magic wand, symbolize magic control: That which destroyed is restored and assures the owner of his omnipotent power. Or, in Ella Sharpe's words: "A delusion of omnipotence finds a reality channel" (Sharpe 1950:128ff.). The artist restores in the object what his hostility had destroyed. But the destroyed object is now incorporated in order to guarantee the owner omnipotent control and to nullify his castration phobia.

The idea of this magic control can be distinguished in the artistic activity of the Vatshiokwe in West Africa. There the anthropologist Baumann learned that the masks are named after the dead: "I heard time and again that the masks are identical with the deceased ones." They are made by the novices while in seclusion.[3] At the termination of their seclusion the young men dance opposite their mothers and offer them a wooden knife. During another performance the initiated ones give the women wooden dolls (*mwana watundanži,* i.e., child of the circumcized). Other dancers use a mask and an artificial phallus and perform in front of the women. They are called the "with the women playing masks."

We can recognize that the same incentive has even influenced a certain style development, at least among some tribes in Oceania and West Africa.

In a rather large region of New Guinea, between the Geelvinck and the Humboldt Bay, we find the so-called *korwar* figures. (See Plate 36.) These images have a big head set on a tiny

---

[3] "Somebody will make his own *mutšiši* (ancestral image); then he will call him (with the) name of the one who died, perhaps (his) uncle, perhaps (his) father; then he will call the name of the *mutšiši* so that the women get afraid; they (the women) say: it is really a *mutšiši tšišanguke* (a related ancestor); the one who died is resurrected. . . ." Hermann Baumann (1935:105 ff.).

body, often in a crouching position. Now the shape of the head is curiously rectangular, with a sharp horizontal mouth that runs parallel to the chin. These figures are usually not as old, historically, as their predecessors. Like their neighbors in the Sepik region, originally these people preserved skulls. They were sacred since they were their father's. However, they did not decorate them with clay and shells and resin as did the Sepik people, but they carved small shrines for them in the shape of little wooden figures in the crouching or standing position—the dead are buried in the foetal position—with an opening in the head in which they kept the original skull. This is a perfect combination of skull and image ritual, and may be seen as a next step toward sculptural art. Now the fact that this little shrine had to hold the skull dictated the style. It is, to be sure, a style which we find spread over the vast area of southeast Asia and Oceania, from Cambodia to Easter Island and, as we learned from the recent discoveries, even in northern Australia (Muensterberger 1945:VII, 63; Speiser 1941).

There are other provinces of primitive art which have objects that resemble, stylistically speaking, this rectangular shape, for example the famous heads and hermae of the Pahouin in West Africa. Von Sydow, who gave the first psychoanalytic interpretation of primitive art, spoke repeatedly of the "truly cubist style" of these figures. But it seems questionable to me whether or not this style was a deliberately chosen one. We have reason to assume that the style was dictated by the development from the skull ritual to the image ritual whereby the image clearly enough became a substitute (Von Sydow 1928). The skull ritual then disappeared or, more correctly, was replaced, but it left its distinct mark in this style and in the belief in the potency of the image.

II

In studying these phenomena we wonder who the artisan or woodcarver is. What is his personality, his social status and position, his role? Are there craft distinctions among these so-called primitive peoples? Unfortunately, we do not possess much information of psychoanalytic value about the individuality of aboriginal artists. Usually the explorers paid very little attention to the art objects, and rarely even mentioned their makers.

In trying to gain access to the artist's personality we have to rely mainly on deductions. From the Batak of Sumatra we have already learned that the shaman is at the same time the artisan who executes the sacred objects. Among other tribes it is to a craftsman or professional woodcarver to whom people turn in ordering a boat or asking for help in building a house or making an ancestral figure. In other cultures every man is a potential artist or at least skilled enough in order to carve the objects necessary in ritual and dance. I know of only one tribe in which women are permitted to be sculptors.

The person combining the abilities of a craftsman, a dancer and a singer, a poet and an actor, as we see him quite frequently among primitives, is, as Marcel Griaule described him correctly, "the complete artist" (Griaule 1947:105). He encompasses what in more differentiated societies became specialized functions.

In these homogeneous societies the artist plays a conspicuously important part because his work is linked with the determinative issues of the tribal life. So the Bushongo ranked their artists immediately under the king. Among the Bambara, the smith who is at the same time the artisan and the woodcarver, is the center of religious and social activities (Griaule 1947:95). Elsewhere the male members of entire groups or families are able craftsmen. Linton gives an extended description of the *tuhungas,* the master craftsmen, in Marquesan society:

> At the upper end of the scale of master craftsmen were the house and canoe makers, who were also organizers and directors, and the artists, who were master carvers. These *tuhungas* worked mostly on order; they joined the employer's household, received food during the time they were working on a job, and were presented with a liberal gift on departure. The *tuhunga* could afford to be temperamental, for because of the peculiar religious sanctions, no other man could carry on a job which one man had

started. . . . A part of the *tuhunga's* training was the learning of the chants that accompanied the creation of an object. A food bowl made without the proper magic ritual would be just a bowl. It would have no real place in the universe and consequently no value. . . . The magic chants were in part a formula for the work, so that if a man knew the charm he could not forget the process, but the ritual was also part of an actual creation, beginning with the genealogy of the universe, building step by step, and finally calling upon the essence of the things to make their contribution to the art of creation, which was regarded as a sexual act (Linton 1949:145 ff.).

We then might ask whether or not there is a connection between creative activity and the pursuit of the man's aims? The natives of New Ireland tell a legend about the first woodcarver who learned his craftsmanship from a ghost. This first woodcarver trained pupils who then became famous artists. Women were absolutely excluded from art and ritual. They were not permitted to see the objects nor were they allowed to use the sacred word for these images, *alik* or *uli*. If they did so, they would be choked to death by the men. These figures as well as the *malanggans* are made in absolute seclusion. The natives explain that these images ought not to be seen before they are exhibited during the ceremonial rites for the deceased fathers. The artists are very anxious not to let anybody copy their individual ideas and innovations.

It is quite surprising that the fact of the particular exclusion of women has not been discussed until now, although it has been mentioned in a number of field reports.

In southern New Ireland, the natives make rude figures of chalk called *kulab*. These are representations of the ancestors which are kept in huts strictly forbidden to women (Parkinson 1907:654ff.). This rule we notice in Africa as well as among the Eskimos, in Australia as well as in the Americas. The explanations for the exclusion of women are varied. A Kuskokwim Eskimo told Himmelheber: "It is against the man's dignity that a woman should paint. I want to reserve this for me" (Himmelheber 1938:57). In the New Hebrides, the men who are engaged in the creation of their ancestral images have to spend the nights in the men's house until the work is finished. They are strictly forbidden to have sexual intercourse with any woman and may not even enter houses where there are women. The objects they make are absolutely taboo to women. "The masks are constructed out of their sight and, were a woman to look while they were being made or while the mask dance *navel* was being practiced, she would die" (Deacon 1934:397, 432). In West Africa the situation is not different. The Ashanti claim that there are no female carvers because women menstruate. In former times, a menstruating woman was not even permitted to approach the artists while at work, "on pain of death or a heavy fine. . . . If any wood-carver's wife was unfaithful to her husband, and the latter, being unaware of this, went to work, then 'his tools would cut him severely.'" (Rattray 1927:271.)

Alike circumstances seem to have existed among the Maori of New Zealand. Woodcarving, which included the building of a house or a canoe or the making of a sacred object, was considered a ritual process whereby no woman was permitted to approach the scene. Here again the artisans were held in high esteem and ranked next to the priests. (Firth 1925:XLIV, 277; Mead 1945:6ff.)

A similar attitude in connection with artistic activity can be inferred from aboriginal Australia. The artist has to be an adult, i.e., initiated man, who carves the sacred and secular objects in seclusion. For that purpose he retreats to a tabooed hut or a special shelter, constructed for this particular work. "This hut *is* the womb," Elkin and R. and C. Berndt write. "There the *rangga* are stored, and from it men emerge with them for the ritual dance" (Elkin and Berndt 1950:31, 34, 48ff.).

III

Without intimate knowledge of the native artists' personalities it is, of course, difficult to reconstruct the underlying mental fabric of the phenomenon of artistic activity among these people. Can we make comparisons with artists of our own environment? Are we permitted to call "art" what often enough was not meant to be art at all, in the Western sense of the word? I do not intend to answer these questions nor will it be possible to make statements about artistic creativity in general. I merely pose these questions because they point up the unavoidable imperfections of our case. The initial lack of information adds to our difficulties. Still, we can focus our attention on some patterns which seem to be almost universal among primitive tribes.

We have seen the widespread connection between death (often actual murder) and the making of an image. The idea of an "ancestral image" or the "ancestral mask" has been recognized by field observers for a long time. There is the obvious and acute relationship between oedipal strivings and the making of these objects. The man who makes the image of the deceased father; the one who wears his father's skull as a mask can, and is even expected to, identify with him in ceremonies and at times in status and position. He takes his father's potency over. The matter of oedipal aggression seems to become more obvious when we see that the artistic creation is not merely confined to activity after the person's death but that, as was pointed out, someone has to die in order to make the object potent. This is an almost reversed mechanism: it is not the ancestor's passing away which stimulates the making of an image, but rather the destructive impulses which are linked with the artistic drive. Destruction and creation go hand in hand. Through this interaction of destructive and restitutive tendencies, the artist is able to channelize his impulses and gain mastery over his aggression.

But these are not the only conditions under which the primitive artist creates his work. It would seem that those who wear the masks and who dare to make them are able to mobilize their oedipal strivings against their superego. It is this ability which permits the artist to free himself, at least temporarily, from the burden of the inhibiting superego.

Not only does it give him the opportunity to enjoy, on occasions of ceremonial or festive wantonness, his unconscious fantasies, his omnipotent creative imagination, but also his desires for a reunion with the mother.

At this point we ought to inquire further into the function of the isolation of the artist. We may ask whether it is the channelization of the oedipal impulses only, to which can be attributed this prerequisite to creative activity. Since killing is so often actually connected with the activity of the primitive artist, the work itself seems to be an attempt at restitution. This is solved by libidinizing the artistic activity.

The attempt at restitution is linked with the detachment from tribal life. The overanxious exclusion of women discloses the regressive tendency involved. The artist relinquishes communication with an inhibiting or disturbing environment. Women are phobically avoided. "If I want to work I forget about them," a present-day West African artist told me. "I feel depressed before I get (an idea). But when I've got it, I enjoy it. . . . If I have a girl, I ask her to go. I get fed up with her. I boot her out."

How can we understand these desperate defenses? The oedipal aggression is not as strongly repressed in these societies as it is in Western civilization. The regressive tendency for isolation is a security measure. Affect is being avoided. Objective reality is denied while strength is gained from the narcissistic retreat to a level of omnipotent fantasy. The Australian artists who work in a specially built hut which they call a womb; the African artists who go to an isolated spot from which women are kept away; Melanesian woodcarvers who work in the men's house or somewhere away from the village; my West African informant Barutu who, if a woman would approach him, would "boot her out"—they all use the seclusion as a matter of self-reassurance, for their avoidance of castration phobia, for their omnipotent fantasy and narcissistic autonomy.

If these are the conditions under which artistic activity among primitive peoples is possible, then two seemingly contradictory tendencies are at work: the necessary isolation indicates that distance from the oedipal mother is sought. The menstruating woman is avoided or even dangerous. On the other hand, reunion with the *giving* mother of the preoedipal phase is wanted. This is clearly pronounced in the statement of the Australian craftsmen with regard to the "primeval" times: "Then we had nothing, no sacred objects (*rangga*-penis), no sacred ceremonies; the women had everything" (Elkin and Berndt 1950:29ff.). The determining factor is that the men who retreat into the "womb" make use of their pregenital defenses and "steal" the phallic mother's paraphernalia. Under the threat of being overpowered by their oedipal desires, the artists temporarily abandon reality. This can be interpreted as a regressive step toward an early phase in which the attachment to the nursing mother was the source for hallucinatory fantasies and creative imagination. Stealing her paraphernalia would then mean stealing the penis which was originally in her. The creative act would be a form of aggression against the phallic mother, so that the later act of killing could be interpreted as an oedipal repetition of preoedipal impulses.

STUDIES ON MIDDLE AMERICAN ART

Tatiana Proskouriakoff

I THINK many of my colleagues will agree that critical study of art is not for the archaeologist. Aesthetic values have little bearing on immediate archaeological problems, and their elucidation in works of art has always been and should remain the function of art critics and art historians. Few of us can bring to bear on these subjects the heightened perceptions and the intuitive interpretations that they require. Occasionally there are persons who do encompass both points of view successfully. Such studies as Spinden's (1913) on Maya art, or Covarrubias's (1946) on the Olmec style, are both critical and anthropological. The synthesis, however, rests on conclusions reached independently by the two disciplines and does not of itself offer a practical method of research. In the field of art criticism, our responsibility ends with supplying for the critic the necessary information on chronology and cultural affiliation of works of art and in publishing them with the least possible loss of aesthetic values.

This, of course, has posed problems that are becoming increasingly serious, but they are obvious problems of which everyone is acutely aware, and which are largely matters of funds and techniques. In spite of all difficulties, the best of Middle American art is now well enough known and readily enough available to give a seriously interested art student plenty of scope.

As a student of culture, the archaeologist is concerned pri-

Reprinted from *Middle American Anthropology,* Social Science Monograph V, 1958, pp. 29–38, published by the Pan American Union, General Secretariat of the Organization of American States, Washington, D.C., by permission of the authors and the Pan American Union.

marily, not with the creative and expressive aspects of art, but with the incidental anthropological information it contains and with the stable artistic conventions, techniques and mannerisms by means of which he can trace continuities in tradition.

Middle American art furnishes us with three distinct kinds of data. The first comprises ethnographic details presented in a realistic manner. Thus Tozzer (1930), on the basis of sculptures at Chichen Itza, distinguished the Maya and the Toltec peoples. Thompson (Ruppert, Thompson, and Proskouriakoff, 1955), in a more recent paper on Bonampak, discussed the ethnographic implications of the detail drawn on the murals. Although such grand pictorial scenes are rare in Middle America, its minor arts are full of scattered ethnographic data, constantly used to amplify interpretations of ancient customs and to trace their continuity in time.

Even richer than the descriptive content, though much more difficult to interpret, is the symbolism of Middle American art, and this constitutes another field of interest, closely akin to an interest in epigraphy. Caso and Bernal's (1952) presentation of the funerary urns of Oaxaca leans heavily on this approach. Rand's (1955) study of the water symbol is an attempt at a more analytical method, which follows a single symbol in its variations. Occasional fantastic excursions into this field do not detract from the more serious work on which archaeologists habitually rely.

It is the third kind of data, however, that I would like to stress in this discussion: data inherent in the formal properties of design, considered without reference to aesthetic values or to symbolic meaning. In Middle America we have scarcely begun to explore the potentialities of this field, although it is directly applicable to archaeological problems.

A number of years ago, several studies attempted to deal with the distribution of certain specific forms such as the stepped fret, but no results of consequence seem to have been achieved, probably because these studies made no attempt to define the significant variations in these forms. To find what sort of variation may have significance, we must turn to studies dealing with specific problems.

One of the earliest attempts to utilize form as a criterion of chronological changes was made by Spinden when he estimated the dates of Copan stelae by progressive modifications in the pose and proportions of the human figure. The changes are actually somewhat less uniform than his postulate stated, but the soundness of his approach is beyond question and pointed the way to further investigation. Applying the method to a larger body of material, and expanding it to include a variety of forms, I followed Spinden's lead in my *Study of Classic Maya Sculpture* (Proskouriakoff, 1950). In the course of this study, I found that the most consistent changes observed were in certain qualities of delineation and elaboration of forms that were the same for a large range of specific forms. Although the changes did not progress with perfect uniformity, trends could be clearly defined by a combination of several factors. I found no way, however, to predict changes by formal analysis or to infer their direction without a detailed chronology derived from other sources. If it is not possible to do so, the application of this method in Middle America is strictly limited.

Analytical description of forms has also been used to define regional styles and schools of art, and in this has proved very useful. Drucker's (1952) admirably precise description of the style of La Venta brings into focus discussion that formerly was carried on in such ambiguous terms that the arguments had little cogency. Drucker's definition enables us to refer to a definite constellation of traits where formerly there was only a nebulous Olmec style that each person was free to conceive in his own way.

Actual difficulties that arose in respect to the relations between the Tajin style and Kaminaljuyu prompted me to try a tentative classification of Veracruz ornament, which brought to light two distinct types of decoration and made it unnecessary to link Tajin with the Esperanza Phase. Haberland (1953) has used the form of minor detail on Maya stelae to distinguish regional schools and to infer contacts between them. His method suffers from what I would call the "dissecting" approach, in which the finest possible distinctions are drawn and each variation is isolated for comparison with others. Clearly it is impossible to handle very large collections of data in this manner. The need for finding general qualities of form which have cultural and historical significance has been felt by all investigators who attempt to deal with design.

When Brainerd (1942), some years ago, tried to describe simple band designs on Yucatan pottery, he first published a brief paper on symmetry in primitive conventional design. Shepard (1948) took up the subject and pursued it more deeply in a paper on the symmetry of abstract design with special reference to ceramic decoration. In this paper she touches on several other aspects of design, and I believe that her work on ceramics (Shepard, 1956) contains a separate chapter on ceramic decoration.

These studies suggest to me the possibility of building up an organized body of descriptive categories that could be applied to a large range of designs and adapted in different ways to the solution of specific archaeological problems. Such a structure need not be theoretically perfect or exhaustive. Miss Shepard's analytical treatment of symmetry is admirable, but we cannot hope that all qualities of design we might wish to use will be so restricted in range of variation. In some ways it would be more advantageous to have a flexible theoretical structure deriving from the material one studies and specifically adapted to it, for it is important to keep the system simple and as fully effective as possible. Consequently, I don't want to suggest in advance precisely the form it should take, but to illustrate more concretely what I have in mind, I will take a hypothetical example of how one may choose to describe style of two-dimensional ornament.

First, we might have an inventory of standard invented forms, or, as I call them, ideal forms, which have a wide geographic distribution and are definable by simple geometric structure: the step, the fret, the guilloche, the scroll, etc. These forms in themselves will yield no evidence of specific cultural contacts but, in a sense, their variety may be a measure of the range of such contact that the culture had enjoyed. Since they are widely distributed, it is convenient to use them, when possible, for direct comparison of more abstract properties. The latter could be grouped into several categories. Principles of arrangement might include symmetry, types of rhythm in spacing, delimitation of field, etc. Principles of form definition would distinguish between forms of definitely delimited area, forms indicated by partial outlines, forms suggested by directional lines, and forms in themselves linear. The degree of the isolation of elements and the relation of field and form may be also capable of precise formulation. A third category might comprize qualities of delineation, for example, character of curvatures and typical devices of form distortion, which are very distinctive sometimes and are an excellent criterion of style. Finally, we may add qualities of elaboration, such as the use of interior or exterior ornament, the degree to which the detail is adapted to the form, as well as more specific types of elaboration.

Any of these qualities, or any group of them, can be investigated independently and in the context of a specific problem, probably only a very few will assume importance. The brevity of this paper precludes a discussion of how this will work in practice or of the numerous problems to which form analysis could be applied, but let me mention briefly three formal properties that seem to distinguish the high Classic development in Mesoamerica.

As you probably know, we have no fixed system of style designation, but habitually refer to nine major styles in the high culture area. These have been given ethnic names, and in spite of many objections, the names have persisted. The four lowland styles are the Olmec, the Totonac or Central Veracruz style, the Huastec and the Maya. In the highlands are the Zapotec, the Toltec, the Mixtec, the Aztec styles and the style of Teotihuacan, which is the only one that lacks an ethnic designation. In addition, there are less well-defined styles such as that of the Danzantes of the Monte Alban and the style of Santa Lucia Cotzumalhuapa, as well as innumerable styles of figurines and of ceramic decoration.

The most striking quality of the great styles of the Classic Period is the rhythm of the curves that delineate their forms. The true circle is rarely used and volutes almost never have constantly increasing curvature. Lines tend to fluctuate from straight line to curve at definite intervals, creating such forms as the squarish Maya cartouche and the undulating serpent. Purely angular forms are also very rare in the lowland styles, though somewhat more prominent in the highlands. The rhythmic quality of curvatures is most pronounced at the height of the Classic development, weakens with the advent of the Toltec, and is all but imperceptible in Aztec sculpture and Mixtec painting. Circles and circular volutes are used freely in the Aztec style.

Another property of Classic styles is their adaptation of the grotesque to ornamental uses. What I call the Middle American grotesque is primarily a symbolic structure which deliberately combines elements incongruous in nature in order to define a supernatural world. It is quite distinct from mere conventionalization of animal forms. The jaguar-human infant motif of the Olmec, the feathered serpent motif of the Toltec, and the saurian monster on yokes from Veracruz are examples of the grotesque. In Classic times, certain grotesques are used freely for subordinate elaboration appearing in such a great variety of contexts that we may infer they had little if any specific connotation. Maya serpent heads, for instance, are ubiquitous in design and adorn the most trivial detail. Sometimes the grotesque is disassociated into elements which are woven in with abstract ornament or completely divested of its significant forms, retaining only its general structure which serves to animate the design. No such liberties are taken with the grotesque in Aztec art, where each grotesque represents a definite symbolic entity.

A third feature of Classic styles is the dominance of the scroll form in ornamental design, particularly in the Maya area and in central Veracruz. Its absence in the Olmec style, noted by

Drucker, is perhaps one of the principal reasons for the tendency to assign a pre-Classic date to this style even before its associations at Tlatilco were known. The scroll is also little used in the monumental sculpture of the Zapotec, though it forms the basis of decorative forms on pottery from Monte Alban. The Maya scroll begins to lose its characteristic structure in the period of Toltec domination, and only primitive forms used as symbols survive at Mayapan. The Veracruz stylistic sequence can only be conjectured, but there is reason to think that here, too, scroll arrangements are simplified and gradually disappear. The scroll plays no great part in Aztec art, and occurs only in certain minor symbols in the art of the Mixtec.

These observations suggest the possibility of characterizing the Classic development in Middle America by the dominance of definitive artistic qualities or modes, and of arranging the recognized styles in respect to their participation in the general development. We can also attempt to trace back this development into the pre-Classic period to see where its essential features originate.

As we look back in time, there are no recognized monumental styles unless we choose to regard the Olmec style as pre-Classic. This style has two of the major properties of the Classic development, but lacks the ornamental scroll. Through figurines, it is definitely linked with the remains at Tlatilco, but the range of its monumental sequence is not known precisely. The Danzantes of Monte Alban and the early monuments of Guatemala are so far only isolated examples of unknown styles. Neither show markedly rhythmic curvatures or ornamental adaptations of the grotesque, though simple scrolls and grotesques are present.

Nevertheless, rhythmically delineated scroll designs of definitely Classic character can be traced back on minor carvings at least as far as the Miraflores Phase in Highland Guatemala. In their report on Structure E-III-3, Shook and Kidder (1952) published a bone spatula and a stone vessel with intricate scroll designs executed in rhythmic line. One of these even shows a coupled arrangement and an imperfect symmetry characteristic of the earliest known Classic designs from Veracruz. Simpler scrolls of the same type are carved on pottery vessels in a plano-relief technique which appears here for the first time. This association of the designs with a newly introduced technique, and the fact that they stand out sharply from their Miraflores matrix, makes it clear that they originate elsewhere, and it is possible to predict that we will some day find a contemporaneous culture in which the essentials of the Classic stylistic development are highly advanced.

The fact that Classic features are first observed in the minor crafts brings us to the intensely interesting problem of the role that minor arts play in the development of the great monumental styles and the subsequent interaction of crafts and fine arts. We know that the relationship between pottery decoration and monumental sculpture is not constant and raises provocative questions. In the Peten, Early Classic polychromes are intimately related in style to the monumental arts, although the designs are specifically adapted to pottery forms. Pictorial art appears sometimes on a coat of stucco added to the vessel, forming a surface on which a hieroglyphic scribe would have been accustomed to work, and on which a mural painter could have practiced his technique in miniature. Only in the Late Classic Period does fired decoration on pottery take the form of figure painting indistinguishable in style from the monumental arts. At the same time there appear many designs that have no discernible roots in the dominant art style. At Copan, the figure painting on Copador pottery remains uninfluenced by the city's great sculptural style. Kaminaljuyu in Early Classic times has no distinctive style of its own, and Maya and Teotihuacan designs coexist on pottery that is all apparently locally made.

Do these circumstances reflect differences in the composition of the societies involved, differences either of class relations or of ethnic background? Can the existence of folk cultures in ancient societies be demonstrated by showing the independence of popular art traditions in certain periods? Are such arts the source, perhaps, of the so-called Archaistic traits that we find in decadent periods? Such problems perhaps cannot be approached or solved directly; but, indirectly, we can infer a great deal from artistic styles provided that we can describe them definitely and accurately, for the work of artists reveals more clearly than any other human activity the character of their training, the traditions they follow, and in some degree their status and function in society.

Whether our interest is centered on historical chronology or on the sociological implications of art, our first objective must be to find an efficient way to deal with the rich variety of designs that we find in Middle American collections. If we are not to be overwhelmed by the impossible complexity of methods of direct comparison, or diverted from our main concerns by the still largely esoteric problems of aesthetics, it seems to me that our only course is to study the general properties of forms and to find among them significant features that can be compared in different designs. Only then can we proceed to define styles by the pattern of their formal properties, to organize them into a unified system implying their degree in interdependence, to explore the nature of the stylistic influences we observe, and ultimately to discern some general patterns in the development of the arts and to study their implications in respect to other factors in Middle American culture.

DISCUSSION OF PROSKOURIAKOFF'S PAPER

Robert L. Rands

As Proskouriakoff has indicated in her stimulating and important paper, artistic investigations may be directed toward varied ends. Thus, Middle American art has been studied by the art critic for its aesthetic values and by the archeologist in order to obtain information of an ethnographic or symbolic nature. In proposing a program of research which concentrates on the formal properties of design, she has emphasized the value of studying "ideal forms"—

elements or motifs—which are widely distributed; her investigation of them would be in terms of their general stylistic properties (rhythm in spacing, the different uses of line in indicating form, the character of curvatures, and so on). If I do not mistake her emphasis, Proskouriakoff comes close to ruling out the value of formal analyses which are not rooted directly in style. At least, it is apparent that in the study of the stylistic aspects of form she sees the grestest contributions being made.

I suspect that few will take issue with her general position. Results of great practical use to the archeologist stem from the systematic analysis of stylistic factors, as has already been demonstrated in Proskouriakoff's masterful study of Classic Maya sculpture (1950), with its tangible results embodied in a bettered chronology. Indeed, when it comes to chronological refinement, it is in style that the archeologist has a particularly sensitive tool at his disposal. This has long been recognized implicitly, and archeologists have become accustomed to working in a context of style. To no small degree, archeological periods, areas, and certain artifact types are defined on the basis of stylistic factors. However—due in part, perhaps, to a fear that we would become too subjective—we have characteristically shied away from a consideration of the qualities and mannerisms which permeate an art style. In so doing, we have surely missed much that is of temporal and cultural significance. It is in coming to grips with this problem that Proskouriakoff, here as elsewhere, has made her special contribution.

I would like to suggest that the susceptibility of style to change may not hold equally true for other aspects of art. For purposes of the present discussion, we can recognize several semi-distinct components of formal artistic analysis. These may be termed *element, motif,* and *style.* The first two, which intergrade, deal with the units or building blocks of form. Another such unit, third in a hierarchical series, would be *subject matter,* although its inclusion introduces a new dimension of interpretation. Style, on the other hand, concerns the execution and patterns of arrangement of these units—i.e., the way they are handled. Schapiro

(1953, p. 288) has voiced the prevailing assumptions that "every style is peculiar to a period of a culture and that, in a given culture or epoch of culture, there is only one style or a limited range of styles. Works in the style of one time could not have been produced in another." Can the same be said of element, motif, and subject matter?

It would seem not. While little systematic research has been directed along these lines, numerous examples exist of motifs or subjects which have outlasted their original stylistic settings. To argue contemporaneity because of the occurrence of a particular motif or subject is to invite error, as is well shown by the existence of the jaguar and eagle complex on an early, pre-Toltec monument at El Tajin (Proskouriakoff, 1954, p. 85). To be sure, cases of styles outlasting motifs can doubtless be found, but in general the latter do not seem to be as usable as style for the chronological refinement which is one of the foremost aims of archeological research.

Nevertheless, if we grant that the fullest possible reconstruction of past culture history is a basic aim of archeology, there is a place for the detailed consideration of element, motif, and subject matter. Historical contacts are involved in the spread of these attributes, and it is probable that for certain types of contact they are more revealing than is style itself. Thus, it would appear that once the basic Mesoamerican art styles of the Classic Period had been established, the spread of certain theocratic, ideological innovations within Middle America would be more readily discernible through a study of motifs than through sheer stylistic analysis. This is to say that sporadic contacts of a specialized sort might leave few recognizable traces in the configuration of habits and mannerisms which constitute an art style, although still being reflected in other formal aspects of the art. This would be significant not only for the somewhat specialized problem of symbolism but for time-space reconstructions, as well. Let us bear in mind, however, that such contacts might well be of a somewhat different order than those which are normally revealed through basic similarities in style.

It is perhaps when we deal with relationships between distinct culture areas that motif and subject matter have their greatest advantage over style in revealing the existence of diffusion and contact. Time does not permit a detailed consideration of this suggestion, which after all lies somewhat outside the subject of a symposium on Middle America. An example must be sufficient. Stylistically, the feathered serpent of Mesoamerica and the winged serpent of the Southeastern United States are quite distinct, yet they almost surely represent historically related artistic concepts. We may perhaps postulate a tendency for motif and subject matter to diffuse more widely than style. This, if true, could in part be related to the previously-proposed tendency for motifs to persist over longer stretches of time, thereby providing an opportunity for them to spread more widely. It may also be that other aspects of culture, such as mythology and folklore, provide media for sustaining and perpetuating artistic motifs and subject matter—something not true in the case of style.

Two additional remarks must suffice. (1) Proskouriakoff's discussion of stylistic properties characterizing the Classic cultures of Mesoamerica gives added demonstration of the essential unity of the area. Note again how an historically integrated region may be defined in terms of a climax style or group of closely related stylistic features. (2) Although in these analytical remarks style has been separated from other aspects of art, it is clear that working with concrete data will almost invariably force the investigator to consider the various components of form. Yet there is practical value in keeping the theoretical distinctions in mind, and they may be accorded varying emphasis. Insofar as this is done, it seems clear that Proskouriakoff's stress is on that component, style, which is most usable and fruitful for general archeological purposes. No matter how good an approach is, however, I feel there is danger in regarding it as the only one to be used.

ART STYLES AS CULTURAL COGNITIVE MAPS[1]

John L. Fischer

STUDENTS of the history of the visual arts have long postulated connections between art form and sociocultural conditions. Such a connection is often obvious in respect to overt content: e.g., the religious art of the Middle Ages. But connections between social conditions and general features of style have also been postulated: romanticism versus classicism, for instance, have been explained as related to the position of the individual in society and to the rapidity of social change. While these explanations of style are often convincing and appear profound, from an anthropological point of view they suffer from being limited, for the most part, to artistic data from various branches of European civilization, or in some cases certain other extremely complex societies such as the Oriental civilizations. The study of art in a widely distributed sample of primitive, relatively homogeneous societies would seem to offer valuable evidence for testing theories of the relationship of art style to social conditions. This

---

Reprinted from *American Anthropologist*, Vol. 63, No. 1, 1961, pp. 79–93, with the permission of the author and the American Anthropological Association.
[1] I wish to thank the following persons for reading a draft of this paper and offering helpful suggestions and criticisms: Herbert Barry III, Irvin L. Child, Clyde Kluckhohn, George P. Murdock, David Riesman, and John Whiting. This paper is a revision of a paper presented at the annual meetings of the American Anthropological Association in Mexico City, December, 1959. I also wish to thank a number of people who made verbal comments at that time, some of which I hope I have heeded, even while lacking adequate notes to give them credit. Barry deserves special thanks for making his findings available to me.

paper is intended as a modest contribution in this direction, making use of objective statistical tests.[2]

Two sets of variables are used in the tests reported below. The judgments on the art styles were made by the psychologist, Herbert Barry III, and formed the basis originally of his undergraduate honors thesis at Harvard carried out under the direction of John Whiting. Barry later published some of his findings in a paper on "Relationships between Child Training and the Pictorial Arts" (1957). Judgments on the social variables are from Murdock's "World Ethnographic Sample" article (1957). Since both sets of judgments were made independently without, moreover, any intent to test the specific hypotheses to be discussed below, it can be fairly stated that the positive results are not to be explained by bias of the judges in favor of the hypotheses.

The sample of primitive societies used below is determined by the overlap of Barry's and Murdock's sample. Thanks to the large size of Murdock's sample all except one of Barry's societies are also represented in Murdock. Barry's sample itself consists of those societies with sufficient art data from the larger cross-cultural sample of Whiting and Child (1953). It is somewhat biased geographically in favor of well-covered parts of the world—North America and the Pacific, but I personally doubt that this seriously affects the validity of the conclusions, since for many of the art variables both extremes of values can be found in the same continental area. A total of 29 societies are available for testing, although for stratification Murdock makes no rating for the Thonga for lack of specific data.

The general theoretical position behind this paper is that in expressive aspects of culture, such as visual and other arts, a very important determinant of the art form is social fantasy, that is, the artist's fantasies about social situations which will give him se-

---

[2] For useful discussion of the methodological problems involved in investigation of this type see Murdock (1949), Whiting and Child (1953), and Whiting (1954). For further information on the statistical methods used see Siegel (1956).

curity or pleasure. I assume that, regardless of the overt content of visual art, whether a landscape, a natural object, or merely a geometrical pattern, there is always or nearly always at the same time the expression of some fantasied social situation which will bear a definite relation to the real and desired social situations of the artist and his society. Incidentally, while this point of view that man projects his society into his visual art will not seem especially revolutionary to many anthropologists or to psychoanalysts, it is one that is by no means universally accepted among art critics, who often emphasize historical relationships, the stimulus of forms in the natural environment, or the limitations of the material worked with. I would not discount these other influences entirely but would point out that almost any society has a variety of materials to exploit, and cultural and natural forms to serve as models. It may be more important to ask not "What is in the environment?" but "Why do these people notice items A and B and ignore items C and D in their environment?"; to ask not "What materials do they have to work with in their environments?" but "Why have they chosen to work with wood and ignore clay, even though both are available?"

In a sense, the hypotheses tested below may be said to deal with latent content of art as opposed to the overt ("representational") content. I do not assume that the artists themselves are necessarily or usually fully aware of the significance of their art as representative of fantasied social situations. There is, on the contrary, reason to believe that this awareness is usually repressed. On the other hand, if some sort of fairly regular connection between some artistic feature and some social situation can be shown, this would constitute plausible evidence for a repressed significance to a work of art which the artist might deny if questioned directly, although one would assume that further and better confirmation of the repressed meaning could be obtained by psychiatric interviews, life histories, projective tests, etc. from individual artists and their public.

A word about the assumed relation of the artist to his society is in order here. It is assumed that the artist is in some sense keenly aware of the social structure and modal personality of his culture, although of course he cannot necessarily or usually put his awareness into social science jargon or even common-sense words. It is not assumed that the artist's personality is a simple duplicate of modal personality for the group; in fact in many societies artists appear to have rather unusual personalities. However, I do assume that all sane persons inevitably participate to a considerable extent in the modal personality of the group, and that the successful artist has a greater than average ability to express the modal personality of his public in his particular art medium. Perhaps under special circumstances he would also have the ability to express his private personality too, but in most societies there are fairly strict social and traditional controls on art production; personal isolation of the artist and encouragement of individual expressiveness to the degree typical of modern Western society are not found to my knowledge in any of the societies in Barry's sample.

I assume that the latent social meaning of visual art refers primarily to people, especially to characteristic physical configurations and to characteristic gestures and motor patterns. Conceivably socially important objects may be also involved to some extent, although because of the variety of artifacts and possessions in most cultures it would probably be hard to pick out general Gestalten from material objects which could influence art styles.

Two examples will be given of the ways social conditions may be reflected in art. The first and statistically more striking involves the reflection of the development of social hierarchy. We may postulate two ideal types of societies with respect to the development of social hierarchy.[3] In the authoritarian type, social

---

[3] These ideal types are set up for the purpose of simplifying the exposition and derivation of hypotheses. There is no intent of course to claim that any real human society can be categorized as purely hierarchical or egalitarian. On the contrary, all real societies fall at various intermediate points along a continuum between the two poles. On an impressionistic basis I would guess that if there is any tendency of societies to cluster it is near the center of the continuum—a balance between the two structural

hierarchy is positively valued. Society is seen as differentiated into groups of people lower than ego, who will serve ego and whom in turn ego must protect and help, and others higher than ego, whom ego must serve but who also in return will help and protect ego and glorify him by their association with him. These groups of higher and lower people, of course, are further differentiated internally along the same lines: there are those in both the lower and the higher group with whom ego has direct and regular contact; there are others too low or too high with whom contact is most often through intermediaries. The comfortable, secure situation in such a society is one where the relative rank of each individual is known and is distinct from the rank of each other individual.

The opposite ideal type of society is the egalitarian society. In this type of society, hierarchy as a principle of organization is rejected. While differences of prestige between individuals inevitably exist, it is bad taste to call attention to them. Work involving two or more people is organized as cooperation between equal partners rather than as service upwards or help downwards. A "bossy" individual is seen as a threat to security rather than as a strong and wise leader.

If we assume that pictorial elements in design are, on one psychological level, abstract, mainly unconscious representations of persons in the society, we may deduce a number of hypothetical polar contrasts in art style. These are listed below, briefly discussed, and the results of statistical tests of them given in Table 1:

1 Design repetitive of a number of rather simple elements should characterize the egalitarian societies; design integrating a number of unlike elements should be characteristic of the hierarchical societies.

---

principles—rather than near either or both extremes. Even in this central group, however, any two societies can be compared as to their relative nearness to the two poles, and their art styles can then be investigated to see whether they differ in the predicted direction. The statistical summaries given herein do this on a group basis.

2 Design with a large amount of empty or irrelevant space should characterize the egalitarian societies; design with little irrelevant (empty) space should characterize the hierarchical societies.
3 Symmetrical design (a special case of repetition) should characterize the egalitarian societies; asymmetrical design should characterize the hierarchical societies.
4 Figures without enclosures should characterize the egalitarian societies; enclosed figures should characterize the hierarchical societies.

The reasoning behind the first hypothesis, an association between visual repetition and egalitarian societies, is perhaps obvious. Security in egalitarian societies depends on the number of equal comrades ego possesses. By multiplying design elements one symbolically multiplies comrades. That the repeated design elements themselves will tend to be simple rather than complex also follows from the basic assumption that design elements are symbolic of members of the society, since, first, it is easier to maximize repetition with simple elements than with complex elements, and second, with the need to de-emphasize actual interpersonal differences in the society, typical persons would be conceived of as relatively simple, with emphasis on their relatively few near-uniform features, and will be symbolized in art accordingly.[4] Conversely, in the hierarchical society, security depends on relationships with people in a number of differentiated positions in a hierarchy. In art these can be symbolized by a

---

[4] Although of course important individual personality variation due to differences in inherited constitution and life history is to be found in all societies, this simplistic conception of people postulated here, I believe, has a definite effect in actually reducing personality variation among members of egalitarian societies. Therefore, even though simplicity in art design is far from a complete representation of the personality of its producers and consumers, I believe that the relationship between simplicity of art design on the one hand and personality and social structure on the other should be, as the data cited suggest, positive (the more A, the more B), not negative or antithetical (the more A, the *less* B).

design integrating a variety of distinct elements. Moreover, the more complex the elements in the design representing members of the society, the greater the possible differences between elements of the design, and the greater, therefore, the symbolic emphasis on personal differentiation. Note that even if one does not accept the human symbolism of the design elements but regards them instead as symbolic of valued objects or artifacts the argument leads to the same results: in the egalitarian society group harmony is promoted by an abundant supply of the same property for everyone—plenty of the same shelters, clothes, etc.; in the hierarchical society group harmony is promoted by every member keeping his place and having his own distinctive paraphernalia.

The second hypothesis, the association of empty space with egalitarian societies, assumes that for members of such societies other people are either comrades or nothing at all. If they are not comrades one tries to avoid contact with them. This implies a shrinking away from members of other groups, from foreigners. There are several reasons why one would be led to postulate that egalitarian societies tend to be more fearful of strangers. For one thing, such societies are necessarily small, and hence it is more likely that external aggression can totally disrupt them. Also, small societies are on the whole economically independent with respect to subsistence and therefore have less positive attraction to foreigners to counteract their fear. From a sociopsychological viewpoint, in small, close-knit, cooperative societies with intense face-to-face contact with a limited number of people, one would expect the generation of a considerable amount of in-group aggression which could not be directly expressed, and would in consequence be projected (in the technical psychoanalytic sense) onto foreigners and supernaturals—anyone outside the in-group—with resultant fear of the supposedly hostile out-group. The ideal situation for security is then one in which one's own group is numerous but well isolated from other groups. This isolation presumably can be symbolized by an empty space around the design.[5] In the hierarchical societies, on the other hand, security is produced by incorporating strangers into the hierarchy, through dominance or submission as the relative power indicates. Isolation of one's group implies that there may be other groups whose relative position is unclear. In fantasy the hierarchical society seeks to encompass the universe.[6]

---

[5] One might be tempted to argue that enclosed figures should characterize the art of egalitarian societies as a means of symbolizing the isolation desired and often achieved relatively well. However, one must consider that the isolation desired by these people is isolation of the whole in-group, while within the in-group close contact is desired with other individuals. At most this might lead one to hypothesize a tendency to frame the entire design in an enclosure but not to enclose separate figures within the design, I believe. For reasons too lengthy to discuss here I am doubtful about hypothesizing even the framing tendency.

[6] Clyde Kluckhohn has pointed out that empty space is characteristic of at least some Japanese pictorial art and asked how this may be reconciled with the interpretation given here. One question which arises is whether Japanese art is really characterized by empty space in terms of Barry's scale. As it happens, Barry did include Japan in his initial ratings but later dropped it because he felt that the country was too diverse and there was no guarantee that the art works rated were characteristic of the particular segments of the society from which the Whiting and Child socialization data came. Barry put Japan on the "crowded" side of the dichotomy, about intermediate between median and extreme. This suggests that while Japanese graphic art has much empty space by Western standards, it is still relatively crowded compared to the art of many primitive societies.

Another problem which arises is that Barry's sample was limited almost entirely to simple and middle-level societies. The only literate society included was Bali (also, incidentally, on the crowded side of the dichotomy). Perhaps in stable, large-scale, literate societies relationship to a social hierarchy is taken for granted more than in middle-level hierarchical societies. If so, the artist might safely engage in compensatory fantasies of temporary withdrawal from the hierarchy, the withdrawal being represented artistically by the empty space. But one would not expect this withdrawal to be extreme. The withdrawal of the simple primitive from foreigners should be more drastic psychologically than the withdrawal of man in civilized society from his obligations and restrictions. If this reasoning is correct the emptiest art should be found in simple societies, the most crowded art in middle-level societies, and somewhat emptier art again in complex, stable societies.

The third hypothesis, an association of symmetry with egalitarian societies, is posited on grounds similar to the first, symmetry being a special case of repetition. However, since symmetry tends to put a limit on the number of repetitions, one might expect that the association would not be as strong. Note also that bilateral symmetry can be said to involve an "original" image and a mirror image which is the opposite or negative of the first. This could suggest an egalitarian society perhaps but with an emphasis on competition between ostensible equals, i.e.,

TABLE 1. RELATION OF SOCIAL STRATIFICATION (MURDOCK COL. 14) TO VARIABLES OF ART STYLE (BARRY)

STRATIFICATION OF PEERS

Art Style	Low (A, O)	High (W, C, H)	
Simple design	13	1	p is less than .005
Complex design	6	8	

(NOTE: Since there are in fact more societies with low stratification than high in the sample, one would expect more with simple art styles. If one increases the number of societies with simple styles by moving the point of dichotomy up the scale of complexity, the distribution is as follows:)

	Low	High	
Simple design	16	1	p then becomes .000045
Complex design	3	8	

	Low	High	
Space empty	12	2	p is less than .05
Space crowded	7	7	

	Low	High	
Design symmetrical	12	2	p is less than .05
Design asymmetrical	7	7	

	Low	High	
Enclosed figures	7	7	p is less than .05
No enclosed figures	12	2	

Fisher-Yates test used for probabilities.

some interest in establishing a hierarchy, but without success in stabilizing it.

The fourth hypothesis, association of enclosed figures and hierarchical society, assumes that in the hierarchical society boundaries between individuals of different ranks are important. Higher are protected from lower and vice versa by figurative boundaries of etiquette and prescriptions of time, place, and nature of association, and also often by physical obstacles such as walls and fences, doors, moats, etc.

As is shown in Table 1, all four of these hypotheses are supported at statistically significant levels, especially the first.[7]

A second variable of social structure of considerable psychological importance is the relative prestige or security of the sexes. As a measure of this, types of residence as categorized by Murdock may be used. These may be dichotomized into those which favor male solidarity in residence strongly and those which do not. The former are patrilocal and avunculocal, while the latter are all others occurring in our sample (Murdock column 8:P, A vs. V, Z, N, B, X, M). The hypotheses below assume that individuals of both sexes find it advantageous to live with their own blood relatives if possible. Even where, as is usually true, the younger relatives must serve and obey the older, the younger have their own old age to look forward to, when they will be honored and cared for. In general, the spouse living with blood relatives has an advantage over the in-marrying spouse in obtaining support from other members of the household or family, so the side of the family chosen by married

---

[7] If one tests a large enough number of hypotheses it is to be expected by chance alone that one will receive confirmation of some of them at "significant" statistical levels. Statements of probability levels of confirmation of hypotheses are therefore questionable unless accompanied by a statement as to the total number of tests from which the reported significant tests were selected. For this paper the total number of hypotheses from which the 6 tests reported in Tables 1 and 2 were selected was 20. None of the other 14 hypotheses was supported or contradicted at a statistically significant level.

couples to reside with would seem to be a sensitive index of the relative security of the sexes. This choice is also a measure of the prestige of the sexes, insofar as one measure of prestige is deference to the wishes of the person with higher prestige by persons of lower prestige. There are often sound economic reasons, of course, which influence residence choice, as well as other rational and irrational considerations, but even where these exist I believe that there will *also* be an interpersonal prestige significance of considerable weight to the decision. From this reasoning two hypotheses were made, as follows:

1 Straight lines, representing the male form, as opposed to curved, should be associated with societies which strongly favor male solidarity in residence.
2 Complex, nonrepetitive design, representing a hierarchical society, should be associated with societies which strongly favor male solidarity in residence.

Reasoning behind the first hypothesis was that if the society gave high prestige to males and favored close association of males, a fantasy suggesting numerous males should produce security.

The reasoning behind the second hypothesis involved an association between male dominated and hierarchical societies. In man and the primates generally, dominance hierarchies are most developed among males. Also, it seems more likely that the man-wife relationship will be regarded as hierarchical in societies with male solidarity in residence. The data on complexity of design cited above already suggest that hierarchical societies are associated with complex design.

Testing of these two hypotheses yielded the results shown in Table 2.

As will be seen, the first hypothesis is strikingly *dis*confirmed and the opposite association supported. The second hypothesis is confirmed at a more modest statistical level.

TABLE 2. RELATION OF MARITAL RESIDENCE (MURDOCK COL. 8) TO VARIABLES OF ART STYLE (BARRY)

MALE SOLIDARITY IN RESIDENCE

Art Style	Low (M, X, B, N, Z, U)	High (A, P)	
Straight lines	14	1	p is less than .005
Curved lines	6	8	
	Low	High	
Simple	13	2	p is less than .05
Complex	7	7	

Fisher-Yates test used for probabilities.

An ex post facto explanation of the association between curved lines and male solidarity on residence is slightly more complicated but, I believe, more plausible. We may assume that when an adult individual is psychologically secure he will be extroverted and look for pleasure by seeking out members of the opposite sex. In fantasy a man will be creating women and vice versa. When, on the other hand, one sex is relatively insecure psychologically, members will be introverted and more concerned in fantasy with improving their own body image and seeking successful models of their own sex to imitate. Thus, to take polar extremes, in societies favoring male solidarity (and socio-psychological security) the men are looking for women as love objects and the women are looking for women as models for self-improvement, while in the societies favoring female solidarity in residence both sexes are looking for men. In visual art, I assume, this concern manifests itself as a relatively greater concern with curved and straight lines respectively.

The reader may have noted that I have grouped with matrilocal residence here some forms of residence, such as bilocal and uxoripatrilocal, which are logically intermediate between matrilocal and patrilocal residence. In the initial test I regarded these as intermediate but on examination found that they grouped with matrilocal rather than patrilocal residence, and amended the hypothesis to its present form. I believe that this finding suggests that the presence or absence of peer support may be more important for adult men than for adult women. If the woman is in an equal position with her husband as far as support of adult relatives goes, as would be the case in bilocal residence, for instance, she is still in a favorable position in the family because of the support of the children. In the family, it would seem, the wife tends to have the children more strongly on her side, the Oedipus situation being generally more severe for males, because of the strength of early ties to the mother of children of either sex.

On reading an earlier draft of this paper, Irvin Child, Professor of Psychology at Yale, has called my attention to two psychological reports bearing on sex difference in preference for shapes. One of these (McElroy 1954) reports a study of Scottish school children in which it was found that significantly more boys than girls preferred designs with rounded shape and more girls preferred designs with straight, angular shapes; also that the difference between the sexes in preference became significantly more marked after puberty. The other (Franck 1946) dealt only with college girls but included a questionnaire designed to get at attitudes towards sex roles as well as asking for preference of paired similar pictures differing only in respect to abstract sex symbols in the design. In this the investigator found that those girls who were more accepting of their own sex role significantly preferred more of the "male" pictures. The findings of both of these studies would fit in with the point of view reached above that sexual instincts affect preference for visual forms differently for the two sexes, but that these preferences can be reduced or even perhaps reversed by socially induced sexual conflict.

As an extension and further test of the above theory it later occurred to me to investigate the relationship between form of marriage (monogamy, polygamy, etc.) and art style. One might assume that in societies where one man may marry two or more women the heterosexual drive of the men is more freely expressed

TABLE 3. RELATION OF FORM OF MARRIAGE (MURDOCK COL. 9) TO VARIABLES OF ART STYLE (BARRY)

FORM OF MARRIAGE

Art Style	Nonsororal polygyny (GNL)	Sororal polygyny (ST) Polyandry (Y)	Monogamy (M)
Simple design	2	7	6
Complex	10	4	—
Straight lines	3	5	6
Curved lines	9	6	—

Using the extremes and omitting the middle column p is less than .005 for both hypotheses using the Fisher-Yates test.

and the men more secure than in those where a man may marry only one woman at a time[8]; that therefore there would be more curved designs in polygynous societies and more straight-line designs in monogamous societies; likewise in the polygynous societies there should be more complex design as a consequence of male hierarchical dominance. Both of these hypotheses are in fact supported by the Barry and Murdock ratings at a satistically significant level, as shown in Table 3.

There is, however, one important qualification. This is that societies with sororal polygyny are distinct from other polygynous societies. In their preference for curvature of line sororal polygynous societies are roughly intermediate between the extremes, and they go with monogamous societies rather than other polygynous societies as far as simplicity of design is concerned. Sororal polygyny is different from ordinary polygyny in that the wives

---

[8] There are grounds for questioning this assumption also. Some might argue that polygyny is comparable to what the psychoanalysts have described as Don Juanism; that it is a sort of overcompensation for feelings of sexual inadequacy. This is a complex question, but I would simply suggest here in reply that there may be a considerable difference between a Don Juan who conquers many women only to spurn them and a polygynous husband who has lasting responsible ties with two or three wives.

tend to form a united front against the husband in case of conflict. The husband cannot so easily play one off against the other, and is not in such a secure position as other polygynous husbands. Sororal polygyny can be regarded as a compromise between the man's desire for heterosexual relationships and the woman's desire for congenial comrades and co-workers of her own generation. The intermediate position of societies with sororal polygyny in respect to curvature of line seems therefore reasonable.

However, evidently sororal polygyny can work well only in relatively simple egalitarian societies, with at most age-grading as the main legitimate manifestation of the hierarchical principle. In hierarchical societies competition between siblings tends to be too severe to permit sororal polygyny to function: a wife would get along better with an entirely new rival than with her sister, an old rival from childhood. This, I believe, is why the societies with sororal polygyny nearly all have relatively simple art styles, as do the monogamous ones in this sample.

Incidentally, it is not necessary to assume that most men in a polygynous society have more than one wife in order to affect the socio-psychological security of the sex roles. As long as it is understood by a married couple that the husband may legitimately take a second wife, or probably even a mistress, if his first wife is not agreeable enough, this gives even the men in monogamous marriages a considerable psychological advantage. Relatively speaking, in a society in which polygyny is common, a second wife is usually available sooner or later to a man who wants one badly enough, regardless of the lack of a demographic surplus of women. This is so because there is usually a marked difference in marriage age between the sexes, women marrying earlier. In a manner of speaking, young men pay by prolonged bachelorhood for the polygyny of middle-aged men. The characteristic age difference between spouses where polygyny is common gives the man another psychological advantage.

Moreover, in the relatively complex societies which have non-sororal polygyny the best art is generally produced for the upper class and must be adapted to their taste. If upper class people have polygyny while lower do not, it will probably be the upper class polygynous art which gets collected for museums and reported in ethnographies on the whole. In such societies one would expect distinct class differences in art consistent with the findings about cross-cultural differences described here. Fieldwork directed at this question in a series of appropriate societies would provide a useful further test of these hypotheses.

My colleague, Henry Orenstein, has noted that it would be desirable to have information on the sex of the artists in testing cross-cultural hypotheses about sex symbolism in art. I can only agree that this would be highly desirable, but plead that the ratings were not available in advance. In addition to the considerable work involved, if I made them now myself I would be in danger of biasing ratings in favor of the hypotheses or overcorrecting for impartiality. I would, however, expect systematic differences to show in the use of curved and straight lines by the sexes in most cultures. Incidentally, I might report a casual observation that at a recent exhibit of contemporary American artists at the Newcomb College Art Department (Tulane University) I found myself able to predict fairly well from a distance without reading the labels whether the artist was male or female by noting the relative predominance of curved or straight lines. The men seemed to have more straight lines and the women more curved. One might conclude from this that both sexes in modern American society are insecure in their sex roles. One could also guess that the form of marital residence favored solidarity of relatives for neither sex, as is of course the case.

The question arises as to the relationship between Barry's published findings on art style (1957) and the findings reported here. As his title implies, his original study was concerned with predicting aspects of art style from socialization data. Barry concluded that, in his sample of societies, complexity of art style was positively related to general severity of socialization as rated by Whiting and Child (1953), and notes that this measure of severity of socialization applies especially to severe pressure on the child towards independence rather than towards obedience.

This is consonant with the interpretation offered here of the relationship between art complexity and social stratification. In the cooperative, egalitarian society there is a fear of the independent, self-reliant person as well as of the "bossy" person. Strength and success are achieved by unity of approximate equals, who must be regarded as powerless alone, for if some one felt competent working by himself he might not cooperate with others when needed. Moreover, since directions for work are given on the whole as subtle suggestions rather than as firm commands, a strong trait of obedience and responsiveness to the wishes of others is highly valued and useful. In the hierarchical societies on the other hand, at least those in which there is substantial practical opportunity to improve one's place in life, obedience and responsiveness to others does not have to be strongly ingrained, since there are public and explicit means which can ensure compliance. Commands can be stated clearly, with their punishments and rewards. The proper working of the hierarchical society depends on the presence of interested and efficient people in a variety of different independent statuses. This means that each person must be trained to be self-reliant within his own special sphere of competence, and widespread personal ambition is useful in ensuring that the key positions are filled with competent people.

It is interesting to note that Barry conceived of a sort of relationship between social complexity and complexity of art, on the grounds that technical artistic development might accompany general sociocultural development. To test this he examined the relationship of his art complexity ratings to thirty variables of Murdock's "World Ethnographic Sample," at the time in a preliminary unpublished draft. Barry observed that the relationships of art complexity to social stratification and also to nonsororal polygyny (as well as to two other variables, discussed below) appeared to be significant at the 5 per cent level. He did not, however, pursue the significance of these relationships, I gather because the results on many of the variables were poor and because statistically more satisfying results were obtained by choosing socialization severity in advance as an independent variable. One of the statistically significant results he obtained by this wholesale testing, an association of complex art with root rather than grain crops, seems on the face implausible to me and I assume it is a sampling accident. The other result, an association of complex art with sedentary rather than nomadic residence, fits in with the social stratification hypothesis in an obvious way.

Barry may have also felt that if socio-economic variables were relevant to art style, they exercised their effect through their influence on child training and personality, not directly. He and his colleagues have since pursued the question of the relationship of child training to subsistence economy with notable success (Barry, Child, and Bacon 1959).

The general point of view of art styles exemplified here, and in Barry's work from which this is derived, gives high emphasis to social conditions of various sorts as determinants of artistic fantasy or creativity. As such it is in opposition to those views of art which see the development of art style as primarily a matter of technical evolution, or of historical diffusion, or of the influence of the physical environment as model or source of materials. If art style is determined primarily by current social factors this does not invalidate the study of relatively trivial technical details as evidence for historical connection between cultures, and I would not deny the great usefulness of such evidence for some purposes. It does, however, cast strong suspicion on the use of general features of art style to establish historical connections, or on the use of known historical connections alone to explain the similarities of art styles of two distinct cultures. Practically all cultures are evidently exposed to a variety of art styles among their neighbors, and also possess within their own tradition a variety of models which could be developed in various directions. If a neighboring art style at a certain period of history proves congenial no doubt the society will adopt it by importation and imitation, but we must still explain why culture A rather than culture B provides the model, and why the diffusion of style did not proceed in the reverse direction. It is here, I suggest, that similarity of social conditions, and relative order of development of these, plays a major role.

These findings suggest that we may regard a work of art as a sort of map of the society in which the artist—and his public—live.[9] To be sure, unlike a geographic map, a wide, though not unlimited, variety of concrete works of art may represent the same social structure. Also, even in a fairly abstract sense, the works of art are not always isomorphic with aspects of social structure. One would not conclude, for instance, that a preoccupation with rounded female forms indicated a numerical preponderance of women in the society; one would simply conclude that the social structure encouraged the artist's interest in women. We might then speak of a work of art as a selective cognitive map of the society with predictable distortions.

The question may be raised whether the artist should not be said to be depicting a wish rather than social reality. I would concede that the wish-fulfillment aspect of art is in some sense primary, but would at the same time urge that wish-fulfillment and reality are closely related, even in fantasy. For art to be effective as wish-fulfillment it must attain a certain degree of plausibility by at least making a rather close compromise with reality. If the artist in a simple egalitarian society finds

---

[9] I do not intend to claim that the social factors identified here as relevant to various factors considered in art design are the sole relevant factors. Art is a complex enough phenomenon so that I would not expect to be able to comprehend thoroughly and explain even a fairly limited aspect of it within the scope of a study of this size. The evidence cited suggests, however, that I have a plausible explanation for a good part of the variance for specific factors studied. Of course, as in all statistical studies of phenomena with complex causes, decisions as to the validity of a hypothesis are unaffected by limited numbers of contradictory cases, and such cases can be expected to occur unless the factor one is studying is unusually strong. Also, it is generally true that a statistical relationship can be interpreted as evidence for more than one set of theoretical explanations, although by no means for just any set. If the reader can propose another set of assumptions which is congruent with the findings reported, further investigation will be required to determine which set is the more powerful.

pleasure in repeating the same simple design over and over again, it is because he can in reality find whatever security and pleasure he knows in a repetitive, undifferentiated social structure. If the artist in a polygynous society becomes preoccupied with curved female forms it may be because he knows he has in the long run a good chance of obtaining security and pleasure from relationships with women. Of course, the questions of relating to peers in an egalitarian society and obtaining women in a polygynous society are also frequent sources of frustration. Problems as well as sources of pleasure are involved, but there are also culturally prescribed solutions which, if not infallible, are usually seen as the best possible.

For an anthropologist, one of the most exciting possibilities that the study of art styles and social conditions opens up is the application to extinct cultures known only through archeology. If we can learn enough of the pan-human implications of art styles for social structure and the resulting psychological processes, we should eventually be able to add a major new dimension to our reconstruction of the life of extinct peoples known only from their material remains.

APPENDIX: BARRY RATINGS OF PICTORIAL ART VARIABLES USED IN THIS PAPER

NOTE: For a description of the manner in which the ratings were made see Barry (1957). In the following lists the order of the societies corresponds to their rank with respect to the art variables, the most extreme being at the beginning and end of the lists. The ratings deal only with graphic art, not with three-dimensional sculpture. For ratings on the social structure variables consult Murdock (1957). The Kwakiutl, while rated by Barry and listed below, are not included by Murdock and not used in the statistical tests above.

Simple	Empty	Symmetrical	No Enclosed Figures	Lines Straight
Andamans	W. Apache	Yakut	Andamans	Navaho
Chenchu	Chenchu	Teton	Ashanti	Ashanti
Masai	Chiricahua	Omaha	Chenchu	Teton

Art Styles as Cultural Cognitive Maps 161

Yagua	Comanche	Ainu	Yagua	Thonga
Paiute	Omaha	Paiute	Zuni	Yagua
Papago	Ainu	Comanche	Murngin	Paiute
Thonga	Paiute	Navaho	Navaho	Marshalls
Navaho	Thonga	Zuni	Comanche	Hopi
Murngin	Yakut	Hopi	Thonga	Ifugao
Marshalls	Teton	Arapesh	Hopi	Chenchu
Hopi	Hopi	Andamans	Maori	Maori
Zuni	Marshalls	Thonga	Masai	Zuni
Comanche	Masai	Marshalls	Paiute	Omaha
Omaha	Zuni	Yagua	Papago	Andamans
Ifugao	Ifugao	Chenchu	Omaha	Samoa
Ainu	Navaho	Kwakiutl	Teton	Ainu
W. Apache	Papago	Samoa	Alor	Marquesas
Chiricahua	Dahomey	Maori	Trobriands	W. Apache
Ashanti	Andamans	Marquesas	Marshalls	Masai
Teton	Ashanti	Murngin	Ainu	Comanche
Arapesh	Murngin	Papago	Ifugao	Murngin
Maori	Arapesh	W. Apache	Marquesas	Papago
Trobriands	Kwakiutl	Chiricahua	Dahomey	Yakut
Kwakiutl	Yagua	Ifugao	Kwakiutl	Chiricahua
Alor	Alor	Trobriands	Arapesh	Alor
Dahomey	Samoa	Ashanti	W. Apache	Arapesh
Samoa	Trobriands	Masai	Bali	Kwakiutl
Bali	Maori	Bali	Yakut	Bali
Yakut	Bali	Dahomey	Samoa	Dahomey
Marquesas	Marquesas	Alor	Chiricahua	Trobriands
Complex	*Crowded*	*Asymmetrical*	*Enclosed Figures*	*Lines Curved*

Part III ∥ THE PRIMITIVE ARTIST

THE ESKIMO ARTIST

Edmund Carpenter

Nowhere is life more difficult than in the Arctic, yet when life there is reduced to its barest essentials, art and poetry turn out to be among those essentials. Art to the Eskimo is far more than just an object: it is an act of seeing and expressing life's values; it is a ritual of discovery by which patterns of nature, and of human nature, are revealed by man.

As the carver holds the unworked ivory lightly in his hand, turning it this way and that, he whispers, "Who are you? Who hides there?" And then: "Ah, Seal!" He rarely sets out, at least consciously, to carve, say, a seal, but picks up the ivory, examines it to find its hidden form and, if that is not immediately apparent, carves aimlessly until he sees it, humming or chanting as he works. Then he brings it out: Seal, hidden, emerges. It was always there: he didn't create it; he released it; he helped it step forth.

What emerges from the ivory, or more accurately from the artistic act, is not simply a carving of a seal, but an act which explicates, with beauty and simplicity, the meaning of life to the Eskimo. Let me illustrate from personal fieldwork and from an exceptionally brilliant manuscript, *Freedom, Being, and Necessity* by Paul Riesman (1960):

Originally published as a "Comment" on H. Haselberger's "Method of studying ethnographic art," *Current Anthropology* 2 (4) 1961:361–63, by permission of the author and the editor, *Current Anthropology*.

In the Eskimo language little distinction is made between "nouns" and "verbs," but rather all words are forms of the verb "to be" which itself is lacking in Eskimo. That is, all words proclaim in themselves their own existence. Eskimo is not a nominal language; it doesn't simply name things which already exist, but rather brings both things and actions (nouns and verbs) into being as it goes along. This idea is reflected in the practice of naming a child at birth: when the mother is in labor, an old woman stands around and says as many different eligible names as she can think of. The child comes out of the womb when its own name is called. Thus the naming and the giving birth to the new thing are inextricably bound together.

The environment encourages the Eskimo to think in this fashion. To Western minds, the "monotony" of snow, ice and darkness can often be depressing, even frightening. Nothing in particular stands out; there is no scenery in the sense in which we use the term. But the Eskimo do not see it this way. They are not interested in scenery, but in action, existence. This is true to some extent of many people, but is almost of necessity true for the Eskimo, for nothing in their world easily defines itself and is separable from the general background. What exists, the Eskimo themselves must struggle to bring into existence. Theirs is a world which has to be conquered with each act and statement, each carving and song—but which, with each act accomplished, is as quickly lost. The secret of conquering a world greater than himself is not known to the Eskimo. But his role is not passive. Man is the force that reveals form. He is the force which ultimately cancels nothingness.

Language is the principal tool with which Eskimo make the natural world a human world. They use many "words" for snow which permit fine distinctions, not simply because they are much concerned with snow, but because snow takes its form from the actions in which it participates: sledding, falling, igloo-building, blowing. These distinctions are possible only when experienced in a meaningful context. Different kinds of snow are brought into existence by the Eskimo as they experience their environment and speak; the words do not label something already there. Words, for the Eskimo, are like the knife of the carver: they free the idea, the thing, from the general formlessness of the outside. As a man speaks, not only is his language *in statu nascendi,* but also the very thing about which he is talking. The carver, like the poet, releases form from the bonds of formlessness: he brings it forth into consciousness. He must reveal form in order to protest against a universe that is formless, and the form he reveals should be beautiful.

Since that form participates in a real situation, the carving is generally utilitarian. One very characteristic Eskimo expression means "What is that for?" It is most frequently used by an Eskimo when he finds some object and stands looking down at it. It does not mean "What can I use that for?" but rather something closer to "What is it intended to be used for?" That portion of the antler, whose shape so perfectly fits the hand and gives a natural strength as well, becomes, with slight modification, a chisel handle. Form and function, revealed together, are inseparable. Add a few lines of dots or tiny rings or just incisions, rhythmically arranged to bring out the form, and it's finished.

Here, then, is a world of chaos and chance, a meaningless whirl of cold and white; man alone can give meaning to this—its form does not come ready-made.

When spring comes and igloos melt, the old habitation sites are littered with waste, including beautifully-designed tools and tiny ivory carvings, not deliberately thrown away, but, with even greater indifference, just lost. Eskimo are interested in the artistic act, not in the product of that activity. A carving, like a song, is not a thing; it is an action. When you feel a song within you, you sing it; when you sense a form emerging from ivory, you release it. It's senseless to assume that when we collect these silent, static carvings, we have collected Eskimo art, even if we record date and provenience. Measurements of size, diagrams of diffusion, and seriation studies of chronology do nothing to correct the initial error here. However, the approach I have recommended is generally called "mystical" or "subjective" or "insight without method," while this latter method is called "objective" or "scientific." That competent fieldwork should be called "mystical" and incompetent fieldwork called "scientific" is one of the more remarkable features of our profession.

"It's the power of belief," writes Rainey (1959:13), "which makes all the difference between original native art and contemporary native souvenirs." This difference becomes most apparent when we study the artistic act, rather than just the artistic object. Haselberger refers to Schaeffer-Simmern's *Eskimo plastik aus Kanada* (1958) but fails to note that the souvenir art which this volume describes is strictly post-1948, Western-designed, Western-valued, and some of it Hong Kong-made. There's a difference between the carver who would stop carving tomorrow if the market failed, and the carver for whom art is a necessary part of being human.

I think it's important that we systematically collect and document souvenir art, but I have no time for the Winnie the Pooh nonsense which is written about most of it. A Canadian official recently stated that "contemporary Eskimo prints are related to the Paleolithic art of Altamira and Lascaux" and from another authority we are advised that contemporary Alaskan carvers "still use the basic principles . . . of the ancient master engravers who produced the 'Okvik Madonna'."

A serious study of Canadian Eskimo souvenir art would tell us much about the modern Eskimo. It would note that art is now a thing, an object, no longer an act, a ritual; that most pieces are now characterized by a base, a favored point of view, three-dimensional perspective, etc., all of which reflect growing individualism, an aggressive self-concept that seeks to possess and control the external world, in contrast to the traditional, aboriginal techniques of multiple perspective, visual puns, three-dimensional X-ray or openwork sculpture, etc., which reflect a less assertive, less individualistic self-concept. A serious study would also include details of the Department of Northern Affairs and National Resources' strong opposition to any study of, and publicity on, aboriginal Eskimo art—an opposition that does not stem from any fear that such studies would diminish souvenir sales, but lies in the fact that the stone carvings are taken by many as evidence of government respect for, and encouragement of, aboriginal Eskimo culture. This might lead to the question: How closely does this propaganda coincide with reality? This in turn will immediately open unexpected apertures, vistas, break-throughs—especially in the field of finance, or the fact that Canadian anthropologists-apologists involved in this situation are as contented as Coolidge in the Harding cabinet—but you're laughing, aren't you? You're laughing at the notion of art as something more than a kewpie nude with a clock in her belly on the television set.

Often we can better understand an art form when we see what happens to it in translation, when, say, in the interplay of cultures, an old art is expressed in a new medium. Thus photographs of minute Dorset carvings reveal that all share a quality of sizelessness: each can be blown up to monumental size with no qualitative change of effect, for the artists reduced each form to its basic essentials.

The tension and beauty which a raindrop possesses just before it falls, and loses when it does fall, was captured by the artists of the steppes who drew, separately or closely locked in combat, "armored" animals: poised, each with suggestions of power about to burst forth, but not yet in operation. Recently, Soviet film-makers employed this art in an animated fairy tale. Still scenes were superb, but when the figures moved, the art was destroyed. Sketches made by Eskimo on two-dimensional surfaces, however, can be animated without violation. This difference in adaptation offers a clue to a major difference between Okvik-Ipiutak art and that of the Eskimo.

I do not think it accidental that it is in Paul Klee's work that we see the closest parallels with Eskimo art, for in both there is a structuring of space by sound. Klee was the son of a music teacher and himself so good a musician he had difficulty deciding whether to devote his life to music or painting. He said his works owed more to Bach and Mozart than to any of the masters of art. He wanted art "to *sound* like a fairy tale," to be a world in which "things fall upward." He was bewitched by the dreamlike universe underwater, the aquarium in which fish and flora moved like phantoms through lyrical light.

We often have difficulty in understanding a purely verbal notion. In *Alice in Wonderland* ". . . the patriotic archbishop of Canterbury found it advisable—."

"Found *what?*" said the Duck.

"Found *it,*" the Mouse replied rather crossly: "of course you know what 'it' means."

"I know what 'it' means well enough when *I* find a thing," said the Duck: "it's generally a frog, or a worm. The question is, what did the archbishop find?"

We feel happier when *it* is visible; then we feel we can understand it, judge it, perhaps control it. In our workaday world, space is conceived in terms of that which separates visible objects. "Empty space" suggests a field in which there is nothing *to see*. We call a fume-filled gasoline drum or a gale-swept tundra "empty" because nothing is visible in either case.

The Eskimo do not think this way. One hunter I knew, when assured by a White man that a gasoline drum was "empty," struck a match and peered inside: he bore the scars for life.

With them the binding power of the oral tradition is so strong as to make the eye subservient to the ear. They define space more by sound than sight. Where we might say, "Let's see what we can hear," they would say, "Let's hear what we can see."

In the beginning was the Word, a spoken word, not the visual one of literate man, but a word which, when spoken, revealed form: "And God said, Let there be light: and there was light." The Eskimo speaker imposes his will diffidently upon unbounded reality. Form is temporary, transient; it exists, as the Eskimo poet says, ". . . on the threshold of my tongue." Nothing has a definite, invariable shape.

In our society, however, to be real a thing must be visible, and preferably constant. We trust the eye, not the ear. Not since Aristotle assured his *readers* that the sense of sight was "above all others" the one to be trusted, have we accorded to sound the role of dominant sense. "Seeing is believing." "Believe half of what you see, nothing of what you hear." "The eyes of the Lord preserve knowledge, and he over-throweth the words of the transgressor" (Proverbs 22:12). Truth, we think, must be observed by the eye, then judged by the "I". Mysticism, intuition, are bad words among scientists. Most of our thinking is done in terms of *visual* models, even when an auditory one might prove more efficient. We employ spatial metaphor even for such inner psychological states as tendency, duration, intensity. We say "thereafter," not the more logical "thenafter"; "always" means "at all times"; "before" means etymologically "in front of"; we even speak of a "space" or an "interval" of time.

To the Eskimo, truth is given through oral tradition, mysticism, intuition, all cognition; not simply by observation and measurement of physical phenomena. To them, the ocularly visible apparition is not nearly as important as the purely auditory one.

The essential feature of sound is not its location, but that it *be,* that it fill space. We say "the night shall be filled with music," just as the air is filled with fragrance; locality is irrelevant. The concert-goer closes his eyes.

Auditory space has no favored focus. It is a sphere without fixed boundaries, space made by the thing itself, not space containing the thing. It is not pictorial space, boxed-in, but dynamic, always in flux, creating its own dimensions moment by moment. It has no fixed boundaries; it is indifferent to background. The eye focuses, pinpoints, abstracts, locating each object in physical space, against a background; the ear, however, favors sound from any direction.

I know of no example of an Eskimo describing space primarily in visual terms. They do not regard space as static, and therefore measurable: hence they have no formal units of spatial measurement, just as they have no uniform divisions of time. The carver is indifferent to the demands of the optical eye: he lets each piece fill its own space, create its own world, without reference to background or anything external to it. Each carving lives in spatial independence. Size and shape, proportions and selection, these are set by the object itself, not forced from without. Like sound, each carving creates its own space, its own identity; it imposes its own assumptions.

Superb examples of this are the great Alaskan Eskimo mobile-like masks in the Heye Research Center. Such masks were not the result of lack of large pieces of wood, but a deliberate effort to let the mask assert its own dimensions. This is in contrast to Northwest Coast Indian carvers who worked within enclosed space.

Other features of Eskimo art, alien and puzzling to us, become comprehensible if we recognize that the ear to them is the primary sense; it imposes its bias over all other senses. Take an obvious example: lack of verticality. The value we place on verticality (it even influences our perception) stems from the strength of literacy in our lives. Children must be taught it. Natives do not know it. And when the mentally ill in our society withdraw from the burdens of literate values, and return to non-vertical, non-lineal codifications, we call them child-like, and even note parallels with primitives. To lack of verticality can be added multiple perspective, visual puns, X-ray sculpture, absence of background, and correspondence between symbol and size: all examples of non-visual structuring of space.

Models in the social sciences come, without exception, from the world of literacy. That Joyce, Pound, and Klee offered models, based on the electronic media and sharing much with oral culture, that are applicable to pre-literate data and relevant to a contemporary audience, has escaped anthropologists. The natural sciences, however, and even certain of the humanities, decades ago turned to post-literate models and found them fruitful.

The only persistent archetypes may prove to be those formed by the interplay of the senses themselves, as in the case outlined

The Eskimo Artist

above. The interplay of cultures does not produce persistent archetypes. The electronic media, regarded as extensions of our senses, can, in their interplay, have archetypal results. As cultural forms they can provide interplay with other whole-cultures. Most studies of archetypes are limited to the archetypes arising from the interplay of the private senses, and thus break down completely when confronted with the interplay of cultures.

ARTIST AND CRITIC
IN AN AFRICAN SOCIETY

Paul Bohannan

CROCE, in what is undoubtedly his most widely read statement, in the *Encyclopedia Britannica,* insisted that it was neither enough to use art objects to explain the ethos of an age, nor yet enough to subject the objects to "aesthetic" judgment without reference to the ethos of the age in which they were produced. Rather, art is of a piece with the rest of an epoch, and in order to understand the aesthetics behind the art, we must understand the attitude toward art, as one of many attitudes which make up the ethos of the epoch.

Translated into terms of a student of primitive art, Croce's dictum would read something like this: it is not enough to use art objects to explain an exotic culture, nor yet to subject the objects to aesthetic judgment without a knowledge of that culture. Rather, we must understand the attitude toward art which is a part of the culture in question.

It has been repeatedly stressed that in order to reach this desired end, we must discover the background, social position, training, motivation, and aesthetic principles of the artist. Only a few anthropologists have in fact investigated these difficult matters in the field, and rather fewer have published their findings, but

---

Reprinted from *The Artist in Tribal Society,* Proceedings of a Symposium held at the Royal Anthropological Institute, Marian W. Smith (editor), London: Routledge and Kegan Paul, 1961, pp. 85–94. With the permission of the author, the Royal Anthropological Institute of Great Britain and Ireland, Routledge and Kegan Paul, and the Free Press of Glencoe, New York.

the precept is put to us insistently. It is, perhaps, the oldest precept now before students of primitive art.

Therefore, heeding Professor Whitehead's advice that we are likely to make most progress if we question the assumption longest unquestioned, it might be well to take a new look at what we mean by "studying the artist" in primitive societies. Will "studying the artist" really provide the information we need in order to evaluate primitive art?

Ask the same question about contemporary art: can "studying the artist" in contemporary society explain contemporary art? By itself it undoubtedly cannot. It elicits the artist's motivation, it elucidates his personal aesthetics, and it clarifies technical problems. It may even help to solve some of the many difficult Western problems about "creativity." But it cannot explain the reason that some art is accepted and other is not, nor why some is considered better than others.

It would seem—and again the point is Croce's—that there is a dimension in art evaluation which goes far beyond the artist. It is the dimension which is added by what we today would call contemporary criticism. Surely, we need both the study of the contemporary artist and the study of the contemporary criticism to arrive at aesthetic principles. We might, for our purposes, even define aesthetics as the relationship between criticism and art objects, for the relationship between artist and the objects is the problem of "creativity." (Obviously, some and perhaps the most telling art critics are artists themselves. For analytical purposes, however, we can divide these functions.)

The question is, then, are we interested in comparative creativity? If, as Westerners, we probably are, we must go to the creators of art for our information. But where do we get our information on comparative aesthetics? Aesthetics means the study of the relationships between art and all that bundle of attitudes and activities which we in the modern world call criticism. Comparative aesthetics would surely establish means of classification of such relationships and, on a practical level, means by which one set of relationship ideas can be made to supplement and differentiate any of the others.

In so far as we are interested in studying the aesthetics of primitive art, then, we need several sorts of things and information: (1) the art objects, (2) a wide knowledge of the general ethnography of the people who made the objects, (3) a rather specific knowledge of the criticism of the objects by members of the society which used them, and (4) a general knowledge of comparative aesthetics. Now all of these different things, ideas, and disciplines are available to the student—except the third. While it is true that we know very little about artists in primitive societies, it is safe to say that we know very much less about criticism in primitive societies.

These problems did not occur to me while I was in the field. I was following the "oldest precept." Therefore, while I was studying the Tiv of central Nigeria, I kept chasing artists. Tiv produce no really great art in the sense that the Yoruba and some Cameroons peoples do produce great art. But art of one sort or another enters into many phases of their lives, and some of it pleases Europeans, a little of it is even compelling.

Tiv artists are not as easy to find as they were fifteen or twenty years before I worked among them. Mr. K. C. Murray of the Nigerian Museum in Lagos has much more information on them, gathered in the 1930's, than I was able to get in the late 1940's and early 1950's. I never found a first-rate wood carver who was willing to be watched at work, though I have watched three mediocre ones at work. Nor have I ever seen Tiv brass casting, although I know several men who worked at it sporadically.

Nevertheless, I saw quite a bit of Tiv art. Even so, I originally thought that I had nothing to say about it because I had not seen and made minute notes on the processes. Then, as I went through my notes for other purposes, I began to find an occasional reference to art—not to artists, but to the art objects themselves. As I found more, I began to realize two points: that these comments formed the core of a critical system which might (with systematic field investigation) be turned into a fairly complete Tiv aesthetic, and that Tiv are interested in the art—not in the artist.

The viewpoint of Westerners, interested primarily in creativity, is completely different from that of the Tiv in this respect. Tiv, indeed, use the word "create" (*gba*) for working in wood—its only other use is for God's creation of the World.[1] But the primary field of Tiv interest is not on the verbal notion of *gba* or creation, but rather on the objects which are the result of it. Tiv are more interested in the ideas conveyed by a piece of art than they are in its manufacture, just as in their religion they are far more interested in the Creation than in the Creator.

This capacity on the part of Tiv to come to grips with a piece of art as it is in itself rather than as tangible result of creation, gives their critical ideas a forthrightness which we might well envy: it resembles that "firm and sure judgment in artistic matters . . . never raised to the level and consistency of a theory" which Croce ascribes to the ancients before they were bothered by the Christian notion of soul.

My most vivid encounter with such art criticism among the Tiv came when I was watching an artist—not a very good one—carve a wooden figure of a woman. The carving, which I had commissioned from him, was about eighteen inches high and, like all African sculpture, was worked from a chunk of log while it was still green. As he worked, and I sat by silently watching, a youngster from his compound appeared.

The youngster said, by way of greeting, the equivalent of "Grandfather, you are carving [creating—*gba*] a woman."

The old man replied that such was indeed the case.

"What are those three bumps on her belly?" the youngster asked.

The old man laid down his adze and eyed the youngster who had interrupted him. "The middle one," he said impatiently, "is her navel."

---

[1] There is a homonym, *gba*—iń so far as one can distinguish homonyms in an unwritten language—which means "to fall" and "to suffer (an act)," but the two sets of ideas are said to be utterly unrelated.

The boy was silent for a moment but spoke again just as the old man reached for his adze, "Then what are the other two bumps?"

The old man barely concealed his contempt for questions about so obvious a point. "Those are her breasts."

"Way down there?" the youngster asked.

"They've fallen!" the artist fairly shouted.

"But, grandfather, even if they had fallen, they would not . . ."

The old man grabbed up his adze. "All right, all right," he muttered, and with three perfectly aimed blows the three bumps came off.

I noted, when I wrote up this incident, that the youngster, who had been three years in school, had acquired an aesthetic of naturalism, and that the elder had not. I was annoyed that my carving was no longer "purely" Tiv and failed to consider the incident as an interaction of artist and critic.

When the artist had finished his work, and I had paid him for it, his only comment was, "It did not turn out too badly" (*iduwe vihi yum ga*). I recorded this comment at the time only because I did not really agree with it.

This incident should have told me that Tiv, in many instances at least, care who creates a given object as little as they care about the creative process. Art is, among them, an epiphenomenon to play, religion, prestige and most other aspects of life. Indeed, much of it is a sort of "community" art, a true folk art in which the artist is as unimportant as the composer of folk music.

It was several months later, in another part of Tivland altogether, that I became fully aware of this communal aspect of Tiv art, and that I again noted the phrase, "It didn't turn out too badly." This new area was swampy, and I cut myself a stick to help me traverse the slick swamps without falling. After a week or so, a young man from a nearby compound told me that I must not use that stick any longer: it was an old woman's stick and did not become a man of my position. When I asked what sort of stick I should have, he replied that he would make me one which was suitable. A few days later, he returned with a staff which he called a "stick of a young elder." It was about six feet long; on it were several bands blacked with soot which he had set with the sap of the *ikpine* tree. Into the black, he had carved several series of designs.

The stick was very handsome, and before long almost every male in the countryside was making himself a stick of this sort. I copied several of the designs and watched a number of them being made. The most astounding feature, to me, was that comparatively few of the designs were made by a single individual. As I sat watching a young man of about thirty carve a stick one day, he was called away. He laid aside his stick and the double-edged knives with which he was cutting the design. A guest came in a few moments later, picked up the stick, and added a few designs. A little later, he handed it on to someone else. Four men put designs on that stick before the owner returned and finished it. When he had done so, he held it out for me to copy and said, "It turned out pretty well, didn't it?" Fig. 1 (*b, c*) shows two of these "communal" designs on walking sticks.

This "communal" aspect of all work, whether artistic or utilitarian, showed up again when I bought a couple of adzes, got some wood, and tried to make sculpture of my own. Since I have no talent whatever for sculpture, I was very soon disgusted and turned to making stools and chairs instead. But I was not allowed to do it myself. The moment I rested, some bystander would take up the adze and get the work a little farther forward. I, in Western tradition, had a feeling of complete frustration because my "creativity" and my ability were being challenged. For a few days I tried to insist that I wanted to do the work myself, but soon had to give it up because everyone thought it silly and because no one could remember my foible. Eventually several of our chairs and stools "didn't turn out too badly." I had a hand in all of them, but they are not my handiwork—the whole compound and half the countryside had worked on them.

Most Tiv men are competent at turning out these chairs, stools, walking sticks, and the like. They appreciate a "good one" but they take comparatively little pains to plan them so that they will be good. There are, however, a few men who work alone and insist on doing all the work; they are regarded as specialists. I knew one man who made chairs from *gbaiye* wood, when he could get it. He refused to let anyone else touch a piece he was working on. He charged about ten shillings each for making a larger Tiv chair; the price was very much higher than usual, but the chairs always "came out well," as was recognized throughout the countryside.

Weaving, like stick carving, is very often a communal activity. However, preparing the cloth for resist-dyeing is not. Tiv today sew patterns into the cloth with raffia rather than tie them as they did when Mr. Murray made his observations (Murray 1949). Although some men sew their designs in a pre-planned fashion, many others do not. The first time I saw a man sewing raffia almost at random on to a cloth he was preparing for resist-dyeing, paying attention to a political discussion rather than to any pattern and obviously having no plan, I was upset. I finally interrupted the business at hand to ask him why he did not pay attention to what he was doing. He told me, and though I understood his words I did not grasp their full meaning until later, that one does not look at a pattern until it is finished: then one looks to see if it has come out well. If this one does not come out well, he said, "I will sell it to the Ibo; if it does, I shall keep it. And if it comes out extraordinarily well, I shall give it to my mother-in-law."

Figure carvings are almost always made by an individual artist. In their religious rituals, Tiv need a certain number of stakes to represent females and another sort to represent males. The only requirement is that the stake be of a particular shape (pointed for the female principle, rounded for the male), and that they have representational eyes and mouth (see photograph facing p. 192, East 1939). Some people, even today, however, pay comparatively large sums (up to ten shillings) to artists to make figure carvings to be used as such representational stakes. The figurine, of course, is ritually no more effective than a stick with three holes gouged in it, but figurines bring prestige to the owner and, even more importantly, they "please the eye."

In the criticism of these pieces, two points are stressed: first, that the owner was thoughtful enough to want to please himself and everyone else, and second that it makes a "better" stake (*ihambe*). I have little doubt that had I asked questions and primed conversations, I could have gathered (from some people at least) lists of traits and characteristics which were approved and reasons why they were approved. Unfortunately, I did not do so. With my own cultural biases, I thought this was the sort of question one asked artists.

My most revealing experience in the matter of art criticism among the Tiv passed, like some of the others, in misunderstanding and a minor annoyance. A man named Akise, who was of my true age-set (not one of the men some fifteen years older with whom I was associated, by Tiv themselves, on a prestige basis), told me that his kinsman from central Tivland was coming to see him and to sell decorated calabashes in the local market. I said I would like to meet the kinsman and watch him work. Akise told me to come up to his compound the evening before market.

The artist kinsman was friendly, but not very communicative about his work. He showed me his tools and his wares. He reconvinced me of something I knew already: Tiv designs have no mystic or religious symbolism, and are at most only a stylization of natural elements like lizards, swallows, and drinking gourds. When asked when he worked, he said, "When my heart tells me"—a standard Tiv answer for anything they do which they have not particularly thought about. When I asked him what his favorite design was, he said that he usually liked the one he was working on, so he liked them all. When I asked him why he carved calabashes instead of carving wooden figures, he replied that he did not have any talent or training for carving wood (literally, he did not "know the root" of it), and in any case wooden carvings were sometimes used by the *mbatsav,* or witches, and carved calabashes were only used as gifts to girl friends. This man, I decided, had no aesthetics.

At the time, I was a little put off by Akise, who insisted on breaking into the conversation. During my questioning of his kinsman, he carried on a long harangue about which of the calabashes he liked best, and which one least, and placed the two dozen or so in a row, in order of merit. I asked the artist if he agreed in Akise's judgment. He said he probably did, but he liked them all well enough. I noted (without realizing its full implications) that Akise considered himself a considerable art critic, and I finally turned to copy some of the designs and some of the reasons why he liked them. We were unfortunately interrupted when I had completed only one copy, and we never returned to the subject.

I have reproduced my copy of the design on the calabash (Fig. 1, *a*). The decorated surface was divided into quarters, and I have shown the numbers indicating Akise's preference. That marked No. 1, he said, was best because the black spots (made by burning with the flat of a hot knife) were in the right place. That marked No. 4 was least good because there were too many black places and they did not balance. The artist agreed but said that if you removed any of the black on No. 4, it would be worse. The lid, as a whole, was considered better than the calabash itself, because the balance of black was better and because the two sides were alike.

Either in my notes or in my memory, I have other references to people who have expressed choices and criticism, giving reasons: I have on several occasions heard winnowing trays praised for a tasteful pattern in the weaving or because they were absolutely round. I have also, on one occasion, heard a man say of a winnowing tray (which I also admired) that it was attractive because it had a very fine bulge on one side. I have heard people praise Tiv chairs because of their symmetry, but also because interesting shapes in the wood were retained.

Tentatively, from what I remember, it seems to me that Tiv admire symmetry, but also admire what they consider tasteful assymmetry. They admire pieces of sculpture which make an idea more intense. Further than this I would not want to go until I have returned to Tivland to discuss the matter.

However, I did learn this: I was wrong in my field work because, Western fashion, I paid too much attention to artists, and when the artists disappointed me I came away with nothing. When I return, I shall search out the critics. And in Tivland, almost every man is a critic. Because there are no specialists in taste and only a few in the manufacture of art, every man is free to know what he likes and to make it if he can. It seems to me that as many Tiv are aware of why they like something as are aware of the implications of any other aspects of their culture. In all spheres, this is a faculty which varies greatly from person to person. There are as many reasoned art critics in Tiv society as there are reasoned theologians or political theorists, from whom we study Tiv ideas about their religion and politics.

Problems of creation in primitive societies are interesting, but they may be overshadowed, from the standpoint of their significance in the societies concerned, by the problems of criticism. We can arrive at an aesthetic for a people by studying the relation of criticism among them to the art objects somewhat more successfully than by studying the relation of creation to the art objects.

THE CULTURAL CONTEXT
OF CREATIVITY AMONG TIWI[1]

Jane C. Goodale and Joan D. Koss

RECENT DISCUSSIONS of art in anthropology have emphasized the need to study the processes of art in tribal societies to complement available studies of art objects. In a pioneering paper d'Azevedo correctly notes that in the anthropological literature "the processes of art are obscured by an emphasis upon its formal products and their value as a source of information about other things" (d'Azevedo 1958:703). This emphasis has emerged from the joining of two views which have influenced anthropological studies of art: One, a "collector's approach" which has focused on "primitive" art products as objective evidence for cultural difference or pan-human similarity; and two, a seemingly widespread agreement among contemporary western artists, critics and audiences that the goal of art is an object able to perpetually elicit an esthetic response when assisted by special rituals (e.g.,

---

Reprinted from Proceedings of the 1966 Annual Spring Meeting of the American Ethnological Society, *Essays on the Verbal and Visual Arts,* Philadelphia, 1966, pp. 175–91; distributed by the University of Washington Press, 1967. With the permission of the authors, the American Ethnological Society, and the University of Washington Press.

[1] Fieldwork on the Tiwi was undertaken in 1954. Goodale, a member of the National Geographic Expedition led by C. P. Mountford, obtained additional support from the University of Pennsylvania Museum. This paper is the result of a suggestion by Koss to explore Tiwi creativity in retrospect.

We wish to acknowledge our appreciation to Dr. Nancy Munn for reading and commenting on a first draft of this paper. She is not responsible, of course, for our final treatment of this subject or our conclusions.

art shows) designed to enhance the visual effect. The central place that art as "product" or "object" occupies in our thinking about tribal art and our neglect of artistic process have led to some rather unproductive treatises on the definition of art, the nature of the "art object" as distinct from the non-art object, the locus of art and so on. Part of the usefulness of a processual approach to art lies in our being able to focus on separate dimensions for study and thereby widen our understanding of art as a distinctive type of social activity.[2]

A beginning may be achieved by attending to the cultural microcosm of particular art forms and noting what *are* the relations that characterize artistic activity. Then one might profitably study other dimensions of art such as the mode and content of the communication between the artist and his audience, and the uses and functions of the completed product within a system of social relations.[3] In this paper we attempt to view one art form as the result of a particular kind of artistic act and have proceeded from the basic assumption that this act depends upon certain psychological characteristics of creative processes.

---

[2] We suggest in passing that a processual approach might shed some light on some frequently noted but rarely explained aspects of "primitive" art forms. A partial list would include: (1) those forms in which the transmission of effect depends on tactile as well as visual qualities of the object (examples are Eskimo carvings as discussed by Carpenter [1961] and New Guinea sculpture—korvar figures—as discussed by Wingert [1962]; (2) those forms in which the transmission of effect depends on special placement of the art object as when it is presented in motion (examples are Ifo masks and Bambara headdresses); (3) those art forms that assume important functions in rituals and are designed for a brief viewing and an initial dramatic impact, e.g., New Ireland malaggan (Lewis 1961); and (4) when much or most of the intent of the artist is conveyed while he is at work; therefore the effect may depend on a sequence of renderings (some examples are Arnhem Land bark paintings, ground and body painting in Central Australia [Strehlow 1964] and Navaho dry painting).

[3] In addition to d'Azevedo, Munn (1962), Carpenter (1961), Mead (1959), and Bohannan (1961) present discussions that follow from a concern with the processes of graphic and plastic art.

THE CREATIVE PROCESS AND THE ARTISTIC ACT

We are immediately forced to identify a creative enterprise in order to single out a particular class of acts for discussion. It is necessary to refer to the expressed views of individuals within a society since only they can point to activities that yield a product with qualities of interest and surprise, i.e., an idea, event or object that affords some individuals a means of going beyond common ways of experiencing the world (Bruner 1963). Therefore, any set of activities—involving one or more individuals—that has as its primary goal the construction of some things considered to be different in form and meaning from all other things—objects or events that are novel in structure and yet exhibit significant new connections with current, important and interesting ideas—can be said to result from and/or incorporate creative thinking.[4] Art forms depend, primarily, on a particular kind of connectedness that is metaphoric involving two or more widely separated domains of experience brought into relation with one another. Other creative products may also exhibit this unsystematic type of connectedness with ideas but not to the extent that they evoke an affective response which art forms achieve, perhaps, by insisting upon a circuitous path of psychic imagery in order to make the necessary connections.

Obviously, the artistic act is only one type of event that displays certain critical features common to creative processes. Following the extensive yet largely explorative discussions of creativity

---

[4] In thinking about the essential features of those phenomena we call "innovations," "inventions," and "creations," we have arrived at a tentative formulation of the kinds of differences these terms may denote for heuristic purposes. Using Linton's aspects of form, meaning, use and function it can be said that "innovations" may exhibit aspects of novelty in all of these features; "inventions" may exhibit aspects of novelty in their form, use or function; and "creations" exhibit features perceived as novel only in form and meaning. Following Barnett's definitions (Cf. Barnett 1953:7) which equate "innovation" with novelty, "creation" and "invention" can be thought of as special cases of innovation.

we will point to social and psychological modalities of the artistic creative process that receive repeated emphasis in the literature. In order to discuss the creative process in one cultural setting—that of the Tiwi of Melville Island—we have made the following assumptions: (1) The key aspects of the processes of creating graphic and plastic art forms are basically similar wherever artists work. (2) Each cultural milieu provides a particular set of contexts within which the artistic act takes place. (3) These contexts are structured in ways to facilitate the production of traditional art forms. The contexts may be viewed through a number of interrelated dimensions (e.g., the social settings for artistic activity; the verbalized motivations of the artist and his audience; the particular choice of materials, tools and subject matter; the symbolic media which are incorporated in the art form and the ideological background of creative activity). We suggest that whatever the content of these contexts certain general conditions of creativity must be fulfilled. Our discussion of these conditions draws upon Bruner (1963), Henle (1963) and Rogers (1959).

CONDITIONS OF CREATIVITY

We suggest six sets of conditions that affect creativity, conditions generally recognized as paradoxical in nature by writers on the subject.

1. As an initial condition the creator must divorce himself from the mundane and the usual and maintain a deep commitment to his chosen work. Although the artist's state of immersion deepens as the work develops and his attention is concentrated on the task at hand, there must also develop a desire and need for partial detachment from the product of creation so that a critical attitude is part of the ongoing experience.

2. There is paradox in the second set of conditions, those involving "passion and decorum" (Bruner 1963:12–13). The artist must allow his impulses free range of expression through his work; interest growing as he proceeds. But these impulses must take on formal qualities and arrangements that are congenial to

preconceived images carried by both artist and audience. Symbolic currency must be subtly manipulated and care and attention lavished on techniques, tools and materials, as these are crucial to accomplishing the formal outcome.

3. When he begins his work the artist appears to guide its development in a thoroughly conscious way manipulating and planning its components to conform to a predetermined image or idea. However, at some point in the work scheme the form and arrangement of the work seem to develop their own requirements; the work appears to "take over" the role of formulating subsequent additions and substitutions and thereby determines its own direction toward completion. It follows from this condition that the artist must be relatively free to judge, critically, his effort at creating—at least during the initial stages of production prior to and during the "take-over" phenomenon. There is some indication, however, that after the work of art assumes a quasi-independent existence, evaluation by both artist and critic is of much less importance to the final stages of creation.

4. The creative act seems to demand an immediacy of fulfillment, lest, it would seem, the initial impetus be dissipated before the expression is cast in external form. However, a period of quietude—frequently referred to in the literature as a "period of incubation"—appears to be necessary to the creative act so that too-early completion can be avoided and first statements matched to the original image. This slowdown of artistic activity is important if we consider the artist's ability (or perhaps need) to play with elements of design, color and composition. This play may produce almost bizarre effects—at least initially—and these must be corrected in order to actualize or improve upon the original image. The incubation period may well be the period of selective correction leading to the retention or accentuation of new and surprisingly pleasant effects and the cancellation of the bizarre and unacceptable.

5. Bruner (1963:16–17) lists as one of the conditions of creativity the externalization of a rich internal cast of characters, idealized figures that are representations of the identifications of

the artist and mythological and fantasied figures with whom there is special identification. The expression of these figures (or aspects of them in opposition or combination) provides grist for the artist's mill and a main source of inspiration. But it is also true that the expression of the "internal cast" would seem to have as its condition a climate of approval of the artist's endeavors—prior to the beginning of a particular work. Before the internal cast is exposed to criticism there must be some tacit acceptance of the artist as artist. This climate of approval should include the attitude that the artist is at least partially free to receive and juggle those ideas he finds most congenial to his work at any given time.

6. We might also include as a condition of creativity, a period of contemplation and inspiration prior to the enactment of the artistic act. Although this condition is most difficult to pin down, it is possible to consider certain activities prescribed as procedural "oughts" by a particular culture such as a method for choosing materials or discussion with patrons. But a consideration of these activities can only account for the complicated well-springs of inspiration in a limited way; obviously an explication of inspiration requires a study of the modes of expression of the individual artist and their relation to his conceptual system.

THE TIWI BURIAL POLES[5]

We have singled out for discussion one Tiwi art form, the burial poles, and have asked two related questions of these data on their construction: Are there indications that these conditions of creativity are relevant to the Tiwi artistic act? And what distinctive contexts of the Tiwi milieu would seem to foster these conditions? Before these questions are considered we will briefly describe the process of making the poles and consider the values that are accomplished through their creation.

---

[5] For additional discussion and illustrations of Tiwi burial poles and ceremonies see Mountford (1958, 1961), Spencer (1914) and Goodale (1959a, 1959b).

1. When a Tiwi dies he is buried the same day in an area close by the graves of previously deceased kin.

Subsequent to the burial grave area (one mile in radius) is tabu to all members of the deceased's matrilineal and patrilineal kin groups. The ghost is given exclusive hunting rights to this area.

A date for the final *pukamani* rituals is set approximately two to four months hence.

2. One to two weeks before the set date pole cutters are ritually commissioned by members of the patrilineal kinsmen of the deceased. The white-painted ax symbolizes the work to be done.

Pole cutters must be members of the local group who are owners of the land in which the deceased died, for they alone have the rights to the natural resources of the area, including the trees from which the poles will be made. In addition the workers must be selected from those members of the local group who are neither matrilineally nor patrilineally related to the deceased, for the grave area is still tabued to those so related to the ghost.

The workers are therefore selected primarily on the basis of kinship and residence and only secondarily on the basis of past performance or skill; some who have never carved a pole before may be selected.

The workers are commissioned as a group and at the time of the commissioning they are given general directions as to how many poles should be cut and how big they should be, directions which indicate the employers' wishes and abilities to pay for the work done.

3. Although the workers are commissioned as a group and work together to prepare the required poles, each worker is completely responsible for his own pole. He selects his own tree and carves it using only the ax to shape the desired form.

With the necessary help of others he cooks it—a process which dries the surface and at the same time produces the desired black undercoating upon which the designs in natural ochres are painted.

4. The poles are then set upright in the first formation—a

straight line some short distance from the actual grave. Those that can be easily painted in this position are left.

5. Those too large to paint upright are removed and placed in a more convenient position for the addition of the painted design.

6. In the painting, as in the carving, the individual is completely responsible for his own creation, however the artists are within sight of each other and may frequently discuss their work with others.

7. When all the poles are completed, the workers clear the area around the poles for the coming dances.

8. Although the worker's efforts have been under critical view of fellow workers during their production, the important criticism—that of their employers—comes when the final ceremony begins and the employers approach the grave for the first time since the burial.

For the next twelve to fourteen hours the collection of poles displayed in a linear arrangement are the center of intensive dancing during which they are viewed collectively and individually as the dancers circle around and through the formation. (See Plate 9.)

9. At times the poles are used as props in the telling of a particular story in dance form.

Finally as the ceremony draws to a close the employers judge each pole individually and lay out their payment (in goods) according to their evaluation.

10. As each artist accepts his payment he dances his acceptance. His pole is carried to the grave and set up in formation encircling the mound. The arrangement at the grave is determined by the workers, not the employers.

11. The visual effect of this second arrangement is one where the individual pole is subordinated to its relation in a group, a variable effect as the viewers circle the entire group while performing the final dances.

The grave is then abandoned, the tabu lifted, and the poles left to the elements. No subsequent care or interest in the grave and its poles is taken except that they serve as markers of ownership of the land by the descendants of those buried here.

TIWI VALUES

An art object is not simply a means to a particular end but represents the incorporation of a number of values, sought or achieved during the process of creation as well as after it (Munro 1963: 376–77). Descriptions of art objects frequently fail to consider the ways in which initial values associated with or achieved in the construction process influence terminal values associated with the finished product.

The values related to the Tiwi creation of burial poles fall under three broad types: those instrumental to ceremonies meant to appease the ghost of a deceased individual; those related to Tiwi ideology and standards of prestige; and those which relate to Tiwi esthetics.

A Tiwi ghost is a lonely being; he has been suddenly separated from those kinsmen with whom he has been most recently associated—those still-living. He has yet to learn to live with those kinsmen who were once-living, his kinsmen in the parallel world of the dead. While his living kinsmen are performing the *pukamani* rituals at his grave side, he and his once-living kinsmen are similarly performing the rituals at the same time and place. The poles, their number and size at once symbolize the social importance of the deceased both to the living and to the once-living and thus facilitate the transition of the ghost from a status among the living group to a similar status among the once-living. Having satisfactorily achieved his new status on the completion of the *pukamani,* ideally, he is no longer interested in the affairs of the living.

There are a number of values defined by the structure of the *pukamani* ceremony. It is obvious that the poles are meant to be viewed as a configuration even though they are free-standing separable units. Moreover, they are not meant to be viewed statically since their main function relates to various and complex movements of Tiwi dancing, running, and walking among them. The poles are arranged in two formations: the first formation is a straight line of two segments, the arrangement for the initial presentation and the payoff ceremony. Each segment of the line formation corresponds to the activities of a dance group from a particular locality. This type of formation seems related to the evaluative setting since payment is based primarily on the size of the pole. The onlooker's judgments of the "goodness" of the poles are expressed at this time and each pole is associated with its creator as evidence of his ability. In these events both the configurational and the individual aspects of the poles receive attention.

When the poles are moved to the grave site the second formation is arranged—this time in one or two oval or round figures. The dancers again use the poles as props employing the projections and openings as accessories to their movements. Although part of the total configuration of dancers, their movements and other poles, the dancer uses individual poles in ways that emphasize their sculptural three-dimensional aspects.

Finally, the spouse of the deceased uses the poles to hide his (or her) movements as he crouches or walks on the grave in a parting gesture of extreme grief. By doing so he defies a most important tabu on his contact with the sacred ground. The poles can be thought of as symbols of this profanation as well as a means to lessen the danger that he courts.

In regard to those values which relate to the individual as "artist" we might first consider the very general and broad emphasis placed upon originality in Tiwi society. This is expressed in the frequent reference to Purakapali, a Tiwi culture hero, who is said to have invented many behavior patterns including the first funeral ceremony. Purakapali enjoined the Tiwi to cut poles and to represent the things around them in their singing, dancing, carving and painting. They interpret this statement as a mandate to express their personal thoughts and experiences through original verbal and visual art forms.

There are two main paths to prestige in Tiwi life, one through the acquisition of wives (Hart and Pilling 1960), the other through artistic activity. Some Tiwi seek to transverse both paths; however, each requires somewhat different characterological attributes. These attributes appear related to contrasting behavior orientations, cooperative manipulation of interpersonal relations and personal autonomy. In Tiwi terms one behavior orientation does not necessarily preclude the opposite type although at any given time one cannot assume both. All Tiwi are expected to attempt success in both paths to prestige since opportunities for the attempts are mainly dictated by duties assigned to kinship statuses. Attempts are expected, successes are not; thus a successful Tiwi gains prestige.

Therefore, to be selected as a worker is to be given a duty, as well as an opportunity to attempt success and achieve prestige. It is an opportunity given to all male Tiwi a number of times throughout their lives. This particular opportunity includes interested immediately available audiences to receive the objective forms of the individual's artistic efforts as well as a training experience for young aspiring artists who are not yet technically proficient. And it also includes a chance to fulfill obligations to kin in assisting close relatives of the deceased in honoring an important number of their kin group. (Since the number and size of the poles are indices of the social worth of the deceased, kin able to pay many skilled workers for big poles advertise their affluent position and the reflected social importance of one of their group.) Moreover, the worker plays a special part in a community effort to pacify a potentially dangerous ghost.

Esthetic values are those which orient the artist in his selection and patterning of elements in the composition of an objective art form. The Tiwi artist appears to imitate shapes, colors, textures and formal relationships among these elements, all of them separable attributes of objects he finds in his environment. He never assigns meaning to these elements but uses them solely for expressive purposes (Arnheim 1954:430–31). Transmission of effect seems to depend on the artist's use of expressive qualities

Cultural Context of Creativity among Tiwi 193

in the form patterns he constructs.[6] In traditional Tiwi art the designs do not have a pictorial function; therefore, there are few limits to the selection of elements for recombination.

The poles may be thought of as artistic vehicles designed to achieve a particular style—a plastic, special kind of environment—for the ritual, the participants and the deceased. In this sense the poles are symbols even though their constituent elements do not have referents. Their significance is linked with the process of bridging the world of the living and the parallel world of those who have once lived.[7]

THE TIWI ARTISTIC ACT AND CONDITIONS OF CREATIVITY

We can now consider the relevance of the conditions of creativity discussed earlier in this paper.

1. In regard to the first—a deep involvement in the work tempered by partial detachment—the Tiwi explicitly provide for a condition of commitment in four ways: The workers are com-

---

[6] Arnheim's discussion of expression (1954:425–43) seems to fit the Tiwi case—admittedly based on incomplete factual evidence. For Arnheim, "expression can be described as the primary content of vision" (p. 430). ". . . expression is conveyed not so much by the 'geometric-technical' properties of the percept as such, but by the forces they can be assumed to arouse in the nervous system of the observer. Regardless of whether the object moves (dancer, actor) or is immobile (painting, sculpture), it is the kind of directed tension or 'movement'—its strength, place and distribution—transmitted by the visible pattern that is perceived as expression" (p. 429).

Whether or not we agree with Arnheim that the origin of the expression can be found in the perceived pattern as well as in the mind of the perceiver, we can acknowledge that formal patterns reveal themes related to the nexus of forces set up by a particular arrangement of elements.

[7] We cannot discuss here the complex symbolism that surrounds the poles. We wish merely to point to the role the artistic approach of the Tiwi plays in relation to this symbolism. The deceased individual is no longer available to the usual sense impressions but his ghost—which is one of his aspects—participates and presides over the *pukamani* rites. Therefore, the deceased *is* and he *is not* during the time of the ceremonies; the poles seem to be related to this symbolic theme. Obviously, the *pukamani* can be analyzed in the manner suggested by Turner (1964).

missioned in a special ceremony; they are freed from the daily food quest; their patrons supply them with hard-to-obtain materials and tools (in recent times steel axes and yellow ochre from the Imilu locality); the work-area near the grave is tabu to all except the workers. Commitment to work is encouraged through temporary identification with a special group of workers who are also relatives. But the nature of social relations in this group permits of the alternation of two patterns: One, the involvement of the worker with his own pole—when he selects the tree, carves it and later paints it; and two, cooperation among workers—when the poles are moved, when they are "cooked" and when the workers join in a search for materials that are locally available. Thus the making of the poles requires intervals when the worker can detach himself from his work and in fact *must* do so to bring it to successful conclusion.

The workers can be said to be separated from the mundane on at least four different planes: They are physically separated from the other members of their local group; they stand apart through their claim to a particular kin status and the obligation they have assumed; their activities relate to sacred affairs of death and ritual; and they are enjoined to display their individuality through the product of their efforts. All of the above would seem to foster concentrated involvement countered at intervals by the detachment that group interaction demands.

2. To consider "passion and decorum" as conditions of the creative act the limitations and freedom from limitations of the artist might be assessed. In the Tiwi case the artistic enjoinder by Purakapali—"use your experience"—may be considered freeing for the Tiwi artist because it is unaccompanied by explicit rules related to representation or graphic signs. But there are many limitations: The materials are specified; the tree must be of bloodwood or ironwood; it must be selected from those available in the vicinity of the grave and within specified limits of length and diameter. Before housepaint was introduced the palette was limited to natural ochres. Before the steel ax was introduced early in this century, the stone ax imposed its own technological

limitations. And the work must be completed within a specified period of time.

There are other kinds of limitations: The size of the pole and the type of effort required of the worker are suggested by an informal leader of the work group in accordance with general instructions given by relatives of the deceased. Restrictions on the size of the pole determine restrictions on the complexity of the carver's efforts. Moreover his reputation as a worker depends on the response of the commissioning relatives; a pole that is too surprising to elicit interest will not accomplish the admiration the worker seeks.

There is a third type of limitation imposed by the technical processes customary in the production of the poles. After the projection to be planted in the ground is shaped the basic geometric solids are carved. The heavier solid forms must complement the hollowed-out sections of the trunk which are formed through the intersection of slender rods and solid masses. Since the poles are erected upright the upper sections must not unbalance the lower.

Subsequent to carving the pole is evenly smoked and blackened. This serves not only to dry the surface but also to create a background for the painted design. After the blackened surface is prepared by an application of fixative of either turtle egg or crushed orchid roots in water it cannot be erased in any way or the total effect of this method of underpainting will be destroyed. Therefore, when the first elements of the painted design are laid in a dynamic relationship between design and background is created which can only be built upon or rendered more complex—but never completely or drastically changed. The artist may work on his pole as a single unit or complete one section before moving on to another but his efforts at pole painting are in large measure irreversible; elements can only be added to the painted design and undesirable effects can only be countered or canceled through addition.

3. When these general features of the technical processes of carving and painting are considered, the third set of conditions—

careful planning superseded by a "take-over" phenomenon—appear relevant. Since very false starts are not permissible and each new effort at design limits the variation possible, the pole-cutters work slowly and carefully in the initial stages of their work and appear to hesitate less in the concluding stages. As they proceed the carved form determines the general arrangement of the painted design; the first bold outlines of the painted design (usually line elements) frame the geometric shapes that are subsequently painted and these shapes structure the arrangement of the dots and small linear filler elements that complete the design. The graphic process is complemented by the simultaneous application of color which adds variation and complexity but also limits the range of variation possible at each stage of composition.

Workers vary in the extent to which they plan their compositions before executing them. In any group of pole artists there are some who are experienced and have already achieved success. These men formulate more detailed plans but because of the value of originality as a means of expression, the "take-over" effect is as apparent in their work as in that of the less experienced.

4. There is no doubt as to the demand for immediacy of fulfillment since the worker is placed in a position where he must produce. But there are sources for cessation of activity during which contemplation and criticism are introduced. Some work with little relief except when their co-operation is needed to move a pole from one position to another. Others pause frequently to relax and smoke, and confer. There is an atmosphere of conviviality and fraternal criticism among the workers; they frequently announce their next planned move opening the way for suggestions from fellow workers. In the vocabulary of the work-group hollowed-out sections are referred to as "windows," knobby projections as "breasts," and the narrow single and dual projections as "masts," terms which relate to the exchange of advice and criticism and, most importantly, to verbalized play with elements of design and composition necessary for the Tiwi artist.

There are three types of workers in the pole-construction groups: Those men who are regarded as expert neither give nor receive advice freely but proceed according to well-formulated plans and develop a distinct personal style. A second group of experienced and skilled (but not expert) workers supply advice and limited supervision to the third group of workers (the inexperienced); the former are the informal leaders who decide matters such as the placement of poles. It is difficult to determine the extent to which the poles and procedures of the experts are used as models by other workers but the performance of the experts is available for this use at critical stages in the production process.

5. In regard to the fifth condition—the externalization of an internal cast of characters as a main source of inspiration—we can only point to the obvious—that the less expert carvers may be modeling their behavior on that of admired workers in their midst. Certainly the quality of the work-setting and the air of congeniality lends itself to free verbal expression. Since this setting is not formally constrained in any way the worker may frequently be able to select the mode of behavior he prefers at a given time—modes ranging from almost complete personal isolation and autonomy to extensive co-operation and frequent interaction.

The special aspects of the commission insure the worker a climate of approval of his efforts; moreover, he is largely competing with himself in the effort to best his earlier efforts at pole-making. (The skills that he has demonstrated in the past have been judged and accepted; even the non-expertise attributes of the unskilled are given a place.) So great is the conviction of the artist that his work should be given the admiration it deserves that he can refuse the payment presented and the use of his pole. This extreme reaction seems related to the attitude that the worker has expressed himself through his work—not simply fulfilled a specified task in making a standard implement. This reflects the high value placed on individual achievement aside from other ends that pole-making serves.

6. We assume that at the base of artistic activity there is a contemplative process—the sixth condition—during which an individual formulates his pole-making plans on both conscious and unconscious levels. Whatever the inspirational source this

process is evident during the Tiwi carver's search for a tree and his later manipulation of material media. Although work with these materials may lead to modifications and changes in the original plan, brushes, palettes and painting implements (e.g., wooden combs, etc.) are spontaneously constructed from leaves, twigs and cast-off materials at hand as if to facilitate the realization of a prior image of a painted design. It appears likely that designs from other art forms are utilized by the worker—particularly those from body and basket painting which are closely associated with the *pukamani* ceremony. (There may be a system of design elements shared by these art forms.) We might also note that poles from other *pukamani* rites are within sight of the worker and may influence his present composition.

THE RECOGNITION PROCESS

A discussion of creative process would be incomplete without some consideration of the ways in which creative (in this case artistic) activity is reinforced by norms of expectation and evaluation in a given social setting (Lasswell 1959:206ff.).

Every Tiwi individual is encouraged to participate in the various art realms—song, dance, body painting, ceremonial basket-making and the carving and painting of ceremonial spears and poles. Tiwi feel that the individual develops and matures through his efforts at creating. Both formal and informal methods of cultural transmission involve a grounding in symbol and technique, and children of both sexes are encouraged to learn. Moreover, children are *expected* to be present at any and all ceremonies and their efforts at imitation are generally rewarded. Participation in ceremonies—the most important settings for formal instruction—is open to everyone regardless of age or sex, but the parts assigned are matched to age and ability.

Children also carry out mock ceremonies in which they approximate adult behavior. Although these early childhood occasions include young females later contexts of artistic activity generally involve only males—unless a woman shows a special interest and ability. Should this be the case she too will be given the same opportunities.

There are many important social contexts in which prestige can be realized through successful artistic activity. For example, one phase of the Kulama ceremony demands the singing of new songs for three consecutive days. There is definite approval for those participants who present original material. During the initiation rites one of the standard tests presented to the initiates is the composition of an original song. Every man meets this test; some are far more successful than others. It may be noted that women are not enjoined to compose but may assist their husbands.

What is important for our consideration is the extent to which artistic activities pervade social relations so that a wide range of possibilities is open to individuals. Not only are creative activities accessible by their abundance but they are thoroughly approved as direct or necessary modes of individual achievement. Moreover, when viewed cross-culturally, the number of modes of achievement in Tiwi life is distinctly limited.

SOME IMPLICATIONS

We suggest that some old problems be reconsidered in the light of the foregoing discussion. For example, discussions of style might be assisted by knowing how the artists work. In Tiwi pole production the "style" of any one grave group depends in part on the role of the skilled worker in the group and the extent to which his pole and other visible examples are used as models. Regional styles may mirror the influence of a small number of "expert" pole carvers who work in particular localities. Although formal roles defining masters and apprentices are not specifically recognized by Tiwi the structure of interpersonal relations both within the pole-cutters group and the local community lends itself to the patterning of artistic efforts. The selection of workers on the basis of local residence and kin relationship heightens this effect on regional style.

Analysis of change in art forms—both with regard to extensive stylistic change and the number of artistic enterprises must include the changing microcosm of social relations embedded in the artistic act as well as the changing milieu as a source of inspiration. We suggest that, despite change in other aspects of the culture, if the need and desire for burial poles remain they will be gratified in the traditional way with the customary fervor unless events disrupt the contexts for creative activity. Given the same opportunities for artistic activity, the same values and approximately equivalent patterns of social relations in art-producing contexts, introduced tools, techniques and ideas will yield stylistic variation but little change in the basic pattern of the art form. Among Tiwi, steel axes, manufactured pigments and new items of material culture have led to a greater number of sculpted and painted elements on the poles yet little extensive change. However, while this particular type of work-group can be a handmaiden to tradition, the presence of a prestigious innovator who has experienced the unusual and expresses this experience artistically could lead to a marked change in a local style.

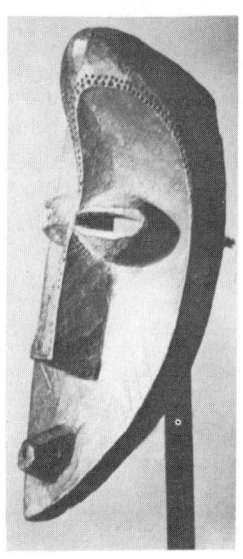

Plates 1, 2 and 3 by courtesy of the Museum of Modern Art, New York.

PLATE 1   Modigliani: Head (1915).

PLATE 2   Wooden mask, from Itumba region, border of Gabun and Congo. Note the stylistic similarities of Plates 1 and 2, as described by Fraser (2).

PLATE 3 Picasso: "Les Demoiselles d'Avignon" (1907). This work reveals the influence of Ivory Coast masks, especially in the two female heads on the right.

PLATE 4 "Horseman," from the Village of Nini, Mali. Although not the identical work to which Redfield (3) refers (his first two illustrations being unavailable), this Dogon piece conveys the same "general impression of balanced verticality" of which he writes. Courtesy of Musée de l'Homme, Paris.

PLATE 5 "Seated ancestral couple," Dogon. Much of Redfield's article is concerned with this well-known piece of sculpture. Courtesy of The Barnes Foundation, Merion, Pennsylvania.

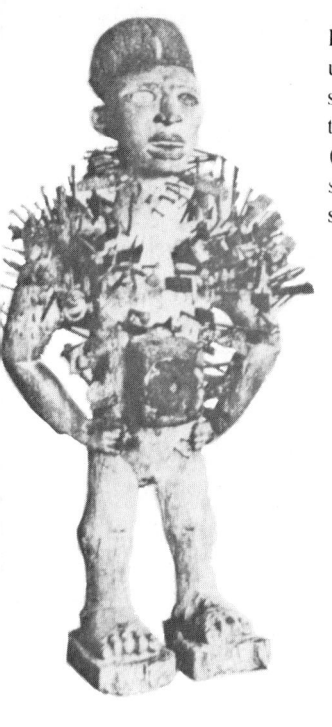

PLATE 6 "Nail fetish" from the Lower Congo, used in juridical procedures and in extracting services from the carving, which is challenged to action with each added nail. Muensterberger (6) describes their making. Courtesy of Museum für Völkerkunde u. Schweizerisches Museum für Volkskunde, Basel (111 2807).

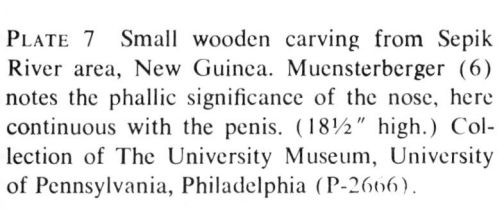

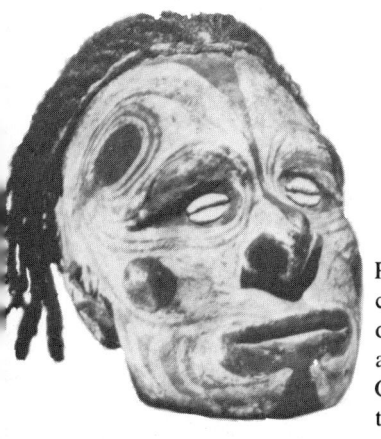

PLATE 7 Small wooden carving from Sepik River area, New Guinea. Muensterberger (6) notes the phallic significance of the nose, here continuous with the penis. (18½" high.) Collection of The University Museum, University of Pennsylvania, Philadelphia (P-2606).

PLATE 8 Skull of ancestor, modeled over with clay and painted. These skulls, common to much of Melanesia, are associated with head-hunting and honoring the spirits of departed ancestors. Courtesy of The Field Museum of Natural History, Chicago (275-702).

PLATE 9 A group of Tiwi burial poles which have been moved to the graves after payment. Dancing and wailing by the employers take place here, with the poles on view. Courtesy of Jane C. Goodale and Joan D. Koss.

PLATE 10 One of the bistre and black horses in the Cave of Lascaux, surrounded by "arrows." Above the horse is a geometric sign of the "latticed" type, discussed by Ucko and Rosenfeld (15). Courtesy of Archives Photographiques, Paris.

PLATE 11 Imaginary animal in the Great Hall of Bulls, Lascaux. This strange horned creature with lozenge-shaped spots has been pointed out as demonstrating the capacity of Paleolithic man to abstract specific features and recombine them imaginatively. Courtesy of Archives Photographiques, Paris.

PLATE 12 Black and red horses in the cave of Pech-Merle, surrounded by stenciled hands. Notice the use of natural rock formation in the head of the horse on the right. Photograph and copyright by Carl Nesjar.

PLATE 13 Jade effigy celt showing characteristic Olmec traits of crying baby mouth with toothless gums in were-jaguar face. This piece is typical of early La Venta style, discussed by Willey (16). Courtesy of The British Museum, London.

PLATE 14 Stone mortar in the form of a jaguar. The exact provenience is unknown, but the subject is easily identifiable as the feline motif of Chavin, with interlocked fangs. (13" long.) Courtesy of The University Museum, University of Pennsylvania, Philadelphia (SA 4627).

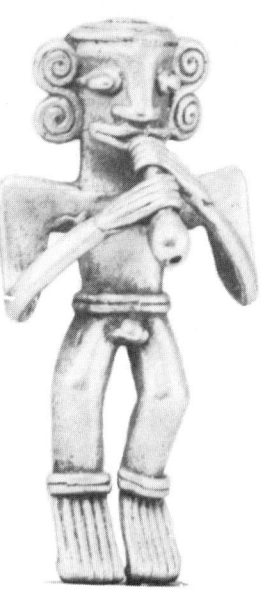

PLATE 15 Pendant of cast gold, of a figure playing a flute. Found at the site of Coclé in Panama, this little fellow (2⅝″ high) is a good example of the fine workmanship of Coclé goldsmiths, who practiced from the fifth century A.D. until the Conquest. Easby (17) describes the process. Courtesy of The Art Institute of Chicago (96, 115).

PLATE 16 Headpiece of crown of hammered gold, from Chongoyape, Lambayeque Valley, Peru. This piece illustrates well the intricacy which could be achieved in hammered gold, as well as the familiar features of the Chavín feline. Courtesy of the Museum of the American Indian, Heye Foundation, New York (16/1972 B).

PLATE 17 Seated female effigy figure of cast gold, Quimbaya culture, Central Cauca Valley, Colombia. The gold work of this area presents the greatest stylistic variety of all pre-Colombian metalwork. (9″.) Courtesy of The University Museum, University of Pennsylvania, Philadelphia (SA 2751).

PLATE 18 A standing warrior in colored clay, from the island of Jaina, showing typical detail of dress and virtuosity of modeling. (12½".) Courtesy of The Art Institute of Chicago (1963.272).

PLATE 19 The so-called "Okvik madonna," a remarkable human figure carved in walrus ivory. The moderate abstraction and style of engraving relate it to the early Okvik tradition of St. Lawrence Island. Rainey (20) discusses the find. Courtesy of the University of Alaska Museum, College, Alaska (UA #8-(4-1934) 607).

Part IV | ACCULTURATION

THE ARTS AND THEIR CHANGING SOCIAL FUNCTION

Roy Sieber

IN ORDER to discuss the changing social functions of art it is first necessary to posit a definition of art that can include the concept of social function as an essential aspect. Only then will it be possible to examine, briefly and in general terms, the character of a few of the changes in the arts and their social functions.

"In the widest sense . . . art is to be thought of as *any embellishment of ordinary living that is achieved with competence and has describable form*" (Herskovits 1951:380).

This statement by Herskovits will serve admirably as a basic and useful definition and as a point of departure for this paper. However, it is necessary to add that this embellishment of life, that is, its beautification or adornment, can and, indeed, usually does sustain a level of meaning. In short, there are two basic aspects of art: its esthetic or presentational context comprised of form and skill and embodying style, and its meaning context comprised of subject and symbolic associations.

Furthermore, the term art has been defined by estheticians to refer either to a process, or to the product that results from that process. Both are implicit in the first definition. The product is usually referred to as the "work of art" and the process somewhat oversimplified as "skill," or as the "creative act." Again, however, I must add a third aspect. Studies of the work of art, as an object or an event, tend to be concerned with the technical

---

Reprinted from *Annals of The New York Academy of Sciences,* Vol. 96, Art. 2, January 20, 1962:653–58, by permission of the author and The New York Academy of Sciences.

aspects of form, style, and symbolism or with the basic data of art history: such as date, place of origin, and name of artist. Studies of the process tend to focus on the training and skills of the artist, the sources of his "inspiration" (at best a vague term) or his position and role in his culture. At times, of course, these are more broadly interpreted, but they do not normally include what I consider to be a crucial part of the study of the arts: its impact on its audience.

Thus in addition to the undeniably important studies of the works of art and of the artist and his techniques, it is necessary to become more acutely aware of the affective character of art, of the associations it arouses, and the responses it elicits from its audience. In contemporary Western esthetics these are usually presented solely as esthetic and individual, yet they can be, and often are, utilitarian and plural.

I must note that it would be impertinent in this paper to distinguish between the fine arts and the useful arts. I emphatically do not use the word art to imply "fine arts" as it does in the Western world. African modes of distinguishing relative esthetic importance have not been recorded. Until they are, the problem is best left open. I might add that in practice it is often difficult to distinguish whether a piece is admired because it is esthetically good or because it is useful or important in a nonesthetic context.

The title of this paper indicates that the arts have one or more social functions. As I have indicated, this is a point not necessarily accepted by all who concern themselves with the arts. Extreme, individualistic romanticism of the sort current today tends to treat the arts as if they were somehow independent of their cultural origins. The art-for-art's-sake attitude deliberately and categorically rejects the point of view that the arts relate to the normative values of the culture in which they arise and that they play a useful role within that culture. The suggestion that the arts are, or can be, the handmaidens of religion or prestige or politics is firmly resisted. I am convinced that this attitude, of fairly recent manufacture, is a deterrent to a full understanding of the role of art and is not supported by historical evidence.

It is worth noting that an antithetical point of view, that of Platonic Idealism, suggests that esthetic excellence, beauty, is an absolute that lies outside human experience and is, by definition, unchanging. Far from being based on human values, ultimate beauty is untouched by the vicissitudes of human history or cultural changes. Historical evidence, again, would seem to indicate that this is, in fact, far from the case and that the history of cultural changes is echoed in changes in the arts. Not only do the facts of art, style, and type change but the concepts and definitions of beauty change.

I subscribe to what is, I think, a more useful, and, indeed, a more accurate premise; one supported by historical and anthropological evidence. It is that the arts, taken as defined above, are symptomatic of cultural values and that they are for the most part oriented positively, that is, toward man's search for a secure and ordered existence.

I have elsewhere discussed the evidence that establishes that this is the case with traditional African arts; that, for the most part, they can be considered positive, integrated cultural manifestations, reflecting and reinforcing the basic values of the cultures that gave rise to them (Sieber 1959).

From this point of view there is a level at which the social function of the arts is constant. The arts at any time or place, in reflecting cultural values, evolve what might be called the "value image" that culture has of itself. That image can become objectified (perhaps reified is a better word) so that it stands as a symbolic reinforcement of the values it reflects. (One of the best examples of this is the Medieval cathedral. In its architecture and decoration it presented—either symbolically, or in quite literal depictions—all of the accepted major areas of knowledge, history and dogma, and even had room for bits of grotesque fun.)

In this sensitive balance the arts quickly respond to changes in the value climate of the parent culture. In times of relative stability the arts evidence a compensatory adaptation, with a seeming deliberation that echoes with some accuracy the pace of other cultural changes. However, cultures in relatively more rapid or more total transition exhibit certain significant modifications in the arts: the arts become less integrated and less pervasive in character, in short, less meaningful; a broadening of choice mechanisms undermines the commitment to traditional styles and motifs; in many cases, the patron-artist relationship is altered, and a tendency to lower standards of critical judgment develops.

All of these phenomena have occurred or are occurring in Africa with reference to the traditional arts. They may be discerned in the disappearances of styles, motifs, and skills, in the substitutions or additions of imported objects, skills, materials or techniques, and in the confusions, contradictions, and syncretisms that result.

This is obviously not the first time that foreign influences or local events have affected African history, culture, and art. The moment is, however, exceptional in that a series of massive, widespread changes are taking place with great rapidity.

The traditional round hut with thatched roof is rapidly being superseded by rectangular houses with corrugated tin roofing. Carved wooden doors have not been made for a decade, but have been replaced by locally made carpentry doors; even some masks have been imported from the Ibo to replace traditional types.

The presence of freely imported objects, like freely imported ideas, reflects a freedom from intertribal wars and reflects, as well, improved modes of transportation. By extension, the change reflects the Pax Britannica and British administration with all its concomitants, including law, education, and medicine, thus becoming symptomatic at various levels of quite profound changes.

Thus the tribal image of itself as a relatively self-sufficient, self-sustaining unit is modified. In turn the concept of a tribal art style dependent on that image is modified, losing its sense of fitness and propriety. An element of choice now enters areas where a single type or mode once predominated. Conformity is replaced by variety.

With the widening of the choice factor, the sense of discrimination often becomes confused. The new, the spectacular often acquire a value that is based neither on utilitarian nor on esthetic concerns. Thus, for example, the carpentry doors that replace the older carved doors are of decidedly inferior manufacture as art or as carpentry.

In addition it should be noted that a new economic scheme is implicit in these observations, and with it new modes of acquiring wealth, and, with wealth, prestige.

The Igala carved doors were once used to enhance prestige. Their replacements still serve as external indications of status but, as noted, their esthetic connotations are minimal, if not nonexistent, not only to us, but to the Igala. In checking this point I discovered that, although the younger Igala men admired the carved doors and to some extent lamented that none were being made, they found them inadequate as status symbols and therefore would not themselves commission them. Beier perhaps overstates the case when he writes ". . . no literate or 'successful' Nigerian will ever employ a traditional carver." (1960:7.)

On the other hand, I found that many of the older men rarely wore the local hand-woven cloths publicly, preferring Hausa or European imports. Nevertheless they insisted that they would be buried in an Igala cloth and they did wear them in their own compounds. Evidently the demands of prestige were here offset in part by a strong tie with tradition.

Thus it seems evident that the loss of the self-image of this tribe as a unit and, concomitantly, the individual's inability to identify himself with an image that no longer exists is reflected in the loss of a commitment to a given artistic style and in the weakening of esthetic discrimination in the face of broadened choice mechanisms.

Every disappearance of a type or a mode and nearly every imported substitute means a lost or diminished skill or a shift to an area of specialism not necessarily related to the arts. The quantitative loss of Igala carvings, destroyed either accidentally or under missionary influence during the past generation, is, according to reports, great. Moreover, most significantly, they have for the most part not been replaced.

Elsewhere in Northern Nigeria (among the Idoma, Goemai, and Montol, for example) there are numerically about as many carvings as there were a generation ago. However few are owned, carved, or commissioned by men under forty. Another generation will most probably see a sharp decrease in the number of carvings in use; and unused carvings rapidly vanish under the effects of climate, insects, and fire.

In the attempt to investigate and relate these phenomena to crucial shifts in value patterns certain problems arise.

One might quite profitably seek out evidence of change in such fields as religion, economics, social organization, medicine, and then seek reflections in the arts. However, to an art historian such an approach seems inverted. Furthermore, the relation of art to the various aspects of culture is not fixed. For example, herbalism might be a secular and casual concern in one culture, as it seems to be among the Idoma, or intimately related to a men's society, divination, and a complex of figure carvings as it is among the Montol. As a result, the introduction of European medical practices has had quite differing effects in these two tribes.

Similarly the art historian's usual trilogy of style, subject matter, and iconography are of little use. To be effective in the analysis of change these demand a sufficient supply of objects and data to establish a base line. Few artistic traditions in Africa are sufficiently studied or are collections exhaustive enough to establish that base line. Unfortunately one cannot use informants to obtain data on style changes, or subtle shifts in subject matter and symbolism.

It seems expedient for the moment to take a number of instances of change observable in the arts in certain tribes in Nigeria, to attempt to relate them to changes of a nonartistic nature, and to make tentative observations concerning the shift in "value image" these tribes hold of themselves.

In reconstructing the role of the chief mask of the Igala it is evident that, in the recent past, it served as a major agent of social control. For example, endowed with spiritual authority, the mask acted in cases of murder. It could quarantine a family, even a village, until the murderer was given up, and it authorized a member of the victim's family to execute the murderer. Furthermore, it adjudicated complaints of debts and empowered a lesser mask to force payment.

Matters of theft, however, were not reported to this mask. Instead, a person accused of theft was required or volunteered to take an oath of innocence on a carved figure of a particular type. Illness or madness descended on one who swore falsely.

The mask and the figure have lost much of their traditional power: cases of theft and of debt are now heard in a local magistrate's court where judgments are based in part on Koranic and in part on British law, and murder trials are held in a court that, geographically, lies outside the territory inhabited by the Igala.

As agents of social control reflecting the ethics of the tribe and embodying in esthetic forms the spiritual forces that were believed to sustain law and order, these works of art have been vitiated by an alien concept of law. With the reasons for their existence gone, it is no surprise that they have nearly disappeared. The shift is from a spiritual *cum* esthetic form to a predominantly secular concern, and even where the law is Koranic and religious, it expressly forbids imagery. It is thus evident that the associations aroused by the mask and the figure have changed and that the new sense of law admits of no continuing role for these works of art. The loss is, or shortly will become, total.

A number of other changes in the arts are also evident among the Igala. Wooden clog sandals have been totally replaced by European shoes, by sandals of North African type dispersed by Hausa traders, and by locally made sandals manufactured of old tires. Wooden bowls have been replaced by Japanese enameled tinware and European glass; pottery, too, is nearly gone. Handwoven cloths of local cotton have been almost totally replaced by Manchester cottons and Hausa cloth, except that the old cloth type is still used for shrouds.

Those carvers who work in traditional modes are, for the most part, elderly men working in a vanishing milieu for a steadily decreasing audience. This, of itself, indicates a major change in the arts. Many younger men who traditionally would have become artisans have moved to other areas of specialism that now carry the prestige and the financial and social rewards that were once accorded the artist. This, of itself, reflects a changed status of the arts as a necessary aspect of tribal values.

However there does exist in Nigeria a younger generation, trained either in traditional modes or in arts and crafts schools, who produce tourist or export objects. These objects, unlike the tribal arts, are produced not on commission but in quantity, for an unknown clientele. Although financial rewards can accrue from this activity, the traditional tribal recognition and the patron-artist relationship have vanished. Thus, perhaps inevitably, esthetic standards have weakened and the products, for the most part, are esthetically inferior.

Another younger group of artists produce painted signs, grave sculpture, or architectural decorations in cement for the new middle class. For the most part they work in European modes with varying degrees of skill and usually with no formal training. In general their products reflect an imported aesthetic put to the use of transplanted ideas. Until those ideas and the associated esthetic become more fully assimilated and integrated the effect of these new forms will remain obscure. Those artists who use traditional modes to express new values, as for example with Father Carroll's group of Christian Yoruba carvers, have transplanted the traditional styles but without their vitality (Beier 1960:15). This may well be because the traditional styles developed in a particular context which lent them their vitality. There exist as well a few artists, primarily painters and sculptors trained in the Western manner, whose esthetic orientation is European but whose sympathies are African.

It is uncertain at this point where we must look for a future art as varied, as African, and as rich in its reflection and contribution to social values as were the traditional arts.

Finally, there is one aspect of this problem that has not been mentioned: art itself can have a social value. That is, in addition to the utilitarian or associative character of the arts, their very existence indicates that a premium is placed—to some degree, and at some level—on the esthetic of and for itself. The excitement, delight, and admiration visible in an Igala audience at the appearance of a mask was elicited not only by functional associations but, as one informant put it, by its "well-carved goodness." The sheer quantity of traditional arts that once existed best attests to the presence of the esthetic as a social value.

Nevertheless, this—to return to our first definition—"embellishment of ordinary living" as a social function of the arts is also undergoing change. For the most part the African feels he urgently needs roads, hospitals, and schools but not the arts. In short, he has created a self image that, despite all the important values it does contain, largely fails to include the arts.

ON THE COLONIAL EXTINCTION OF THE MOTIFS OF PRE-COLUMBIAN ART

George Kubler

THE EDITORS originally requested an article on "the survival of native art motifs into the Colonial Period." Such survivals are so few and scattered that their assembling requires an enormous expenditure for a minimal yield, like a search for the fragments of a deep-lying shipwreck. Therefore, I renamed the study as above, so that its readers would not expect any large remnants of the wreck of pre-Columbian civilization.

The extinction was gradual but its pace changed. In the sixteenth century the rush to European conventions of representation and building, by colonists and Indians alike, precluded any real continuation of native traditions in art and architecture. In the seventeenth century, so much had been forgotten, and the extirpation of native observances by the religious authorities was so vigorous, that the last gasps of the bearers of Indian rituals and manners expired unheard. Following the exploratory fervor of the first two generations of colonists, it was not until after 1750, when the Enlightenment reached the American cities, that any close attention was paid to the ruins of American antiquity. No finds of monumental sculpture were reported in Mexico until the excavations of 1790 in the cathedral square of Mexico City (León y Gama 1832).

One is reminded of the mystifying inability of Europeans to see

---

Reprinted by permission of the author and publishers from Samuel K. Lothrop and Others: *Essays in Pre-Columbian Art and Archaeology*, Cambridge, Mass. Harvard University Press, Copyright 1961, by the President and Fellows of Harvard College. pp. 14–34.

Colonial Extinction of the Motifs of Pre-Columbian Art

or remark upon prehistoric cave paintings until late in the nineteenth century. The intellectual climate of the Enlightenment in Mexico, however, could favor only an archaeological autopsy. Survivals were by then beyond recall, and it is an autopsy that all posterior research has continued to perform. We shall not here be concerned with any stage of this prolonged dissection of the corpse of a civilization, but only with the exceptional occasions when pre-Columbian themes continued in the artistic utterance of the peoples of Latin America.[1]

These utterances were like death cries, and their study pertains to eschatology, or the science of the end of things. Very little is known about the termination of art styles, or of the cultural configurations for which an art style is often the only proof of existence. The case of the pre-Columbian civilizations of America is a peculiarly abrupt example of the termination of cultural entities. We shall later comment on the general significance of the extinction of American antiquity.

Works of art are symbolic expressions. They evoke a reality without being that reality. Buildings, statues, paintings and tools all suggest so powerfully a specific time, place and attitude, that they are among our most tangible and permanent manifestations of culture. "Enemy" works of art are destroyed during cultural conflicts. The triumph of one culture over another is usually marked by the virtual cessation of the art of the vanquished, and its replacement by the art of the conqueror. When the offending objects and monuments finally cease to correspond to any living behavior, they become symbolically inert. They then are "safe" to play with in recombinations emptied of previous vital meanings, as in tourist souvenirs, antiquarian reconstructions, or archaizing revivals.

Under the conditions of colonial life in Latin America, nearly all symbolic expressions of native origin were suppressed by the

---

[1] An account of these survivals in Mexico is scattered through the work of Weismann (1951). See also Grajales Ramos (1953:75–100); Gomez de Orozco (1939:48–50); Romero de Terreros (1923); Moyssen (1958: 33–46).

colonial authorities as well as by native leaders whose positions depended upon conforming obedience.[2] Only the practical or useful items of behavior were eagerly adopted. Hence the utility of any native behavior and its colonial survival are closely linked.

The survival of the native languages is only an apparent exception to the rule of symbolic extinction. Without knowing Indian languages, the colonists could not attain their ends. Indian language was purified of its native symbolic content, and in the seventeenth century it became an acceptable vehicle for Christian belief and ritual. The linguistic separation of the populace into Spanish- and Indian-speaking groups strengthened the emerging division of colonial society as exploiting and exploited groups. Under these conditions, all symbolic expressions, including those of native origin, eventually became reinforcements of the power of the colonial state. As such, they are extensions of European art rather than native survivals.

For example, in Mexico and in Peru, the earthen platforms of the pre-Conquest peoples could not be dismantled, and they still stand as tokens of the power and grandeur of ancient religions. The Christian churches erected upon their summits symbolize the conquest of pagan observance by Christian ritual, like early Christian temples which mark triumph over the monuments of the ancient Mediterranean world. The idea of triumph probably also appears at many pre-Columbian sites where the superposition of earthen platforms records distinct cultural periods as at Cholula. The several structural stages in the great pyramid form a layered record of cultural succession, which concludes with the Christian church built atop the entire complex in the seventeenth century, as if taking symbolic possession of the entire vast accumulation of human effort (Marquina 1951:115–28; de la Maza 1959).

Before treating other visible survivals of art motifs, we should carefully examine one supposed class of forms which have been treated as survivals, although clear evidence of preconquest themes

---

[2] For the best account of early colonial methods of colonialization, see Ricard (1933). For Peru see Kubler (1946:331–410).

has not been shown. We might here designate these types as "formal" survivals. During the past decade, much has been written about a "Mestizo art" in colonial Latin America (Neumeyer 1947: 104–21; Wethey 1949:8; Kelemen 1951:167).[3] Alfred Neumeyer, its principal proponent, postulated that mestizo art was unified by "admixtures of Indian pre-Conquest tradition," taking the form of "flat, grooved, or embossed designs" in "two-dimensional, symbolically abstract modes," analogous to the folk art of Central Europe or North Africa. In short, the "survivals" are formal rather than thematic. These "admixtures of pre-Conquest tradition" are not shown in thematic detail, but other writers have adopted the thesis of survival on the basis of mere formal persistence without closer scrutiny.

As to the persistence of formal types of design independently of symbolic content, it is perhaps more plausible to suppose that we are confronted with examples of provincial or folk art, which are the end products of frequent copying. For example, the arabesques and grotesques of Italian Renaissance architectural ornament were copied in Spain and transmitted to Mexico in book illustrations and wood engravings, which then were turned back into relief sculpture by native craftsmen, as at Tlalmanalco, southeast of Mexico City. In this process the original design loses articulation, hierarchy, variation and individuality in increasingly schematic stylizations. This degradation of form has nothing to do with racial symbolism. It occurs independently of race and class, wherever a given form is required to serve many needs by frequent repetition. . . .

The other principal modes of the survival of ancient forms are in reality the modes of extinction. The native symbolic system

---

[3] On Peruvian notions of race and caste, see Kubler (1952). H. E. Wethey, writing on colonial architectural decoration in southern Peru, and seeking a thematic survival, connected certain carvings of fruit and flowers in the portals of Arequipa with Nazca pottery designs from the south coast valleys. Nazca pottery, however, was unknown until about 1900, when the cemeteries of the ancient Nazca people, who flourished early in the first millennium A.D., were first discovered.

was first broken into disjoined parts, of which a few were gradually assimilated into the colonial fabric. The process can be classified as follows:

Juxtaposition: among the same people, coexistence of forms, drawn from two different cultures, without interaction. Only here has native culture any chance of intact survival.

Convergence: unconnected cultural traditions produce similar behavioral patterns which are interchangeable in the colony for aims approved by the ruling group.

Explants: connected portions of native behavior continue to evolve for a period under colonial rule.

Transplants: isolated, but meaningful parts of native tradition are taken into colonial behavior, without major changes or development.

Fragments: isolated pieces of the native tradition are repeated without comprehension, as meaningless but pleasurable acts or forms.

These all have in common some participation by native peoples, who brought to the work those residual preferences and symbolic forms which might pass the filter of colonial institutions.

Juxtaposition is a rare accommodation between colonists and natives. For instance, the Portuguese in India and Japan (Boxer 1948) so adjusted their ways to native habits that their message or action was transformed, as much to secure native compliance as to impose the will of the colonizers. In Asia, the colonist often assumed many new habits, as if to compensate the native for having been obliged to adopt an alien faith. Under these conditions extensive portions of native culture survived, and the extinguishing action of colonial institutions remained minimal.

In America, only the Franciscan missions among the Pueblo Indians of the southwestern United States can be considered under this head. The Pueblo peoples of the Rio Grande Valley and the Hopi lands in northeastern Arizona have massive and integral survivals of prehistoric urban life, rimmed with only a thin accretion of European culture until this century (Kubler 1943:39–48).[4] In discussing the Pueblo tribes, to speak of acculturation is less relevant than *juxtaposition* of distinct kinds of culture. For example, in the pueblos the Christian church usually stands at the periphery of the densely built town, where the underground ceremonial chambers of the men's societies, the kivas, still are in use. Each adult is likely to have two modes of religious life: one Indian and the other Catholic, with few evidences of reciprocal influence. The Catholic churches have always been there on sufferance and it is instructive to see how their structure reflects the profound indifference of the Indian communicants, who refused the technical novelties of European building traditions. In this matrilocal society, ownership of buildings was vested in the women, who built the walls and maintained the surfaces, while the men cut the timbers, formed the adobes and transported the building supplies. All pre-Conquest construction was of post-and-lintel type, and when the Franciscans brought knowledge of arches and domes in the seventeenth century, these were refused. Although adobe brick is well suited to dynamic structural devices, arches and domes were generally refused because they would have upset the traditional division of labor by sexes. The women were accustomed to build the walls, and to keep up the surfaces. The men assembled the materials.

However, the friars countered this passive opposition among their charges by transforming European structural habits to accommodate Indian tradition, resulting in a reciprocal acculturation of which there are very few examples in the history of Christianity. In such an acculturation, the behavior of the missionaries is altered by colonial contact as well as the behavior of the natives themselves. . . .

Convergence. The celebrated "open chapels" of the sixteenth century in Mexico and Yucatan have been the subject of much

---

[4] Detailed study of a single edifice: Montgomery, Smith, and Brew (1949). For other ancient traits in modern Pueblo culture, see Warburg (1938–39: II, 277–92).

discussion, centering upon the question of origin (Kubler 1948; Palm 1953; Guerrero Lovillo 1949). Some writers assert the transfer of ancient Mexican habits of outdoor worship to Christian ritual. Others prefer to regard open chapels as functional necessities with ample precedents in Mediterranean antiquity, in Early Christian art and in Islamic worship, as well as in Mexican religion. Since the open chapel usually includes a courtyard or atrium like that of Early Christian churches, and a covered sanctuary like the Syrian *kalybe,* its Old World derivation seems assured under favoring conditions in the early colonization of the huge urban congregations of Mexico. Hence the open chapel is best classed as a phenomenon of convergence between ancient Mediterranean types and more recent Mexican habits, with its structural features deriving from nearly forgotten European antecedents. . . .

No . . . doubts arise in connection with the many colonial examples of heraldic and commemorative records in which pre-Conquest themes appear. Pre-Columbian examples are common. The Tizoc stela in the Museo Nacional is a commemorative relief: it records a date (1486) and it shows the rulers Tizoc and Ahuitotl drawing penitential blood from their ear lobes. Heraldic forms, such as personal name-signs and as place-names, were the principal substance of pre-Conquest picture-writing. Thus the name-glyph of Tizoc was the picture of a bleeding leg and foot. The emblem of Tenochtitlan was a cactus plant (*nochtli*).

The convergence of native emblems and European heraldry was inevitable. They are comparable stages in the history of writing, especially useful in the making of maps. For example, the name of Tenayuca, near Mexico City, signifies "walled place" and its Aztec glyph shows the outline of a crenelated wall. This glyph survived in colonial usage, and it appears over the church doorway at Tlalnepantla as part of a Renaissance architectural composition. Personal name-glyphs recording Indian sounds continued in colonial use through the sixteenth century in tax records and genealogies,[5] and they were replaced by written names in the Spanish phonetic system only after 1600.

Explants. The descendance of a small piece of embryo chicken heart has flourished since 1912 at Rockefeller Institute in New York as an explanted tissue. It has been kept alive outside its organism in an appropriate medium. (Lecomte du Noüy 1936: 102f.) The term can be borrowed to describe certain phenomena of native survival in colonial America, as when an isolated theme flourished for a period within the supporting medium of colonial institutional life.

An example is the continuing development of one aspect of pre-Columbian calendrical symbolism under colonial conditions for two generations after the Conquest. No regular sequence of glyphs designating the 20-day months of the native calendar of Mexico and Central America was used in Central Mexico until some Indian scribe devised a sequence of month-glyphs in connection with historical records of the Conquest and colonial taxation periods (Kubler and Gibson 1951). The appearance of these 19 signs coincides with the introduction from Europe of an archaic form of the farmer's calendar and a group of Renaissance menological symbols based upon Roman prototypes.

The glyphs themselves depict the Mexican names of the months, but the forms of panel composition derive from European models. In short, the cells of the tissue are Mexican, but their medium is European. These early colonial efforts to perpetuate the use of the Indian calendar died out about 1600.

Indeed, the entire "native" illustrated manuscript production of the metropolitan region surrounding Mexico-Tenochtitlan can be regarded as an explant. All these manuscripts, with only one possible exception—the *Plano en papel de maguey*—were made after the Conquest. Early colonial illustrated texts, made either on European paper or on a new colonial variety of native paper prepared from the fiber of the maguey cactus, (Lenz 1948; Von

---

[5] E.g., *Codice Xolotl* (1951).

Hagen 1945) were commissioned for the use of the Crown and for the information of colonial administrative officers when considering new legislation or matters under litigation.[6] They were not made for publication or for general use, and they all remained lost to view in archives and private collections until the modern era. Many are faithful copies of pre-Conquest books, like Codex Borbonicus, whose colonial date is betrayed by certain European conventions of draughtsmanship, with rounded contours suggesting three-dimensional bodies. The Aubin tonalamatl is also a colonial manuscript, because it contains a depiction of a European species of pig. At the other extreme, the Europeanized illustrations for Sahagún's great encyclopaedia of Mexican ethnography were painted by Indians, but the graphic conventions are those of sixteenth-century Spanish art. An exception is the group which illustrates the *Primeros Memoriales,* circa 1558, in a manner still retaining some habits of pre-Conquest drawing. Occasionally, a graphic style of some expressive power arose from the compounding of Indian and European conventions, as in the Lienzo de Tlaxcala (ca. 1558), but it was inevitable that the flat manner of Indian painting, fenced about by straight lines and abrupt curves, with color in ungraded local tones, should disappear in favor of the far greater descriptive power of European drawing and coloring. The appearances of solid bodies could only be shown schematically in the Indian conventions and the Indians themselves eagerly learned the new European system of perspective construction by line and graduated color relations.

Another instance of the colonial expansion of pre-Columbian themes appears in the highland Peruvian manufacture of lacquered wooden drinking vessels called *keros* and *pakchas.*[7] Many hundreds of them are known, showing Indians with elaborate colonial costumes, engaged in ritual actions of pre-Conquest types. The *kero* is a vessel form of flaring beaker type. Examples have been

---

[6] Robertson (1959) gives the most complete account of these materials.
[7] Keros: See Rowe (1961:317); Schaedel (1949:17–19). On pre-Conquest examples, Valcarcel (1932:11–18). Pakchas: Joyce (1923:761–68). On both, Lothrop (1956:233).

found at Inca sites of fifteenth-century date, but they lack the elaborate figural compositions of the colonial examples. The *pakchas* are complicated carvings in which the vessel is separated from the drinker's mouth by a more or less elaborate channeling of the liquid along a carved handle or stem.

These painted wooden vessels, together with the remarkable seventeenth-century manuscript by Felipe Guaman Poma de Ayala (Guaman Pomo de Ayala 1936; Porras 1948) are the principal pictorial documentation of Inca culture known today. Though colonial conventions of representation are predominant, the subject matter is indigenous, so that the class as a whole, of which the manufacture endured far into the nineteenth century, can be regarded as an explanted survival of native themes in colonial forms.

Transplants describe the inclusion of pre-Columbian symbols among the configurations of colonial art. Such grafts of pre-Columbian material upon the colonial matrix are uncommon, because of the general tendency toward the symbolic extinction of pre-Columbian values in colonial life. When transplants can be identified, they enjoy an exceptional dramatic status, as much because of their rarity as because of their intrinsic interest.

An example is the occasional use of obsidian inserts on colonial sculpture to symbolize the vital principle, as in pre-Conquest statuary, when an obsidian disk set into the chest of a stone figure represented the heart and therefore the life of the image. Two stone churchyard crosses of sixteenth-century date in Michoacán, and one at Tepeapulco in Hidalgo, bear such inserts at the intersection of the arms. There can be no doubt that the pre-Conquest symbolism of heart sacrifice was intended, in order to reinforce the Christian meaning of the crucifixion among recently converted natives.[8]

---

[8] Garcia Granados (1940:54–56) and Weismann (1951:190) recall that jet was similarly used in Spain, citing A. K. Porter (1928:11). If this use was present to the minds of sixteenth-century friars, we should regard the crosses inset with flakes of obsidian as examples of convergence between Spanish and Indian customs.

Many opportunities for this kind of reinforcement were present, but in practice the parallels were not drawn close enough for use. Thus the ritual of Xipe Totec, with human flaying to symbolize the renewal of vegetation, had a Christian parallel in the martyrdom by flaying suffered by St. Bartholomew. The apostle is often represented in colonial art, and many churches are dedicated to him, but no allusion to the pre-Conquest symbolism of flaying is ever apparent, nor is any conflation of Xipe symbolism with that of St. Bartholomew known.

Fragmentation. Survivals of odds and ends of native ornament, torn from context and repeated as "empty" decorative themes, rarely appear in sixteenth-century art. One example is convincing: in the mural paintings at the Augustinian cloister of Culhuacán, south of Mexico City, painted about 1570–80 (Gorbea 1958) the borders are repetitions of the pre-Conquest stepped-fret meander, or *Xicalcoliuhqui*. This symbol appeared most frequently in Cholula polychrome pottery designs. The form is properly listed among the most common and widespread of pre-Conquest geometric decorations. Its wide diffusion suggests that even in pre-Conquest time no highly specialized or restricted symbolism was read into it.[9] Such forms are comparable to the flotsam of a shipwreck, to the wooden fragments and buoyant objects washed ashore and preserved as mementos by uncomprehending foreigners.

Bits of empty decoration like the Culhuacán borders are important, however, as early dated examples of the most abundant category of "survival art" in existence, the category of tourist souvenirs decorated with archaeological themes. Enormous amounts of textile, pottery, jewelry and painting have been emblazoned with the Aztec calendar disk or with the Tiahuanaco "sun-gate" figure. These empty revivals, without meaning beyond the vague evocation of place, first appeared as an industrial phenomenon about 1875. A transformation in the direction of upper-class taste began after the First World War, when ex-

---

[9] *Editor's note:* Possibly the last unrevived native use of this symbol is to be found in modern warp-pattern belts from southern Peru.

patriate artists, like William Spratling in Tasco, made use of rural artisans for the execution of designs aimed to appeal to the moneyed and discriminating traveler (Spratling 1955:63–90). Truman Bailey in Lima is another such director of revival design, using highland artisans brought together from many provinces. Many items of native technology, like the dye-stuffs of the central Andes, have thus been recovered from obscurity and probable oblivion, to be mixed into the immense technological repertory of modern industrial art.

Thus the principal native survivals in post-Conquest life are nearly all useful and technical, pertaining either to language or economic life. Other than in language, symbolic and expressive behavior of all kinds was discarded early in colonial history never to be recalled or revived unless as documents by modern students of the history of culture, long after the extinction of native art.

If we now return to the eschatological theme, of the ways in which cultures terminate, it is instructive to compare the end of the American Indian society with the end of the Roman Empire. The events are comparable as to magnitude alone; otherwise they differ most radically. The end of the Roman state was gradual, enduring several centuries, unlike the nearly instantaneous conquests during one generation of the principal American Indian peoples. The Roman Empire was slowly flooded by barbarians and by eastern Mediterranean mystic religions. Its aristocracy was ruined or destroyed by a barbarianized army (Rostovtzeff 1927:Vol. II). The American peoples were conquered by the emissaries of a unified nation possessing more viable ethical and technological resources than their victims. The survival of Roman antiquity in Europe was generally regarded by the historically conscious ruling classes both as a guiding heritage and as a burdensome model of superior achievement, which mediaeval men struggled to equal or surpass until the Renaissance. The survival of antiquity in America rapidly faded into oblivion, as all peoples gravitated into the domain of European technology and of Christian ethical standards, often of their own volition, and as if in flight from the limitations of pre-Conquest cultural life.

In short, the differences are those of termination by gradual dilution and replacement in the Roman case, as contrasted with integral transformation into the European model in the American case. The ethnic dilution of the Roman state facilitated those massive survivals of superior ancient knowledge among disoriented peoples that animated the Middle Ages until the Renaissance. In Europe, the technology of the Roman could only be imperfectly imitated during the Middle Ages. The symbolic forms of classical antiquity could be used to implement and propagate the ethical system of Christian religion. But the integral transformation of America required the destruction of all symbolic expressions of Indian intellectual tradition, and the Spaniards permitted only the technologically useful elements of economic behavior to survive.

The slow ending of Greco-Roman civilization was the end of a system of political control. After its disintegration, the spiritual and technical achievements of antiquity survived as living traditions of overwhelming superiority. Of this mode of survival there is practically no trace in America, unless it is in an illusion of Indian superiority held among the more sentimental or opportunistic followers of the twentieth-century movement of *indigenismo*. *Indigenismo* seeks to establish the economic and political rights of the native peoples of America. The intellectual foundations of *indigenismo*, however, are built upon the political theories of the eighteenth and nineteenth centuries in Europe and upon humanitarian demands for victims of racial and economic oppression. There is no native philosophical or religious tradition upon which *indigenismo* rests. Its intellectual boundaries are those of European thought alone.

The end of American Indian civilization came by total replacement in symbolic matters with significant residues surviving only in economically useful products, like corn, peanuts, chocolate, and tomatoes and potatoes (Nordenskiöld 1931). Are there other examples of this mode of ending in history? Probably not,

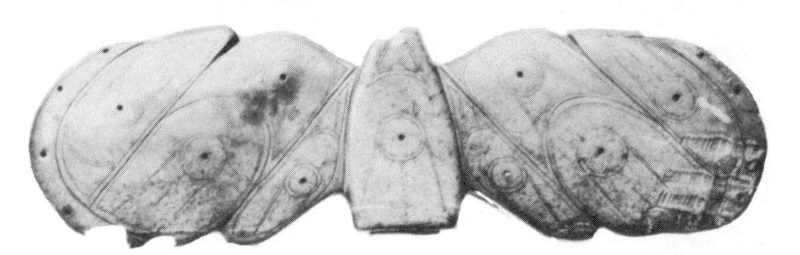

PLATE 20 Old Bering Sea winged object of walrus ivory, from St. Lawrence Island, Alaska. The original use of these pieces is unknown; they may have been part of spear-holding equipment carried on kayaks, or part of spear-throwers.

PLATE 21 *(left)* Ivory socket-piece for a harpoon, modeled in the form of a reptile head, Old Bering Sea tradition. Both Fig. 1 and 2 are discussed by Rainey (20). Both are reproduced by courtesy of the Smithsonian Institution, from the collections of the U.S. National Museum, Washington, D.C.

PLATE 22 Fantastic wooden Eskimo "spirit mask," of Lower Yukon, Alaska. This particular mask is said to represent the bad spirit of the mountain. (See Introduction and Rainey.) Courtesy of the Lowie Museum of Anthropology, University of California, Berkeley (2-6920).

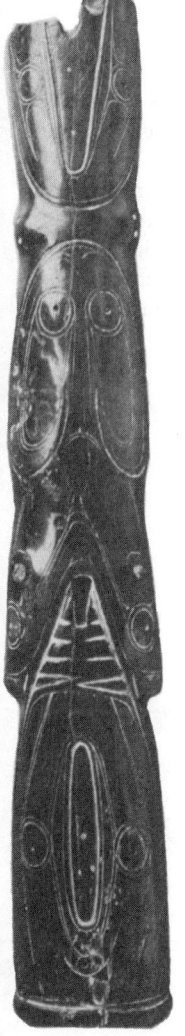

PLATE 23 Haida "totem poles" from Skidegate, Queen Charlotte Islands, British Columbia. Rather than totemic representations, these are family crests with their associated myths. The wide boards across the top of the "moon crest" pole signifies a burial pole; behind the boards a box holds the body of the deceased. The taller pole at the right is probably a commemorative pole. Courtesy of the Field Museum of Natural History, Chicago.

PLATE 24 Carved wooden ceremonial hat, worn as part of a dancing costume, probably Tlingit. The basketry rings indicate high status, and the number of potlatches given. The figure represents a wolf. Courtesy of the National Museums of Canada, Ottawa.

PLATE 25 Kwakiutl Komokwa mask. The many round protuberances indicate its undersea nature, and are identified as "octopus tentacle suckers" and "sea anemones" by Indian informants, according to Audrey Hawthorne (1967: 240). Courtesy of the Field Museum of Natural History, Chicago (19266).

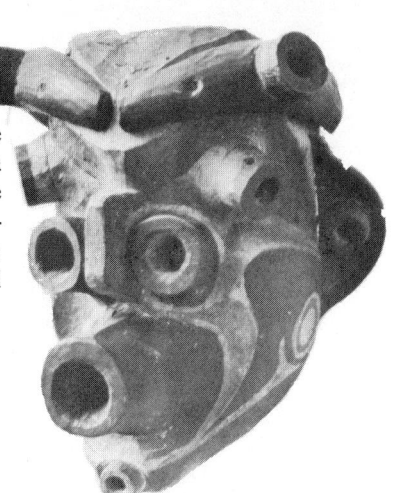

PLATE 26 Tsimshian round rattle, in an old style. This type was used by shamans, the hawklike face representing one of his spirit helpers. Courtesy of the National Museums of Canada, Ottawa.

PLATE 27 Unfinished Haida grave figurine, known as "the dead shaman in apron." He holds gambling toggles in his hands. This work, which illustrates the best of Haida realism, is attributed to the carver Charles Edensaw (1839-1924). From the Reverend Sheldon Jackson collection, by courtesy of the Museum of Natural History, Princeton University, Princeton, New Jersey.

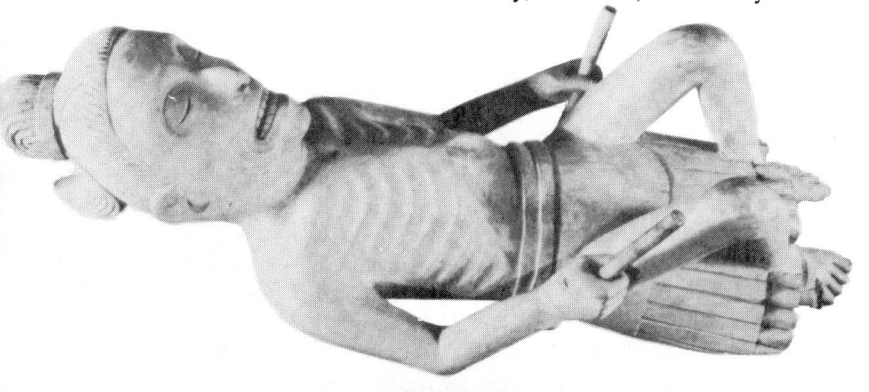

PLATE 28 Terra cotta head from Tare, Nigeria. The flaring pierced nostrils, pierced eyes, and conical form of the head are characteristic of Nok style (6½").

PLATE 29 Magnificent terra cotta head from a royal figure, found at Ita Yemoo, 1958, where it was impacted in the potsherd pavement.

PLATE 30 Brass head from Wunmoniji Compound, Ife. Traces of paint are still visible around the eyes. The head is now in the Ife Museum. (11¾".) All three figures are by courtesy of Frank Willett, who discusses them (21).

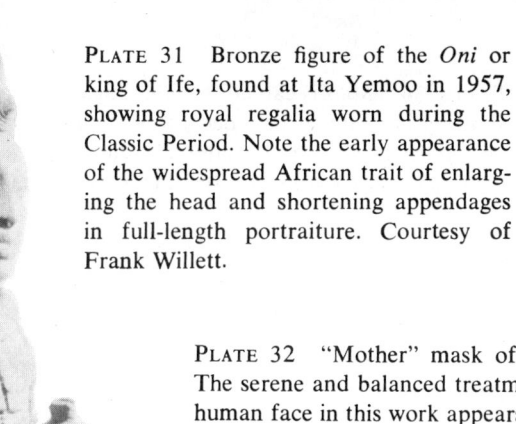

PLATE 31 Bronze figure of the *Oni* or king of Ife, found at Ita Yemoo in 1957, showing royal regalia worn during the Classic Period. Note the early appearance of the widespread African trait of enlarging the head and shortening appendages in full-length portraiture. Courtesy of Frank Willett.

PLATE 32 "Mother" mask of the Dan. The serene and balanced treatment of the human face in this work appears to reflect its function of settling strife and protecting the newborn. Gerbrands (22) discusses the making and uses of these masks. Courtesy of Sammlung für Völkerkunde, der Universität, Zürich (10032).

PLATE 33 Reliquary figure, Bakota, Gabon. This wooden figure covered with copper and brass sheeting manifests a spirit of the dead, and acts as "guardian" of the skull basket. It illustrates the extreme abstraction of the human face and figure of some African works. (30¾".) Courtesy of Sammlung für Völkerkunde, der Universität, Zürich (8286).

PLATE 34 Maori carved wooden figure, apparently unfinished, showing intricate surface decoration characteristic of New Zealand and much of Polynesia. Tattooing utilized the same curvilinear all over designs. Courtesy of the Field Museum of Natural History, Chicago (273933).

PLATE 35 Wooden image of a deity, Caroline Islands, which exhibits the tendency to simplification and geometric abstraction characteristic of Micronesian art, (15½".) Courtesy of the Honolulu Academy of Arts, Hawaii (HAA #4752).

PLATE 36   Mortuary figure (korowaar, korwar, or korvar) from Dutch New Guinea. These were regarded as residing places for the dead, and highly sacred. The figure was carved during life, so as to be ready to receive the spirit at the moment of death. See Muensterberger (6) and Linton and Wingert (23). (12″ high.) Courtesy of The University Museum, University of Pennsylvania, Philadelphia (P 3587).

PLATE 37   Ancestor tablet of carved and painted wood from Maipua, Gulf of Papua, New Guinea. These sacred boards are kept in the men's houses; many have secret names with magical properties. Courtesy of the Field Museum of Natural History, Chicago (142390).

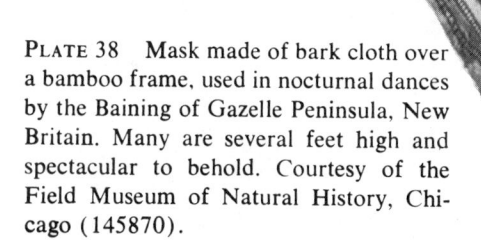

PLATE 38   Mask made of bark cloth over a bamboo frame, used in nocturnal dances by the Baining of Gazelle Peninsula, New Britain. Many are several feet high and spectacular to behold. Courtesy of the Field Museum of Natural History, Chicago (145870).

PLATE 39 Ancestor figure *(uli)* of carved and painted wood, New Ireland. They are used in highly sacred rites for males, discussed by Linton and Wingert (23). (48½" high.) Courtesy of the Field Museum of Natural History, Chicago (144001).

PLATE 40 Large carved and painted mask in the form of a wild pig's head, New Ireland. This is an excellent example of the exuberant and violent style, a riot of clashing forms, movements, and colors, which characterizes the art of the area. Courtesy of the Field Museum of Natural History, Chicago (138855).

for only in the period of the voyages of discovery, could such disparate cultures as those of Spain and America be brought into contact. At all other times, the differences between more advanced or urban peoples have been more gently graded, and more slowly resolved. Never before and probably never again will a nation be able to profit from such a tremendous potential energy of difference between national and tribal cultures as in Renaissance America, when the confrontation of Spaniards and American Indians produced a reaction violent enough to strip apart the symbolic system from the practical behavior of an entire continent. Save for rare exceptions, the pre-Columbian arts are gone. Only the practical economic behavior, and a few superstitious rites survive among the rural proletariat. These parts of pre-Conquest life were enriched in most respects by European imports, and they are overlaid altogether by European symbolic patterns.

Our demonstration that symbolic forms are perishable, while utilitarian traits, like hardy weeds, may infiltrate situations where symbols cannot survive, has some bearing upon the issue between diffusionists and independent inventionists (M. W. Smith, ed. 1953). The traits enumerated by the new diffusionists pertain mainly to symbolic expression. The diffusionists have never given any explanation of the absence of large-wheeled vehicles and of Old World beasts of burden in America. Would these powerfully useful instruments not have survived the displacement more readily than Hindu and Buddhist symbols? Between equivalent peoples of differing traditions, tools and useful ideas travel much more quickly than symbolic forms, as we are witnessing today in the massive flow of useful ideas between Russia and the West, in contrast to the negligible exchange of symbolic forms in art, philosophy, and religion.

In respect to colonial action, differing graduated scales can be suggested for the survival of various items in the cultural repertory. The scales vary according to the magnitude of the intrusion. Most likely to weather a great displacement in the hands of a few stragglers would be useful plants and animals (index 5).

Useful crafts would be next most likely to attain perpetuation if any one survived (index 4). Then, useful symbolic knowledge such as language, explanatory myth or animalistic accounts (index 3). Aesthetic symbols would come next, in the arts of time and space (index 2). Religious beliefs: the accounting of the unknown in nature and in perception would have the lowest value (index 1).

An inverted index order attaches to these same items when a conquering people, strong in numbers and tenaciously persistent in its colonizing ambition, rules a subject population of retarded culture. Thus with Spain in America: religion came first to Indian notice; then art; then the useful skills and crafts.

The viability of native symbolic matter varied therefore inversely with the magnitude and staying power of the intruder. Powerful and numerous invaders can impose their religion at once upon a retarded and conquered people, whose own religious tradition then withers away. Art is the symbolic expression accompanying this displacement. Utility and practical need probably governed the later sequence of adoptions, rejections and displacements. For early man in America, and for all the principal regions of pre-Columbian life, we have no evidence that any Old World invader other than the conquistador was ever numerous enough to impose his religion to the exclusion of his useful knowledge.

AFRICAN INFLUENCE
ON THE MUSIC OF THE AMERICAS[1]

Richard Alan Waterman

THERE ARE two reasons why African musical elements have influenced the musical styles of the Americas. In the first place, American Negro groups have remained relatively homogeneous with regard to culture patterns and remarkably so with respect to in-group solidarity. This has almost guaranteed the retention of any values not in conflict with the prevailing Euro-American culture pattern. Second, there is enough similarity between African and European music to permit musical syncretism. This has put some aspects of African musical style in the category of traditions not destined to be forced out of existence because of their deviation from accepted norms. The first factor has been dealt with adequately by Herskovits (1937, 1941; Herskovits and Herskovits 1934, 1936, 1947). The second, less well

---

Reprinted from Selected Papers of the XXIX International Congress of Americanists, *Acculturation in the Americas,* Sol Tax, editor, University of Chicago Press, 1952, pp. 207–18, with permission of the editor, the University of Chicago Press, and the author.

[1] The writer gratefully acknowledges the aid of the Carnegie Corporation of New York in providing a field grant for ethnomusicological study among African-derived religious cults in Cuba during the summers of 1946 and 1948, from which stemmed many of the insights documented in this paper. He is even more deeply indebted to the Social Science Research Council of Northwestern University and to the Graduate School of that institution for their financial support over a period of years of a program of research which has resulted in the establishment of the Laboratory of Comparative Musicology and in most of the work in the field of Afro-American music which is summarized here.

known because of the lack, until recently, of reliable data concerning the music of Africa, will be given consideration here.

In some respects, the western one-third of the Old World land mass is musically homogeneous, for it is set off from the other major musical areas by the extent of its reliance on the diatonic scale and by its use of harmony. Although the former appears sporadically elsewhere, as, for example, in China, it has not, except in the West, been used as the basis for musical development, and is to be distinguished sharply from the microtonal scalar system of the Indo-Arabic area. Harmony, on the other hand, appears in aboriginal music nowhere but in the western one-third of the Old World, where it is common in European folk music and African tribal music. Three points must be made here in amplification and clarification of this statement. In the first place, no reference is intended to the European school of literate music and musical theory; this has developed many aspects of music, and harmony in particular, to a point of complexity where it can scarcely be compared to either European folk music or African tribal music. Second, there exists a broad intrusive belt of Arabic and Arabic-influenced music which stretches across the middle of the western area, along both shores of the Mediterranean. Since the times of ancient history this alien musical outcropping has masked the fact of the previous existence of a continuous harmony-using bloc of cultures established earlier in the area.

The third point concerns the oft repeated assertion that Africans, except those who have been in contact with European music, use harmony only as the accidental result of polyphonic overlapping of leader and chorus phrases. This last fact merits closer examination, since it contradicts—by fiat, as it were—the evidence now available in many recordings of African music. It seems to have stemmed from certain preconceptions concerning the evolution of music which have proved inapplicable to the present case. The argument, in terms of these preconceptions, is simply that Africans had not developed enough culturally to be expected to have harmony. Given this bias, it is easy to see, in view of some factors immediately to be adduced, how an ethnomusicologist of a decade or two ago could have listened to African music, and even have transcribed African music, without ever hearing harmony used, even though harmony may actually have been present.

Let us first consider the nature of the machines used in gathering early recordings of African music. These necessarily were acoustical rather than electrical. A singer whose voice was being recorded had usually to be carefully placed in front of the horn. He had to sing loudly, and, even so, a deviation of any magnitude from the correct position might serve to put his voice out of collecting range. Since the usual field musicological task is looked upon simply as the collection of melodies, it is not difficult to comprehend how choral backgrounds, possibly harmonized, could elude the ear of the laboratory musicologist who heard only the recorded result, although he might be making use of the best equipment available at the time. Coupled to this consideration is the circumstance that most studies of African music were done by trained music analysts using phonographic materials provided by other, perhaps even "non-musical" researchers. Purely as a practical matter this division of labor between the collector in the field and the analyst in the laboratory, so unfortunate for the development of ethnomusicology as a branch of cultural anthropology, has been, until recently, a standard arrangement for the conducting of research in this discipline and is, of course, very effective in those rare cases in which true collaboration has been achieved between collector and analyst.

The fact that many African tribal styles actually do not use harmony to any great extent bolstered the accepted position. "Negro Africa" encompasses a number of peoples, and while, as will be seen presently, certain generalizations may be made concerning the musical style of the whole area, the great variety of styles actually present must never be lost sight of. The peoples of a large section of Dahomey, for example, manage to do almost entirely without harmony, while the Ashanti, in the neighboring West African territory of the Gold Coast, seem to employ at least two-part, and frequently three- and four-part, harmony for almost all of their music. It may be, therefore, that the notion of the absence of harmony in African music was connected initially with the fact that early samples came from non-harmonizing areas. Also, although this can by no means be used as a valid explanation of African harmony, it is true that the ubiquitous "overlapping call-and-response" pattern provides many instances of a sort of sporadic, although accidental, harmony when the beginning notes of the chorus refrain happen to harmonize with the simultaneously sounded terminal tones of the soloist's phrase.

That a hypothesis concerning the absence of harmony in African music could have been framed on the basis of early data presented, then, is completely understandable; how the hypothesis came to be accepted as fact and how it managed to persist to this day are less readily understood. Yet we must realize that not only in ethnomusicology does it occur that an authoritatively stated, although invalid, generalization comes to have considerable inertia of its own. Nevertheless, facts, in the form of phonographic recordings, indicate that singing in harmony is common among African tribesmen. The presumption that the development of African music must of necessity be following the same evolutionary path blazed by European academic music is, furthermore, seriously undermined by recorded examples of the facile use by non-Europeanized African tribesmen of intervals considered extremely "modern" when encountered in European harmony.[2] African harmony, while it has remained simple, as has that of most European folk songs, nevertheless seems in some areas to have had certain striking autonomous developments.

The presence of the same basic concept of scale and the use of harmony in both Europe and Africa have made easy and inevitable the many varieties of Euro-African musical syncretism to be observed in the New World. It is, for example, easy to

---

[2] Observe, for example, the use of parallel seconds in the choral music of the Babira of the Belgian Congo in "The Belgian Congo Records," *Denis-Roosevelt Expedition Album,* New York: General Records, Inc. Side No. 2.

understand how, to a member of an early American Negro group steeped in the value and behavior patterns of West African musical tradition, the European music which came to his attention must have appeared mainly as a source of new musical ideas to be worked out in terms of African concepts and techniques. Almost nothing in European folk music, to phrase the matter cautiously, is incompatible with African musical style, and much of the European material fits readily into the generalized African musical mold. An indicator of the fact that this is not true of any two styles of music taken at random is afforded by the rarity of examples of genuine syncretization between American Indian music and the music of either Europe or Africa.

Thus, in the United States as in other New World areas controlled by English-speaking Europeans, folk tunes and hymns stemming from the British Isles were often seized upon by African slaves and their descendants and, after suitable remodeling, adopted as American Negro tunes. The remodeling process was one of Africanization, and the tunes which emerged are best to be interpreted as European-inspired African music. In the Iberian-controlled areas of the New World, an additional factor facilitated the process of syncretization. The fact that the music of Spain and Portugal had already, over a period of several generations before the beginning of the slave trade with the Americas, been influenced by African musical traits imported along with West African slaves, was something that gave Euro-African musical syncretization in Latin America a head start, so to speak.

Both of the criteria offered above for the persistence of a tradition in an acculturative situation are thus seen to have been fulfilled in the case of the African musical style in the Americas. There has been sufficient density of Negro population, sufficient Negro group-consciousness, and sufficient homogeneity with respect to African musical values in most of the Negro areas of the New World to permit the transmission of these values to the young in consistent fashion. The sociological isolation of some of these Negro groups without relation to the actual proportions of African ancestry in the genealogies of members of the groups, as is the case in the United States, must not be overlooked as an important factor in maintaining relatively inviolate the African musical values in spite of a considerable infusion of non-African genetic strains. The ease with which many European musical traits could be incorporated into the African patterns simply permitted, through the processes of reinterpretation and syncretization, a retention of African musical formulae in bodies of New World Negro music which have become, if we start with African music, more and more European with each generation as the blending progressed.

This statement has been intended to show how African musical tradition, or at least, certain aspects of it, could persist in the New World. There would be no reason for the explanation, since such persistences of tradition are commonplace in acculturative situations, were it not for the fact that a sort of *academic* tradition has been in force which, placing emphasis on the many changes in the lives of the American Negroes brought about first by slavery, and later by the exigencies of life as a member of a minority underprivileged group, has systematically denied both the fact and the possibility of such persistence of African tradition.

This is not to say, of course, that American Negro music must be derived entirely from Europe or entirely from Africa. Since the music actually is, for the most part, a blend of both African and European idioms, the answer to the question of derivation may well depend largely on the initial direction of approach to the problem. Thus, Negro spirituals have been pronounced by some scholars to be derived solely from Europe because they contain a great many Euro-American elements; the problem of the provenience of jazz, on the other hand, has been muddled by the proclamations of certain writers who, discerning Africanisms in that form of music, insist that jazz is purely African.

Attention thus far has been concentrated upon the aspects of African music which coincide with European; however, African music, obviously, is not European music. The European folk song is typically more complex harmonically and simpler rhythmically than African tribal song. Modulation from key to key, for example, is virtually unknown in African tribal music, while the consistent use of multiple meter—two or three time-signatures at once, as it were—is equally unknown in European songs. Melodic structure, however, seems to be at about the same level of complexity in both areas, although different forms are utilized.

The outstanding feature of African music which sets it most apart from that of Europe is the rhythm, a focal value which is implemented in a great number of ways. As Herskovits (1950:3) has written, "for the African, the important thing about rhythm is to have it, regardless of how it is produced." African rhythms have been spoken of (Jones 1949:51) as "incredible and incomprehensible to us." While this may be rejected as the counsel of defeat, it is undoubtedly true that the appreciation of African rhythms requires the development of a musical sense that, in the individual conditioned only to the norms of European music, usually lies somewhat dormant.

This may be spoken of as the *metronome sense*. Until it is developed, much of the aspect of African music most important to the African may well remain incomprehensible to the most careful investigator. From the point of view of the listener, it entails habits of conceiving any music as structured along a theoretical framework of beats regularly spaced in time and of cooperating in terms of overt or inhibited motor behavior with the pulses of this metric pattern whether or not the beats are expressed in actual melodic or percussion tones. Essentially, this simply means that African music, with few exceptions, is to be regarded as music for the dance, although the "dance" involved may be entirely a mental one. Since this metronome sense is of such basic importance, it is obvious that the music is conceived and executed in terms of it; it is assumed without question or consideration to be part of the perceptual equipment of both musicians and listeners and is, in the most complete way, taken for granted. When the beat is actually sounded, it serves as a confirmation of this subjective beat. And because it amounts to an unverbalized point of view concerning all music, this traditional value which differentiates African from "pure" European systems of musical appreciation is a typical example of the variety of subliminal culture pattern most immune to the pressures of an acculturative situation.

The metronome sense is not limited to the African; one variety of it is necessary in playing or listening to Hindu music, for example. But complete reliance on it, as a part of the standard musical equipment of every individual in making music, is an exclusively African musical trait. The metronome sense, in an extremely limited way, is also necessary in appreciating European music, particularly European social dance music and marching tunes. The rhythmic music of Europe, however, is so structured as to emphasize the very metric elements which African music is most likey to take for granted—the up-beat and the down-beat. The assumption by an African musician that his audience is supplying these fundamental beats permits him to elaborate his rhythms with these as a base, whereas the European tradition requires such close attention to their concrete expressions that rhythmic elaboration is limited for the most part to mere ornament. From the point of view of European music, African music introduces a new rhythmic dimension.

Additional features of African music which set it off markedly from that of Europe may be summarized as follows:

Dominance of percussion. Most African music includes, and depends upon, percussion instruments. Indeed, most African musical instruments are of this type, including a bewildering array of drums, rattles, and gongs. These are the necessary implements for the peculiarly African elaboration of rhythmic and metric constellations. Melodic instruments, also, are utilized for their percussive values, as in the case of "thumb pianos," xylophones, and, for the last three centuries or so, the European guitar. Conversely, the gongs and drums frequently have melodic and harmonic importance. The percussive effect of hand-clapping, often in intricate rhythmic patterns, is also utilized constantly in African music.

Polymeter. European rhythms are typically based on single metrical schemes, more or less elaborated according to the types of music the rhythms are used to reinforce. In European folk and popular music, particularly that used as accompaniment to the dance, the tempo is steady; in academic forms, the tempo may be varied greatly. African music, on the other hand—based, as we have seen, on the invariant or accelerated tempo consistent with the metronome sense—uses the interplay of two or more metrical frameworks as the primary material out of which the music is built. While the individual components may be quite simple, the combination is likely to sound to European-trained ears completely puzzling, particularly when, as often happens, rhythmic emphasis shifts back and forth from meter to meter. Anyone who cares to attempt to perform a $6/8$ beat with one hand, a $4/4$ beat with the other, and a $3/4$ tap with the toe of one foot will be convinced of the complexity, and will learn something about the character, of African multiple meter. This particular relationship of time signatures is a common pattern in African musical rhythm. The various rhythms are usually expressed by drums or other percussion instruments, but they need not be. Signs that these complex patterns pervade all of the African feeling for music are to be read in the accent patterns of melodies both instrumental and vocal and are likewise evident in the motor behavior of participants in African dance.

Off-beat phrasing of melodic accents. From the African tradition of taking for granted the presence of a basic musical beat in the mind of the performer and auditor alike has stemmed not only the elaboration of meters just discussed, but also a quite different artistic technique completely dependent for its effect on the metronome sense. Syncopation, as utilized in European music, is in a way the simplest form of this technique, but in the absence of the metronome sense further development could hardly occur. In popular writings on the subject of jazz, the term "syncopation" has been used to characterize the technique as it appears in that form of music. However, in terms of total musical effect this label is felt to be misleading, and the more cumbersome but more general designation, offbeat phrasing of melodic accents, is preferred by the author.

In transcriptions of African music this pattern appears in the form of notes tied together across bar lines or across other main beats. Melodic tones, and particularly accented ones, occur between the sounded or implied beats of the measure with great frequency. The beat is, so to speak, temporarily suspended, i.e., delayed or advanced in melodic execution, sometimes for single notes (syncopation), sometimes for long series of notes. The displacement is by no means a random one, however, for the melodic notes not coinciding with the beat are invariably sounded, with great nicety, precisely on one of the points of either a duple or a triple division of the beat. Viewed a different way, this may be seen as a placement of tones *on* the beat of an implied meter at a tempo twice or thrice that of the controlling rhythm.

Certain psychological aspects of African off-beat phrasing must be considered if the pattern is to be fully understood. The maintenance of a subjective meter, in terms of the metronome sense, requires effort and, more particularly, a series of efforts regularly spaced in time. The regular recurrence of these "rhythmic awarenesses" involves the expectancy, at the moment of any beat, that the next beat will occur precisely at some succeeding moment determined by the tempo. Subjectively, the beat does occur. If it is reinforced by an objective stimulus in the form of a percussive or melodic tone, the metronome sense is reassured, and the effort involved in the subjective beat is masked by the effort of perceiving the objective pulse. If the objective beat is omitted, however, the co-operating auditor becomes very much aware of the subjective beat, which thus attains for him greatly increased significance. If the objective beat occurs ahead of time, the auditor, unprepared for it, perceives it and assigns to it the additional importance always accorded the unexpected, further reinforcing it with his subjective pulse which occurs at the "proper" time in terms of his experience. If the objective beat is delayed, the period of suspense between subjective and objective beats likewise increases the auditor's awareness of the rhythm. When the objective, audible beat occurs halfway between two subjective pulsations, as is frequently the case, both mechanisms operate to give the off-beat tone heightened significance.

On the other hand, it is apparent that if a whole tune were to be sung in such a way that each note occurred a half-beat ahead of a corresponding beat established by the subjective metronome on the basis of cues from, say, the initial beats of a percussion instrument, the subjective beats would sooner or later, depending on the degree of intransigence of the metronome sense of the auditor, come to be interpreted as off-beats, and hence would be realigned so as to coincide with the new beat pattern. In other words, complete "off-beating" has the same effect as complete lack of off-beat patterns; it is, in these terms, meaningless.

The off-beat phrasing of accents, then, must threaten, but never quite destroy, the orientation of the listener's subjective metronome. In practice, this means that a sufficient number of notes of varying degrees of importance in the structure of the melody must coincide with the auditor's rhythmic set to validate the gestalt through reinforcement of key points. A very few notes so placed will suffice for a listener whose metronome sense is highly developed, particularly since at least one percussion instrument is likely to reinforce the main beat. Occasions where melodic notes are on the beat, and percussion notes are off, are more trying to the metronome sense than the usual situation just sketched, and, of course, melodic notes may be in an off-beat relationship to one meter in such a way as to suggest even more complex relationships with other simultaneous meters. Theoretically, elaborations of the combination of polymeter with off-beat phrasing are almost endless. In practice, however, limits are set to this development by the fact that, regardless of conditioning, no musician's and no listener's metronome sense operates beyond a certain point of complexity. This point, however, is likely to be far beyond anything the European tradition would consider rhythmically intelligible.

Overlapping call-and-response patterns. While antiphonal song-patterning, whereby a leader sings phrases which alternate with phrases sung by a chorus, is known all over the world, nowhere else is this form so important as in Africa, where almost all songs are constructed in this manner. A peculiarity of the African call-and-response pattern, found but infrequently elsewhere, is that the chorus phrase regularly commences while the soloist is still singing; the leader, on his part, begins his phrase before the chorus has finished. This phenomenon is quite simply explained in terms of the African musical tradition of the primacy of rhythm. The entrance of the solo or the chorus part on the proper beat of the measure is the important thing, not the effects attained through antiphony of polyphony. Examples of call-and-response music in which the solo part, for one reason or another, drops out for a time, indicate clearly that the chorus part, rhythmical and repetitive, is the mainstay of the songs and the one really inexorable component of their rhythmic structure. The leader, receiving solid rhythmic support from the metrically accurate, rolling repetition of phrases by the chorus, is free to embroider as he will.

The metronome sense, then, together with these four basic characteristics related to or derived from it, accounts for the major differences between tribal African and European folk and popular music. In attempting to trace the influence of African musical ideas on the music of the Americas, we must, therefore, pay particular attention to these features. The extension of purely rhythmic aspects of African musical style to Western Hemisphere music has already been discussed at some length (Waterman 1948:3–16). Certain additional musical and allied practices of that area may, however, be mentioned here, and the fact of their appearance in the Americas simply indicated. While, as has been mentioned, the African scale is diatonic like that of Europe, the tendency toward variable intonation of the third and seventh of the scale has occasionally been noted in West African music.[3] This is the "blues" scale. West African song often utilizes the device of contrapuntal duet, with or without a recurrent chorus

---

[3] For a typical example of this, hear *Tribal, Folk, and Cafe Music of West Africa*, New York: Field Recordings, Inc. 1950. Album I, Song 5C.

phrase.[4] This pattern is important in the religious singing of southern United States Negroes. The use of song as a device for social control and for the venting of aggression and the traditional contests of virtuosity in singing and playing are functioning elements of West African culture today, as they are of such musical styles as the Trinidad "calypso" in the New World. The counter-clockwise circle dance, in which the dancers make up a part of the singing chorus, is common both in West Africa and in the New World, as is the custom of singing in falsetto. Finally, there is, in West Africa, little difference, in purely musical terms, between sacred and secular usage; this is mirrored in all the areas of Negro settlement in the Americas.

There are two aspects of the problem of African influence on the music of the Americas. One concerns the music of predominantly Negro populations, the other the spread of stylistic elements from American Negro music to the music of New World populations in general. Also, two distinct geographical areas—roughly, North American and Latin American—must be considered separately, since they have had different acculturation histories.

In the Negro population of Brazil all traits[5] of African music have been retained, and many songs are sung in West African languages (Herskovits and Waterman 1949:65–127).[6] Negro songs of Dutch Guiana exhibit all the listed traits of West African music; they are, however, sung in a creolized language compounded, for the most part, of English vocabulary and West African phonetics and grammar (Herskovits and Herskovits 1936; Kolinski 1936). In Haiti, songs of the Vodun cult show all traits of African music, as do many secular songs (Courlander

---

[4] *Ibid.* Album II, Record 6.
[5] "All traits" of African music, in the present list, must be taken to mean those basic traits discussed above as distinguishing tribal African from European folk music: the metronome sense, dominance of percussion, polymeter, off-beat phrasing, and overlapping call-and-response patterns.
[6] Subsequent research by Alan P. Merriam, using a larger sample of Afro-Bahian cult music, confirms these findings (Waterman 1951).

1939).[7] In Jamaica, both sacred and secular songs of the Negroes of the Port Morant district frequently show the five "basic" African traits.[8] Found here also is the use of a large African vocabulary, both in songs and in actual conversation. Negro music of the Island of Trinidad ranges from the religious songs of the Shango Cult of Port-of-Spain, conceived in purely African style, through the various urban secular styles, including the "calypso," in which all the basic African traits are to be observed, to the "reels," "quadrilles," "bongos," and "beles" of the rural districts, in which European and African traits are commingled, although all the basic African traits are likely to appear (Waterman 1943). Most of the folk music of Puerto Rico is derived from Spain, although the style called "la bomba" is of purely African conception, while the popular urban Negro style, the *plena* (Puerto Rican equivalent of the calypso) sometimes shows all the African traits.[9] Percussion instruments of African origin are used in connection with all the above styles.

In United States Negro musical styles, one of the main African components, polymeter, is usually absent except by implication, and there is a dearth of African-type musical instruments.[10] Metronomism, however, is present in all Negro sacred and secular styles, as is the importance of percussion (wherever percussion instruments or effects are not proscribed by circumstances) and the overlapping call-and-response pattern.

In modern American Negro spirituals and, to a greater degree, in the urban gospel hymns, percussion effects are stressed even in

---

[7] And hear his *Folk Music of Haiti*, Album No. 1417, New York: Ethnic Folkways Library.
[8] Recorded 1950, by Joseph G. Moore. To be deposited with the Laboratory of Comparative Musicology, Department of Anthropology, Northwestern University.
[9] See Richard A. Waterman, *Folk Music of Puerto Rico* (Library of Congress, Archive of American Folk Song, Album XVII). Washington, D.C., Government Printing Office, 1947.
[10] See, however, Courlander's convincing derivation of the United States Negro washtub bass fiddle from the West African "earth bow," in the pamphlet accompanying *Folk Music of Haiti*, Albums Nos. 1417 and 1418. New York: Ethnic Folkways Library.

the absence of actual instruments, and the instruments (sometimes, but rarely, the pipe-organ, usually the piano, and frequently the guitar and tambourine) used are, in general, exploited to the full extent of their percussive possibilities (Waterman 1951). The overlapping call-and-response and the off-beat phrasing of melodic accents are important features of the religious music of the United States Negro, and a well-developed metronome sense is required for its appreciation. These same traits, appearing in secular music—for the distinction between sacred and secular styles in this music is generally to be made on the basis of the words rather than the music—characterize the kind of Negro music known commercially as "rhythm and blues." In the 1960s, under the generic term "soul music," this Negro style, with its characteristic melisma and consciously varied tonal qualities, attained considerable popularity both as religious and as secular music.

It is evident, then, that in the regions mentioned, which span the habitat of the Negro in the Americas, music associated with Negroes is, in terms of the five dominant values listed, predominantly African. There are, even in the United States, cases of Negro songs with melodies almost identical to recorded African songs.[11] These identities must be laid to the fact that the songs have sprung from similar roots.

The music of these same areas which is *not* specifically identified with Negro populations likewise shows, in many instances, the same African traits. The diagnostic rhythm schemes of the Brazilian *samba* and the Cuban *rumba* and *conga,* to mention only three examples, are common in West African music. In general, most styles of popular dance music in these Latin Ameri-

---

[11] Hear, for example, "Run Old Jeremiah," in John A. Lomax and Alan Lomax: *Afro-American Spirituals, Work Songs, and Ballads.* (Library of Congress, Archive of American Folk Song, Album III) and compare it with "Bahutu Dance," in "The Belgian Congo Records," *Denis-Roosevelt Expedition Album.* New York: General Records, Inc. Also compare "Long John," from the Lomax album with "Mossi Chant," in *Tribal, Folk, and Cafe Music of West Africa* (Album I). New York: Field Recordings, Inc., 1950.

can countries where the Negro population is at all dense have been strongly influenced by the basic African musical patterns listed, and many African musical instruments, such as drums, calabashes, etc., are used.

The areas referred to are those in which research has been done specifically from the point of view of African acculturation. There are undoubtedly many other instances of African musical influence in Latin America. For example, the Guatemalan "national instrument" is the *marimba*—an instrument certainly derived from Africa. In Mexico, especially in the region of the former slave port of Vera Cruz, African elements appear strongly in the rhythms of the folk music. The Argentine *maxixe*, to mention another example, probably can be considered as of partly African origin.

A major artistic product of the United States is the music called "jazz." Jazz is an intricate blend of musical idioms and has also had its own evolution as an art form. It is, of course, no one thing; yet any attempt to frame an all-inclusive definition points up the fact that those elements that mark off any kind of jazz from the rest of the popular music of the United States are precisely those we have cited as diagnostic of West African music.

For example, jazz depends, for its effect, largely on the metronome sense of its listeners and its players. Jazz terminology makes constant reference to this metronome sense. Musical terms like "rock" and "swing" express ideas of rhythm foreign to European folk tradition, and stem from African concepts, as does the extremely basic idea of the application of the word "hot" to musical rhythms. The development of a "feeling for the beat," so important in jazz musicianship, is neither more nor less than the development of the metronome sense.

The tremendous importance accorded to complex percussion patterns is another basic trait of African music to appear in jazz. An appreciable proportion of African dance music is entirely drum music; the tradition of long drum solos appears in all jazz styles, and, in the United States, only in the jazz styles.

The overlapping call-and-response pattern has, in jazz, been reworked in accordance with jazz instrumentation and orchestration. Typically, a soloist plays the call phrases as an improvised variation on the melody, while an appropriate section of instruments plays the chorus pattern, repeated with only those minimal changes forced by the changing harmonies, as a "riff." Most jazz band records contain examples of this use of the riff; since it is a pattern which gives a good deal of "rock" to the music, it is frequently reserved for the last, hottest chorus.

The off-beat phrasing of melodic accents is a stylistic trait which functions in jazz in unusually clear-cut fashion perhaps because of the absence of polymetric formations, which tend to make the off-beats equivocal. Syncopation has often been spoken of as an earmark of jazz melodies; of importance here is the fact that, in addition, jazz makes constant use of the more extended off-beat phrasing patterns. It is these, rather than syncopation per se, which give to the melodic line of jazz its characteristic impelling rhythmic quality.

In the middle years of the century, largely as a result of the influence of "soul music," several varieties of "rock-and-roll" music succeeded jazz as a popular dance music. Some stemmed from jazz, which had, by the 1960's, evolved into a type of rhythmic chamber music; some, called "folk-rock," came from folk music; and much was inspired by British and Continental versions of American Negro "rhythm-and-blues," altered, simplified, and fed back into the United States musical stream by imported musical groups. The rock-and-roll styles, by contrast to jazz, involve much singing and a reliance on highly-amplified guitars and other electronic effects, together with simple, but forceful, and very prominent, percussion. They all share the African-derived musical characteristics we have noted for jazz.

In this short paper it has been possible to illustrate in only the most general way the character of African influences on the music of the Americas. To summarize: in areas (e.g., in Brazil, Haiti, and Cuba) where the official European religion permitted the syncretism of deities with the saints of the Church, African religious music has persisted almost unchanged, and African influence upon secular music has been strong. In Protestant areas where such syncretism has not been possible, the influence of African musical patterns on both religious and secular music has hinged upon a more extensive process of reinterpretation but is nonetheless considerable, in that fundamental characteristics of West African music have been retained.

In the case of the music of the Negro in the New World, we have an ideal situation for the study of musical change. We know, in general, the African side of the equation, although much field work must be done before specific tribal styles—the real raw data for our study—can be described. We also know the European side, and we are in a position to study the American results of musical acculturation. We also know enough about the general cultural contexts of the various American Negro musical styles to be able to assess both historical and contemporary factors bearing on change. Furthermore, among the less tangible aspects of culture, music is unique in that it can readily be quantified and submitted to rigid statistical analysis, although nothing of this sort has been attempted in this paper. The objective demonstration of the retention and reworking of West African tribal musical styles in the Americas, which seems likely to follow the collection of sufficient field data from specific African groups, may be expected to have relevance for the study of other cultural intangibles which, while not so easily subjected to quantitative treatment, are, like musical patterns, carried largely below the level of consciousness.

Part V ‖ ART AREAS

CRITICAL ANALYSIS OF INTERPRETATIONS, AND CONCLUSIONS AND PROBLEMS FROM *PALAEOLITHIC CAVE ART*

Peter J. Ucko and Andrée Rosenfeld

ETHNOGRAPHIC PARIETAL ART

ARTISTIC ACTIVITY is not the prerogative of any one people, group of people or area of the world. 'Primitive' and 'peasant' groups perform an enormous variety of decorative and representational practices, varying from the striking sand paintings of the North American Navaho Indians to the crudest small figure of unbaked clay among, for example, many African tribes as well as Spanish peasants. Painting also (but less so engraving and relief-work) has a very wide distribution in the 'primitive' world, an activity which is the response to many different situations. Paintings on house walls are very frequent in many areas of the world and the motifs employed for this purpose are usually abstract designs or representational items (such as hands) chosen for their visual effect, although in some cases a symbolic content has been presumed for ceremonial house-wall and door decorations. Equally frequent is the use of painting and engraving for the decoration of functional utensils or for the further embellishment of a modelled figure or carving. Except in terms of the generalised ethnographic parallel these practices are too diverse and the activities too general to have much relevance to the

---

Reprinted with abridgments by permission of the authors, Weidenfeld and Nicolson, Ltd., London, and McGraw-Hill Book Company, New York.

parietal art of Palaeolithic man, except for the parietal art in association with habitations (and possibly for mobile art). . . .

Australian aboriginal art is similar to the rock art in various different areas of the world (such as those in East Spain and those made by the Bushmen) in that human representations are frequent as are also vivacious narrative scenes usually connected with economic activities, and on both these counts it differs from Palaeolithic parietal art with its apparent absence of narration and its paucity of anthropomorphs. Australian art is not, however, the solitary response to totemic practices which it is so frequently accepted as being. Australians paint and engrave on rock walls for many different purposes. According to many statements by Mountford and McCarthy (e.g. Mountford 1961:7–8; McCarthy 1958:9; McCarthy 1960:299) Australian aboriginal art is often carried out purely for pleasure (Art for Art's Sake), to illustrate statements and stories, to record historical events of both economic and mythical/ceremonial importance (Totemic) and to act as teaching aids during initiation. Aboriginal rock art has also, sometimes, a (Sympathetic) magic importance both in the context of sorcery and increase rites. The information regarding sympathetic hunting magic is, however, less clear for although many authors believe that some Australian art has this significance 'no direct proof of this assertion has yet been obtained from native informants' (McCarthy 1965:90). Some of the difficulties involved in interpreting the significance of Australian rock art are neatly summed up in an experience recorded by Mountford (1961:13)[1] who 'found a cave painting which pictures the chase, the capture, and the cooking of an emu, a painting which should have contained all the elements of hunting magic. On questioning the aborigines about the meaning of the painting, [he] was told that it had no magical significance whatever; it was simply the record of a successful hunt. If, [his] informants explained, they wanted to catch an emu, they chanted

---

[1] A somewhat similar situation exists among the now sedentary East African Sandawe (TEN RAA, personal communication).

a magical song which made the bird so stupid and sleepy that they could approach and spear it without difficulty'. In many cases the problem whether the pictures were concerned with hunting magic or were records of a successful hunt is largely a 'question whether a painting was made before or after the incident portrayed took place' (McCarthy 1960:389) and this information is largely lacking for Australia. The information available from a few areas in Africa clearly shows that some representations were made for hunting magic, some were 'doodles' and some were executed as part of initiation ceremonies.

In all these forms of Australian aboriginal art animals, humans, weapons and vegetation feature predominantly. How far this should be taken as indicative of a significant difference from Palaeolithic parietal art is not easy to decide for interpretations by the aboriginal artists themselves make it very evident that what appears 'naturalistic' to the modern observer is very far from being the same for the aboriginal artist and it is not inconceivable that Palaeolithic 'signs' might in fact have clearly represented vegetation or humans to the Palaeolithic artists. What does seem certain is that the obvious 'pictorial compositions of everyday life' (McCarthy 1958:12) in Australian art is absent in Palaeolithic art. . . .

When it comes to more specific points about the ethnographic representations (such as their orientation, their localities within particular shelters, or their superpositioning) they share many features with the Palaeolithic parietal representations and it may, therefore, be instructive to note what is known about these aspects of living peoples' artistic works. The evidence regarding superpositioning reflects the variety of practices which exist in different parts of the world where rock art is carried out. In Australia alone it is possible to find some shelters in which representations are few and far between and others in which 'it is difficult to find a space entirely devoid of any [representations] . . . and the work of hours must have run into the labour of years, yea, of generations, because . . . one design has been carved over the top of another, time after time, until eventually the ground appear[s] as though it were covered with an elaborate carpet . . .' (Basedow 1925:303). In some cases it appears that the Australian aborigines painted or engraved over older representations without any regard for them and without caring that they were obliterating them; indeed there are examples known where red ochre has been applied to obliterate previous works and to provide the canvas for new representations. In some cases it is suggested that 'newer paintings derive some merit or value from being painted over . . . older paintings' (Macintosh 1952:269) while it is also the case that superpositioning in other cases (but by no means always) indicated meaningful associations to the aboriginal artist.

Although in most cases known the rock art of 'primitive' peoples is placed on the most suitably available vertical faces of rock outcrops, often shelters beneath which they camped or worked, there are some instances from Australia where the localities chosen for artistic representation as well as the orientation of the pictures recall some of the peculiarities of Palaeolithic parietal localities. Thus in some Australian rock shelters paintings are placed high on the shelter ceilings while others are hidden under recesses and in narrow cavities so that in each respective case the artists must have clambered up the rock walls or squeezed through narrow passages and lain on their backs to carry out their art works. Unfortunately there is very little certain information about Australian parietal localities; it has been tentatively suggested that in one particular cave a decorated recess itself signified the female womb and that the representations within this recess were chosen with this symbolism in mind, while in other cases it seems probable that the particular totemic or historical myths with which the artistic representations are connected themselves influenced or dictated the choice of locality. There are occasions where the associated myth appears to have influenced the orientation of representations and many other occasions where it is the available rock surface which has conditioned orientation.

Only for the Australian art works on rocks which are connected with totemic 'maintenance' rites is there evidence of regular retouching of paintings, for the addition or improvement of representations for critical reasons of inaccuracy or technical incompetence must be an occasional and irregular occurrence. In certain parts of Australia where rock art was used for totemic ceremonies the act of retouching or renovating a painting or engraving was the mechanical means of ensuring the reactivation of the totemic 'magic' so that, for example, the retouching of certain paintings causes the rain to fall and the plentiful supply of food animals and plants.

In Australia and Africa the available information suggests that anyone (at least any male) can be an artist although, everywhere, some people are well known as more skillful than others and their paintings and engravings are easily recognised and are fully appreciated. There seems very little standardisation in Australia regarding who is allowed to see rock wall representations; in many cases it has been claimed that shelters which contain totemic paintings and engravings are sacred spots into which few are allowed, but examples are frequent where there is no such selectivity and anyone is free to admire the representations. The variety of Australian artistic practice is again seen in the situation where some shelters are 'owned' by a particular person to whom payments are made before anyone is allowed to paint or engrave in his shelter, while other shelters contain not only totemic representations but also (sometimes superimposed on the totemic example) 'casual' representations whose aim is no more than to give aesthetic pleasure, to indicate that a particular person had been there, or to illustrate a particular domestic episode.

Rock paintings and engravings undoubtedly play an important part in initiation ceremonies in both Australia and Africa. . . . In Australia there are places where engravings were shown to initiates as aids and explanations for the teaching of tribal myths and beliefs. In one example these engravings were laid out in galleries along which the initiates were led, but here, too, it is interesting to note that intermingled with these didactic engravings were many examples of 'casual' art. . . .

ART FOR ART'S SAKE

The idea that Palaeolithic men were artists simply because they appreciated beautiful things, and that therefore their artistic work had no special functional aim, was rejected very early on, mainly on the basis of one simple argument. As pointed out by Reinach (1903), the context of Palaeolithic art precluded any such interpretation for no one would go deep down into caves which were not used as living places in order to decorate walls which would not often be looked at, unless they had a very special reason for so doing. The important reason could not be simply that they were 'artistic' for they would then have carried out their artistic works in places where they could at least see the results. . . .

Assumptions about the necessarily simple nature of Palaeolithic man and his inability to evolve religious concepts were disproved by the ethnographic practices of the very hunters and foragers which supporters of the Art for Art's Sake theory had themselves originally drawn upon. The reasons for the Australian aboriginal paintings were not at all 'primitive', nor were they the simple expression of man's innate artistic nature, but some at least were acts of specific intent. Supporters of the Art for Art's Sake theory of Palaeolithic art also conjured up a luxurious Palaeolithic environment to explain artistic activity. In a sense such an environment may have existed, but it was also shown by the Australian aboriginal parallel not to be a prerequisite for painting. The Australian aborigines were not living in luxury. Of course no one will paint if they have no time to do so; but studies of modern hunting and gathering peoples have shown that, despite relatively inhospitable environments, these people generally still have time for leisure activities (and even exercise considerable selective choice as to the particular animals and berries that they will or will not eat (McCarthy, McArthur 1960:147, 190–92). The idea of a particularly rich environment is, therefore, largely irrelevant for the Art for Art's Sake interpretation.

The existence of two very different contexts of Palaeolithic art as stressed by Laming, already made the situation considerably more complex than that assumed by Reinach and others, while the threefold classification of parietal art followed in this book: —1 associated with a living site; 2 starting within or near the living area of the cave, but also penetrating beyond this into the darker regions of the cave; and 3 in no way associated with habitation debris, complicates the picture even further. The existence of the first category of Palaeolithic parietal art, which includes Laming's 'open-air' sites, has removed the ground from the argument that some very important, non-materialistic, driving force must necessarily be the basis for all of Palaeolithic man's art. For the category of parietal art associated with habitations, therefore, there is no reason to reject out-of-hand an Art for Art's Sake interpretation. It is a remarkable fact that the original supporters of this Art for Art's Sake interpretation have almost entirely ignored the reasons why the Palaeolithic artists should have chosen such contexts for their works; indeed, this is the reason why the adverse arguments of Reinach etc. were almost immediately accepted. Only Piette (1907:106) offered a specific reason for this context of parietal art. According to him, the Palaeolithic artist first carried out his parietal works near the openings of caves where he lived. However, the frost destroyed this work and the artist was forced to go deeper and deeper into the cave to find spots where his art could safely remain. It is, of course, impossible to accept this view for all the Palaeolithic representations, for although in several caves works of art begin at or near the entrance and continue far into the dark passages (category 2), there are also caves in which works of art are found only far inside the cave (category 3). Although it may sometimes be argued that works of art near the entrances have been destroyed, there are many cases in which this appears very unlikely.

Even in some of the category 2 caves, where Piette's suggestion might at first sight seem plausible, difficulties arise in the interpretation of these works as purely Art for Art's Sake. It would have to be assumed that the dark cave passages which were not inhabited were kept scrupulously clean and perhaps even lit as some sort of art gallery, or were decorated places used for sleeping or other leisure activities only. A more serious objection to Piette's thesis lies in the distribution of paintings and engravings within these galleries. Representations do not follow each other in some ordered way down the passages, and many apparently suitable wall or ceiling areas were not decorated, whereas on other areas representations were superimposed. Assuming that representations in the blank spaces had not perished (and there is no reason to assume that they have; indeed Piette's argument presupposes that the Palaeolithic artist had chosen a spot where this would not happen) it would follow that superpositioning was intentional, as suggested by Laming and Leroi-Gourhan, and that there were certain places (possibly defined by cavern features and relationship to other representations) which dictated the irregular spacing of artistic works in these passages; a sort of 'art gallery' with rigorously observed codes of 'hanging'. . . .

It would seem, therefore, on the basis of these arguments, that this second category of parietal art should, in the main, probably be grouped with the third category of representations not associated with habitation. It is necessary to stress the words 'in the main', however, for it is not at all impossible, or even improbable, that from time to time a Palaeolithic man moved a little way away from the strict area in which he worked and ate, and painted or engraved an animal, sign, or anthropomorph. . . .

The technically most difficult works, the bas-relief sculptures, are almost exclusively found in daylight shelters with habitation debris but, as in the case of Commarque, they occasionally extend beyond the entrance shelter into the dark regions of the cave just as the various engraving and painting techniques do. . . .

Thus any interpretation of Palaeolithic art must recognise that the most difficult technique was used to carry out detailed representations of animals and humans for works which were placed in association with, or near to, habitation. Deep outline engraving, light engraving and painting were also used in these contexts. How far it is possible on this basis to carry inferences about the relative importance of the representations is very difficult to assess. It may be argued that as the most difficult techniques were used where they were either close by or in full view of everyone, such works were considered more important than the less accessible ones on which less energy and skill were expended. It could also be argued that whereas category 1 and 2 works were so important that a difficult technique was used for them, the art of deep caves was equally important but that, for definite reasons, other techniques were preferred. . . . Where two techniques, painting and engraving or bas-reliefs and painting were employed for a single representation it is strong evidence that the visual effect of the work was the overriding interest of the artist concerned. . . . The significance of superpositioning is crucial to this argument; if superpositioning means that previous, but more or less contemporary, representations were disregarded then it seems plausible that in some cases the act of painting and engraving was more important than the final visual result; if, on the other hand, superpositioning is a means of indicating composition the final effect was clearly significant, and it remains difficult to explain why sculpturing techniques were not normally used on suitable rock. Again it may be significant that some Australian superimposed representations may sometimes indicate meaningful association in the same cave as representations superimposed for no artistic purpose. . . .

TOTEMISM, SYMPATHETIC HUNTING AND FERTILITY MAGIC

As was stressed, the totemic and sympathetic magic interpretations of Palaeolithic art were originally one and the same. Although acceptance of totemism as the *raison d'être* of Palaeolithic art was short lived and found few supporters the grounds for originally accepting it were much the same as those for accepting sympathetic magic. The fertility magic and hunting magic interpretations are usually combined together as one Sympathetic Magic interpretation. In themselves, however, the totemic and fertility magic interpretations are the most closely related. . . .

The argument that Palaeolithic art was hidden away deep inside caves, while delivering the death blow to the Art for Art's Sake interpretation, proved at the same time to be the corner stone of the totemic and magical interpretations. . . . the widespread belief among living primitive peoples in sympathetic magic by which the human could gain control over, or at least exercise a fundamental influence on, whatever subject was represented. For early ethnographers, no less than these early archaeologists, the subject of magical beliefs was of paramount interest, and led to Frazer's (1911:52) classic division of all magic into two 'principles of thought'—1 'that like produces like, or that an effect resembles its cause' and 2 'that things which have once been in contact with each other continue to act on each other at a distance after the physical contact has been severed'. As one of numerous examples of 1, Frazer mentioned the North American Indians who 'believe that by drawing . . . in sand, ashes or clay . . . and then pricking it [the representation] with a sharp stick or doing it any other injury, they inflict a corresponding injury on the [subject] represented'. For Reinach it was the first of these principles of sympathetic magic, 'homoeopathic' magic, which underlay the phenomenon of Palaeolithic art.

It is important to realise when considering such early interpretations that in the early part of the twentieth century the concepts of magic and totemism were not divorced.

Thus acceptance of totemism as a fundamental form of religious expression, recognition of the vital role of sympathetic magic within the context of totemic ceremonies and the knowledge that Australian aborigines painted complex scenes in the course of totemic rituals are the factors which, as has been seen above, influenced a few authors to make allusion to totemism in the course of their expositions of magical interpretations. Previous arguments in this book have shown that all Palaeolithic art is not of necessity to be found in the most inaccessible parts of caves for much is in open-air sites, much in galleries leading off from inhabited cave entrances, and only little completely separated from habitation areas. To explain these contexts, some supporters of the sympathetic magic and totemic interpretations (notably Breuil) postulated different functions for the hidden and the daylight art (daylight sites for totemism [or Art for Art's Sake] and hidden sites for initiation). It is a strange fact that the ethnographic parallels on which both the totemic and the sympathetic magic interpretations relied do not, in fact, suggest that these activities, which may or may not be associated with artistic expression, need necessarily be hidden away from the general public. Only when it comes to considering Australian totemism in connection with initiation ceremonies (see above) is 'discreetness' a vital feature; and even so the point is not necessarily to hide away the initiation region but only to delimit it and to forbid the presence of the uninitiated in the delimited area. Thus the fact that Palaeolithic art is found frequently in or near to habitation does not rule out a secret or non-profane significance. . . .

The second feature of Palaeolithic parietal art which was isolated by the protagonists of the sympathetic hunting or fertility magic interpretations was that the representations were not primarily intended to be looked at and that the artists were not primarily concerned with aesthetic appeal. At a later date these features were used as strong arguments against a totemic interpretation; since in Australia, for example, totemic localities were often visited and totemic representations often viewed.

The evidence regarding all these points is anything but clear. How frequently Palaeolithic man visited the parietal representations inside caves rests on the evidence of footprints in the localities concerned and the evidence of representations of different dates in these localities. . . .

What is clear from the evidence of footprints in several caves is that both adults and children penetrated into the dark regions of caves, both into areas where parietal representations existed and into areas where there was no parietal art. To try to see in this evidence the after-effects of initiation ceremonies or of children wandering away from the 'beaten tracks' is to read much into the partial information available. Some Palaeolithic representations were intended to be viewed and these argue against the assumption of followers of the sympathetic hunting and fertility magic interpretations that it was the act of representation itelf and not the visual effect that was important; they can, however, be seen as meaningful within a totemic interpretation which assumes the religious importance of the representations which would be often revisited and admired. . . .

The meaning of superpositioning remains fundamental to any interpretation of the significance of the locality and relationships of individual Palaeolithic parietal representations, for it is this frequent and characteristic superpositioning in Palaeolithic parietal art which would appear to support the contention that it was the act of representation itself, and not the final visual result, which was important to the Palaeolithic 'artists'.[2] It is natural that discussion at this point turns to the work of Leroi-Gourhan and Laming for it is they who have made it possible to look again with an open mind at the possible significance of superpositioning: whether it be evidence of later work placed on top of much earlier work, or whether it be a Palaeolithic artistic convention to denote association. It is significant that neither of these authors pose the question in this way. To both of them superpositioning of Palaeolithic parietal art may reflect either of these two alternatives; to distinguish them is only possible when dealing with works of clearly different styles and techniques. In other words, unless the style or technique of two superimposed works is different both authors assume that superpositioning was a conscious act of association by the Palaeolithic artists.

The basis of Laming's argument lies in her observation that, with all the blank spaces available on cave walls or nearby blocks of stone, Palaeolithic man superimposed representations without first removing or covering earlier representations, while

---

[2] The fact that, as seen in the Art for Art's Sake section, some category 1 art was allowed to become covered with habitation rubbish cannot in this connection be taken as strong evidence against a visual intention for Palaeolithic art, for many thousands of years may have elapsed between the original act of representation and the covering with habitation debris.

Leroi-Gourhan simply states that Palaeolithic man only superimposed representations when he desired association or when no available blank spaces existed within a cave. These two sets of reasoning are not exactly equivalent, but both clearly rely on the evidence of the modern investigator being able to isolate correctly the various different styles and techniques employed at different times by many different Palaeolithic artists. . . . As Laming has correctly shown there are many examples of Palaeolithic parietal art where representations of seemingly similar techniques and styles appear intentionally superimposed (Laming 1959:105-11) and various combinations of animals often repeated in various different regions of the same cave as well as in different caves, although sometimes only by superimposed silhouettes (Laming 1959:184), support the view that certain animals were often associated together. There are, therefore, some powerful indications from the art itself that much superpositioning of Palaeolithic parietal representations was intimately concerned with the visual effect of the art.

From all that has been said above it would seem, therefore, that facts revealed by the art itself suggest that many Palaeolithic representations were intended to have a visual effect, despite their situation in regions of caves where normal domestic activities were not carried out. This evidence does not necessarily conflict with the view that Palaeolithic parietal art was associated with totemic beliefs and actions, but does appear to conflict with the classic view that it was the act of representation itself, and not the aesthetic result, which was the concern of the Palaeolithic 'artists' who were involved in sympathetic or fertility magic rites. It must be emphasised that (as already stated in the section on Art for Art's Sake above), the visual effect of superpositioning even if it was not in the main a question of demonstrating associations between various representations, could well have had the specific aim of creating an impression of 'animalness' or 'vitality' which need not have been due to repeated and unconnected acts of magical representation. . . .

One of the essential features which was isolated very early on and became the starting point both for magical and totemic interpretations was that the majority of representations were of animals. It was the particular range of animals chosen for representation by Palaeolithic artists which supported a magical as opposed to a non-functional artistic interpretation of the art and also argued against a totemic interpretation.

That Palaeolithic man was not just decorating habitation areas and caves with 'scenery' was proved for supporters of the hunting magic, totemic and fertility magic interpretations by the absence of natural objects, such as trees, plants, rivers, etc. from the repertoire of Palaeolithic parietal art and they stressed that all the animals represented could be divided between those which were potential food and those which were dangerous. The facts about the content of Palaeolithic parietal art are, however, more complex than envisaged by most supporters of the magical interpretation and frequently appear to argue against many of their assumptions. Taking first the 'food animals' it is the essential assumption of the magical interpretations that they were represented to ensure either their capture or their increase. If this were a correct interpretation it could be expected that the animals represented in Palaeolithic parietal art would reflect a close relationship with the actual environmental conditions surrounding Palaeolithic man. It is known from actual animal bones that throughout much of the Magdalenian period at least the reindeer was staple food throughout western Europe but it is extremely rare in Palaeolithic parietal art.[3] Throughout the cold periods of the Palaeolithic the saiga antelope was eaten, yet no sure parietal representation of this animal is known. Also in a cave such as Rouffignac where the mammoth is, very exceptionally, a common subject it cannot be concluded that there was specialist mammoth hunting for this animal was extremely rare in western Europe throughout the Palaeolithic period.

---

[3] Reindeer are frequently shown on mobile art. This has led Leroi-Gourhan (1965b:73) to postulate a close relationship between mobile art and parietal art, whereby the respective roles of these two art forms are interchangeable.

Critical Analysis of Palaeolithic Cave Art

Only one explanation for the facts about the food animals represented in parietal art is offered by supporters of the magical interpretations. It has been suggested that it was only worth Palaeolithic man's effort to represent an animal for the purposes of sympathetic hunting magic if that animal was particularly difficult to catch. In this way it could be thought that the reindeer was an easy catch and for this reason not commonly represented in parietal art, but this argument will not bear scrutiny in the case of the mammoth. This animal was certainly a difficult animal to hunt and this could conceivably explain its frequency on the walls of Rouffignac despite its rarity throughout the Palaeolithic period in western Europe. But if this were the correct explanation there is no reason to find the mammoth shown commonly only at Rouffignac for it must have been equally difficult to hunt at other sites in western Europe.

A further embarrassment to supporters of the magical interpretations is caused by the occasional parietal representations of birds. Quite clearly these birds cannot be classified as dangerous so that they must have been represented either to ensure their capture as food or to increase their number as a source of food. It is known from bone debris in habitations that Palaeolithic man did in fact eat birds and it is therefore difficult to explain satisfactorily their extreme rarity in parietal representations. . . .

In the case of the dangerous animals also, supporters of the sympathetic magic interpretation have failed to explain satisfactorily the choice of animals represented in Palaeolithic parietal art. Cave lion and cave bear are known to have been common and widespread during the Palaeolithic period. They are both dangerous animals and difficult to catch but representations of them are very few. Even more peculiar is the fact that there is no single parietal representation which can surely be interpreted as a hyaena although this dangerous animal is known to have existed in Palaeolithic times in western Europe.

Clearly the sympathetic fertility magic interpretation is normally taken to apply only to the representations of food animals. As has been seen, however (Fertility magic), this has been extended by some to apply also to parietal representations of humans. It is instructive to note several facts about the contents of parietal art in this connection. If fertility magic was the aim of many parietal representations it is extraordinary that there is no sure example within Palaeolithic parietal art which certainly represents a copulation scene. . . .

Several parietal representations have been taken to represent pregnant animals. In all the cases referred to in the literature this interpretation has been based on the (slightly) swollen stomachs of the animals concerned. Whether this interpretation is accepted or not depends ultimately on the view taken regarding the likelihood of a modern observer being able to recognise, identify and correctly interpret the significance of a stylistic convention of artists living thousands of years ago, and many Australian aboriginal examples show how impossible this is likely to be.[4]

In this particular case the question boils down to the simple one of deciding whether a particular Palaeolithic representation of a horse, for example, with slightly swollen stomach can be assumed to have been intended to represent a pregnant mare, or whether it should rather be assumed that the Palaeolithic artist conceived the horse to have a more rounded stomach than is commonly assumed by modern western artists and commentators. How important it is for the modern commentator to recognise the fact that he may not only look at a representation with quite different eyes from the artist responsible for the representation but also react in a totally different way from that intended by the original artist has often been discussed (Ucko 1965: discussion and bibliography) and stressed but all too often is forgotten in the interpretation of Palaeolithic art. One of the most ingenious articles

---

[4] E.g. in the cave reported by Macintosh (1952:202–3) are 'two elongated paintings . . . completely infilled with red ochre . . . Without native interpretation they do not suggest any obvious diagnosis to a European, but to the native they are adequate naturalistic representations of long yams.' There is also a representation with 'some superficial resemblance to a female human figure . . . but it was a water lizard . . . a "devil-devil lizard, little weeny one go down waddy then go up trees." '

written about Palaeolithic parietal art, by Leason (1939), looked at the representations with the eyes of a modern game-hunter. He correctly stressed that on many of the animals shown on cave walls could be seen more of the underside of the belly than would be possible if the standing animal had been observed from the side. Leason also drew attention to the fact that many animals were shown on tip-toe or hoof-tip, that very few of the animals gave an impression of body tension, that some of the animals were shown with the feet nearest to the observer at a higher level than the other feet, that some of the animals were shown with raised tail and projecting tongue and that many of the animals were shown with prominent lower jaw.

All these features, according to Leason, were explicable if the Palaeolithic artists' models had been dead animals lying on their sides on the ground . . .

Several other detailed features of the content of Palaeolithic parietal art have been taken as support for the magical and/or totemic interpretations. As shown, many anthropomorphic representations have been interpreted as sorcerers (often disguised) officiating at the magical or totemic rites. Quite apart from the difficulty of correctly identifying many of the features of these 'anthropomorphs' the question arises whether their acceptance as sorcerers makes logical sense within the totemic and magical interpretations. As Laming (1959:160) has cogently argued, 'Why should the sorcerer, who was probably also the artist of the tribe, portray his own image? A ritual ceremony is efficacious in itself, and there would appear to be no valid reason why it should be recorded on the rock surface'. . . .

The identifications which have had perhaps the profoundest effect on the dismissal of the totemic interpretation and the acceptance of the sympathetic hunting magic interpretation are those of arrows and traps. According to the classic view, animals are commonly shown either wounded (sometimes with blood dripping from their mouth) or caught in traps. How difficult it is to identify any particular type of arrow from the parietal representations has already been stated, but two more reasons argue against the acceptance of this identification.

First, there are many representations where the 'arrows' are about to, or have already just, 'missed' an animal. There is no conceivable reason why Palaeolithic man should have wanted to shoot an arrow past a food or dangerous animal or, as it would appear from many representations, wound such an animal just above the ankle! Second, as has been stressed by Leroi-Gourhan (1965b:119) less than ten per cent of animals shown in parietal art are wounded in any way (and less than two and a half per cent of bison, one of the most frequently represented animals in parietal art) so that, following the sympathetic magic interpretation, for the vast majority of parietal animal representations it would have to be assumed that Palaeolithic man had given up any hope of wounding the animal, had resigned himself to some other form of capture, or was concerned with the increase of that species and not its capture (but what about the dangerous animals?).

No less troubling is the question of traps in parietal art for even if all the signs which have been claimed to represent different traps are accepted as such, the number of animals represented neither with wounds nor caught in traps is enormous. Furthermore, Breuil pointed out at a very early date that the number of times when a tectiform or other sign can be certainly said to be associated with an animal representation, and not to be either a later superpositioning or an earlier representation, is extremely small. There seems little doubt, therefore, that the real significance of many of these signs still remains obscure and it is understandable that authors have recently preferred to seek some symbolic, rather than representational, meaning for them . . .

Representations of food animals as such offered no difficulties to those who favoured a totemic interpretation of Palaeolithic parietal art and even the existence of the second group of animals, the dangerous ones, was incorporated into the totemic interpretation. Two of the features incorporated into the sympathetic hunting magic interpretation, however, did appear to rule out a totemic interpretation. First, that animals were wounded or caught in traps in Palaeolithic art, for the Australian evidence, according to those who attacked the totemic interpretation, made it clear that one's totem was never eaten or killed. Second, that caves contained representations of several different species of animals whereas, in a totemic system, each group would have its own distinctive totem.

Totemism is a word applied to concepts relating to many different social activities and institutions and one of the difficulties in using this term is to find a common denominator for the various phenomena which have been included within this categorisation.

What has been established, therefore, is that an intimate relationship between man and animals in primitive societies often exists irrespective of the role of these animals in the actual environment. The discrepancies noted between the animal content of Palaeolithic parietal art and the animal bones found in actual habitation debris would not therefore be inconsistent with a totemic interpretation.

It has been seen in this discussion that both the fertility and hunting magic interpretations of Palaeolithic parietal art include many unwarranted assumptions, several contradictory premises and a considerable number of obscurities. In addition they fail to account for many of the subjects of parietal art. They offer no interpretation for the numerous undeniable cases of representations of files of animals, many of which are not, in nature, found associating together. They offer no explanation for the repeated associations of different animals in different caves and on different walls of the same cave. They fail to explain the instances of intentional superpositioning and care for artistic balance (for example the Lascaux bison) unless some theory is advanced to combine the magical act of representation itself with an inherent human desire to express himself artistically. Finally, they ignore the undeniable representations of imaginary creatures or 'monsters' for there was clearly no purpose in either killing off these animals or increasing their numbers.

Many of these criticisms of the sympathetic magic interpretations cannot be levelled at the totemic interpretation of Palaeolithic parietal art but it is quite another matter to assess whether there are any features positively in favour of a totemic interpretation. Totemism as an aspect of social organisation is not particularly relevant to the interpretation of Palaeolithic parietal art for it cannot be shown that a totemic social organisation existed in Palaeolithic times; there is no evidence available either to support or to deny such a presumption. It is not sufficient to presume such a principle of social organisation simply on the basis of inferences from the parietal art of a close relationship between Palaeolithic man and animals. Such an intimate relationship, in any case, is not exclusive to totemism for it can be found amongst many 'primitive' people, utterly devoid from any totemic beliefs or practices. There is no reason to single out totemism on this basis in favour of cattle cults or sacrificial ancestor cults, etc. Finally, as has been shown at some length above, even among the totemic Australian aborigines totemism is far from being the only incentive to paint or engrave on rocks.

LEROI-GOURHAN

Like many of his predecessors, Leroi-Gourhan bases his interpretation primarily on parietal art for this art alone gives definite contextual evidence whereas mobile art was, presumably, carried about for all sorts of different reasons. Taking only the parietal art Leroi-Gourhan has drawn up a detailed inventory of subjects to be seen in many caves (over sixty-five) and his analysis is based on these facts as well as the contexts of each subject noted.

His analysis has two starting points which come together finally in his overall view of the meaning of parietal representations; the first is the frequency and spatial distribution of animals in caves, the second the analysis of the signs in Palaeolithic art. (See Plate 10.) Leroi-Gourhan notes that well over half of the animals shown are horse and bison. These, he concludes, must represent two coupled or juxtaposed themes, 'A' and 'B' respectively, whereas other animals must have played subsidiary roles.

For the analysis of the distribution of the animals he divided up the caves into seven different regions which are frequently determined by natural topographical features such as sharp bends, constrictions, chambers, etc.: 1 the first point where representations begin; 2 passages and shafts which connect up the large galleries; 3 points at the beginning of fissures, diverticules and alcoves; 4 the furthest region which is decorated; 5 the central part of decorated walls in large galleries; 6 marginal zones around the central part; and 7 points inside fissures, diverticules and alcoves. From the distribution of animals in these seven regions he finds that all the animals represented can be divided into the two groups A and B which correspond to the horse and bison groups and which are consistently used in particular regions of the caves. From this Leroi-Gourhan concludes that caves must have been systematically organised sanctuaries.

Group B animals (which are bison, aurochs and women) are found in the central panels (5 above). In most cases group B is represented by one animal, aurochs or bison, and only rarely by both although in a bison cave aurochs may play a subsidiary role, and vice versa. With one exception group A animals are found in all the other areas (1–4 and 6–7 above) only. The one exception is the horse which is also very commonly found in area 5 together with 'B' animals, thus forming the basic theme of 'man-woman and (or) horse-bison' (1965a: 218).

This fundamental differentiation of group A and B representations is not always easy to make out for animals of either group are frequently shown in twos: 'one sees that it is couples of couples which are represented; male and female bison opposed to mares and stallions' (1964:105).

The whole theme is made much more difficult by the presence in some scenes of a third (or even fourth or fifth) animal belonging to group A which Leroi-Gourhan himself admits may sometimes dominate, numerically, the whole scene (1963:109–13).

On the basis of this dichotomy of parietal representations and the fact that in some places the central 'B' animals' place is taken by the representation of a woman, Leroi-Gourhan sees the whole theme of Palaeolithic 'naturalistic' representations as the 'juxtaposition', 'opposition', 'coupling' or 'association'[5] not of two groups of animals *per se* but of the female and male principle, B group animals representing the female and A group male. It is at this point that the first part of Leroi-Gourhan's analysis joins up with the second part, the analysis of 'signs'.

On the basis of a detailed inventory of the 'non-naturalistic' signs, tectiforms, etc., of Palaeolithic parietal art Leroi-Gourhan has constructed an evolutionary series which he thinks divides up the signs into two groups which show a clear derivation either from the whole female figure and the female sexual organs, or from the male sexual organs.[6] Once again Leroi-Gourhan sees the two groups of signs as opposed, coupled or juxtaposed; those of 'a' (lines, dots, etc.) representing the male, and those of 'b' (ovals, triangles, etc.) representing the female.

As with group B representations 'b' signs are predominantly found in central panels whereas 'a' signs are predominantly peripheral. Leroi-Gourhan sees the relationship between male 'a' signs and female 'b' signs as the same as that between horse and bison. Similarly, signs are frequently coupled; group 'b' signs 'accompanied by "a" signs which complete it'. The place of an animal representation is often taken by an equivalent sign,

---

[5] It is difficult to conclude anything from Leroi-Gourhan's use of these different words. They most likely reflect his cautious statement that he is able only to guess at the vague outline of the main structure of Palaeolithic symbolism and that details of interpretation are bound to remain enigmatic. . . .

[6] In 1965b:107, Leroi-Gourhan states that he has been unable to construct an evolutionary derivation for the male signs, but has identified many of them as male simply because they are found in different positions from signs which he considers female.

while the place of a sign is sometimes taken by an equivalent male or female human representation.

Leroi-Gourhan admits that 'the relationship between the group a-b and the group A-B is difficult to define clearly'. The juxtaposition and coupling of the male and female principles is symbolically expressed not only by group A and B animals but also with group 'a' and 'b' signs, as well as by one group A or B representation with a sign of group 'a' or 'b'.

Leroi-Gourhan's thesis is clearly far removed from all previous interpretations in which the virtual absence of any scenes was considered a significant feature of Palaeolithic art. Both Leroi-Gourhan and Laming, on the contrary, consider that although 'narrative' scenes are uncommon, or even absent, all panels with more than one single representation should be viewed as meaningful scenes (see below). Whereas earlier authors took frequent superpositions to mean that the final appearance of the panel was not important and that the actual act of depicting each individual animal had an essential magical purpose, Leroi-Gourhan and Laming both consider that superpositioning on a panel was used as a means of showing the association between figures, thus forming a composite picture. According to these authors, except in cases where they were short of suitable rock walls, the Palaeolithic artists were careful to avoid destroying earlier works with more recent paintings and engravings.

From his analysis of the distribution of animals and signs within caves, Leroi-Gourhan concludes that the caves were decorated according to a systematic plan and he has reconstructed the elements of the 'ideal' composition in the 'organised world' of Palaeolithic man: 'a group of large herbivores of two species, one of which is nearly always a horse. One of the two species is numerically predominant. This central composition is flanked by complementary animals, most frequently deer and ibex. Juxtaposed with these are the usually abstract representations of man and woman or of the male and female principles' (1958: 395), the whole being a true 'metaphysical system', a mythology based both on the opposition as well as the complementary nature of the two sexes:

Gone are the wounded animals so important to previous interpretations, for wounds are group b signs (female), frequently associated with male signs. Gone are the frightening impersonal caves where magical rites took place, for male signs are frequently placed in particular natural cavern features and the cave itself is therefore female. Gone are the animals which can be classed as edible or dangerous, for the animals themselves are sexual symbols. Gone are the traps for animals or spirits, the houses, weapons or projectiles, for tectiforms etc. are also themselves sexual symbols. Instead Leroi-Gourhan has introduced the idea that Palaeolithic parietal art expresses, in abstract form, a whole complex system of fecundity. 'In the last analysis (which is still provisional) we may conclude that Palaeolithic people represented in the caves the two great categories of living beings, their corresponding male and female symbols, and the symbols of death which feeds the hunter. In the central zones the system was expressed by the aggregate of male symbols around the female principal figures, while in the other parts of the sanctuary the male representations were exclusive, apparently complementary to the cavern herself' (1965b:121). Palaeolithic 'representations are concerned with an extremely rich and complex system, much richer and much more complex than anyone had previously suspected' (1964:151). . . .

From Leroi-Gourhan's new approach to Palaeolithic parietal art several important facts emerge. Certain species of animals are represented markedly more frequently than are others. Within a cave, bison and horse (and possibly ox and mammoth) 'themes' are more frequently shown on the walls of large chambers and passages whereas many 'themes' of other animals are found virtually anywhere and certain other animals (e.g. bear and lion) are usually shown isolated from major concentrations of other animals in a cave. How far this evidence can be taken to show that the compositions within a cave were regularly planned is still difficult to assess, for it is a fact that the two most commonly represented animals are also those which Palaeolithic man is likely to have seen on numerous occasions in large herds. Leroi-Gourhan has shown on a numerical basis that some caves contain certain galleries in which one animal species or sign is numerically predominant, and other caves in which the most frequent representation is of one animal species only. He has shown also that different 'signs' are shown in caves depending on the geographical area concerned and that some types of these signs are more commonly found in certain cave areas than other types. Leroi-Gourhan's numerical analysis has revealed that certain types of representations are not generally found close together; there are very few examples of male and female human representations in the same regions of a cave or shelter and where the bison, for example, is predominant in a central area of a cave it is unusual to find wild oxen in the same region (or vice versa). . . .

From his topographical division of the artistic contents of a cave into two entities, in the lateral and central areas, Leroi-Gourhan infers two symbolic equivalences, the male and the female respectively. This inference is based primarily on the supposed equivalence of central animals (excepting, of course, the horse) and central female human representations. It must be noted, however, that female representations with recognisable sex indicated are extremely rare in Palaeolithic parietal art. Moreover, there is no obvious reason that, just because a certain species of animal and a human representation are found together in the same panel of cave, the two representations concerned should be assumed to have the same symbolic equivalence. After all, in Leroi-Gourhan's own system of equivalences, the horse which is found predominantly in the same panels as bison, is assumed to belong to the opposite sexual group from the bison.

Leroi-Gourhan's interpretation of the symbolism of signs is again partially based on their topographical positions within caves and also on their assumed typological derivation from male and female sexual organs or whole figures. As has been seen above it is undoubtedly true that some signs are predominantly found in areas of caves where other signs are largely absent. It is, however, quite another matter to infer from this distribution that the signs commonly found in central panels have the same symbolic equivalence as the animals and occasional female representations also found in these central panels, or that the signs in lateral areas signify the same thing as the animals and rare male representations found in these areas. . . .

Basically what Leroi-Gourhan is assuming is that Palaeolithic artists made use of several very different symbols to express the 'female', symbols derived either from the vulva or from the whole female figure; it is interesting to note that he derives no symbol from breasts (although several of the supposed derivations from triangles and from the whole figure could as well be derived from breasts as from anything else) although several figurines and low relief sculptures have breasts clearly and prominently marked. . . .

According to Leroi-Gourhan there are three major groups of 'male' signs. . . . Although his work includes tables showing their typological derivations, he has admitted (1965b:104, 107–8, 453–55) that they are really only classifiable on the basis of their different topographical cave positions from 'female' signs. Only the hooked or 'spear' signs have been traced by Leroi-Gourhan to the male sexual organ, a unique representation in mobile art. The other signs classified as male are various combinations and variations of simple lines and dots which Leroi-Gourhan considers are originally evidently male sexual symbols which become very stylised and their typological development unclear. . . .

Perhaps the most worrying feature of Leroi-Gourhan's whole symbolic interpretation concerns the absence of primary sexual organs and the absence of any definite representations of copulation. He is well aware of this for in some of his works he talks about the 'prudishness' and 'discretion' of Palaeolithic parietal art (1965a:234; 165b:120). Leroi-Gourhan is suggesting that the 'female', for example, was symbolised in Palaeolithic art equally by the representation of a female human being, by several different 'signs' (some of which are 'recognisably' representations of the vulva, others derived from it or the whole human figure), by certain animals, by wounds, by the caves themselves, by hands, etc. It is striking that he sees no incongruity in the fact that some of these symbols, such as the female human being and the signs, are by definition female in sex while others, such as male bison and male mammoth, are not. That fertility should be expressed in many different ways according to the context concerned is not in itself difficult to accept; that a complex system of symbolism should be difficult for the modern observer to unravel is very likely. What is much less easy to envisage is a situation whereby people who distinguish the female from the male sex (as proven by the primary sexual organs on many human figurines and some low-relief sculptures and possibly also from the signs in parietal art) should ignore the male and female sex of animals and regard them as equivalent to the male or female human (for a male bison is as much the symbol of the female element as is the female bison). To postulate that the Palaeolithic artists were prudes (and this is the reason, according to Leroi-Gourhan, why sexual signs so quickly became geometrical in form) cannot be reconciled with the fact that some examples of humans and animals are shown with primary sexual organs and that (according to Leroi-Gourhan) both isolated female vulva and isolated male phalli were shown by the Palaeolithic artists.

How difficult it is to accept Leroi-Gourhan's symbolic interpretation of Palaeolithic parietal art is reflected in his statements about the rites. These have virtually nothing to do with his symbolic interpretation and, in fact, are sometimes very similar to sympathetic magic interpretations. Although convinced of the religious nature of decorated caves he cautiously states (1964:148–49) that almost anything could have happened in these caves (except art for art's sake!) but that the evidence is not good enough to tell exactly what. He sees the evidence of cave usage as conflicting, sometimes suggesting that caves had been rarely visited and sometimes that they had been often frequented, and accepts that children, as well as adults, went into the caves and were allowed to wander away from the main passages. He takes the panels of unfinished compositions and meanders as evidence for novices having attempted to copy the subjects on main cave panels (but see their actual positions, above) and points to evidence for retouching, replacement and improvement of old representations. Beyond this he accepts that wounding rituals (or rather theatrical ceremonies) may have taken place inside the caves. Little of this appears to be directly connected with the fertility symbolism which Leroi-Gourhan has induced from Palaeolithic parietal art. . . .

CONCLUSIONS AND PROBLEMS

. . . Perhaps the most important single barrier to an understanding of the significance of Palaeolithic parietal art (and equally to any clear-cut conclusions to a book such as this) is the ignorance which still surrounds the use of caves by Palaeolithic man. Until it is known what exactly Palaeolithic man was doing inside caves, apart from painting and engraving on their walls, all interpretations of parietal art can only be tentative hypotheses. To what extent did Palaeolithic man live inside caves? Did he use caves as storage places (perhaps for sacred objects which have long since perished)? Did he fear to go inside caves unless for a special purpose, or did he nonchalantly and confidently explore their passages? It is, of course, fantastic that such vital evidence is still not available for it is surely context which one hopes will one day, together with the systematic study of content, reveal the best clues to the meaning of Palaeolithic art and it is, after all, the context which distinguishes parietal from mobile art and makes it potentially the most suitable Palaeolithic art form for interpretative studies.

It is possible to guess (but not to prove) that in reality there was considerably more Palaeolithic activity inside caves than is usually thought or admitted in the literature for, from some caves, there is data (largely chance finds) of considerable activity by a considerable number of people (e.g. Montespan—footprints, flints, animal bones; Labastide—hearths, flints, animal bones, engraved plaquettes; and many others). But it is impossible as yet to answer the vital question whether Palaeolithic man went into caves primarily in order to paint or engrave, or whether he went there for some quite different reason, and, while there anyway, took the opportunity to decorate the cavern walls.[7] Footprints have been found in several caves where no parietal art exists (and in several large galleries within decorated caves) and this might support the idea that Palaeolithic man had some other reasons beyond artistic representation, to penetrate caves.

Footprints also appear to prove that both adults and children went into caves. It is, however, again impossible, without knowing more about Palaeolithic uses of, and attitudes towards, caves to choose between the two possible alternative interpretations. Either the children went into caves for a particular purpose, such as initiation, which concerned them as children or they went there just as they would have gone elsewhere with, perhaps, the added appeal of exploration. There is, possibly, a little evidence from the footprints that children did wander quite freely inside parts of the caves and there is a report (Count Begouen 1928:6) from the cave of Le Tuc D'Audoubert that children had, presumably for fun, stuck their fingers vertically into the gooey mud. In this connection it is interesting to note that for amusement children among the Australian aborigines have developed considerable skill in the arts, especially engravings on clay floors.

It is definitely established that Palaeolithic man lived both in open sites and in rock shelters and cave entrances and that he sometimes decorated these areas with paintings, engravings and low-reliefs. It is also known that he penetrated deeper into some of the passages leading off from inhabited cave entrances and decorated these galleries also. On the available evidence there is also a third category of caves in which he did not live but into which he went, sometimes for considerable distances and with considerable difficulty (marks where he slipped on the wet clay are still to be seen in many caves), apparently with the express

---

[7] An extremely important question posed by G. H. Luquet (1930:29).

purpose of decorating walls, ceilings and floors despite the darkness in these regions. If these category 3 caves really do exist then they must be considered strong evidence in favour of there being some esoteric meaning behind these category 3 examples of Palaeolithic parietal art. But until it is finally determined not only whether Palaeolithic man ever lived inside the caves but also where the original entrances were, this problem will not be finally resolved. If they do exist they have no clear parallel in the practices of living 'primitive' peoples. Perhaps some support for an esoteric interpretation of art in this third category is, rather ironically, provided by the unlikely attempts to explain why the Palaeolithic artist should have penetrated so deep. Neither an explanation based on the destructive action of frost (Piette) nor one based on respect for previous work (Leroi-Gourhan) can convincingly explain art in category 3 caves.

Because of the paucity of definite contextual evidence about Palaeolithic parietal art, interpretations must be largely based on the contents of the art. There is, however, one other source of clues towards correct interpretation and this is the locality of representations. There are two striking features about much Palaeolithic parietal art: 1 that representations are often superimposed, 2 that some representations are placed in inaccessible places. There is a small range of possible explanations for these two characteristics; if the art was a response to explanatory myths or traditions which dictated where representations should be placed this would explain both superpositioning and hidden localities (an explanation which applies to some Australian art); the art might have been intended to impress a visitor either by its abundance (superpositioning) or by its ingenuity (placed in localities which were difficult of access); the art might have been concerned with associated subjects shown by superpositioning (a stylistic convention found also among some Australian aborigines); the art might have been the work of people living at different times who had no feeling or respect for earlier artistic representations (an attitude reported both from Australian aborigines and other 'primitive' peoples); the art might have been placed in localities which were considered especially sacred, thus explaining both superpositioning and localities which were difficult of access (an explanation which most probably applies to some Australian aboriginal art). On the evidence of context from some caves and content of some representations, some of these explanations appear more likely than others, but the significant feature may well be, as it is among the Australian aborigines, that more than one criterion was operative at any one time; thus it may well be that association was sometimes indicated by superpositioning (as it was undoubtedly for some Palaeolithic parietal representations) but that at other times, or in other places, superpositioning had no especial significance, indicating only disregard for previous works.

The contents of Palaeolithic art should provide some of the strongest evidence for its correct interpretation. It is a fact that in Palaeolithic art are represented only very few human beings and there are no certain representations of scenery (no vegetation nor natural features such as rivers or mountains). Again, there are several very different possible explanations of these facts; either animals were the predominant concern of Palaeolithic artists for something like fertility or hunting magic for food-animals, or possibly the predominance of parietal representations of animals was bound up with their role as 'background' for actual human participation (as 'actors') during which 'props' may have been brought into the caves for any given occasion (for example, actual vegetation). It is possible also to explain the paucity of human representations and the absence of scenery and vegetation in terms of representational taboos on these subjects, but it is difficult to imagine an explanation which might, in this way, connect humans, vegetation and natural features such as rivers. It is unlikely that the art was exclusively concerned with increase or hunting magic directed at certain animals for this does not adequately explain either the different proportions of animals represented nor the representations of humans and part-humans. The relative frequencies of animals, the absence of representations of vegetation and also the evidence reviewed in previous pages, which shows that many representations were intended to be viewed, suggest that 'theatre' may well be behind some of the parietal representations.

The proportions of animal species represented in Palaeolithic art show conclusively that the Palaeolithic artist was selective in his choice of subjects; how his selection should be interpreted is debatable. At Lascaux virtually only stags and no does were shown on the cave walls; at Covalanas, on the other hand, virtually only does were represented. Obviously this selection did not reflect the actual environmental situation of Palaeolithic times; at Lascaux, perhaps, the choice was based on the impressive antler spread of male deer but at Covalanas it has to be presumed either that the deer represented were males in rutt (without antlers despite their sex), that the artists at Covalanas had some special reason for showing only female deer or that for the artists concerned the female of the deer species had some special attraction (as did the male deer for the artists at Lascaux).

Such selectivity of animal species, as well as the distribution of animals within caves (as documented by Leroi-Gourhan), is not adequately explained by any sympathetic magic interpretation. It is necessary, however, to wait for much more numerical evidence (based upon criteria such as size and numbers of representations and tested by adequate statistical methods) before it is possible to determine whether the distribution of animals and signs within caves are the result of intentional selection, or of haphazard localisation of the animals most commonly encountered by the Palaeolithic artists. At the present time the distribution of human, bison and ibex representations at least, appear to indicate the likelihood of a certain degree of selection and planning by the Palaeolithic artists.

On the basis of the contextual evidence, of the practices of certain 'primitive' peoples and of the content of Palaeolithic art there seems little evidence against the assumption that much of the parietal art which surrounds Palaeolithic habitation (category 1) was intended to enliven and brighten domestic activities.

In most art of this category there is little superpositioning, few enigmatic signs and no particular paucity of human representations.

If this inference about category 1 art should be true it is important to recognise the support that this gives to the assumption that the signs so often interpreted as sexual symbols need not necessarily be concerned with increase ceremonies but may be simply connected with eroticism (Luquet 1930:109–10).

That this may indeed be likely and that fertility magic interpretations of Palaeolithic art need considerable rethinking is supported by the fact that several modern hunting and gathering tribes are known to avoid, as opposed to increase, the possibility of having large families. It is a fact that the Bushmen regularly practice infanticide because, they maintain, a hunting and gathering life is too hard to be able to support many children. Among several tribes of Australian aborigines, also, there is evidence that increase ceremonies are a foreign concept, for the usual level of life is, for them, a normal and natural order of life and 'the need to increase their food supply was not felt deeply enough to appear in their spiritual expressions, let alone in practice' (W. Arndt 1962:316–17; see also M. J. Meggitt 1962: 221).

Indeed it is as likely that Palaeolithic man was not interested in the fertility of the human species as that he was concerned with producing large families.

Although in the literature totemic and sympathetic magic interpretations are usually kept apart, in reality sympathetic fertility magic and totemic interpretations have much in common while sympathetic hunting magic interpretations are based on slightly different evidence. Although totemic practices and beliefs of living 'primitives' suggest that any animal, whatever its prominence or role in a society, may be selected as the subject of totemic practice it does not follow that just because the Australian aborigines are totemic so, therefore, were Palaeolithic men.

Perhaps the most striking feature which argues against a fertility interpretation, outside a symbolic totemic increase function, is that some of the content of Palaeolithic parietal art does not reflect the actual environment and eating habits of Palaeolithic man. This is also a feature which argues against a sympathetic hunting magic interpretation for there is no reason why Palaeolithic man should have been interested either in killing or increasing the number of 'imaginary beings' nor, on the other hand, why he should not have been interested either in killing or increasing the number of reindeer which, it is known, was staple food in one period of the Palaeolithic. Finally, in the context of increase and fertility, it would be strange to find that the Palaeolithic men who lived by hunting animals and gathering wild fruit and berries had no interest in the increase of vegetation. Even if the usual 'increase' interpretation is slightly adapted to fall more in line with the 'maintenance' rituals known from Australia it fails to account for the absence of representations of vegetation and for the not insignificant number of dangerous animals represented.

The choice of animals represented may either be due, in part at least, to actual environmental conditions throughout the vast number of years during which parietal art was made (e.g. the correlation between the actual and the parietal distribution of rhinoceros, bison, deer, etc.) or to the art being a record of myths or symbolism. A numerical analysis such as that attempted by Leroi-Gourhan reveals little to suggest that any underlying symbolism or myth was simple but rather, if it existed at all, that it was a complex system of inter-relationships. With time and more accurate recording of the contents of each decorated cave it may become possible to determine how likely it is that there was such an underlying 'philosophy'; there is little doubt that such analyses will have to take into account not only 'themes' represented (often only recognisable on the basis of rather arbitrary divisions of caves) but also the number, size and prominence of representations. Even on the basis of Leroi-Gourhan's suggestions it might be possible to attempt correlations between such features of the art and his suggested 'juxtapositioning', 'complementarity', 'completions', etc. . . .

. . . Perhaps the main impression gained from visits to many decorated Palaeolithic caves is one of variety. Palaeolithic man was extraordinarily varied in his choice of where to camp, the use he appears to have made of caves, in the selectivity of subjects which he chose to represent, in the localities which he chose to decorate, in the techniques which he used and in the combinations of subjects which he favoured. With this variety in mind it is not at all surprising that none of the interpretations reviewed, adequately account for all the examples of Palaeolithic art known to the modern world; perhaps it is nonsensical to have expected that any one interpretation could be so.

It seems, therefore, that if any of the suggested interpretations have any real validity, with regard to Palaeolithic parietal art each of them is likely to apply to only certain works. There is nothing against assuming that Palaeolithic art, as is also the art of many living 'primitives', is the result of many different interests. Within any one cave, therefore, it is possible to imagine that many of the possibilities outlined in this book apply: that some representations were the work of children (perhaps some of the floor engravings), that some were used in acts of sympathetic magic (perhaps some of the representations pierced with holes), that some were placed in particular situations in order to please (perhaps some of the open-air low-reliefs), and that some were illustrations of myths and traditions (perhaps those which contain imaginary creatures, anthropomorphs and unexpected combinations of animal species). It is very possible, however, that some and perhaps many Palaeolithic representations were made for reasons which still totally escape the modern observer.

THE EARLY GREAT STYLES AND THE RISE OF THE PRE-COLUMBIAN CIVILIZATION[1]

Gordon R. Willey

"Experience has shown that it is hopeless to storm, by a frontal attack, the great citadels of the causality underlying highly complex groups of facts."

A. L. KROEBER

IN NATIVE AMERICA, not a great many centuries after the establishment of a village agricultural way of life, two major art styles of the first rank appear, more or less contemporaneously, in southern Mesoamerica and in northern Peru. These are known as the Olmec and the Chavín. I purpose to consider these two art styles, first, and briefly, as to their content and form and, secondly, but in more detail, in their cultural settings and from the general perspective of New World culture history. For what engages our attention is that both styles occur at that point in time which might be said to mark the very first stirrings of civilization in the Mesoamerican and Peruvian areas. What role

---

Reprinted from *American Anthropologist*, Vol. 64, No. 1, 1962, pp. 1–11, with the permission of the author and the American Anthropological Association.

Read as the Presidential Address at the annual meeting of the American Anthropological Association, held at Philadelphia, November 1961.

[1] The author gratefully acknowledges the critical reading of the manuscript and the suggestions made by M. D. Coe and D. W. Lathrap in July 1961.

did these art styles, or the motivations of which they are the symbols, play in the rise and development of pre-Columbian civilizations? Are they, the styles themselves, the touchstones of that condition we refer to as civilization? What do we know of their origins or, if not their origins, their pre-conditions?

Like most anthropologists who are interested in culture history I am interested in origins and causes, but I am not sanguine about the possibilities of easy or early victories. Certainly the answers to the ultimate causal questions as to why the ancient American civilizations began and flourished where they did and when they did still elude us, and what I can offer here will do little more, at best, than describe and compare certain situations and series of events.

My use of the term "great styles" is a special and intentional one. I refer to art styles and to manifestations of these generally considered as "fine arts" (Kroeber 1957:24–26). Their greatness is judged in their historical contexts, but it is none the less real. These great pre-Columbian art styles of Mesoamerica and Peru are expressed monumentally; they occur in settings that were obviously sacred or important in the cultures which produced them; they are also pervasive, being reproduced in a variety of media and contexts; the products are rendered with the consummate skill of the specially and long-trained artist; they conform to strict stylistic canons; their subject matter tends to be thematic; and finally, the finest monuments or creations in these styles are truly powerful and awe-inspiring. These last criteria are subjective, but I do not think we can ignore them. We see ancient art—the word "primitive" is here most inappropriate—across the millennia and with the eyes of an alien culture; yet we are not unmoved. Man speaks to man through art, and the screen of cultural difference and relativism does not strain out all emotional effect. Olmec and Chavín art measure fully to standards of greatness.

OLMEC AND CHAVÍN

The Olmec style of Mesoamerica has been known for 30 years as such. Stirling (1943) and his associates (Weiant 1943; Drucker 1943, 1952) fully revealed the style in their discoveries in southern Veracruz and Tabasco. They and Caso (1942) and Covarrubias (1942, 1946, 1957) made it widely known and also opened the question of its cultural and chronological position in Mesoamerican culture history (see also Greengo 1952; Coe 1957). Olmec art is rendered in life-size, or greater than life-size, full-round, and bas-relief stone monuments. These include free-standing heads, human and anthropomorphic figures, stelae, and altars. Carvings are also found on natural boulders after the manner of pictographs, but most of these are done with such skill and are so much a part of the deliberate style, that "bas-relief," rather than "pictograph," is the fitting term to describe them. Olmec sculptures also occur as small pieces: jade and serpentine figurines, celts, ornamental effigy axes, plaques, and other small ornaments. (See Plate 13.) Ceramic objects in the Olmec style are less common but include figurines, pottery stamps, and vessels.

The central theme of Olmec art is a jaguar-human or were-jaguar being. The concept is nearly always expressed as more human, in total characteristics, than jaguar. The face is frequently infantile as well as jaguar-like, and in many instances actual human infant bodies are portrayed. But subtle shades of this infantile jaguarism infect almost all human or anthropomorphic representations, ranging all the way from only slightly snubbed, feline noses and down-turned drooping mouths to toothed and snarling countenances. Some stelae and monuments bear another concept, elderly men with aquiline noses and beards who are sometimes depicted with portrait realism; but there is also a fusion of the jaguar-like anthropomorph with the bearded man in Olmec iconography (Coe 1960 ms). Other motifs are rarer: fully animalized jaguars, bird and duck monsters, serpents, and fish.

The formal properties of the Olmec style are highly distinctive. Although the subject matter is to a large extent in the mythological realm the portrayals are carried out with a "realistic" intent. It is thoroughly nongeometric and nonabstract; lines have a slow curvilinear rhythm, and free space balances figures. There is little fine detail (Coe 1960 ms). As a style it is the equivalent of any of the later great styles of Mesoamerica, and in the full-round treatment of the human body it is the superior of all.

The climax region of the Olmec style was southern Veracruz and Tabasco in such ceremonial center sites as La Venta, Tres Zapotes, and San Lorenzo. Insofar as the style is expressed monumentally there is little doubt but that this is its homeland. Elsewhere, Olmec monuments are widely scattered and occasional. Most are bas-relief figures carved on boulder outcrops, as in Morelos (Piña Chan 1955), Chiapas (Ferdon 1953), Guerrero (Jimenez Moreno 1959: fig. 4, Pl. I-a), Guatemala (Thompson 1948: fig. 111a), and Salvador (Boggs 1950). Aside from these monuments, portable objects of the Olmec style, such as jade figurines, ornaments, and small manufactures, are found throughout much of southern Mesoamerica, from the Valley of Mexico and Guerrero on the northwest down through Chiapas and Pacific Guatemala. Covarrubias (1957) held the opinion that Guerrero was the ancestral home of the Olmec style, in its pre-monumental era, but it has yet to be demonstrated that the numerous Olmec figurines found in that region are earlier manifestations of the style than the great sculptures of Veracruz-Tabasco. In any event, for our present discussion, it is sufficient to note that the climax of the "great" aspects of the style are in this latter zone but that the style as a whole is spread over much of southern Mesoamerica. Wherever it can be dated, Olmec art appears in the Middle pre-Classic Period of Mesoamerican history, with an outer dating range of 1000 to 300 B.C., and a probable more specific bracketing by radiocarbon determinations of between 800 and 400 B.C. (Drucker, Heizer, and Squier 1959:248–67).

Chavín style art is named for Chavín de Huántar, an imposing archeological site in the Marañon drainage of the north highlands of Peru. Tello, more than any other archeologist, called attention to Chavín art (Tello 1942, 1943, 1960); subsequently, Bennett (1943, 1944), Larco Hoyle (1941), Kroeber (1944a:81–93), and Carrion Cachot (1948) made significant contributions (see also Willey 1951; Coe 1954). Like Olmec, the Chavín style is one closely adapted to sculptural forms, both monumental and small. The heroic-sized sculptures are mostly free-standing monoliths or stelae, lintels, cornices, and decorative features of buildings. These are executed with a relief-incision and champlévé technique in stone or are modelled in clay. Some full-round carving and modelling is also attempted in heads or figures tenoned or affixed to walls or buildings. Chavín small carving produced stone and bone plaques, stone and gourd vessels, ceremonial stone mortars and pestles, and ornaments. (See Plate 14.) The style also appears in finely modelled and incised pottery vessels, in repoussé goldwork, and even in textile designs. In sum, it enters into more varied media than the Olmec style, but both styles are most at home in carving, particularly in large sculptures and in the work of the lapidary.

The content of Chavín art, like that of Olmec, deals with a few powerful central themes. With Chavín the dominant motif is either the feline or the fusion of feline elements, such as fangs and claws, with other beings, including humans, condors, the cayman, and the serpent. The fantastic beings of Chavín art emphasize somewhat more the animal attributes than the human, in contradistinction to Olmec. Strictly human representations are rare, and none of these have the qualities of portraiture observed in some of the Olmec sculptures. Although firmly set in a unified style, the monster or composite beings show great variations in the combination of jaguar or puma and other animal elements.

The formal properties of the Chavín style, which are its essence, are decidedly different from those of Olmec. No one would mistake the two styles in juxtaposition. Chavín is intricate with detail in a way that Olmec is not. It does not employ free space, but seeks to fill it with such things as small secondary heads and eyes disposed over the body of the central monster figure of the sculpture. There is little mastery of realism or naturalism. It has more features that are stiff and "archaic." As styles the two have common ground only in that they rely upon slow heavy curves rather than straight lines, and both have a quality of the esoteric about them rather than the obvious.

The heartland of the Chavín style, insofar as it is monumental and in stone or sculptured adobe, is in the north highlands of Peru, at such sites as Chavín de Huántar, Yauya, and Kuntur Wasi, and in the coastal valleys of Nepeña and Casma. This is but one sector of the larger Peruvian culture area, and as such this focal concentration is comparable to the distribution of Olmec art in the Veracruz-Tabasco region within the larger sphere of Mesoamerica. The wider compass of Chavín art, as expressed in small manufactures, takes in much of the Peruvian culture area. Formerly thought to embrace only the northern part of Peru, its definite influence is now traced as far south on the coast as the Cerrillos phase of the Ica and Nazca Valleys (Lanning 1959). Thus, in its total geographic extent Chavín outstrips Olmec, the latter being confined to the southern half, or less, of its culture area setting. Chronologically, Chavín art belongs to the Formative Period of Peruvian prehistory and to either the Early or Middle subdivision of that period, depending upon one's terminology. The gross estimated dates for the Peruvian Formative Period are approximately the First Millennium B.C. Within this range, and with the aid of radio-carbon determinations, the horizon of the Chavín art style is narrowed to between 800 and 400 B.C. (Collier 1959, 1960 ms; Lanning 1959). As will be noted, this is identical to the dates for the time span estimated for the Olmec style in Mesoamerica. These two sets of dates, incidentally, were arrived at quite independently by different sets of archeologists.

OLMEC AND CHAVÍN IN CULTURE HISTORICAL PERSPECTIVE

As we have already observed, Olmec and Chavín styles make their first appearance on an underlying base of village agriculture. In Mesoamerica, village agriculture, defined as sedentary life based primarily upon maize cultivation, became established by about 1500 B.C., following a long epoch of incipient plant domestication (Willey 1960). The presence of ceremonial architecture, in the form of platform mounds for temples or other buildings, in the early centuries of Mesoamerican agricultural life is probable, although not well documented. But by 800 B.C., some 700 years or so after the village agricultural threshold, the great Olmec ceremonial center of La Venta was founded in Tabasco. At the same time that these events were taking place in Mesoamerica, similar and related ones were going on in Peru. At about 1500 B.C. a well-developed variety of Mesoamerican maize appeared in coastal Peru and was rapidly assimilated into the local root-crop agricultural economies of the Peruvian coastal communities (Lanning quoted from Collier 1960; Mangelsdorf, MacNeish, and Willey 1960 ms). Soon after this the Peruvians were making pottery and building ceremonial mounds, and to clinch the relationships between Peru and the north at this time, a distinctly Mesoamerican figurine has been found in one of these early Peruvian ceremonial sites known as Las Aldas (Ishida and others 1960, 97ff.). The Chavín style appears shortly after this. During its period, contact between Mesoamerica and Peru continued. For example, among the best known traits that have often been pointed to as linking the Olmec phase of Tlatilco and the Chavín Cupisnique phase are figurines, rocker-stamped pottery, incised and color-zoned wares, flat-bottomed open-bowl forms, and the stirrup-mouth jar (Engel 1956; Porter 1953; Willey 1955; Coe 1960).

In this setting of an almost exact equation in time, and with further evidences of contact in specific ceramic items, can we go further and argue that Olmec and Chavín are definitely related? Drucker (1952:231), Wauchope (1954), and I (Willey 1959) have all called attention to this possibility, and Della Santa (1959) has argued the case in earnest; but on reflection I do not think that the two styles show a close relationship. At least they do not exhibit a relationship which, in the realm of art, is a counterpart to the Mesoamerican maize in Peru or the Tlatilco-Cupisnique ceramic ties. What they possess in common, except for an addiction to sculptural and lapidaristic modes of expression, is largely the concept of the feline being, most probably the jaguar.[2] Therefore, their relationship, if it existed, must have been on a level of concept and mythology, either an ancient undercurrent of belief on which both Peruvian and Mesoamerican societies could have drawn to develop quite different art styles or by a stimulus diffusion in which the source idea was drastically reworked in the recipient setting. In this last connection the example of Mesopotamian stimuli to the rise of early Egyptian civilization comes to mind. If this interpretation of the relationship between Olmec and Chavín is the correct one, I would, all things considered, see Mesoamerica as the source and Peru as in the role of the receiving culture.

An argument against a close, continuous Olmec-Chavín relationship on the level of style is, of course, the absence of either style, or any style definitely related to either, in the Intermediate area of Lower Central America, Colombia, and Ecuador. The San Agustín sculptures of southern Colombia are, perhaps, the only candidates (Preuss 1931; Bennett 1946:848–49); but they are remarkably unlike either Olmec or Chavín, sharing with them only the attribute of feline-fanged beings, and they are only dubiously dated on the same time level as Olmec and Chavín. Further, as a style, San Agustín is considerably below the quality or sophistication of these great styles (Kroeber 1951). This absence of stylistic linkages in the Intermediate area stands in contrast, however, to many of the significant traits of the village agricultural base out of which Olmec and Chavín seem to have developed. Evidence is rapidly accumulating from Ecuador (Evans and Meggers 1957, 1958; Estrada 1958), Colombia (Reichel-Dolmatoff 1959), and Lower Central America (Coe and Baudez

---

[2] M. D. Coe has called my attention to a small but specific design element found in Olmec sculptures and also present on Chavinoid incised pottery from Kotosh, Peru, recently excavated by the University of Tokyo Expedition to Peru but not yet published. This element is a U-shaped figure with what may be a stylized ear of maize emerging from the opening.

1961) which shows the Intermediate area to be a common participant in early ceramic and other traits held also by Mesoamerica and Peru. A notable example of this is the striking similarity between Guatemalan Ocos pottery and that of the Ecuadorean Chorrera phase (Coe 1960). Thus, in spite of this background of apparent intercommunication and interchange down and up the axis of Nuclear America, the entities of style which we recognize as Olmec and Chavín remain bound to their respective areas. They did not spread to the Intermediate area, nor can they reasonably be derived from there.

THE EARLY GREAT STYLES AS PRECURSORS TO CIVILIZATION

We have placed Olmec and Chavín at that point in the developmental history of the Mesoamerican and Peruvian cultures where village farming societies undergo a transformation to become temple center-and-village societies. This event is another major threshold in pre-Columbian life. It is a different kind of threshold than that of village agriculture which precedes it by a few hundred years, but it signals important changes. It is, in effect, the threshold of complex society that leads on to civilization. The economy appears much the same as earlier; it is based on maize, or maize and root crops, supplemented with other American food plants. The technology includes pottery-making, weaving, stone carving —in brief, the village agricultural neolithic arts. Houses were permanent to semi-permanent affairs disposed in small hamlets or villages. The most noticeable difference on the cultural landscape is the ceremonial center. These centers were not urban zones. Heizer (1960) has made quite explicit the nonurban nature of La Venta, and he estimates that the constructions there could have been built and sustained only by the cooperative efforts of villagers from a surrounding radius of several kilometers. Although Chavín de Huántar is situated in a radically different natural environment from La Venta, it, too, appears to have been a complex of ceremonial buildings and chambers without a large resident population in close proximity (Bennett 1944; Tello 1960).

It is in such ceremonial centers that the outstanding monuments of the Olmec and Chavín styles are found. In Mesoamerica it is assumed that this ceremonial center-with-outlying hamlets type of settlement pattern is allied with a theocratic political structure. The assumption derives partly from the nature of the settlement and the feeling that such dispersed societies could only have been bound together by strong religious beliefs, but it derives mostly from our knowledge of the late pre- and early post-Columbian periods in Mesoamerica when lowland ceremonial centered societies were known to have a strong theocratic bias. In Peru this kind of theocratic orientation was not a feature of the Inca state; but there the archeological record shows a definite trend, from early to late times, that can best be interpreted as a movement away from religion as a dominant force and the gradual ascendance of secular power (Willey 1951). In the light of such trends it is likely that priest leadership was more important in Chavín times than later. Thus, archeological inference is on the side of identifying the nonurban ceremonial center as primarily a sacred or religious establishment whatever other functions may have been served there. Olmec and Chavín works of art must surely, then, have been religious expressions. This concatenation of circumstances, the shift from simple village agricultural societies to complex temple-centered ones and the appearance of the two great styles, suggests that Olmec and Chavín are the symbols of two ecumenical religions. These religions lie at the base of the subsequent growth of pre-Columbian Mesoamerican and Peruvian civilizations (see Bernal 1960).

This fundamental underlying nature of Olmec and Chavín art is revealed in the later cultures and styles in the two areas. For Mesoamerica, Michael D. Coe (1960 ms) suggests that all known major art styles of the southern part of the area have an origin in the Olmec style. Most directly related among these would be the styles of the slightly later "danzante" monuments at Monte Alban and the Monte Alban I phase effigy incensarios

(Caso 1938), the Olmec-derived sculptures from the later pre-Classic Period levels at Tres Zapotes, the Izapa style stelae in Chiapas, and the closely similar Late pre-Classic monuments found recently at Kaminaljuyu. More remotely, but nevertheless showing affiliations with Olmec art, especially through the link of the Izapa style, would be the Classic Maya and Classic Veracruz styles (Proskouriakoff 1950:177; Covarrubias 1957:166). Further afield, the derivative influences are dimmed or uncertain. Classic Teotihuacan art stands most apart in showing little Olmec influence, and perhaps this may be correlated with the relatively slight impress of Olmec art on an earlier level in the Valley of Mexico where it is known mainly in the occasional Tlatilco ceramic objects. But that some connections, however indirect, did exist between Olmec and Teotihaucan iconography is shown by Covarrubias (1957: fig. 22) in his diagram of the stylistic evolution of the Teotihuacan and other rain gods from the prototype of the Olmec baby-jaguar face.

For Peru, the story is much the same. There, the distribution of the Chavín style was more nearly area-wide. Perhaps as a consequence, nearly all post-Chavín styles show some Chavín feline elements (Willey 1951). Mochica art, of the north coast, depicts a feline or anthropomorphic feline as an apparent deity. Feline symbolism has an important part in Recuay, Pucara, and Nazca cultures. It is present in Tiahuanaco art, although not as the dominant motif.

CONSIDERATIONS OF CAUSALITY

We see Olmec and Chavín styles at the root of civilization in Mesoamerica and Peru. We also note, in the wider perspective of Nuclear America, that contemporaneous and related societies of the geographically intervening Intermediate area do not possess comparable great styles. Neither do they go on to civilization. From these facts I think we may reasonably conclude that Olmec and Chavín art are in some way involved with the rise to the status of civilization in their respective areas. But these are observations of history, or prehistory, and like all such observations it is difficult and perilous to attempt to read causality into them. In pointing to what I think is a special relationship between the early great styles and civilization, am I not merely defining civilization in terms of itself? In a partial sense I am; great art styles are one of the criteria by which the condition of civilization may be judged (Childe 1950). But it is not, however, altogether true in that many of the criteria of civilization are not yet present in either Mesoamerica or Peru at the time of Olmec and Chavín art florescence. Certainly one of the most significant of these, urbanization, is not; writing and metallurgy, if present, are only in their infancy; and the institution of the state, in any extensive territorial sense, is highly unlikely. The appearance of the first great styles, then, comes early in the growth of these American civilizations. By the time a full civilizational status has been achieved in either Mesoamerica or Peru these styles, as organized entities, have vanished, leaving only their residue in later styles. Nevertheless, styles themselves cannot be reified into civilization builders. They are, as I have said, symbols of institutions, attitudes, beliefs. Is, then, a belief system, a religion, a prime causal force as Toynbee has stated? I would think so, or at least I consider it near enough to a causal core to speculate on the processes whereby fundamental beliefs and their representative art may promote the growth of civilization.

In making these speculations let us consider a hypothesis about culture development in native America and particularly in the Nuclear American areas. Casting back to earlier chronological ranges than I have been talking about, it is now becoming evident that man changed from a collecting-hunting mode of existence to one of food plant cultivation by a process of introgression. The term is a botanical one, and it applies to what happened to plants over the several millennia leading up to village agriculture in Mesoamerica; but I also think it applicable to the culture change that went along with the gradual domestication of plants. The studies of Mangelsdorf and MacNeish (Mangelsdorf, Mac-Neish, and Willey 1960 ms; MacNeish 1958 and personal communication 1961) have shown that original wild plants were found in a great many small locales where they were gathered and used and where seeds were eventually sown and plants tended by small, local populations. With contact between two such small communities, of plants and people, plant introgression and hybridization ensued with a genetically improved result. This process continued among enclaves with both hybridization and with the interchange of different species as well. Present investigations indicate that primitive maize, beans, and squashes do not follow the same sequence of occurrence in incipient agricultural stratigraphies in all parts of Mesoamerica but that the order varies from region to region (MacNeish, personal communication 1961). This diversity in development led, eventually, to the New World complex of food plants and to village agriculture. I would suggest that culture, too, evolved along with plants in much the same way, by introgression or interchange and by hybridization or fusion. This, I believe, is an aspect of what Lesser (1961) is saying in his concept of social fields. To follow the analogy, I think that this is what continued to happen in the development of cultures and societies after the attainment of village agriculture. Regional interchange or regional symbiosis provided an important impetus for change and growth. Sanders (1956, 1957; Braidwood and Willey 1960 ms) has detailed this process for parts of ancient Mesoamerica. It led to civilization.

In this hypothesis an obviously crucial factor is natural environmental setting and a multiplicity of varied settings in relatively close juxtaposition to one another. As has been pointed out by various authors e.g., Wolf 1959:17–18), Mesoamerica is well suited in this regard. It is a land of climatic, altitudinal, and vegetational variety; it is rich in natural resources. Further, the archeological record shows trade and contact among distinct natural environmental and cultural regions from early times. Peru, as well, although not quite so varied, has dramatic regional differentiation, particularly between coast and highland; and the prehistory of that area may be read as a kind of counterpoint between the regional cultures of these natural zones (Kroeber

1927). Contrast the potentialities of these two areas with others of the New World which also had a basis of village agriculture. The natural environmental and cultural contours of differentiation within the Amazon basin or the Eastern Woodlands of North America are low in comparison. Products from region to region were the same or similar. Perhaps this homogeneity discouraged exchange (Coe 1961 ms).

Are we, now, at a nexus of causality in the rise of pre-Columbian civilizations in certain areas but not in others? Although conceding the importance of intra-areal cultural heterogeneity, and realizing that such heterogeneity must be to a large extent based in natural environment, I am not convinced. What of the Intermediate area which lies between and close to both of our areas of high civilization and which did not match them in these conditions of civilization? It is an area of spectacular regional environmental differentiation, tropical and semi-arid coasts, tropical lowlands, semi-tropical and temperate valleys, cool-temperate uplands. It has them all, and it is not an area poor in resources. We also know that the communities of this area were in possession of agriculture about as early as those of either Mesoamerica and Peru. These village agriculturists were similarly skilled in pottery making and, probably, the other neolithic crafts. In fact, they participated in the same technical traditions as their Mesoamerican or Peruvian contemporaries. Where then is the lack? What are the essential differences between the Intermediate area and its native cultures and those of the Mesoamerican and Peruvian areas?

I return, again, to the great styles, to Olmec and Chavín, for which there is no counterpart from Honduras to southern Ecuador. I have suggested that they, in themselves, are but the symbols for the religious ideologies of the early farming societies of Mesoamerica and Peru. I would further suggest that in these ideologies these early societies had developed a mechanism of intercommunication, a way of knitting together the smaller parts of the social universe of their day into a more unified whole than it had heretofore been or would otherwise be. In a way similar to that of the interchange of objects, plants, and techniques which had previously prepared the village agricultural threshold, the sharing of common ideologies led to the threshold of civilization by enlarging the effective social field. By this enlargement more individuals, more social segments, more local societies combined and coordinated their energies and efforts than at any time before. Regional differentiation in culture is an important precondition to cultural development insofar as differences contribute to the richness of the larger order, but without union the different parts remain isolated and in danger of stagnation. There are various ways by which man has promoted such union, but mutually and deeply held beliefs seem paramount. Such belief systems were, I think, the distinguishing features of the Mesoamerican and Peruvian societies of the first half of the First Millennium B.C., and the great Olmec and Chavín art styles are our clues to them.

Yet, even if my thesis is accepted thus far, have we done more than follow the chimaera of causality into one more disguise? Why did Mesoamerica and Peru develop early great religions and art styles and other areas not? What was the reason for their genius? I do not know. I do not think that it sprang from a seed planted by Chinese voyagers—or from two seeds brought by two such sets of voyagers—despite the facts that the Chou dynasty is replete with prowling tigers and that the time element is right for such a transference (Heine-Geldern 1959). It does us no good to deny the sudden mutation of creative change to the aborigines of America. It is no easier to explain elsewhere than it is here. What we are seeking is probably in New World soil, but genius must arise from preconditions which to our eyes do not foreshadow it. Local prototypes of Chavín and Olmec may eventually be found, although these will only carry the story back a little in time and leave the startling florescences unexplained.

I do not reject in their entirety any of the factors or forces we have been discussing as having had possible important influence in the growth of New World civilization. Climate, soil, agricultural potential, natural regional variety, all undoubtedly were significant. I am hesitant, however, to pinpoint any one of them as *the cause*. I am equally hesitant to advance my thesis of an early, prevailing, multi-regional ecumenical religion in either Mesoamerica or Peru as a *sole cause* of later civilizational greatness. I ask, rather, that such phenomena as I have directed attention to be considered as a step in the process of cultural development— a step which almost certainly was taken in these two areas of native America. For it may be that we phrase the problem wrong, that the search for the very well-springs of origin and cause is meaningless, and that the limits of anthropology are to appraise and understand the continuum of process as it is disclosed to us rather than to fix its ultimate beginnings.

ANCIENT AMERICAN GOLDSMITHS

Dudley T. Easby, Jr.

CELLINI, the celebrated Renaissance goldsmith, is said to have tried in vain to discover exactly how a jeweler of ancient Mexico had made a fish of silver with a delicate inlay of gold (Westheim 1950:300). And Albrecht Dürer, another Renaissance master, frankly marveled at the talent of the Aztec craftsmen (Thausing 1884, Vol. II:183). Even today, experienced metallurgists have questioned whether modern jewelers, with all their twentieth-century equipment, could duplicate some of the masterpieces turned out by the Indians before the Spaniards conquered them.

In ancient Mexico, gold was highly regarded as an item of tribute and also had religious connotations. Its Aztec name was *teocuitlatl,* literally "excrement of the gods." The goldsmiths had their own special deity, *Xipe Totec,* and anyone guilty of stealing a gold object was flayed alive to propitiate this bloodthirsty god.

The goldworkers, a highly respected group, came to exercise their skills to the exclusion of all other work. By the time of the Spanish Conquest, they had achieved a degree of specialization that would put any modern labor union to shame. (See Plate 15.)

Friar Sahagún, the sixteenth-century historian, mentions two main categories: the smith who hammered or beat gold and the founders who cast it. Within those categories the craftsmen had separate names, depending on the kind of object they made

---

Reprinted from *Natural History* 65 (8), 1956:401–9, by permission of the author and editor of *Natural History.*

(1959: Book 9, chapters 15, 16). In Montezuma's time, the goldworkers had their own center in Azcapotzalco, a short distance from the capital. Unhappily, however, no remains of their workshops have survived.

Goldworking does not seem to have reached Mexico until the Toltec Period, about A.D. 900. The Mayas to the south, with all their mathematicians, astronomers, architects, sculptors, and lapidaries, produced no goldworkers. The gold hoard dredged from the Sacred Well at Chichén Itzá in the Yucatán peninsula was probably brought in by trade. It consisted mainly of thin gold plaques, imported from farther south, to which local workers added low relief or repoussé decoration. The craftsmanship is superb, but even this relatively simple technique was unknown before the Toltecs of Mexico introduced it at the end of the tenth century. Some goldwork from the Valley of Mexico resembles jewelry from as far away as Panama and Costa Rica. And, curiously enough, legend has it that the god of the goldsmiths, *Xipe,* came from the south.

The small drawing below shows that the office of goldworker was hereditary in Mexico. These artisans were free to barter their products in the fabulous market place of Tlaltelolco, described by Cortes, (1519–1526), Bernal Diaz del Castillo, The Anonymous Conqueror (1917), and other eyewitnesses. There were booths for trading gold objects, and also those that handled the raw material, gold dust and nuggets.

Not so at the other end of the Golden Axis of the New World. In the highly organized state of the Incas of Peru the goldworker (*kori-camayoc*) was not a trader but is said to have been a full-time government worker in the local bureaucracy. Goldworking began in Peru about 1,000 years before the birth of Christ, but almost nothing can be surmised about the workers before the Incaic Period in the fifteenth and sixteenth centuries. As in Mexico, the office was probably hereditary.

Fine metalworking reached a high degree of proficiency among the Chimus of the desert coast of northern Peru. Their kingdom arose about A.D. 1200, and when they were finally conquered by the Incas, around A.D. 1450, their best goldsmiths were carried off to work at the court in Cuzco. At the Chimu capital of Chan-Chán, near present-day Trujillo, some remains of an extensive metalworking industry are still visible, but no representation of a metalworker has ever been found. This is curious, considering that the many products of the potter's art portray almost every other aspect of daily life.

Colombia has long been distinguished for the excellence and variety of its ancient gold ornaments. (See Plate 17.) There is a museum in Bogotá devoted entirely to ancient indigenous goldwork.

A somewhat apocryphal tale persists in Colombia that throws light on the esteem in which the craft was held. A local chieftain had many skilled goldworkers, whose services were in great demand. He refused, however, to lend any to a neighboring ruler unless he received two hostages for each artisan. The neighbor, being crafty and ambitious, conceived the idea of sending two of his best and bravest warriors in each of the many exchanges that followed. Then, at a given signal, his "Fifth Column" suddenly rose and seized the domains of the goldworkers' chief. (Simón 1953:303.)

Apparently commerce flourished between the Chibchas on the plains of Bogotá and their neighbors. Unworked gold was sometimes exchanged for salt and emeralds. In fact, the god of the merchants, *Chibchachun,* was also the deity of the goldworkers and was propitiated with gold offerings. The Spanish authority José Pérez de Barradas (1954, Vol. I:38,261) mentions special places known as *Patios de Indios* where the Indians set up their forges and foundries for working gold, and he laments that not one has been excavated scientifically.

The fine jewelry of Ecuador has been described by archeologists and metallurgists, but little can be said of the men who made it except that they were several hundred years ahead of the rest of the world in using platinum. A temperature of 3,223.8 degrees F. is necessary to melt platinum, and the Indians had no way to produce such heat. But they were able to use platinum by mixing fine grains with gold dust and alternately heating the mixture with a blowpipe and hammering it until it became a homogeneous mass.

This was the first crude beginning of "powder metallurgy," arrived at independently and then lost, to be re-invented in Europe in the nineteenth century. Today, powdered metal is forced into strong molds under hydraulic pressure (replacing the Indians' repeated hammering) and heated to incipient fusion— or, as we say, "sintered."

The products of the aboriginal Panamanian and Central American goldworkers, like those of Colombia, show great talent in casting and then forging to stretch certain flat elements. . . . In this area pieces were set with precious stones occasionally, a technique also used in Peru and Mexico.

People express surprise that gold should have been worked in these regions before copper, which was the first metal used in Egypt and North America. The explanation is simple. Gold in a relatively pure state was conspicuous and readily available in stream beds. It was pretty and caught the sun's rays. It was easy to work, and it did not oxidize or corrode. The Indians worked virgin gold, not gold won from auriferous ores by smelting. Despite early Spanish tales of gold mines worked before the Conquest, there is no proof that gold ore was ever smelted in pre-Columbian America.

The volume and value of gold jewelry produced in America before the coming of the Europeans was enormous. The Spanish chronicles give inventories of loot *ad nauseam,* running into the millions of dollars. But next to nothing was recorded on techniques. The one truly outstanding contribution is Friar Sahagún's sixteenth-century description of casting from wax models, written in a phonetic transliteration of the Aztec tongue. If one has patience to unravel the original version with an Aztec grammar and vocabulary, it is an astonishingly accurate job of technical reporting. With very few changes it might have been written yesterday or today.

Fortunately, the objects themselves tell their own story of how they were made. The rarest treasure house of technical information is the partially worked or unfinished piece. Certain gold-platinum pieces from Ecuador are in this category, and so are the twin warriors with paddle clubs from Panama.

Without doubt, the first step in the long evolution of working gold was the crude shaping of a nugget by grinding and hammering. It is almost too much to expect to find many such objects at this late date, but George Grant MacCurdy described two in 1911 in his monumental study of the Chiriqui part of Panama.

ANNEALING DISCOVERED

The early craftsmen could produce ingots of workable size by fusing gold dust and small grains, with a blowpipe to quicken the flame. Aztec drawings show goldworkers using the blowpipe, and Sir Walter Raleigh reports its use in the Guianas. The earliest work on metallurgy in the New World (Barba 1640) mentions blowpipes, adding that bellows were unknown before the Europeans introduced them.

Some long-forgotten smith in Peru or Colombia must have observed that after cold-hammering an ingot for awhile to stretch it into a sheet, the metal began to get springy and unworkable. We call this "strain hardening" and now know that it is due to changes in the microstructure of the metal caused by hammering. The Indian worker did not know why, but he observed that his hammer would just bounce off the metal without affecting its shape. If he struck harder blows, it became brittle and cracked. At some stage in his effort to escape from this blind alley, he may have remembered that the metal was pliable when it first came from the fire in ingot form. In any case, he found out that if he heated the strain-hardened metal, it lost its springiness and hardness and became as easy to work as it had been at the start. True, it would become springy again under hammer blows, but he now knew that the remedy was to heat it. He had discovered the process of annealing.

Hammer-hardening was the "secret process" used by the ancients in both the Old and New World to temper copper and bronze weapons and tools. (See Plate 16.) The craftsman simply refrained from heat-treating the objects after the last hammering. The gold-copper tools found in Colombia were hardened in the same way. In fact, a springy gold ornament like the famous Huarmey collar in the American Museum of Natural History requires no laboratory examination to establish that, although repeatedly hammered and annealed, the final step was hammering.

The discovery of annealing enabled the smith to "raise" cups and produce other forms previously impossible but it brought him a new crop of headaches. For example, if certain alloys were overheated, they got "burned," and no amount of heat treatment would restore their malleability. All the smith could do was to abandon the work and melt it down. Also, if gold were not watched carefully and removed from the fire when it reached a dull red, it would collapse suddenly. As Herbert Maryon, the British Museum's authority on ancient metalwork (1954) has pointed out, gold gives almost no warning in color change before reaching its melting point. In fact, today gold is often annealed in a dark corner so the craftsman can perceive the subtle change to dull red and withdraw it from the fire.

Annealing ushered in another problem with alloys of copper with silver or gold, which were common in the New World. Heating such alloys in the open air produced a thin scale of copper oxide, which impeded further work and had to be removed. Today this is done by putting the piece in a mild acid bath, or "pickle," while still hot. Spanish chroniclers report that the Indians in Colombia used organic acids from plants.

In discovering how to dissolve the copper-oxide scale, the ancient workers also found that by alternately heating and "pickling" a gold-copper or silver-copper alloy, they could impart the color of the noble metal to the finished product. This was coloring by concentration, not plating. The repeated action of forming and dissolving the copper oxide without affecting the gold or silver in the alloy left a surface richer in gold or silver each time it was carried out.

The extent to which true plating was practiced in America before the coming of Europeans still remains to be established by competent metallurgists. Paul Bergsöe (1937) has reported some pieces from Ecuador that show signs of fusion gilding, a process in which a molten gold-copper alloy is flowed over preheated copper and then hammered. At one time archeologists here and in Europe unquestioningly accepted the theory that the Indians knew and used mercury for amalgam plating, a case of relying on familiarity with modern methods to attribute to the Indians a technique they did not possess. That this belief should have gained such a foothold is strange; for in 1653, Father Cobo wrote that, although cinnabar was used as a pigment in Peru, the Incas did not know how to extract mercury from it. And William H. Holmes (1887), writing of the Chiriqui of Panama in 1887, noted that there was "no evidence whatever that these people had any knowledge of mercury." Modern spectroscopic analyses, made by Paul Bergsöe, of ancient American pieces confirm Cobo and Holmes.

Another armchair theory about plating was that models or molds were coated or lined with gold leaf before a casting was poured. But as William C. Root has pointed out, "This is impossible, as the molten metal would dissolve the gold leaf before it solidified."

The high point of hammer work in raising a vessel from a flat disc of sheet metal was reached by the Peruvian smiths in making high-relief effigy beakers. The technique was well known in the ancient Near East and Greece and is still used by art metalworkers. It requires that the metal be kept pliable by repeated annealing. It also calls for the greatest skill and care in hammering to avoid cracking or tearing the thin metal. No metalworker today would undertake such a job with the rudimentary equipment of the Indian smiths, and few could do it even with twentieth-century tools.

TWO-PIECE MOLDS USED

Once it was found out that solid nuggets could be liquefied by the application of sufficient heat, the discovery of casting was inevitable. Probably molten metal was first poured into shapes hollowed in the surface of flat stones, or "open molds." Next in order of complexity came the two-piece "closed mold" for ax blades, knives, and the like.

The first step in a two-piece mold was to make a model or pattern to the exact shape of the finished piece. This was pressed into a slab of clay to about half the thickness of the model. A second slab of clay was then laid over the first and pressed down on the model. The two slabs or halves of the mold were then separated and the model removed, leaving a cavity of the same shape. A pouring channel for the metal was hollowed in the mold, which was then fired to harden it. The two halves were bound together, and the molten metal was poured in to fill the cavity.

To avoid having to take the mold apart to remove the original model, some aboriginal genius hit upon the idea of making the model out of wax or resin so it could be melted out. All that was necessary was to leave a hole in the one-piece outer shell or mold. The same hole later served as an entrance channel for the molten metal. When the metal cooled its mold was broken away, and inside was an exact facsimile of the wax model reproduced in solid metal. This was "pickled," sharpened up with tools where necessary, burnished, and polished.

Many persons seem to have gained a mistaken idea of the "lost wax process," as this technique has been called. The phrase has been taken to mean that the *process* was lost and rediscovered, whereas it simply means that the *wax* is lost in the process.

Wax was easy to model, and this process made possible single-piece castings of the most complicated sort. When a gold pendant with twin warriors was reproduced recently, the caster took the easy way out; he made it in two parts and soldered them together.

In a mold for a complex shape like the one just mentioned, there were many recesses where air would be trapped when the molten metal was poured in, so the caster had to provide for its escape. He therefore attached a series of wax rods around the outside of the original model before enveloping it in the clay. When the wax was melted out, these rods left hollow channels through the outer shell. The molten metal would flow part way into these, leaving tiny bars projecting from the cast object. These were usually cut off and burnished down in finishing the piece, but traces of them in the twin warrior pendant prove that air vents were used in casting this object.

In addition to facilitating the flow of the molten metal by these air vents, it was customary to preheat the mold just before pouring to prevent the metal from cooling and setting before the cavity was filled.

To assure a smooth surface on the finished casting, Sahagún reports that the surface of the wax model was coated with a paste made of water and finely powdered charcoal before the outer shell was applied. Today, an aqueous emulsion of graphite is used for the same purpose in precision industrial castings.

The true culmination of casting from wax models in pre-Columbian America came when this method was elaborated to produce hollow objects. The method was fully described by Sahagún in his sixteenth-century account of the Aztec goldworkers. It differs in only one major respect from the method for making solid castings.

The starting point was to make a porous core or nucleus that could be broken up and removed from the object at the end of the process, leaving it hollow inside. According to Sahagún, this was made of clay and crushed charcoal; and analyses of core fragments confirm this.

After the core had dried thoroughly in the sun, it was covered with a coating of wax. The thickness of this wax represented the thickness of the metal in the final hollow casting. Using little pellets and threads of wax for decorative details, the founder completed his model with sharp tools just as a sculptor works in modeling clay.

From this point on, the steps in the process were identical with those described above for making a solid casting. Of course, something had to be done to keep the core from slipping out of position after the wax was melted out and before the metal was poured into the mold to replace it. This was accomplished by piercing the wax model with wooden pegs or thorns, such as maguey spines, which penetrated into the core and projected above the surface of the wax. These projecting ends would be embedded in the outer shell when it was applied and would hold the core in place. A simplified version of the various steps in the process of casting a hollow bird ornament is shown in Figs. 23–26.

Herbert Maryon has suggested that the discovery of soldering probably came when someone first noticed that some nuggets in a crucible melted before others. Having once noted the color and source of these early-melting nuggets, the craftsman was able to procure a naturally alloyed solder merely by separating them out of future lots before anything went into the crucible. Their lower melting point was due to a higher content of silver or copper or both.

Solder in goldwork does not mean the familiar tinsmith's alloy of lead and tin that melts around 330 degrees F. but a series of alloys of gold and copper, with silver sometimes added. These are called "hard solder" by jewelers and have melting points in the neighborhood of 1,500 degrees F.

The joints on many pre-Columbian pieces are so strong and so close in color to the parts joined that there has been speculation about "welding," just as there has been in ancient metalwork in the Old World. The explanation of these perfect joints is to be found in part in the earlier discussion of "coloring," or enriching the surface of gold-copper alloys by heating and "pickling." A well-burnished joint on a soldered piece treated this way will be exceedingly difficult to detect. Soil acids have the same effect as pickling on the surface of a gold-copper object buried for centuries. Detection is also made difficult because some of the solder

308   *Anthropology and Art*

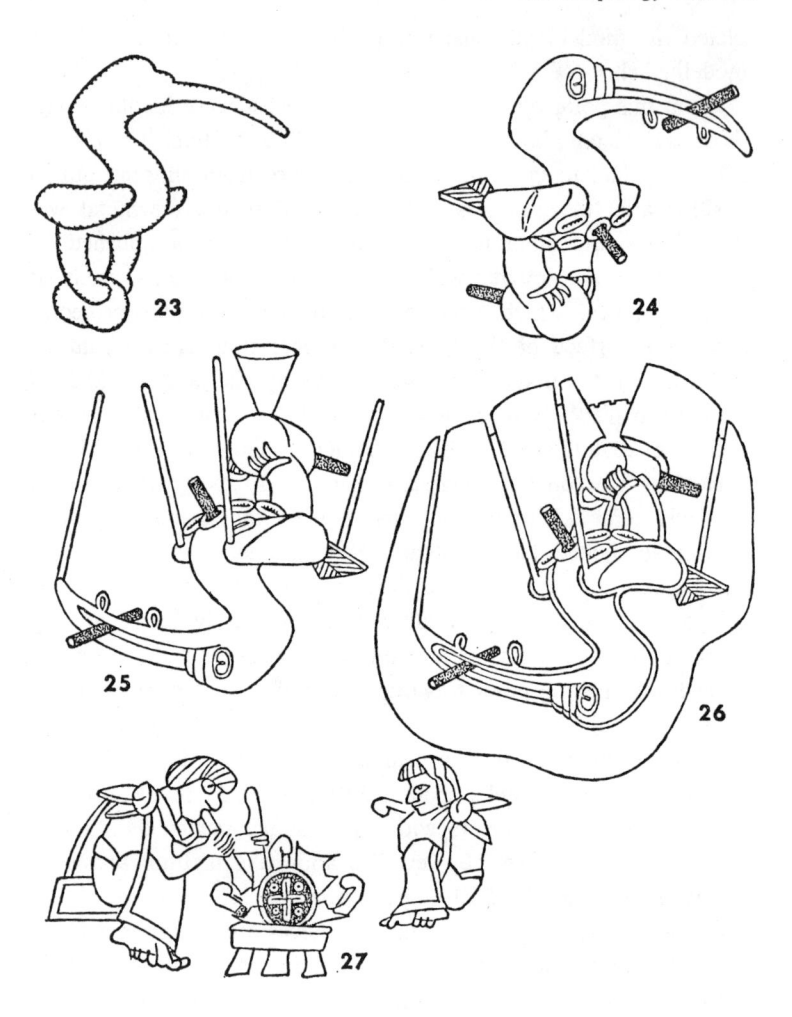

Fig. 23. This rough core, made of clay mixed with charcoal, will be broken up and removed after casting, leaving the piece hollow inside. This saves gold and also permits the making of hollow vessels.

Fig. 24. The rough core is first covered with a uniform coating of wax. The eyes, talons, suspension rings under the bill, and decorative holes have been added in the form of wax threads. The founder finishes the details on the wax model with sharp tools. The three

will have penetrated the metal in the parts joined, tending to produce a uniform color.

To summarize, although goldwork that has come down to us shows that the ancient goldworkers of the New World had mastered other techniques, the principal ones were: (1) stretching and shaping by hammering, with the indispensable step of repeated annealing to keep the metal pliable; (2) casting in open and closed molds; and (3) soldering. Of course, many pieces, like the pendant from Colombia (See Plate 15), show the use of combinations of these techniques. In addition, there are the strictly decorative-techniques, many of which are also shown in the accompanying illustrations, such as repoussé, chasing, incising or scratching with a sharp point (true engraving requires a steel tool and hence was unknown), inlaying with other metals, setting with precious and semi-precious stones, sheathing wood, bone, shell and resin objects with gold foil, trimming and openwork, and painting metal. Enameling, electroplating, and centrifugal casting are about all we have been able to add.

A final and, unhappily inconclusive, word about the tools of these forgotten jewelers. Not one of their workshops has been excavated scientifically. However, there are examples or reports of clay braziers and crucibles; blowpipes; stone and metal punches and chisels; carved stone and wood models and patterns; stone

---

black bars are the pegs to keep the core from slipping out of position during the work.

FIG. 25. The casting will be done in an inverted position. Before enveloping the model in clay, a cone of wax is added to provide a pouring channel. And four wax rods have been added to provide air vents when the metal is poured in.

FIG. 26. This drawing represents a section through the mold after the wax model has been melted out. The colored portion shows where the gold will form rods that will be later cut off and burnished. The core is finally broken and removed through the hollow bill and the holes in the breast and the back of the perch.

FIG. 27. The fact that gold working was hereditary in ancient Mexico is deduced from this illustration from the Mendoza Codex showing a metalworker teaching his son the use of the blowpipe.

anvils; and stone and metal hammers. No tongs have been found or described, but unquestionably the ancient workers used some sort of lifting sticks to handle hot crucibles and to remove annealed metal from the fire when it reached red heat.

These unknown craftsmen were scarcely the subhuman barbarians many have considered them from the sixteenth century on, nor do they fit the eighteenth-century poet's concept of that simple unspoiled child of nature, "the poor Indian, whose untutor'd mind sees God in clouds, or hears him in the wind." Plenty of free time and patience were not the only advantages these workers enjoyed over their modern counterparts. They possessed an almost matchless dexterity and ingenuity that enabled them to turn out with rudimentary equipment masterpieces that hand workers today would be hard put to imitate.

CLAY SCULPTURE FROM JAINA

Luis Aveleyra Arroyo de Anda and Gordon F. Eckholm

JAINA (pronounced HY-nah) is a small, low, mangrove-bordered island lying just off the gulf coast of Mexico, thirty miles north of the city of Campeche. Roughly a square mile in size, it is separated from the mainland of the Yucatan Peninsula by a channel about 150 feet wide.

Unimpressive in size and appearance as it is, Jaina is a world-renowned archeological site of the ancient Maya, and is specially famous as the source of great numbers of those minor Maya masterpieces known as Jaina figurines. (See Plate 18.) These beautifully executed little figures of the Mesoamerican Classic Period have been recovered from innumerable burials that are found there, for the island is a great cemetery of simple, shallow graves in which pottery vessels and ornaments, in addition to the figurines, were placed with the bodies. The island is unique among Maya sites, for even in those that boast magnificent buildings and great stone sculptures, graves are not often discovered, and complete clay figures are rarely found. More well-preserved Maya figurines have come from Jaina than from all other Maya sites combined.

Despite its archeological riches, Jaina has been little known to the archeologist. Although hundreds of the figurines can be found in museums and in private collections, they have, for the most part, been excavated by illegal diggers and disposed of through commercial channels. This grave looting has been going on for a

---

Reprinted from *Natural History* 74 (4), 1966:40–46, by permission of the authors and the editor of *Natural History*.

long time; the French explorer Désiré Charnay, who in the 1890's provided the first published account of Jaina archeology, reported that the island was then being dug into by treasure hunters. Undoubtedly this has continued intermittently, but the phenomenal growth of interest in pre-Columbian art during the last thirty years has caused an acceleration in the ransacking of the island by commercial diggers.

It may seem strange that Jaina has received so little archeological attention in the past, but it must be remembered that it is only one of a tremendous number of Maya sites, and that many major problems of Maya archeology can be attacked in other places to greater advantage. Jaina has also been a difficult place to reach and to work. There are no roads by which one can approach the island by land, the most feasible route being by canoe from Campeche. All drinking water and other supplies must be brought in the same way, although one could depend for food on the plentiful fish that are easily caught in the vicinity. Despite its inaccessibility, several groups of Mexican archeologists investigated the site for short periods in 1941–42, and later in 1947 and 1957, but all were working with limited facilities and personnel.

The most recent expedition to the island, and the one that has accomplished the most extensive work there, was a by-product of the planning and building of the magnificent new National Museum of Anthropology in Chapultepec Park in Mexico City. The museum was an all-out effort by the Mexican government to establish a new and adequate center for its extraordinary archeological treasures and for studies relating to the country's many native Indian groups. Architect Pedro Ramírez Vásquez, designer of the new building and head of the council created for planning the museum, realized the need to enrich the collections. He helped to send out several archeological and ethnographic expeditions to make possible full coverage of all aspects of Mexican anthropology.

Jaina was an obvious choice as a source for enriching the museum's exhibition materials, and the expedition sent there remained in the field from mid-April to mid-June of 1964. Equipment and supplies, a powerful motorboat, and a barge were provided. A modern camp was established by setting up several prefabricated steel structures and by constructing large water-storage tanks. The installation, which has accommodations for fourteen persons, includes a kitchen, dining room, laboratory, and storerooms, and was designed both to accommodate this expedition and to be a permanent structure for future use by archeologists. It also furnishes quarters for the guards who remain in residence to protect the site from further depredation by clandestine diggers.

The expedition was conducted by the archeologists Román Piña Chan, who was in direct charge of the field activities, and Luis Aveleyra Arroyo de Anda, at that time Secretary General of the museum planning council. Two physical anthropologists, Roberto Jiménez Ovando and Sergio López, collaborated in the excavations and undertook the preservation of skeletal materials. Fifty laborers were hired for excavation work; twenty others were employed as cooks, fishermen, and administrative and maintenance personnel. With this staff it was possible to excavate extensively at several places on the island.

Nearly four hundred burials were methodically explored during the season. They provided an invaluable corpus of information on burial customs, and the largest and most spectacular collection of figurines and other objects, as well as osteological materials, ever gathered at Jaina. This great amount of excavated material awaits detailed classification and study, and should result in a new understanding of the sequence of grave and artifact types and of the history of the site's occupation. It is most important that precise information on the associations of various types of objects in graves will now be available.

The people of ancient Jaina deposited their dead directly in the ground, the body either extended full length or, more frequently, in a flexed or natal position, with knees drawn up to the chin. In nearly every instance a heavy tripod ceramic bowl was inverted, as if protectively, over the head. In some cases the body was painted red with iron oxide, indicated by remnants of this durable paint adhering to the bones. Occasionally a jadeite bead was placed in the mouth. Many kinds of funerary offerings are found with the skeletons, including pottery vessels of various kinds, ornaments and necklaces of stone and shell, and generally one or more of the terra-cotta figurines that have made Jaina so justly famous—the latter usually on the body's chest or arms. The infant dead were placed inside large pottery jars with inverted tripod bowls serving as lids. Many of the finest figurines were found with this type of infant burial. The skeletons at Jaina indicate that these people followed the usual ancient Maya custom of deforming the skull—a method of modifying the shape of the head by the application of pressure during infancy—and that tooth mutilation was in vogue. The incisors were filed in various ways; sometimes their outer surfaces were inlaid with small disks of iron pyrites or of semi-precious stones.

The quantity of graves on the island is nearly unbelievable, for while working in only relatively small areas the expedition excavated four hundred of them—a number limited only by the time available. Considering the large areas still untouched, it is conservatively estimated that there must be more than 20,000 burials still remaining. This is most remarkable in view of the large numbers that must have been rifled over the years by the treasure hunters. To everyone's surprise, however, these grave robbers have been able to accomplish only minimal damage, simply because of the incredible volume of material available.

The figurines that appear in the burials are of great variety and of extraordinary interest. Most of them represent human beings in ceremonial regalia, much like the figures on Maya stone monuments. There are warriors, ball players, priests, and perhaps deities dressed in robes and high, elaborate headdresses, decked in all the symbolic accouterments of their religion. There is far more freedom of representation, however, than was apparently allowed in the supposedly stricter conventions of stone carving, and we find realistically modeled animals and men and women in a variety of poses, often simply dressed and occupied with what can only be described as everyday activities. A great many of the figurines accent the more human qualities that are usually absent in Maya art.

The figures are made of a fine clay, fired to a light tan or pink color. A majority of them are moldmade by the use of a single-piece mold that served to fashion the entire front surface. The back was probably applied when the front was still in its mold by fitting onto it a thin sheet of clay and welding it around the edges, leaving a hollow interior. Often there were pellets of clay left inside this hollow to make the figurine into a rattle, or in some cases, cuts or perforations transformed it into a whistle. Other figures were made entirely by hand modeling, or the faces were moldmade while the bodies and headdresses were individually modeled and attached. The figurines were often covered with a white slip—an over-all coat of liquid clay—before firing, and then were painted with brilliant colors. These colors are often preserved and add greatly to the beauty of the objects.

It is the hand-modeled pieces that are the high point in Jaina figurine art. Here the artist could develop his forms with great freedom. (See Plate 18.) It is easily understood why these figurines are the most coveted by collectors and museums. Certainly they compare favorably in interest and esthetic quality with the elaborate Tanagra figurines of Classic Greece or the best of the clay sculpture of early Egypt or China.

Jaina has become so famous for its burials and its figurines that little attention has been paid to the fact that the island also supports a good-sized Maya ceremonial center. There is a large plaza surrounded by a number of mounds, and preliminary tests have shown that these contain temples and other buildings in which there are indications of several phases of construction. There are two higher mounds, known as the Zacpool and the Zayosal, that must have been the principal temples, the larger

Zacpool being about sixty feet high. There are few standing walls, however, and nearly all of the buildings have been divested of their stone facings. Some time earlier in this century the island was occupied by an industry engaged in the burning of lime, with the ruins serving as convenient quarries. Limestone was available in small-sized pieces that had been used in the ancient buildings. The burning of limestone to produce lime was facilitated by the fuel at hand in the mangrove wood that could be cut on the island or along the shore of the mainland.

It is difficult to know just how to interpret the archeological remains of Jaina. While this location on an island could mean that it was a fishing and perhaps a trading station for coastal canoe traffic, it is unlikely that these were its primary functions, because of the presence of the ceremonial buildings and the extensive burial grounds. It appears more probable that Jaina was, at least in part, a kind of mecca for the deceased, and that the dead and perhaps the dying were brought from the surrounding country of the mainland for burial in a place that was thought to be specially sacred or favorable. This would be consonant with practice in other areas in Mesoamerica where special reverence was seemingly accorded to particular bodies of water or islands. Such a hallowed site is the sacred *cenote,* or natural well, at Chichén Itzá, famous as a place of sacrifice. Evidences of similar rites are found in the numerous ceremonial vessels that have been recovered from Lake Atitlán in Guatemala. We know too, from historical accounts, that at the time of the Spanish Conquest, the Isla de los Sacrificios—in what is now the harbor of the city of Veracruz—was a place of reverence, and that pilgrimages were made to it from distant points. In a similar fashion, Jaina may have figured in a form of water cult that was of greater importance at an earlier date than it appears to have been at the time of the Spanish invasion. Whatever its function in Maya society, Jaina was occupied only during the latter half of the Classic Period and perhaps to some extent into the Post-Classic. This would span the period between the sixth and the tenth or eleventh centuries A.D.

Despite the recent studies, many questions remain concerning the Maya occupation of the site. It is uncertain, for instance, if the island is a natural formation or if it was built by man. There are some geologists who have suggested the latter because the island is underlain by a thick layer of white, sticky marl, perhaps composed of what is known locally as *sascab*. This is a soft, crumbly form of unconsolidated, limey material found in cavities in the Yucatan limestone and used by the Maya in their construction work. Certainly, huge quantities of limestone were brought from the mainland for the construction of the buildings, and, if a good portion of the island itself is artificial, Jaina saw the expending of tremendous amounts of human labor. There are also traces of what might have been a stone bridge crossing the channel that separates the island from the mainland, but they have not yet been investigated.

Obviously much remains to be done at Jaina before all aspects of its culture are known and its role in the florescence of Maya civilization is fully revealed. Through its miniature clay sculptures, however, it has already provided a greater visual understanding of the appearance and activities of the ancient Maya people than have the materials from any other Maya site.

NORTHWEST COAST INDIAN ART

Erna Gunther

THE COUNTRY AND ITS PEOPLE

THE COUNTRY and the life developed by the Indians of this region are strikingly different from Indian settings in other parts of America. The coastal strip from the mouth of the Columbia River to southeastern Alaska is broken by deep bays and inlets, and heavily wooded with conifers that cover the high mountains. Sheltered coves into which fresh water streams empty provided ideal locations for villages where a society based on a plentiful, dependable food supply and an equitable climate developed. The mountain barrier to the east and the rough seas to the south isolated this region from the main currents of cultural development on the continent and gave opportunity for the creation of an original and independent way of life. This resulted in a society that developed many of the culture traits generally associated with the presence of agriculture, which they did not have, although this economy had a similar rigid seasonal aspect. Village life gave opportunity for social interaction within and created a unit for intergroup relationships.

Ethnographic work on the Northwest Coast and study of its cultural relationships began when George Steller in 1741 prowled a village on Kodiak Island from which the natives had evidently fled, and there recognized some greens which were drying to be used as food, similar to ones in Kamchatka. The observations of these visitors to the coast are excellent and as modern eth-

---

Reprinted from *Northwest Coast Indian Art:* Catalogue of the Exhibit at the Seattle World's Fair Fine Arts Pavilion, 1962, pp. 9–38, by the permission of the author.

nographers increase their knowledge these early records become more understandable and useful. In world culture history, a story that begins in the 18th century does not seem of much consequence. Even on the North American continent this is almost a century after the Pueblo revolt against the Spaniards and coincides almost exactly with the history of the United States as an independent nation. While archaeology can trace this culture much farther into the past, it is still a very fragmentary account.

The highly complex society of the Northwest Coast is based on a fishing, gathering, and hunting economy which established an annual cycle of activity. During the winter, life went on in small villages, each consisting of a few large houses or a large one and a number of smaller dwellings. However many, these always stood in a single row facing the beach and as close to it as the tides would allow. On the beach, the canoes were lined up, piles of shell accumulated from the eating of shellfish, fire pits were seen here and there, as well as other signs of community life. These villages were all conspicuously lacking in any planned arrangement, this haphazard appearance even extending to the placing of their great totem poles.

The ground upon which the houses were built was never owned by an individual. In the northern villages with their more complex social organization an area might be considered as being associated with a social division such as a lineage, clan or phratry, and in the simpler societies a family may traditionally occupy a certain stretch of beach, but if a house was not occupied and fell apart, anyone in the village might clear it away and build there. Houses were built by a group of male members of a family, brothers or cousins, and each then occupied a section of the house. The larger houses were from 60 to several hundred feet long and appropriately wide. They were built of cedar planks, either vertically or horizontally placed, on a framework of great uprights supporting cross beams. The framework belonged jointly to the builders, but the planks were the personal possession of the cooperating individuals and might be removed at will. In case of a quarrel this could lead to a chilly situation.

Inside the house a bed platform was built along the two long sides and across one end. On this the families slept, and when the house was used for ceremonial occasions the audience sat here. This culture was very conscious of relative social position and this was reflected in the placing of families in the house both for permanent occupancy and for guests at a social gathering. The places of honor were across the back of the house, farthest from the door, and from there positions were graded down to the slaves who gathered beside the door. Fires located in the center of the house supplied heat and light. The monumental character of these houses was typical of the spirit of Northwest Coast society, which was carried on in a large and affluent manner.

In the spring when the salmon runs began the villagers departed for the fishing grounds. The family possessions were loaded into canoes whose capacity was expanded by fastening two together and setting a platform of planks between them. For this purpose the wall planks of the house were used and during the summer they also formed the base of a rectangular tent, the upper part of which was covered with mats. The better fishing places were near the mouth of a river and belonged to the wealthy men of the village, in fact were one of the sources of their wealth. When the owner had taken all he needed he invited people who did not have such privileges to use his site. Such a gesture was expected of him and if he failed to make it, his prestige suffered.

The basis of Northwest Coast plenty was the presence of two fish, the salmon and the halibut which could be dried and kept for long periods of time. At the fishing station they were prepared and dried by the women and at the end of the season carried back to the winter village by the canoe load. During the summer season wild vegetables and fruits were also gathered, some to be eaten at once and others to be dried for winter use. After returning to the village short trips for food in season were always taken and shellfish were part of the daily diet. When a village was preparing for a great feast these food-gathering activities were intensified, for several hundred guests need quantities of food.

The 18th century explorers generally came to the coast in

late April or early May and often recorded that they found many abandoned villages. These, of course, were the winter villages which had recently been left for the fishing grounds. By the early 19th century the abandoned villages, however, bespoke the tragedy that was overtaking the coast in the form of introduced diseases that took on epidemic proportions.

Transportation in this area consisted of canoe travel and the "Grease Trails" leading to the interior. In canoe building the only possible rivals to this coast were the Polynesians. The canoes, like the houses, were made of red cedar, hewn from a single log and ranged from 10 to 70 feet in length. There were a variety of models, each made for a specific purpose. Whether the sail had been developed before it was seen on European vessels is a matter of dispute and unless some unexpected evidence is found, it is doubtful that the matter can ever be settled. Even without the sail these canoes covered distance and their seaworthiness was often praised by the men in broad-beamed, high-decked sailing vessels that tossed their way along the coast.

The "Grease Trails" connected this isolated area with the region across the coastal mountain barrier and the continent. These routes were used for trading, for the different environments on the east and the west sides of the mountains offered products that each group desired from the other. Dried fish, shellfish, oolachen grease (from which the trails take their name) from the coast were exchanged for mountain sheep horns, caribou skins, ermine skins, mountain goat horns and wool, all materials important in the economy of the coast. Trade southward extended to the mouth of the Columbia River where the Chinook controlled the products from the upper river and California. In the 18th century when the Europeans came, hungry for furs, the wealthy men of the villages where they stopped became the middlemen for collecting skins and exercised their skill at trading to the chagrin of the fur traders. In this way they laid the basis for the final development of Northwest Coast culture in the early 19th century, the climax and end of a colorful society.

It is reasonable to assume that the long strip of land, extending hundreds of miles from south to north was not homogeneous in its cultural development. During the historic period it appears that generally the simpler cultures were in the southern area among the Coast Salish and the more complex societies in the north as exemplified by the Haida, Tsimshian, and Tlingit. This seems to be true of art styles as well as other features of culture. The problem of tracing the development of this culture could be partially solved by more extensive work in archaeology, but these finds represent only a small part of the total culture. A theory has been advanced that much of the population of the coast came originally from the interior, moving slowly down the river valleys and then adapting themselves to a maritime culture on reaching the coast. However, it has been shown by archaeological studies of the Vancouver area that the earliest stratum seems to indicate a maritime culture already there and one that has some features in common with the maritime life of the Eskimo. The question this raises is whether there was once a uniform type of culture along the entire North Pacific Coast which later was changed by the up-river people who came in and then as they adapted themselves to maritime living, some of the older features again rose to importance. For such changes at least one millennium should be allowed. Since this exhibition does not stress the archaeological side of Northwest Coast life, but rather the art of the historic period, these theories are offered to indicate a trend of thought, but are not a major part of the discussion.

One standard feature of the whole coast was the basic economy with little change in the kinds of food available and the manner in which they were procured. Generally the tribes living upstream used less shellfish and did more hunting, but these specialties became articles of trade, so the products were present everywhere to some degree. The villages were physically very much alike, except in the north where the totem poles gave them a distinctive appearance. If one investigated further into village composition, one found that in the south, among the Coast Salish, the houses were occupied by kin groups of a different nature from those of the north. Here descent was reckoned, like ours, on both sides of the family, whereas in the north among the Tlingit, Haida, and Tsimshian, descent was counted principally on the mother's side and the child was raised in the house of his mother's family. With this alignment of descent there went also an inheritance that was largely intangible. It consisted of the rights to use certain crest designs and to perform certain dances involving the use of masks and specific songs. Furthermore, it determined the place in the ceremonial house to be assigned during ceremonial and social occasions. These patterns of social behavior in the northern tribes of the Northwest Coast affected the art in the demand for graphic symbols of the inherited social privileges such as crests on ceremonial regalia, feast dishes, house decorations, and totem poles. (See Plate 23.)

The Nootka-Kwakiutl group and the Bella Coola developed a system of their own which elaborated the practices of the south and incorporated some of the unilateral kinship concepts of the north. When ethnography was first recorded in this region they appeared to be in a period of transition with the newly acquired means of increasing wealth spurring them on toward more complex ceremonial and social activities. Meanwhile among the Coast Salish some ideas of social stratification based on wealth existed, but in the presence of the bilateral family where descent was counted on both the father's and mother's side. Most frequently it involved members of two village groups because the choice in marriage was to marry outside of one's own village. The word tribe is being avoided because such a concept was almost totally lacking in this area. The languages of the Coast Salish can be subdivided into mutually understandable groupings and this relationship was recognized but was rarely the basis for any concerted social or political action. Missing almost completely from this society was a concept of political unity beyond the village. The socially prominent families tried to arrange marriages for their sons and daughters in other villages with people of their own status. This gave them the social alliances that could be called upon for help in great feasts, and provided relatives to visit, and sources of trade. Family crests were not developed here, but the basis for the arts came from the religious concept of the guardian spirit. Many of the myths, related here as an origin tale of the village, were also told in the north as the adventure leading to the establishment of a family crest. Both adventures were with supernatural spirits, one taken as an individual for spiritual strength, the other as a family property to be inherited and not acquired through personal effort. This brief mention of the social structure would not be included here if it were not important in a consideration of the art of the Northwest Coast.

A unifying factor in Northwest Coast Indian culture is the basic concept of the universe and the relationship with the supernatural as expressed in all the arts. The concept of an individual guardian spirit is found in many American Indian societies but each group has developed it in a specific local manner. The clearest example of the guardian spirit cult on the Northwest Coast is found among the Coast Salish where it was not so heavily overlaid with ceremonialism connected with the social structure as is found farther north. Throughout the area there is a fundamental belief in powerful spirits that live beyond the sea, under lakes, under the earth, and in the atmosphere who can bestow on human beings some of their power to be successful at those activities which are socially sanctioned by the group. These powers are granted when they are sought in a spirit quest of fasting or, in the socially more complex groups, they are inherited as ceremonial rights. Spirits are nearest this part of the earth during the winter months and when they revisit the people to show they once appeared they must be exorcised by song and dance. It is in these arts that the Coast Salish excel rather than in the graphic and plastic arts.

Since the spirit quest is individual, the costumes used in the dancing are devised by the dancer according to his vision. They are ephemeral in character, made of shredded cedar bark, feathers and human hair, or robes of painted skin, but no masks. The exception to this is the Swaixwe mask used by the Cowichan of the east coast of Vancouver Island. From there northward as the Kwakiutl influence grows stronger occasional masks appear, but they are not part of the Salish pattern. The Swaixwe mask is derived from a myth that clearly shows the merging of the spirit quest and the crest idea of the north. The mask was given by the people who live under a lake to a man who, on receiving it, gave it to his sister as a present for her husband at her marriage. The birds on the mask were described to me recently by a Cowichan as ravens, but there seems to be no mention of this in the literature. They have long beaks, but always sharply bent back. There is nothing in the mask to identify it visually with "people under the lake."

The Coast Salish also stressed the shaman whose rituals were the basis for many ceremonial occasions and whose needs in figures, rattles, and dance wands created demands on the arts. The stark simplicity of the Salish art is perhaps a reflection of a closer spiritual relation between an individual and his guardian spirit compared to the social domination of the arts of the north.

The attention of the Kwakiutl was focused on their many secret societies which have also adopted the same origin myths which are associated with the villages in the south and the clan or lineage in the north. Their social structure was not as fully developed as that of the northern groups and the clan system had not fully taken root so their attention was turned toward the societies of which all the northern groups also had representatives, but the Kwakiutl developed them with an exuberance which is characteristic of them in their 19th century aspect. The societies were stratified as were their social positions, and the highest was the cannibal society represented in the late 19th century art by some of the largest and most elaborate masks of the entire coast. (See Plate 25.) The Kwakiutl dances were also famous for their intricate stagecraft which was enhanced by the dramatic firelight and the use of whistles and percussion sounds on the outside of the houses.

This is the background of an art that is strong, unique, and that has a sculptural quality which can be appreciated even without this brief resume of the life of its creators. It ranges from accurate realism in animal forms to highly conventionalized figures that require the cultural explanation of one conversant with the patterns of life and thought on the Northwest Coast.

THE ANATOMY OF THE ART
ART IS A REFLECTION OF THE ENVIRONMENT IN MATERIALS

The environment gives man an opportunity for life, and regardless of his way of living, he recognizes his dependence on the land, the sea, and the elements. To establish a relationship with his universe, man develops a system of these forces and then seeks to control or placate them. The visible symbols of this supernatural world are man's artistic interpretations of either the supernatural forces in resemblance to the life forms he knows, or his expression of their "essence" as he feels their spiritual or magical power.

In the Northwest these supernaturals are conceived as spirits that move in an annual cycle, coming to the region in the winter months to possess their devotees. At that time all the arts are united to acknowledge their presence, exorcise them and send them off for another cycle of wandering around the earth. The legends connected with these ceremonies reveal the story of an ancestor's experience with a spirit; the mask represents the spirit that possesses the dancer, while the music is recognized as the song given to the seeker by the particular spirit.

The basic figures used by the Northwest Coast artist are drawn from the living world around him and supplemented by the fabulous creatures of his imagination. These are all presented in forms that have a foundation of realism; even the purely imaginary ones still bear resemblance to animal or human forms. The whole figure is seldom carved but the salient features are chosen and often exaggerated. This does not mean that these features are constant and that designs can be "read," but knowledge of the principles and background of the art serves as a guide to its interpretation and deeper enjoyment.

To find materials for the creation of these designs the Indian artist also goes to his environment. It is natural that since the

Indians lived in a heavily wooded area they should use many wood products in all phases of their life. They are fully cognizant of the qualities peculiar to each tree and wood is carefully selected in accordance. The straight grain of the cedar is important in its choice for house planks, canoes, totem poles or house posts, and for shorter, thinner boards used in the making of boxes. Alder is used for food dishes which are carved from a single block. Spoons are carved of maple, chosen for its close grain and hard quality, and yew wood is sought for the carving of beautiful clubs for killing fish and seal, as well as for bows.

Before European contact these materials were worked with many ingenious tools. Beaver teeth were inserted in wooden handles and used as carving knives. The bear's tooth also made a good carving tool. The principal woodworking tool was the adze, used in several forms, but always with a stone blade, carefully ground and polished. When metal was introduced, the Indians reshaped the pieces gotten in trade until they resembled as closely as possible the blades to which they were accustomed. Thus the character of the tool and its mode of handling remained the same. Metal tools made it easier to undertake large pieces and the work could be done faster. However, speed was not important and was not considered by the Indians as a great advantage in this change.

Wood was used exclusively for the monumental sculpture of the Northwest Coast, but it could also be carved with a delicate touch in small, elegant pieces. Very small dishes in the forms of birds or animals were carved, partly for the pleasure of creation and also to be used on special occasions for the serving of small portions of rare foods at feasts. One of the great characters in Northwest mythology is the raven who is represented in such dishes as well as in many other forms of the art. He can always be recognized by his strong, large beak which protrudes straight from his face. Since one of Raven's great feats in the establishment of world order was the stealing of the sun or daylight, he is often shown holding a pellet, symbolizing the sun, in his beak. On the other hand, if Raven's beak projects too far and interferes with the function of the object, the artist employs his considerable skill in adapting the design to a given space, by making the beak its customary size, but bending it downward on the breast of the bird.

Closely related to wood and carved by the same technique and with the same tools are bone, ivory, and horn. Some of these materials are not local in the area of the greatest carving development and must be traded from neighbors. The horn was obtained from the mountain goat and mountain sheep which were hunted by the tribes living inland, up the rivers and near the mountains. The short, black horn of the mountain goat has an elegant curve which was used to great advantage for the handles of spoons, as well as for small objects such as charms and ornaments. One such piece is carved in the form of an eagle, a bird represented also by his characteristic beak. The eagle's beak protrudes from the face and curves downward at the tip. It is strong and large and frequently, if the figure is painted wood, yellow is used to set it off from the face. The Nootka often carve the entire body of the eagle and decorate it with very fine detailed carving of his feathers. Since the eagle is a clan symbol among the northern tribes his figure is often seen on totem poles, headdresses, and other ceremonial objects where family crests are displayed.

Mountain sheep horn is even more difficult to obtain and is used primarily in carving small dishes, some very simple shapes with high squared ends and others having the same essential shape but magnificently carved with intricate patterns. In making spoons the two types of horn are sometimes combined, with the handle of black, polished goat horn and the bowl of light yellow, almost translucent, sheep horn.

The largest skeleton available to the Northwest artist is that of the whale. While the Eskimo used the baleen for baskets, the Indians used the bones for clubs, and the vertebrae for small stools and masks. Such a mask of a bird which cannot be identified is decorated with the tentacles of the octopus, the symbol used for this creature of the sea which really does not have much to recommend it artistically. The treatment of these tentacles bears some resemblance to the nucleated circle which is a favorite design of the Eskimo and is also found on the mountain sheep dishes, otherwise undecorated, which are found among the Chilcat and other groups living up the rivers of Alaska.

The whalebone clubs are characteristic of the Nootka and although made only by them are found both archaeologically and in historic collections everywhere on the coastal strip of the Northwest and also across the Cascade Mountains. These clubs are from 18 to 22 inches long, spatulate in shape with a highly conventionalized eagle or thunderbird head on the hilt. Often joined diamond or circle designs are set in a groove along the center of its length, and these are frequently inlaid with haliotis shell. These clubs were one of the most common items collected by the 18th century expeditions to the Northwest Coast and so serve the ethnohistorian as a guide to the chronology of Northwest art style.

Ivory is perhaps the least common of the materials mentioned above and obtained in trade from the Eskimo walrus hunters. The tusk was never used in its original shape as the Eskimos do, but cut in small pieces and carved into amulets and charms.

In carving texture, a transitional material, from the carving of wood, bone, and other materials just discussed, to work on real stone, is a carbonaceous shale known in the art literature of the Northwest Coast as slate or argillite. It is soft and damp when it is mined and hardens when exposed to the air. This stone occurs on the Queen Charlotte Islands and its carving is a specialty of the Haida who live there. It probably was used occasionally before the 19th century, but at that time it became a prominent item in the trade of the Haida, and has the peculiar status of being perfectly authentic Haida work which, however, was never used by the people themselves except for an occasional amulet or charm. In other words it is a truly "tourist" art and its style changed with the demands and influence of the visitors to the Queen Charlotte Islands. This material was used during the period when the whalers from New England ranged in the North Pacific waters and their scrimshaw carving as well as the new objects which the Indians saw, from the sailors to the sea captains themselves to the wheel houses and cabin details of their ships, inspired the Indians to combine the new ideas with their totemic symbols. In the carving of slate a more involved type of design developed, oriented in a horizontal line rather than the vertical of the familiar poles. Many of these designs were composed to form pipes but few were really functional.

Technically, stone can be worked either by being flaked and chipped if it is flint or a flint-like stone, or pecked, ground and polished if it is an igneous rock. Both techniques were used on the Northwest Coast, not only for tools but also for other purposes. The petroglyphs, which may or may not be very old, were pecked; the great stone mauls used for driving in wedges in splitting planks and as pile drivers in placing the posts for salmon weirs, were often decorated with pecked designs. On a smaller scale, stone was often used for charms and amulets where its weight and strength was not necessary but where the challenge of the material for carving and incising intrigued the artist. Small carvings of stone are also a problem to the student of chronology of the art for since they are of a lasting material, they are difficult to date unless they are found in association with other objects. Consequently, when the stylistic features of Northwest Coast art as it is known in the historic period appear on such a piece it is a temptation to claim antiquity for the style because a work in stone is properly associated with ancient cultures. The choice of stone, however, for charms and amulets is often made because of features of the stone itself, like its shape or coloring, which might be believed to have some magical quality. Of such a nature is a semi-circular charm representing a whale which would be recognized as from the Northwest Coast because of the shape of the eye as well as the filling of space and the "eye joint" near the tail. On the other hand, the selection of stone for a mask seems only a challenge which the artist found in the material, for the finished product was probably never used as its function would indicate. This challenge was evidently only taken up by very fine carvers and the two best known examples are both Tsimshian, one being in the Musée de l'Homme in Paris and the other in the National Museum of Canada, Ottawa.

The stock of materials available to the artist was naturally increased through the contact with Europeans which began in the late 18th century. The question as to whether the Northwest Coast Indians were familiar with iron before the coming of Europeans has been argued both pro and con, with the authoritative work of Dr. T. A. Rickard convincing many that their knowledge of iron came through finding it embedded in the drift which originated in the broken parts of vessels coming across the Pacific on the Japanese current. There is also good reason to believe that copper was known, though perhaps by no means plentiful. Iron came into the culture primarily as tools but occasionally it was used in other ways, as in brightly polished hair ornaments inlaid with haliotis shell which were highly prized by the women of the Tlingit, Haida, and Tsimshian. These metals were not handled with any knowledge of true metallurgy but were hammered as a stone might be pecked. Copper was used for fighting knives which in themselves are beautiful, but which really belong in the field of art because of their handsome handles which are decorated with the head of an animal or bird.

A metal which was not known before the European advent on the Northwest Coast is silver, but according to Cook's journal the Nootka had possession of some very early. Cook visited Nootka Sound in 1778 and believed himself to be the first white man to land there, but he found two Indians wearing silver spoons around their necks. These appeared to be Spanish and the Indians indicated that they had been bought from other Indians who came from the south in a canoe. Later in the 19th century silver was used to make bracelets, brooches, earrings, and hair ornaments. With adoption of a new material, new designs were often used. Many bracelets are beautifully designed with the traditional

Northwest Coast motifs but floral designs appeared as well, which may have been adapted from European patterns.

Bone is available in many forms from large land animals like deer and elk, from sea mammals like the whale, and from birds. Its qualities are carefully studied and the hollow wing bones of birds are made to serve as drinking tubes, while the hollow leg bones of deer and elk supply an important article in the shaman's equipment. When the shaman has found a soul that has wandered away from its body and he has captured it, he carries it back to its owner in a "soul catcher." This is made of a hollow piece of leg bone carved all around, open at both ends, with the design highlighted with inlay of haliotis shell. Another use of the carved and highly-polished leg bone is for the making of amulets or charms. For these the bone is cut in half, for it does not need to contain anything, not even a soul. However, the artist makes use of the curved surface to create the illusion of a third dimension.

One of the first items of trade goods to infiltrate the Northwest was woolen cloth and clothing. The fur traders gave the Indians pieces of their clothing in trade and this was much preferred because, while they wanted the clothes, they of course did not know how to make them from cloth. After some years of contact a purpose for both cloth and blankets was found when the button blanket was designed. This blanket was usually dark blue and it was trimmed with a border of red flannel. Then a typical design, often a family crest animal, was appliqued on the back, filling a large part of the surface. This red flannel applique was stitched down with white pearl buttons and the details of the design were also created with these buttons. Button blankets became the most popular ceremonial garb, especially among the Kwakiutl in the latter part of the 19th century. A native forerunner of this form of blanket was the painted skin robe which was especially known among the Tlingit. On this, the design might be one central piece like the button blanket or a series of smaller designs scattered over the whole surface, or animal motifs along the two borders at the front.

ART IS A REFLECTION OF THE ENVIRONMENT IN DESIGN

This review of the materials that are used in the development of Northwest Coast art shows the close relationship between the people and their environment. They knew everything that was offered and their creative imagination used it to the best of their technical ability. The animals whose forms appear in the art are treated with the same understanding, whether presented realistically or conventionalized. As one artist explained it, "This is not just the animal, it is his spirit. I see only part of him, but that is him." The artist followed the mythology into the world of imaginary creatures and made them familiar to the people of his tribe.

From the environment the artist selects widely among the animals, from the whale to the mosquito. When he wishes to present an animal realistically he generally does it in a single figure, which may be functional but still retains enough characteristics so that it can often be identified as to species. Since actors in the mythology can function either as humans or animals or both, the artist also uses this convention by placing some animal features on a human base figure. Some of the creatures appearing often in Northwest Coast art have been mentioned in preceding paragraphs, but a brief resume of their features will gather together the whole animal world with which the Northwest artist is so familiar.

The raven and the eagle have already been described and the distinction in the treatment of the beak pointed out. It might be added that in many designs the body of the bird is not shown. This neglect of the body is perhaps a reflection of a characteristic of the dance costumes, which is to stress the mask and head but almost disregard the body of the dancer. He is wrapped in a blanket and often remains in a crouching position, imitating bird-like movements. Other birds often used in the art are the hawk, with a beak that returns to the face, and the owl with a similar beak that is more gently curved and which issues from a broader face. The crane is used on dance rattles, with the elegant curve of his neck realistically shown, and on dance staffs where his long tongue is sometimes designed into an elongated human figure. On these pieces the crane always has a ridge of hair on the top of his head.

Not satisfied with the wealth of forms that the natural environment offers, the Northwest Coast artist and story teller created fabulous beings with supernatural power, distinguished symbolically from the realistic forms. (See Plate 26.) For example, the thunderbird looks like an eagle but has much larger talons and has crest feathers on his head. The beak also differs slightly in its downward curve and its relative length. The thunderbird is usually shown with spread wings, especially when painted. The raven and the crane also have supernatural counterparts among the Kwakiutl in the figures associated with the Cannibal Society.

Among the land mammals the bear, the beaver, and the wolf are the most prominent. The beaver is usually shown with his whole body, sitting up with his front paws holding a stick crosswise in his mouth. He always has his large front teeth showing and his scaly tail is lapped forward between his legs and serves as a decorative motif on his otherwise bare abdomen. The bear has several representations, from the simple brown or black bear to the large, dangerous grizzly who can be distinguished by his curling nostrils. Generally the bear has a large mouth with heavy teeth and a protruding tongue. Claws are indicated on both his front and hind feet. If he is presented in two dimensional form he is shown sitting on his haunches and his body is decorated by "x-ray" drawing of his internal organs. The wolf also has a large mouth with prominent teeth, but he has a longer snout than the bear. He has erect ears above his eyes. His body is lithe and his tail is long and full.

The sea with which the Indians of the coast are so familiar adds many interesting forms, both real and imaginary, to the figures of the art. (See Plate 25.) The seal and the sea lion are very realistic, the latter being larger than the former, as in nature. There are no special symbols associated with them. One of the most dramatic, both in nature and art, is the killer whale with its great dorsal fin and its large mouth. It appears in all sizes and in both sculpture and painting. Compared to the killer whale, the great whale itself is very static. The shark is shown commonly with the head only and its characteristics perhaps have a little humor in them. He has a large sad face with a high forehead that always carries three wrinkles. The mouth is filled with rows of teeth and the corners are turned down. Along the sides of the face the gill slits are often marked and two large tears drip down from his eyes. He is by far the saddest of all the familiar characters. The octopus is characterized by his tentacles with suckers on them, and he really has nothing else in his natural form that could recommend him to the artist. A mythical creature of the sea is the sea bear or sea wolf or sea monster. This creature has the body of the wolf with two dorsal fins, and he often holds a fish in his mouth.

The amphibians are represented by the frog, whose presence is disputed in some parts of the Northwest where his kind is represented by the toad. However, a very realistic frog is shown in the art, usually in full form, although the head alone is sometimes used as a mask. He always has very large eyes and a broad mouth.

Even the insects are not forgotten by the Northwest artist. Mosquitos, wasps, and bees are frequently used as the subject of masks. The mosquito's proboscis, which issues from a small face, is as dramatic as the long beak of the crane. Its body is never shown.

When these forms are simply done they are recognizable, but the artist, working within a closely defined tradition, shows his creativity in his variations of his themes so that great liberties can be taken with these figures. When they appear on totem poles it is often thought by the public that if one knows the symbols the "story" can be read. Nothing is further from the truth. The artist does not tell a story but rather draws from the crest myth of the family for incidents which he represents in a single figure or at most a few related figures, but never in a narrative style like the painted robes of the Plains Indians. It is often said that the only person who knows for certain the meaning of the figures on a totem pole is the artist who carved it; even the man for whom the pole was made may not know. The descriptions just given are merely clues to what the artist may have had in mind, for if the viewer can share this with the artist and thus gain insight into the ways of thought in these cultures, a greater appreciation of the artist's work will be one result.

THE USES OF THE ART

The close interrelation between an art and the society in which it functions is apparent in the primitive world and especially among the tribes of the Northwest Coast. In fact, there are few phases of the life of these people which are not embellished by artistic expression. In the winter season, when there was leisure for visiting, the feast was important as a mode of entertainment as well as a means of displaying wealth. Large serving dishes were carved of solid blocks of wood, and delicate little grease dishes took the forms of birds and small animals. Great ladles for serving food were carved of mountain sheep horn and the food was eaten with spoons of mountain goat horn with handles designed in a vertical structure like the totem poles. All this grew out of the need and the desire to share surplus food with others, and out of this generous gesture developed all the striving for social position through control and show of wealth. Invitations to a feast could be issued a year in advance if a potlatch was connected with it, or at a week's notice if only the nearby villages were involved. Preparations for a feast took the time and energy of everyone in the family of the sponsor and often of the whole village. During the previous season the women had dried salmon and halibut as they were caught. They had also collected extra quantities of vegetables and fruits such as camas, brake fern roots, salal berries, and huckleberries. These were stored away in large wooden boxes and baskets.

Just as the feast indicated the ability to provide food for

many people and thus gave the sponsor importance in the eyes of his community, so other symbols of wealth were also prominent in the winter festivities. A leader inherited position, but to keep it he had to give feasts, order decorated objects to be made for him, and acquire slaves, for in this way he could improve his status and gain greater respect from the community for his descendants. Through his ceremonial clothing he displayed his position, his membership in a clan, a lineage, or a society. The frontlet on one type of ceremonial headdress showed his family crest. Another hat with woven basketry rings on top indicated the number of potlatches he had given. (See Plate 24.) The slave killer was used for the sacrifice of a slave at a great celebration to show that he could "destroy property" without suffering from the loss. The copper was the ultimate in the climb to social position, for it could be held only by those who had given extraordinary feasts and improved the family status. It represented wealth as do bonds of high value.

While the art serves the society in many ways, its greatest challenge and accomplishment is the creation of the visual aspects of ceremonialism. During the winter season when the spirits pervade the atmosphere they are brought into the lives of the people by the dancers who, masked and costumed, represent them in dramatic incidents of their encounters with human beings which are part of the origin myths of villages, clans, and lineages. For this purpose, a wealthy family has many masks at hand, for their friends and relatives from other villages often help them with the dances. In the Puget Sound region, where masks were not used but where dancers developed intricate patterns of choreography, a person's esteem was measured by the number of people who followed him when he danced. Many of the masks were heirlooms, used by many generations, but others were quickly carved for a single occasion. Some masks which had good carving were repainted every time they were used. Many of the masks can be identified but others changed hands, often into other tribes, so that their current names were not the original ones. As long ago as the early part of the 20th century, Swanton commented on the variety of names given certain masks by different informants. This is undoubtedly true because of the wider latitude given the artist in mask creation than he is allowed in designing family crests, thus making identification difficult.

The objects used in the majority of Northwest Coast ceremonies are masks, rattles, and dance staffs. The actual wearing apparel usually does not have ceremonial significance; a dancer may be partially naked or wear a cape or blanket which he would also use if he were not actively performing. Masks may belong to a certain dance, but sometimes they were also worn for other occasions; in fact they were even loaned to a relative or given as a present. Under such circumstances the transfer involved also the privilege of using the song which went with the mask and these rights were then relinquished by the former owner. There were many ramifications to the ownership and use of masks, and customs differed among the various tribes along the coast, but the basic rule was that every mask was owned, either by an individual or a family, and its use was limited to the owner.

Certain masks were associated with a ceremony such as the initiation rites of the Cannibal Society of the Kwakiutl or the Wolf Ritual of the Nootka. These societies were present in the majority of Northwest Coast tribes, but among the Kwakiutl and the Nootka their development was outstanding. Alice Ernst, who has made a detailed study of the Wolf Ritual, believes that it was once a warrior ceremony, having as its aim the fostering of bravery and those qualities that make for bodily and mental endurance. She traces its origin to the area of Clayquot influence and northward where the Nootkan-speaking tribes meet the Kwakiutl, represented by the Quatsino. The ceremony was passed from one to another through marriage. While some masks belonged specifically to this ritual, others are family masks which could be used by their owners at their discretion. Such a time occurred in the Wolf Ritual in the procession through the village to the ceremonial house, in which all members participated, wearing masks of their own.

Other masks were called portrait masks, though the title usually given for them was merely "A Dead Man" or "The Spirit of a Tlingit Singing." Many of these show some of the finest and most sensitive carving of the mask-maker and one feels certain that the artist had a specific person in mind. Many masks had the base of a human face but it might be covered with symbolic painting representing someone in a ceremony with clan or lineage symbols painted on the face.

In the regions of the Northwest Coast where the masked dances were not used shamanistic ceremonies were of great importance. In the area of Puget Sound the Salish tribes called several shamen together for the Spirit Canoe ceremony during which these men paddled a spirit canoe to the land of the dead to bring back the soul of a person who was ill because of soul loss. In this dramatic performance the medicine men sang their own songs during the journey. If the shamen were successful in bringing back the soul the patient was apt to recover. The spirit canoe was outlined with spirit boards designed by the shaman according to his dream experience with his "power." These are very simple compared to the elegant art of the northern tribes, but they are in keeping with the Salish style, direct and with a folk art naïveté.

The music accompanying dances was percussion and singing. The instruments consisted of tambourine drums of deerskin and large wooden box drums which were suspended from the cross beams and beaten on the broad sides by the heels of drummers who sat above them. Rattles were made in great variety and show some of the finest carving. They range from the simple realism of the Salish form of a single bird to the complexity of the raven rattle with decorative figures of other birds. The use of the bird figure is a tradition which can be traced to the earliest ethnographic collections. The round rattle is often associated with the medicine man, but this is not consistent. In addition to the carved rattles, some with no decoration are made of pecten shells, dew claws of deer, and the bills of puffins.

The raven rattle was also carried as part of the ceremonial

costume by a family or village leader and sometimes used to emphasize important statements in a speech.

The dance staff was carried by an attendant to help steer a dancer, who was wearing a mask without eye holes, and to keep him away from the audience and out of the fires. In a dance encircling the fires either the leader or the last man would carry a staff to keep the group in line and in motion. Dance staffs were usually very long and decorated along several feet at one of the ends. A favorite figure was the crane or the face of the killer whale with a long dorsal fin on top of his head. In contrast to the long poles, the shaman often carried a short "wand" when he was dancing. It helped him define his gestures and its decoration referred to his spirit power.

The close relationship between the art and the social and ceremonial needs of the Northwest Coast Indians can be compared to the mediaeval arts as they were associated with the cathedral. When new culture patterns developed through contact with Europeans, and when the needs of the society were changed through outside pressures, the arts could not continue alone. The new ways of life which the Indians first saw among the whites who settled around them were those of a rough pioneer society where there was little thought and less time for any of the arts.

THE VANISHING ART OF THE ARCTIC

Froelich Rainey

> *But of the land on the other side of the bald men none can give any trustworthy account because it is shut off by a separating wall of lofty trackless mountains, which no man can cross. But these bald men say—which, however, I do not believe—that men with goat's feet live on the mountains, and on the other side of them other men who sleep six months at a time . . . The whole of the country which I have been speaking of has so hard and severe a winter, that there prevails there for eight months an altogether unsupportable cold . . . even the sea freezes . . .*
>
> HERODOTUS—45TH CHAPTER OF THE 4TH BOOK.
> ABOUT 430 B.C.

> *They first pointed to the ships, eagerly asking, what great creatures those were. Do they come from the sun or the moon? Do they give us light by night or by day? Sacheuse told them that he was a man, that he had a father and mother like themselves; and pointing to the south, said that he came from a distant country in that direction. To this they answered, "That cannot be, there is nothing but ice there."*
>
> JOHN ROSS, FROM AN ACCOUNT OF THE DISCOVERY OF THE POLAR ESKIMO. LONDON, 1819

ALL OF THE desolate shores of the Arctic Sea have now been charted. No lost tribes like the Polar Eskimo remain to be discovered. We now know that men were living along the Arctic shores several thousand years before the birth of Christ and that by 1500 B.C. they lived much further north than any men live today. But the history of man's conquest of the Arctic remains

---

Reprinted from *Expedition*, 1 (2), Winter, 1959:3–13, with the permission of the author and the editor of *Expedition*.

a mystery. Several distinct races like the Lapps, Samoyeds, Yukaghir, and Eskimo have long been adapted to Arctic living. There are students of the northern people who believe that all of these tribes carry on the cultural tradition of an ancient circumpolar stone age which may be derived from the reindeer hunters of Magdalenian times in western Europe. Others maintain that the Eskimo, the most northern and the most famous of all Arctic people, originated in North America and have no connection with other Arctic dwellers in Asia.

No primitive race in the world has been the subject of more study and speculation than the Eskimo. They are the Skraelings who met and fought with the Norsemen in West Greenland in the 13th century, the men who attacked one of the first European ships to pass through Bering Strait, and the men who made it possible for Peary to discover the North Pole. Eskimos in East Greenland speak the same tongue as those at East Cape, Siberia. For the most part they cling to the shores of the Arctic and the Bering Seas, but some manage to live inland on the Barren Grounds of Northern Canada and Alaska. All are hunters of land and sea mammals. We think of them as men of a common language, race, and culture, but find it exceedingly difficult to give a satisfactory definition of Eskimo culture. And there are at least two distinctive physical types.

Some of our Russian colleagues who study the northern people believe that the Eskimo are originally Americans because they find no trace of them west of the Kolyma River on the Siberian coast. None the less, most American experts believe their origin is to be sought in Siberia. Thus, at the present time, they are disclaimed by both the East and the West. In this dilemma, the Russian archaeologist, S. I. Rudenko has suggested that they may be descendents of sea people who moved northward along the Pacific coast of Asia.

In recent years many archaeologists have excavated scores of ancient sites in Siberia, Alaska, Canada, and Greenland, piecing together the tangible evidence of a long history of Arctic settlement, and each year the story becomes more complex. There is today no generally accepted scheme of northern history nor any real agreement on interpreting the evidence in the Eskimo regions. However, in brief, it is possible to say that men had settled the Bering Strait region by at least three or four thousand B.C., that they had settled Greenland by 2000 B.C., and that Arctic culture has not been static. The Arctic has not been a refuge of ancient Stone Age people. Culture change is a characteristic there as it is in the rest of the world.

There is at present evidence of an ancient Stone Age culture related to the Mesolithic of the Old World, a paleo-Eskimo culture characterized by the use of chipped flint tools, and a neo-Eskimo culture characterized by the use of polished slate tools, which survives to the present day. But within these three time horizons numerous distinct stages can be recognized from the remains excavated in many archaeological sites.

Through the technique of radiocarbon analysis we now have some debatable dates for the three time horizons. The ancient Stone Age appears to be earlier than 2000 B.C. (absolute dates are not yet possible), the paleo-Eskimo stage was sometime between 700 B.C. and A.D. 300, and the neo-Eskimo stage represents the period from at least A.D. 300 to the present. But we do not know when the Eskimo first appeared in this time sequence. Skeletons from graves of the earliest neo-Eskimo times found at East Cape, Siberia, very closely resemble those of the living Eskimo. Skeletons from graves of a late paleo-Eskimo stage found at Point Hope, Alaska do not, and therefore suggest that those we have called the paleo-Eskimo are not physically Eskimos, even though they may have spoken the Eskimo language. There are no skeletons from the ancient Stone Age; hence, we have no way of knowing whether the people were physically or linguistically Eskimo. Cultural connections suggested by the kinds of stone tools found in the ancient sites are very tenuous.

If you examine a polar map with the North Pole at its center, a familiar type of map now that air travel across the Arctic has been established, you will see the Arctic Ocean as an enclosed, ice-covered body of water surrounded for the most part by low, barren, tundra lands. This icy basin disgorges floe ice each year through Bering Strait into Bering Sea, and through the Denmark Strait into the Atlantic. Primitive fur-clad hunters have penetrated to the frozen tundra coasts around the entire rim of the sea. They are of different races and they speak different languages but they have in common many cultural traits which may be no more than necessary adaptations to the same environment. Of all these different groups it is the Eskimo who cling most closely to the edge of the ice and who have developed a unique Arctic culture. For most of them seals and reindeer are the bases of life.

But in the region of Bering Strait there is a phenomenon of nature which provides the sea-hunting Eskimo with an abnormally rich harvest. Here walrus and bow-head whales pour through the funnel between the Bering and Arctic Seas, northward each spring and southward each fall. Now depleted by commercial hunters, the yearly migrations give only a suggestion of the vast numbers of these animals which once passed through the Strait. It is thus no accident that large permanent villages of Eskimo are located at such points as East Cape, Siberia and Cape Prince of Wales, the Diomede Islands, and Point Hope, Alaska, where the migrations would be intercepted. Some of these villages may be as old as Rome. Certainly several of them have been permanently occupied for nearly two thousand years. This narrow strait between Asia and America may mark the region in which Eskimo culture, as we know it, originated. At least, this is where we find the most ancient remains, the most complex cultures, and most of the evidence of culture change and development. It is also this region which produces the finest examples of the ancient classic art of the Eskimo.

We Arctic diggers during the past twenty-five years have defined several distinct forms of ancient art work in the Bering Strait region, known as Ipiutak, Old Bering Sea, Okvik, and Punuk styles. All fall within the period of the first millennium after Christ, so far as we can tell at present from radiocarbon analysis of organic material in the ruins excavated about the Strait.

What we believe to be the most ancient style was discovered at Point Hope, Alaska, in 1939 by Dr. Helge Larsen, Dr. Louis Giddings, and me at the largest ruined settlement so far known in the Arctic. More than 600 house ruins extended over an area nearly a mile in length and the graves of these ancient inhabitants were found along the Arctic shore for a distance of about four miles to the east of the house ruins.

We have named this ancient site Ipiutak after an Eskimo name for a section of the Tigara sand spit, and we speak of it as a settlement of paleo-Eskimo people who lived in the American Arctic some centuries before and some centuries after the time of Christ. But the origin and the history of these people remain a mystery. A clue may be found in the distinctive Ipiutak style of sculpture and incised design. Of the 10,000 manufactured objects found in the Ipiutak ruins at Point Hope, Alaska, no single piece is more significant than the small ivory carving of a cub walrus. Across Asia from the Ordos region in China to the shores of the Black Sea, have been found examples of an art form known as the Siberian Animal Style. Originally associated with the Scythian people of South Russia who produced the finest examples in bronze and gold during the 6th and 5th centuries B.C., it is sometimes referred to as Scythian. But with extensive archaeological work in northern Asia it is apparent that many ancient and primitive people in the vast temperate and northern regions of the Eurasian continent produced similar figures of animals in bone and ivory as well as in metal. It is most commonly associated with nomadic people of the steppe regions and with the century preceding the Christian era, but related forms have been found in the northern forested regions of the Ural Mountains and even as far north as the mouth of the Ob River on Siberia's Arctic shore.

At Ipiutak we found numerous engraving tools with an ivory or antler shaft slotted to receive a cutting bit. In some were set a beaver's tooth with the chisel-shaped cutting edge not unlike a dental tool. In others the slot was much too narrow to receive a beaver's tooth. It was obvious that only a metal blade could be used in such thin slots, but only in one engraving tool at Ipiutak did we find the oxidized remains of wrought iron or steel. Later, at Cape Spencer, Helge Larsen discovered another burial site of the Ipiutak period with fragments of metal blades inset in ivory implements. Siberian steel or iron must have been precious on the north Alaska coast in the fourth century after Christ, but it was there in small quantities at least.

Most of the elaborately carved and engraved objects at Ipiutak were found in the burials. Some were exceedingly rich with scores of objects lying about one or more skeletons—others contained no burial equipment whatever. Some skeletons lay in log-walled tombs, others in shallow graves which had been much disturbed by animals or by weathering. Most dramatic were those skeletons equipped with ivory eyes—spool-shaped or conical ivory plugs inset with jet to represent eye pupils—and with carved nose plugs and mouth covers. There was obviously an elaborate burial cult, at least for certain individuals who we assume were shamans, and many of the carvings probably were symbolic of supernatural powers. We know that shamans among many of the Siberian tribes customarily hung about their clothing innumerable figures representing their spiritual powers. Shamanism is an ancient cult in Asia and there is good reason to suppose that many of the Ipiutak carvings have to do with its practice.

In one grave we found the skull of a loon with ivory plugs set in the eye-sockets and an ivory ring about the beak. From this and from the innumerable legends about the loon prevalent among the Arctic tribes, we assume that many of these objects symbolize the loon. The shapes are graceful and light with cut-out sections. Many are engraved with such familiar design patterns as the circle with tangential lines. Normally one surface is decorated and the other flat and plain, which suggests that they were affixed to something like a bag, a box, or a garment.

A set of tubes cut from caribou antlers also suggest the paraphernalia of Shamanistic practice. They were carefully hollowed out so that the walls are exceedingly thin. One was elaborately engraved over most of the surface, others were without carving or engraving.

The strange rake-like object of ivory was found on the Arctic coast of Alaska and probably comes from the Ipiutak cemetery at Cape Spencer. There is no implement made by historic Eskimos which could explain its function. Two similar implements were found at the Ipiutak site at Point Hope but neither of those is carved in such an elaborate form. The guard which fits neatly over the teeth is unique and puzzling. Like the carving of the cub walrus, this has a peculiarly important significance, because the central figure, representing the head of a polar bear face-on, suggests a stylistic connection with bear carvings found in the region of the Ural Mountains. There is an ancient cult and a ceremonialism associated with the bear in the far north which was practiced among many native peoples in Asia and America. It is possible that such a stylized design of a polar bear may indicate a distant cultural connection between northwestern Siberia and northwestern Alaska as well as the existence of the ancient and wide-spread bear cult among the mysterious people of Ipiutak as early as the 4th century A.D.

In 1926 Diamond Jenness of the Canadian National Museum discovered some remarkable ivory carvings at ancient sites on Bering Strait which were so unlike familiar Eskimo work and so distinctive in style that he could assume without further evidence the existence of an Old Bering Sea culture notably different from that of the historic Eskimos. His conclusions were borne out by the work of Collins, Geist, Rudenko, and others on St. Lawrence Island and at East Cape, Siberia. However, strange as it may seem, not a single site or deposit has yet been found which contains only this particular style of art. On St. Lawrence and at East Cape where most of the excavated objects were found, it occurs in houses or sites with later material, and we have yet to discover a "pure" deposit which could clearly isolate this style in a specific period. Hence its relative age in the sequence of northern art styles remains a puzzle. We do know that during the early centuries of the Christian era there lived about Bering

Strait a people who dwelt in permanent houses in large settlements on St. Lawrence Island, East Cape, Cape Prince of Wales, and the Diomede Islands. They were great hunters of walrus, seals, and whales. They were a sea-people who made pottery and polished slate tools not unlike similar utensils found along the northeastern coast of Asia, but very different from the most common tools and utensils made by the people of Ipiutak on the northern coast of Alaska. But like the Ipiutak people they were masters of the art of carving and engraving delicate objects in ivory. Some of the designs are similar although we can easily distinguish them.

The curious winged object is very characteristic of the Old Bering Sea period. (See Plate 20.) Such objects are remarkably like the stone "bannerstones" made by Indians of the eastern United States. There is no certain knowledge of their use or significance but in the collections of the University of Alaska Museum there is a whole series of related objects from Okvik, Old Bering Sea, and Punuk periods which, taken together, give a clue. All have sockets at each end of the central section. It is possible that they are counterweights affixed to the butt of throwing spears, with the larger socket to receive the spear butt and the smaller socket to receive the hook of a spearthrower. The most elaborate and the largest are invariably engraved in the Old Bering Sea style.

One of the finest examples of this style is an ivory socket-piece for a harpoon, now in the collections of the U. S. National Museum. (See Plate 21.) It was affixed to a harpoon shaft to receive the small foreshaft which joins the toggle harpoon head. The modelling and incising delineate reptile-like heads and snouts with raised bosses and sockets in the position of eyes or nostrils. It is this curvilinear style with punctate bosses and concentric circles that particularly distinguishes a specific Old Bering Sea stage in the art of northern Bering Sea. Moreover, most of the objects decorated in this style are now dark brown or black in color which indicates that they have been buried for centuries in the decaying organic matter of ancient Eskimo house ruins and middens. For this reason they are referred to as "fossil ivory" although they are simply discolored by age, not fossilized. When in use they must have been glistening white ivory covered with bold patterns in red or black lines.

The black ivory toggle, from the collections of the U. S. National Museum, may once have hung from the handle of a drum. It is unusually well preserved and ornate—an excellent example of the complex curvilinear designs which distinguish this early period. In this, all semblance of representation is gone and to the uninitiated eye it is purely a geometric design. But to an Old Bering Sea Eskimo the incised figures probably represented recognizable symbols or schematic animal heads similar to those on the socket-piece. Modelling is part of the design but the emphasis, as in most Old Bering Sea art, is upon engraving.

Such elaborate curvilinear designs have suggested to Professor Rudenko and other Russian archaeologists that Old Bering Sea art may have originated somewhere along the Pacific Coast of Asia, perhaps even as far south as Melanesia in the South Pacific.

St. Lawrence Island in northern Bering Sea produces much of the so-called "fossil" ivory which is prized by the Alaskan Eskimo carvers of today. Somewhat more than twenty years ago Eskimos from the village of Gambell on St. Lawrence Island, in search of dark ivory which had been buried in the earth for centuries, found a site on the small Punuk Islands off the eastern end of St. Lawrence which became a rich mine for the village carvers. It is an ancient village site, occupied during the first centuries after Christ, where large numbers of walrus were taken and where masses of walrus bones and walrus ivory have been preserved to the present time.

Otto Geist of the University of Alaska learned of the site from the Eskimos and was able to excavate part of it before it was destroyed by these fossil ivory hunters. With his collection this became the "type site" of what is now known as the Okvik period of early neo-Eskimo culture. The period is characterized by a distinctive art style. Examples of this style have been found in some of the most ancient house ruins at Gambell as well as in two extensive sites in northeastern Siberia.

Judging from the collections from Okvik on the Punuk Islands, carvers of this early period were preoccupied with reproducing human figures, or more particularly the human head. Unlike the Old Bering Sea and Ipiutak people who emphasized animal figures in their sculpture and engraving, these Okvik people seem to have focused on human features and they have left to us a number of remarkable examples of their skill. By all odds the finest of these is a female figure holding a child or a small animal. (See Plate 19.) It was found by Otto Geist at the Okvik site in 1934 and having lain in damp earth for 1500 to 2000 years it literally exploded during the drying process after excavation. Restored with great care it is now intact except for the legs which were apparently broken away in antiquity. Like all such carvings from the site, all of the attention is focused on the head and face.

Perhaps by some odd coincidence the head has a startling resemblance to the stone sculptures from Easter Island and the Marquesas in the eastern Pacific. It is unique in this respect and in the queer twisted smile which lends such a strange expression to the face. The greatly elongated nose, however, appears on other figures.

Engraving on implements of all kinds shows a specific stylistic relationship between the art of this period and that of the other early periods in the far north, but in its simplicity and its general forms it appears to be more closely related to that of the Ipiutak than to the Old Bering Sea people, although the culture in general is much more closely related to the latter. We can be sure that the Okvik people also had small quantities of Siberian iron or steel for cutting tools since some of their knife handles are slotted for metal blades.

At the present stage of our knowledge it would appear that Okvik art is essentially a Siberian style. St. Lawrence and the Punuk Islands are geographically and culturally Siberian and the only known Okvik sites have been found on these islands and

The Vanishing Art of the Arctic

in northeastern Siberia. Only rare pieces have been found on the American side of the Strait.

The Punuk period, terminating about A.D. 1000, is the last recognizable stage in the early art of the North and at this time sculpture and engraving had become much more simple and more crude. Thereafter, with the beginning of the Thule period, very little art work of any kind was produced. Moreover, all of the implements and weapons of the Eskimo were heavier, cruder, and more clumsy than in the early periods. It is a curious fact that most of the manufactured objects of the early periods have a light, delicate, elaborate quality which disappears, at least among the most northern Eskimos, after the wide spread of Thule period culture during the second millennium A.D.

In some regions such as Southampton Island in the eastern Arctic and in the southern Bering Sea region, these lighter, more delicate, and more skilfully designed implements continued to be made, and the skill in producing utilitarian objects was never lost by the Eskimos, but one familiar with Eskimo culture soon comes to distinguish most of the ancient from the modern implements simply by their size, weight, and skill of manufacture.

The "winged figure" is most characteristic of Punuk work in carving and engraving. It is related to the winged objects of the Old Bering Sea period and may have been used as a weight on the butt of a throwing spear since it also has a socket in each end; but it was made at least five or six hundred years later. Engraved designs on this figure are like those on many of the Punuk harpoon heads and can be distinguished easily from earlier styles, although some of the design elements persist to this late date. We know that larger quantities of Siberian metal had reached Bering Strait during the Punuk period and that the idea of slat armor, like that worn by the Japanese, was introduced at this time. Punuk armor was made, however, of bone and ivory slats rather than metal. Considerable fighting must have taken place at this time since the Eskimos developed a particular type of arrow point for warfare alone. They also made wrist guards of ivory which were lashed to the wrist to protect it from the slap of the bow string.

While the really fine work ended a thousand years ago, some of the ancient skill in ivory carving was carried on into modern times, and wood carving, at least as demonstrated in the elaborate dance masks of western Alaska, remained a very remarkable art form. Some Eskimo wooden masks made as late as the beginning of this century, are among the finest examples of contemporary native art to be found anywhere in the world.

All of the wooden masks are of the spirit wood. (See Plate 22.) With each must have gone a vision, a song, and a dance. As a one-time crewman with the whaling boat of the Inyuelingmiut family at Point Hope and, as such, a kind of adopted member of the family, I cannot help but regret that the vast store of legend, learning, and belief which all these masks represent is lost to those who now collect them. Surely we would appreciate them more if we knew the vision behind them.

Old Nashugruk, an Eskimo woman of Point Hope, Alaska, was one of those ancient dames who spend the two summer months excavating ancient house ruins which adjoin her village. Some houses must have been built during the late Middle Ages, others as recently as the last century, but they are now abandoned to burrowing mice and the native collectors of antiquities. In the summer of 1939 she had dug deep into the rotting muck of the old town to the planked floor of a dance house and there she found a cache of some fifty wooden masks nicely preserved in frozen debris from the house roof. Helge Larsen of the Danish National Museum and I bargained with Nashugruk for most of the summer and finally succeeded in closing a trade for the masks with a pound of tobacco after supplies in the village had been exhausted.

The Episcopal Church naturally frowns upon masked dances which are meant to call up a host of pagan spirits, and so the deeply religious Eskimos of Point Hope today no longer carve these symbols of visions evoking the other world. But they remember them. David Frankson's grandfather, Acetchuk, was one of the last great shamans before his conversion to Christianity in 1925 and he has left us a clear account of the vision experience which led to his acceptance into the profession. He was confirmed after he and his friends carved a set of masks with the features of his helping spirit, a man who had recently died and then appeared to Acetchuk as the captain of a skin boat, quietly floating through the air over the tundra. The spirit had a much distorted other-worldly face which the carvers reproduced in their masks, and a personal song which Acetchuk taught his friends so they could sing it with him when they danced his vision in the dance house of the Inyuelingmiut.

Acetchuk became such a powerful shaman that he eventually gave birth to a kikituk, one of those monsters with sharp teeth which were directed to kill opposing shamans in deadly battles between the supernatural powers of the titans in the profession. Such a kikituk was also found by Nashugruk in the old dance house floor and it is now in the collection of the University of Alaska. It is made of wood with teeth of ivory. David explained how Acetchuk gave natural birth to such a creature at will during a seance and how he had used it to kill an exceedingly powerful shaman from Siberia.

Wooden masks are still carved by Eskimos of today and some may have merit as copies of the vital art form developed in the Arctic over the centuries—but they are meaningless in a true aesthetic sense. Today all Eskimos are Christians. The masks are of the pre-Christian period, when the carvers worked with sincere belief in the supernatural forces, not only represented but embodied in such masks. Each is the result of an intense religious belief and the product of an ancient Eskimo world-view which is incomprehensible to the Christian except as a work of art. It is the power of belief, I think, which makes all the difference between original native art and contemporary native craft.

IFE IN NIGERIAN ART

Frank Willett

OF ALL THE ART of Africa, Ife is rightly the most famous. These formal and serene heads were once thought to be Greek, but they are quite unlike the Greek/European tradition of sculpture. The naturalism of the art of Ife probably developed in Nigeria, ultimately from an art style which originated two thousand years ago.

The tin-mining village of Nok, in Zaria Province of Northern Nigeria, was the site of the first discovery of the most ancient African sculpture excepting that of Egypt. It is terra-cotta sculpture, made of pottery materials, and it dates from about five centuries before to two centuries after Christ. Bits of decayed wood found near the sculptures and subjected to the radio carbon dating technique have established its age.

The remains of what has come to be known as the Nok culture have been collected over a wide area, from near Kaduna to the Benne Valley at Katsina Ala, and these tell us that the Nok people knew the use of iron also. The nozzles of bellows and iron slag have been found with the terra-cotta figurines, although the Nok people continued to use stone axes and hoes. They were agriculturalists, probably living close to rivers. They were fond of beads, and their women folk wore lip and ear plugs of polished quartz. Their domestic pottery was solid, heavy, and coarse, but well fired. But the most important aspect of the culture is undoubtedly the terra-cotta sculpture.

Reprinted from *African Arts/Arts d'Afrique,* University of California at Los Angeles 1 (1) 1968:30–34, 78, by permission of the author and the editor of *African Arts/Arts d'Afrique.*

The Nok sculptures vary in scale from human and animal figures a few inches high to human figures approaching life-size. The human heads were very imaginatively treated, with a high degree of stylization necessitating distortion of shapes and proportions, but producing a high degree of liveliness and vigour. One of the characteristic devices was to treat the head as either a cylinder or as a cone (see Plate 28), sitting at an acute angle upon a vertical cylinder which represents the neck. The limbs and trunk were usually treated much more simply, as cylinders. Normally, very elaborate beadwork ornaments were added, including thick rolls of beads around the neck, bracelets, anklets, and elaborate tassels and pendants. At the same time, however, some details were naturalistically treated (i.e., in a way which copies nature) e.g. the lips in one piece, or the nose in another, while as a whole the animal sculptures are noticeably more naturalistic than the human figures.

The great majority of the pieces of Nok sculpture were found by accident, mostly in the course of tin-mining. The finds had usually been washed from the riverside occupation sites into the water and incorporated into the gravel bed of the river. The site at Katsina Ala, however, seems to have been a sacred grove, and the site of one of the Nok villages has been found at Taruga near Abuja.

It is likely that the Nok culture extended more widely in space than it has so far been found, and it probably lasted a good deal later than the second century A.D. The study of younger art styles in West Africa suggests that many of them are derived in part from the Nok culture, or at any rate from a sculptural tradition of which Nok is the only manifestation we know from such an ancient date. Some of the Nok terra-cottas have features characteristic of wood-carving, and a great many small and delicate stone adze heads suitable for carving wood have been found in the same deposits, which suggests that the Nok people may have been skillful wood carvers, too. Of course, this also implies the possibility that there were other contemporary or even older cultures practicing wood-carving, whose sculptures have not survived, but which may have contributed more than Nok did to the development of later art styles.

Whatever may have been lost to the archaeological record, there was clearly a tradition of sculpture in terra-cotta already established in Nok times, probably forming a continuum into later times, of which the best known manifestation is the sculpture in terra-cotta from Ife. The Ife sculptures, although emphatically naturalistic, do have conventional and even stylized elements—there are conical and cylindrical heads, for example— and the eyes and ears are conventionally treated. More striking is the treatment of the human trunk and limbs, which is very close to the treatment of these parts in the Nok sculptures. Moreover, the Ife sculptures show a wealth of decorative beadwork arranged in much the same way as on the Nok figurines: thick rolls of beads forming collars around the neck, bracelets, and anklets, and elaborate pendants and tassels. All in all, the terracotta sculptures of Ife look rather like a more refined version of those from Nok, with an emphasis on the naturalistic treatment of the head.

These are the only two cultures we know of, from the whole of Africa, which made terra-cotta sculptures of complete human figures of anywhere near life size. The many terra-cotta sculptures known from other parts of West Africa are all on a very small scale; if they approach life size, only the head is represented, not the whole body. (There are, of course, smaller scale sculptures at Nok and Ife, too.) There seems therefore to be little reason to doubt that the art of Ife grew from roots in the Nok tradition of terra-cotta sculpture.

When the art of Ife became known to the art world, first in 1910, thanks to the work of the German anthropologist Frobenius, and more strikingly in 1938, when seventeen life-size brass heads were found in Wunmonije Compounds, the Nok culture was still unknown. (See Plate 30.) The art world at large was unable to account for such major works of art in a naturalistic style, quite unlike the general run of African art, but superficially similar to the Greek and Egyptian traditions which had led up to modern European art. Art critics could suggest only that either they were made by a European who had wandered into Africa, or that the Ifes had been taught by the early traders on the coast. Frobenius himself had thought that they were made by Greeks, and that the Guinea Coast was the lost continent of Atlantis, lost when the Greeks, having colonized it in the Thirteenth Century B.C., lost touch with it some five centuries later.

The Ife heads are really quite unlike the Greek/European tradition of sculpture, which is based on careful measurement and accurate proportion. The Ife head-shape is conventional, as is the treatment of eyes and ears. In the 1938 finds, however, the upper half of a figure of an Oni, or King of Ife, showed its African character very clearly. The head was greatly exaggerated in size in relation to the rest of the body, equaling about a quarter of the estimated over-all height of the figure. In the Greek and European tradition, the head would occupy only one-seventh or less of the over-all height. William Fagg of the British Museum first pointed this out, and it was emphatically confirmed by the full-length brass figures discovered in 1957 at Ita Yemoo on the Ilesha Road, Ife. (See Plate 31.) These showed the same proportions, which correspond to the proportions of Yoruba twin-figures (*ibeji*). These proportions certainly prove that the sculptors were African, just as the subjects were, but we must still ask ourselves whether the evidence is clear and positive enough to say that no influence from Egypt or Europe contributed to the naturalism of the art.

We cannot at present give an absolutely certain answer, but we do have a number of pieces of evidence of various types which allow us to formulate a hypothesis. There are strong traditions in Ife of an earlier population already there at the time of Oduduwa, who is usually credited with having made the world itself. This population goes by the name of Igbo, and one of them seems to have been Ore, who is commemorated in the Ore Grove, where the most important stone sculptures in Ife were kept until they were transferred to the Museum for greater safety. It may be that this indigenous population was descended from the people of the Nok culture, on whom the ruling class, represented by Oduduwa and his companions, imposed themselves, producing a social reorganization and eventually, by intermarriage, the emergence of the Yoruba people we know today. Certainly across the forest belt of Southern Nigeria there seems to be a basic homogeneity of culture, onto which, in the case of the Yoruba, other elements have been grafted. These elements seem to have come from further north, from the open grassland country. Indeed, at the height of its power, the Yoruba Empire was clearly of a type which is regularly found in the savanna belt of West Africa, with a strong army based on cavalry which would be of little use in the forest areas.

West Africa throughout the middle ages was in touch with the Mediterranean world by the trade routes across the Sahara, and with the Middle East by routes running east and west along the savanna belt to the south of the desert. It is very likely that not only trade goods passed along these routes, but also craftsmen and most important of all, ideas. Perhaps the idea of the impluvial courtyard, which is very characteristic of the traditional architecture of the Yoruba and the Bini, was one of these ideas which came across the desert, for similar impluvia are found around the Mediterranean Sea, both in Europe and North Africa. The knowledge of metal-casting also appears to have come by one or other of these routes, but this skill must have been brought by the craftsmen themselves, who must for some time have had to import the raw metal for their castings, until they were able to locate sources of ore for themselves.

The ruling group which is represented by the legends of Oduduwa probably came into Nigeria by one or other of these routes, but at present the available evidence is too unsure to allow us to suggest a date. This group no doubt brought new ideas with it, and would have remained receptive to new ideas whilst it was spreading out among the indigenous peoples to found the many city states, with their sacred kings, which composed the Yoruba Empire. They were no doubt quite a sophisticated people who, although maintaining the worship of the indigenous gods through priests drawn initially from the indigenous population, also made provision for their own founding heroes to be worshipped. (The most obvious example is Shango, one of the earliest kings of Oyo, who became a god among the Oyos, but who is not worshipped at all by the Ifes.)

The indigenous population almost certainly had some cult of the ancestors of whatever form, but it was probably affected by the inhibition about the realistic portrayal of the human form which has made African art so rich and varied in its stylizations. The sophisticated ruling class in Ife seems to have overcome this inhibition, if they ever had it themselves, but we do not know for certain whether this naturalistic art derived entirely from their own philosophical concepts, or whether they received some ideas or even models from outside. Certainly there are no really close parallels to the art of Ife outside Western Nigeria. The art of Ife stands alone in its serene, rather idealized naturalism. Such parallels as have been suggested from time to time—ancient Egyptian, Greek and Roman statuary, European Renaissance sculpture—have only a general similarity. After all, if you once hit on the idea of representing the human body as realistically as possible, the resulting work of art will look very similar whether it is done by an African, a European, or an Asiatic, since all are copying the same model—the human body. Thus it is possible to explain the naturalism of the art of Ife as having been developed in Nigeria, ultimately from an art style which originated two thousand years ago. The parts of the world from which any outside influence would have had to come have been closely studied and no convincing evidence to contradict this hypothesis has been uncovered. It therefore seems likely that further work will confirm it.

The naturalistic art style probably developed in terra-cotta. The skill required to build up a life-size terra-cotta sculpture, and in one case a group of figures of probably about life size, was very great, but the skill required to fire them in one piece in a simple wood fire is of a far higher order. To a people capable of controlling fire to the degree required for this, the technical feat of casting a life-size head in brass would be relatively easy. Astonishment at the skill required to make the brasses has contributed to their fame as works of art, although, in fact, both technically and artistically the terra-cotta sculptures are much more important. Being fragile, many of them are incomplete and abraded, and this makes it difficult for the layman to appreciate the quality of the damaged ones. (See Plate 29.)

It has already been suggested that the naturalism of the art may have developed in response to the needs of a cult of the ancestors. Small figures in brass and terra-cotta seem to have been memorial figures used on shrines. The large terra-cotta figures were used in groups in shrines. One such shrine was excavated in 1957 and found to have contained seven figures of Onis and attendants of about two-thirds of life-size.

The life-size brass heads, however, seem to have been used in a different way. There is a widespread custom in Southern Nigeria of having two burials—an interment as soon as possible after the death, then the funeral proper sometime later when sufficient wealth has been saved up for the necessary sacrifices and feasting. In Owo, Benin, and Onitsha, the second burial ceremony for very important people is accompanied by the making of a figure called *ako* to represent the deceased. Offerings are made to the figure which is set up in the compound of the deceased; the figure is then taken in procession around the town and buried. In Owo, for the last 60 or 70 years, these figures have been carved in wood (earlier they were made of straw) with the head, hands, and feet carved most naturalistically whilst the rest of the body is roughly carpentered since it is completely hidden by the clothing. It seems very likely that the brass heads from Ife were used in the same or at least a similar way. All of them have big nail holes in the neck as if they have been fitted to a wooden body such as those used for an *ako* ceremony. The effigies would be dressed up, the small holes in the heads carrying the crown or chief's cap of the deceased and possibly a ritual veil to hide the mouth.

The purpose of the ceremony was more than mere commemoration. The effigy, wearing the symbols of the office held by the deceased during his life time, represented the office itself, rather than its late incumbent. It demonstrated the continuity of the office, despite the death of the mortal holder: the king dies but the Crown endures. The effigy would then be buried, but the damage which many of the brass heads suffered suggests that, at some time after the burial place had been forgotten, the heads were dug up again, perhaps in the course of a search for the beads which were buried with them. The purpose of the heads was no longer remembered, but they were brought together in one place in the palace. Later the palace was reduced in size, so that they were outside the palace wall when they were found. At some stage, presumably before the palace was reduced in size, the building over them collapsed, crushing two of them severely. Perhaps this was during a time of war when people were occupied with other matters. Their existence had been completely forgotten until they were again dug up by accident in 1938.

Until recently there was no direct evidence in Ife itself of the date when the brasses and terra-cottas were made, so we had to rely on evidence from Benin. D'Aveiro who visited Benin City in 1485, reported that on the accession of an Oba of Benin, the new Oba had to send ambassadors to the Oni of Ife to request confirmation in office. To signify his agreement, the Oni sent back a brass hat, staff, and pectoral cross. Thus, we know that brass objects were being made in Ife and sent to Benin already when the first Europeans visited Benin. Another tradition records that the head of the late Oba was sent to Ife for burial and that a brass head was sent back in return to place on the altar dedicated to his memory. The Oba Oguola, who reigned towards the end of the Fourteenth Century, asked if the Oni could not send a brass-smith to teach the craft to his people. Igue-Igha went, and he is worshipped to this day in Benin as the patron of the brass-smiths. This tradition means that brass-casting must have been flourishing in Ife already before the late

Fourteenth Century. How long before is a matter of guesswork, but it seems likely that the brasses were not made over a very long period since they appear to be the work of only two or three artists. We may assume then that brass-casting in Ife flourished during the Twelfth to Fourteenth Centuries, but it may have begun earlier and continued later.

Radio carbon dates from excavations at Ita Yemoo now suggest that sculptures in terra-cotta had been abandoned there during the Eleventh or Twelfth Centuries, thus agreeing with our interpretation of the Benin traditions.

The bronzes found in Benin give support to the tradition of a connection between the two art styles. One small figure seems likely to have been made in Ife and to represent an Oni. The thinnest heads in Benin are in a more naturalistic style than the later ones, which increase in thickness after European trade made bronze easily available.

It is very interesting to see the later development at Benin of the art style which began with something akin to the naturalism of Ife. It is remembered which Obas introduced certain variations into the regalia represented on the bronze heads, so that not only can a typological sequence of development be worked out, but approximate dates can be assigned to it. The increasing stylization can be clearly observed. There is quite a rapid springing away from naturalism into increasing stylization, the heads becoming increasingly heavy in treatment as well as in weight, and increasingly elaborate but at the same time increasingly dull. All real feeling for anatomy is lost; the heads become lifeless symbols, not representing anyone, and are merely furniture for altars which commemorate the deceased Obas.

Of course, the story of brass-casting in Benin is not as consistently depressing as this bald description of the increasing formalism of the ancestor heads makes it sound. There was a tremendously wide range of subjects represented in the middle period (ending about 1700 A.D.), particularly in the scenes from court life which were represented on the plaques which were cast to decorate the columns of the Oba's palace. These were not merely technically excellent, but some, despite their conventions, are by no means completely lifeless. Some of the animals of royal associations—the leopard and the cock—are vigorously portrayed. Moreover, in spite of the disruption caused by the exile of the Oba Ovonramwen in 1897 (for the brass working had been carried out almost exclusively for the Oba's personal requirements up till then) the art never died out completely, and is at present showing a remarkable recovery in the skill of workmanship and in the size of castings made.

After starting the Benin brass-casters on their way, the art seems to have died out in Ife. E. B. Idowu in his book, *Olodumare, God in Yoruba Belief* (1962), records the study of how when one Oni died his courtiers did not wish to announce his death, but persuaded the brass-casters to make a life-size effigy of him which was placed in a dark corner of the reception hall of the palace. The trick was soon exposed, but his successor as Oni was angry at being kept from the throne and had the entire craft-group of sculptors slaughtered. Whether this really happened we do not know, but it does seem that serious brass-casting stopped suddenly in Ife, probably not long after the art was taught to the Binis. Yet in spite of this, the Ife tradition continued to be the inspiring model for later Yoruba sculpture.

At the same time as the naturalistic sculptures were being made, some stylized pieces were being produced. Three of these represent gagged human heads, probably victims for sacrifices; they have bulging eyes, horizontally protruding lips, and very conventional ears. All these features can be found especially clearly in the wooden masks carved for the *Gelede* society in modern Yorubaland, but they are present in most modern Yoruba wood and ivory sculpture. These same features were found also in a large group of terra-cotta heads excavated at Ilesha (20 miles from Ife) in 1959. These can be dated to about the middle of the Nineteenth Century. In time we shall no doubt find yet older examples of the style to demonstrate its continuous history.

These stylizations show a clear connection between Ife and modern Yoruba sculpture, but the naturalism too persists, though in a modified form. The two strands in the Ife art—naturalism and stylization—are woven into a true union in the later Yoruba sculpture. The art is in general stylized but has a strongly naturalistic core. It is quite obvious at a glance what the carving represents—kings, servants, rams, snakes and so on—which is not possible with the more abstract and cubist styles of African sculpture. In effect, the true naturalism of Ife continues under a reduced impetus in more recent work and makes increasing use of stylized elements. This strong tradition noted in the Ife art has made Yoruba sculpture recognizably Yoruba wherever it occurs in the extensive area which the Yoruba people occupy. The different divisions, the different villages, even the different carvers, have their own local or personal characteristics of style, but in spite of this they all have in common a basis of relaxing naturalism which marks them out at once as Yoruba.

In striking contrast to this is the sculpture of the Ibo. Here, where the society was organized into small units based on the clan, with originally no large settlements (in contrast to the veritable city-states of the Yoruba) the sculptors do not share in a unitary stylistic tradition. Styles of sculpture vary from clan to clan, not merely in relatively superficial characters, but in the fundamental way of conceiving the subject matter. In consequence, most Ibo sculptures can only be recognized as of Ibo origin if one has already seen the same kind of object from the same area before. This contrast between Ibo and Yoruba sculpture is a fascinating phenomenon and serves very well to illustrate the great range there is in the artistic heritage of Nigeria. For its area, Nigeria has produced a greater variety of art styles than any other part of Africa, which is a legitimate source of pride to her people. Unfortunately, changes in Nigerian society have upset the balance between the artist and his public. Nigerians who have been through school understandably look down on the traditional art forms as being associated with paganism. If they are interested in art, they tend to seek works which are close to the European tradition. Indeed, most of the rising generation of Nigerian artists use traditional sculptural forms in the same way as European artists have been doing since early in the present century. As a result, they are drawn into the cosmopolitan art world, where the nationality of the artist is of no relevance to his art.

Increasingly, therefore, in order to study specifically African art, we shall have to turn to the past. Material of the recent past is being collected into museums for safety, and there is a comprehensive scheme to provide museums in all the major centres of Nigeria. For the more distant past, we shall have to rely increasingly on archaeology, to throw light not only on the history of art, but on the whole history of human progress in Nigeria.

ART AS AN ELEMENT OF CULTURE IN AFRICA

Adrian A. Gerbrands

ETHNOGRAPHIC MATERIAL

FOLLOWING UP Olbrechts' experiences during a collecting trip in French West Africa in 1933 (Olbrechts 1933 and 1939), Vandenhoute undertook some research among the Dan and Diomande and among the Gere and Wobe in the Western part of the Ivory Coast. The investigation among the first was the most complete, among the Gere and Wobe it had to be broken off because the war broke out.

The object of the investigation as described by Olbrechts (1939) may be summarized as follows:

a. a general examination of artistic activity in the widest sense, but particularly with regard to masks, which are predominant in this area (Olbrechts, 1939:178);
b. a special investigation into the origin of the work of art, integrated as it is in the social, religious and economic life of these communities. For this the artist would be the starting-point: the motives which drive him to create, his sources of inspiration, the way in which he obtains his training, his technique, the economic or other factors which set him to work, his social position within his group (Olbrechts, 1939:180).

Reprinted from Mededelingen van het Rijksmuseum voor Volkenkunde No. 12: *Art as an Element of Culture, Especially in Negro Africa,* Leiden, 1957:78–93, by permission of the author and the Director of Rijksmuseum voor Volkenkunde.

A large part of the information, namely the material relating to masks and the artist, is embodied in Vandenhoute's manuscript thesis "Het masker in de cultuur en de kunst van het Boven-Cavally-gebied" (1945), a copy of which he kindly supplied for the purposes of this study. Much other material was also gathered, e.g. with regard to drawing, ornamenting the walls of huts, casting in bronze, plaiting, making pottery, building huts and bridges, dramatic art and the miming of "clowns", historical and religious data. Though this material remains in reserve up to the present, the mask complex and the activities of the artist which are so intimately connected with it are such dominant factors that a description of them offers sufficient possibilities to illustrate the place and function of art in these societies.

No particular rules can be given why someone becomes a sculptor. It is a free choice, in which many factors can play a part, as family tradition, natural talent or vocation, and the general esteem accorded a sculptor. We must bear in mind, though, that the sculptor is in the first place a farmer and remains one; there is no question of his trade being exercised as a regular profession. This even applies in the North of the area concerned, where the influence of the Bambara and Senoufo may be observed in that the sculptor is also a smith, though not all smiths are sculptors, as they are among the above-mentioned tribes. In the South on the other hand, among the Gere and Wobe, it seems to be a fairly common combination for a man to be a sculptor, cast in bronze, model "fetish" heads in clay (glé cult) and be a medicine-man (in the literal sense of a native doctor). But even then he remains in the first place a farmer. Of course his many capacities often contribute to his becoming a kind of adviser to the chief. In the centre, among the Dan, such combinations are not found. The direct economic advantage of being a sculptor is slight in a man's own community; only rarely his work gain him such favour among the chiefs that they present him with a wife. Besides the greater prestige this gives him in the community, such a gift is of value because she will work for him. A certain economic factor has now been introduced through the continual asking after masks and statuettes on the part of the white government officials, planters and others. This does not mean so much to the sculptor, though, as the orders are mostly placed through the chiefs, who keep the better part of the profits for themselves.

When a man wishes to learn carving, he attaches himself to an established craftsman, though one or two of the artists who were questioned claimed to have taught themselves. As to the duration of the period of training nothing definite can be said, as this depends very much on the talent and perseverance of the pupil. Generally speaking, the elementary technical knowledge needed is communicated in a fairly short time right at the beginning, after which progress continues over a much longer period, during which the master himself undertakes a piece of work at long intervals. There is no question of paying fees, or performing any kind of work, though the pupil will certainly not omit to offer some presents now and again as a polite gesture. One can hardly speak of a definite system of instruction; mostly the pupil just copies, under the master's eye, some piece that he himself is working on, having first looked on a few times. In choosing a teacher the candidate stays in the neighbourhood of his own village if he can, for he is then amongst acquaintances, or even relations.

Though hardly any economic advantage accrues to the teacher from his pupils, yet he likes to have them, for their work makes him better known, and enhances his reputation. Competition is not feared, for it is considered impossible for a pupil to produce as good work as his master, who has the advantage of long years of experience.

The tools are very simple and generally consist of adzes and knives, with sometimes a curved knife for hollowing out and an awl for burning holes round the edge of the mask. If we except a European pocket-knife or two or a big nail to serve as awl, all the tools are of native manufacture; indeed, they are often made by the sculptor himself. There is some difference between the adzes used in the South (bush country) and the North (savanna): in the South the blade has a shaft-hole through which the handle is thrust, and the angle between blade and handle is less acute than in the North, where the blade is inserted into the handle. In so far as the tools are used for making masks they have a pronounced sacral character. The mask is a supernatural being, and the tools play an important, creative part in its formation. Under these conditions it is natural that a certain potentiality is thought to lie in the tools, capable of greatly influencing not only the success of the work, but the health of the artist. Hence the tools are treated with the greatest care, offerings are brought them, and they may not be shown to women or uninitiated persons (no more may the mask itself in any stage of preparation), or the work will miscarry, or great evil will come on the unauthorised persons who saw it. It therefore often proved very difficult to see and study the tools, let alone to buy them.

Various kinds of wood are known, and the choice is determined by the nature of the article to be made. Before going to look for a suitable piece of wood some offerings are made to the ancestors, as their assistance is indispensable for a favourable result. The wood is used while wet and fresh, because dry wood is very difficult to carve, and because a solid block of wood inevitably cracks in drying, thus rendering it useless for making a mask. A finished mask rarely shows cracks, because no heartwood is used. The rule is very strictly observed that neither while searching for the wood nor while carving it may its name be mentioned.

While making a mask the sculptor always works alone in the bush, because women and non-initiates may not see him busy with it, to avoid injury to the work and great harm to themselves. He also prefers to work in isolation because only then can he "think" properly how to make the mask. And this "thinking" is the hardest part of the work, in which he must not be distracted. Besides observing all kind of rules (as not working when there is rain in the offing, not touching salt or lemons) the principal factor for a favourable result is the assistance of the ancestors. To make sure of this the sculptor abstains from sexual relations before beginning the work. Also a sacrifice is offered to the personal or family fetish. The presence of a white man at the work of carving, particularly if a mask is being made, is certain to displease the ancestors extremely. It was only after long negotiations that Vandenhoute did finally obtain permission to watch three sculptors at work, but in each case the work was more or less of a failure. During work offerings of kola-nuts are made now and then to the tools and personal fetish. These rules do not apply to the carving of other things than masks, or only to a lesser extent. After the general shape of the mask has been roughed out on the block of wood, it is finished in detail, smoothed off with a knife, scoured with sand, dried in the sun and finally polished quite smooth with the rough back of the leaves of a certain liana. Then it is coloured black with great care; in the forest by means of pounded leaves, in the savanna area by first colouring it red with the juice of certain roots and then covering it with mud from overgrown swamps: this changes the red into black. After rubbing it up with palm-oil the mask is finished; the inferior wood, now a deep shining black, has been transformed to express a high spiritual value. Sometimes masks are coloured red by means of vegetable dyes or the application of a layer of chewed kola-nuts, which turns a reddish orange after exposure to the air. In the North the mask is sometimes covered with European red felt instead.

The artist, especially as a maker of masks, is in close contact with the supernatural. Because he is very much aware of this, he usually shows a strong sense of self-importance. He knows himself chosen by the supreme power, though this election is sometimes felt as a burden. For the election in itself is no more than a certain spiritual predisposition for the artist's work; material realization depends upon the technical ability acquired, and both physically and mentally the sculptor's trade is arduous. Mentally, because heart and head must always be "thinking", that is one must determine what to make and realize the shape it will have to take. Indeed, some artists really prefer to go hunting, or to work on the land. That one does carving nevertheless is due not so much to the economic benefit, for that is very slight. The increased social prestige is rather more of an inducement, though after all, in the uniform social structure of these societies even the most prominent is little more than *primus inter pares*. The principal motive, however, seems to be a genuine pure joy in finishing a piece of work successfully, satisfaction and an agreeable sense of relaxation after mental and emotional strain when a difficult undertaking has produced a good result, as is only natural from a psychological point of view. There is no doubt that a certain impulse towards creation with its concomitant joy are at work here.

A creative impulse is evident also from the fact that several artists expressly stated that a beautiful face, a handsome man or woman might make such an impression upon them that they afterwards retired into solitude to carve a mask. It is not a matter of depicting the person concerned; that which is made is not a portrait, nor is the mask even intended to represent that man or woman. It is just a spark of inspiration which is imparted by what one happens to see, and which sets the creative process in motion.

In considering which requirements of his society are supplied by the artist's work, we must first remark that there is little sense in arranging the objects produced in strictly separated categories according to their function. In this area the artist's work ranges through the entire scale from sacred to profane. No wonder that under these conditions it is often very difficult to determine which of these aspects predominates in any particular work. Not that a distinction between sacral and profane has much value in his connection, (or religious and utilitarian as Himmelheber called it, 1935:37), for the qualification "profane" only has meaning when contrasted with "sacral", and in itself says little or nothing as to the actual function of the work of art. To make things still more complicated, this function also has social or economic aspects, or may fluctuate between the two.

But let us first take a look at what we might call the "production programme" of the artist in this area. It is an impressive series. Among the Dan we find of course masks in various types, then carved stools the boys sit on for circumcision, "dancing spoons" i.e. an attribute of the first wife of an important chief which she uses during the dance celebrating the return of his eldest son (his successor) from the seclusion of the initiation period, and which is afterwards carried as a mark of honour at all public ceremonies by the mother of the future chief. There are also various other carved spoons for stirring or for serving food. Then there are different kinds of dancing staffs; staffs of office for village chiefs, which are also used by the masked dancer; birds as gable ornaments and little animal figures which the artist sometimes offers the village chief in token of respect. Wooden statuettes have the same function, though nowadays these are also made for Europeans, as they are particularly interested in them. In the North tables whose legs are human figures are also made for sale to Europeans. Approaching the field of decorative art, we have clubs, neck-rests, *mankalla* playing-boards, musical instruments such as whistles and the so-called thumb pianos, wooden bowls, house-posts, and in former times also pipes. Finally wooden sandals, though here there is no longer any question of artistic form, and one can only describe the function as entirely profane.

Among the Gere-Wobe the repertoire appears to be less varied. Besides the masks, which here too are dominant, we find dancing and ceremonial staffs, combs and pins for the hair, occasionally a chief's stool. There is far less production for whites. Casting in bronze, however, seems to be of more consequence here than among the Dan.

This is an impressive array of objects in which the artist shows his skill and talent, but Vandenhoute does not discuss by any means all of them with regard to their significance for the community. One might attempt to gain an impression of this by collecting the remarks about it scattered through his extensive thesis, but this would take us altogether too far afield. Far more results are to be expected from discussing *the mask* as a cultural element which is in many respects dominant in the region of Upper Cavally.

In order clearly to establish the place of the mask in this

society it is necessary first to give a short summary of the religious system. According to the ideas of the Dan, the Gere-Wobe and the respective sub-tribes, life upon earth is only possible thanks to the omnipotence of a unique, anthropomorphous supreme being, the creator of everything that exists, *Zlan* (Dan) or *Nyonswa* (Gere-Wobe). But *Zlan* is too great a "chief", as the Dan put it, to be interested in human doings. Yet it is of vital importance for man that *Zlan's* omnipotence should exercise its beneficial influence upon life on earth, and means are sought to bring this about.

The supreme being is so far exalted above man that this is not possible in any direct fashion. But *Zlan* himself has created the means and indicated the method of attaining this goal.

It is among the Dan that we find the system based on these principles in its clearest form. More to the North and in the South also other influences make themselves felt which have occasioned certain adaptations and changes in the system. We will therefor deal principally with the system as it is found among the Dan and their various sub-tribes.

The most important rôle in coming into contact with the supreme being falls to the *ancestors.*

At death the life principle, the *meni,* which is conceived as anthropomorphous, leaves the body and enters the sphere of the supernatural, where it carries on an existence of the same kind as its life upon earth. The dead retain their terrestrial personality in all respects, so that someone who was an important person on earth will also be one in the afterlife. (See Plate 33.) It depends on the disposition of the ancestors whether all kinds of evil powers will be able to injure a man or not. They can also reward or punish their descendants by direct intervention, according to whether these carry out or neglect their duties towards the community, of which the ancestors also form part, even the most important. Owing to their existence in the supernatural, i.e. their close proximity to *Zlan,* they dispose of special powers, which derive from the omnipotence of *Zlan.*

But even the ancestors cannot be approached directly by man.

The sovereign method to do so, and especially to induce the ancestors, and if necessary through them *Zlan* himself, to take action in favour of the living is by means of the mask. On the other hand the ancestors also make use of the mask to intervene in the life of their descendants, so that in the final instance *Zlan* himself might also be said to do so.

The usual conception is that *Zlan* specially created the mask to enable man to contact his omnipotence on the one hand, and as a means of keeping direct control of man's doings on the other.

The mask, however, cannot simply be used by anyone to influence the ancestors. In principle, the initiative must be taken by the highest spiritual functionary, the *go-master* or *go-priest*. He may be considered as the representative on earth of the ancestors. Yet again as a man, being actually the most important functionary of his community, he is naturally very much concerned with the well-being, in the fullest sense, of his fellow-men, both individually and as a community. In him the divine and the human have a point of contact, and it is from this common centre that he handles the mask as a divine instrument of power. Either as a man on behalf of his fellow-men confronting the supreme power, or as executive of that same supreme power transmitting its commands to individual and community.

The *go-master* is the centre of spiritual power of the community and in this quality has very great influence with the holder of temporal power, here the sub-tribal chief, who is the highest authority, as there is no tribal chief here. This influence is not only a matter of principle, but is often exercised in actual fact. It is obvious, however, that this state of affairs may sometimes occasion strained relations between temporal and religious authorities, all the more so in view of the special qualities required of such functionaries as leaders. We are not surprised, then, to find that in many cases temporal authorities have gradually succeeded in attributing the function of *go-master* to relations or persons without much initiative. This is especially noticeable towards the North. But as a rule these conflicts remain behind the scenes,

Art as an Element of Culture in Africa 375

and generally speaking the *go-master* still represents to the ordinary Dan all that is mighty and most to be prized.

The concept *"go"* has many aspects, and cannot really be translated. It indicates the highest power imaginable, which is of a deeply mystic nature.

The *go-master* lives in strict isolation in a hut standing more or less apart with his first wife, the leader of the women, who is the midwife and carries out the excision of the clitoris at the initiation of the girls. He rarely shows himself in the village, and never appears in public. Except for the highest temporal authorities, all contact with the outside world is through his assistant and future successor, who carries out his orders. Through this helper he has a direct hold on the community, apart from the temporal authority. This influence also has another form, because the heads of families exercise essentially the same function as the *go-master* towards their families, though on a lower plane, and they act as his assistants and keep him informed.

The *go-master* makes himself felt as the omnipresent authority in the background. Never does he enter into direct contact with a white man. Even Vandenhoute was never able to see one, though negotiations for the purchase of masks in the Dan area had to be conducted with him. Not always with success, as appears from an answer Vandenhoute once received: "Tu es encore enfant, et les enfants ne trouvent pas ca!" (1945:167, note 1).

In the *go-master's* hut the source of his authority is to be found in the shape of the *go-fetish* (a conglomerate of all kinds of supernatural ingredients), *and especially in the actual presence of the ancestors.* For prominent persons are buried in the hut of the *go-master.* And not only that, the *masks* they have used during life are put away in the hut, and do not leave it except on most exceptional occasions. In other words, the *go-hut* is the actual centre of the whole enormous potential of supernatural power of the notables buried there and of their masks. We can well understand, then, that even the leading members of the community only enter the enclosure with the greatest diffidence, and that it is a great exception if one of them is allowed to go into the hut itself. Obviously the presence of a white man would be the greatest profanation imaginable.

This brings us to the point where it becomes necessary to discuss the actual significance of the mask in this whole complex as we find it among the Dan.

We must first observe that, apart from those masks which are placed in the *go-hut,* the mask is the personal property of the individual *male* owner. But by no means every man possesses one, and those who do possess one, have usually either acquired it at the behest of the *go-master,* or inherited it from their father. Though the mask is a piece of personal property, the *go-master* has an important voice in the matter when it has to be decided, possibly in consultation with village dignitaries, whether a mask is to appear in public.

As already stated, the mask is the most efficient means of influencing the ancestors. Although in principle every mask has the same power of doing this, in practice they are by no means equal in this matter. The influence of a mask is measured by the social prestige of its owner in his community. For it was only the help his ancestors gave him through the intermediacy of the mask, which enabled him to rise to a place of importance in the community during his life-time. After his death the special qualities are still present in the mask. This makes it very valuable for his family, for it is to be expected that in order to assist his descendants the deceased will by preference make use of the mask which he himself found so helpful. If the deceased was a man of high standing, he will be so too in the hereafter and will be able to induce the other ancestors to add their power to his and make it available through his mask for the benefit of the living. The older a mask is, the stronger, because the potential of several generations becomes concentrated in it. The dignity of the son is added to that of the father, and the mask also grows in power. This power really has two aspects. In the first place the mask in itself is a supernatural being and much feared, like all the supernatural beings created by *Zlan.* It is a materialization of that power which is absolutely indispensable for maintaining contact, through the ancestors, with all powers in the supernatural sphere and with those of the earth. In other words, it is in the final instance the contact with *Zlan* which is maintained through the mask. This contact is a vital necessity both for the individual and the community: without the mask no contact is possible and the community is doomed.

It is true that the wooden mask as we know it from the glass case in the museum is the principal manifestation of this supernatural being, but this manifestation is not truly complete until the mask is being worn by a person in full costume. Together, the wooden mask and the costume which hides the wearer constitute the supernatural being of the mask. This combination is felt as the actual presence of this being, not a symbol or representation of it. It *is* the entity. Whether any distinction exists or is felt between the being manifest in the mask and the wearer of the mask, is not clear. But it is a fact that the wearer is always completely hidden by the costume and remains anonymous, except to a few initiates. Neither may women and children of the Dan ever be present when a masked dancer is being dressed, or see one of the masks without adornment. Possibly we have to do here with a certain rationalization on the part of the men in order to maintain awe and fear of the mask and costume as a supernatural being. The mask is quite definitely not an ancestor, though it may sometimes be regarded as of the same order. Neither is it the portrait of anyone dead or living. Both the Dan and the Gere, however, are very decided in declaring that the mask always represents a human face, though the European sometimes finds it difficult to recognize human features, especially in the masks of the Gere.

The mask itself, as a wooden object, also has a certain power which is mainly apotropaeic and protective, and can be strengthened by the addition of various preparations. This places it in the category of what are commonly called "fetishes" in Africa. "Amulet" is a very inadequate translation of this term. In its function of fetish the mask is often found in the possession of individuals, when it is often of much smaller size than usual. Such masks are preferred for bringing offerings to one's ancestors on, and the owner consults it when in difficulties, or before carrying out some plan. Several artists have one of these little masks, to which they repeatedly bring offerings while at work. Especially with these sacrificial masks it is often difficult in practice to decide whether they are being consulted in their quality of "fetish" or as intermediary with the ancestors. In the North, where the influence of the Islam is clearly to be seen, they have been entirely superseded by texts from the Koran sewn into little leather bags.

Among the Dan we find an elaborate system whereby the masks are classified in various *categories* of higher and lower rank. The neighbouring tribes have something of the same system.

The higher masks include the *ancestor masks,* i.e. among the Dan the masks kept in the *go-master's* hut and among the Gere-Wobe the higher grade *tegla,* with various "panther masks" to second them. Then *sacrificial masks,* on which heads of families or individuals sacrifice to their ancestors. These masks often partake of the character of a "fetish" (see previous paragraph). Among the Gere-Wobe these are represented by lower grade *tegla.* Also so-called *avengers,* particularly malevolent masks, mainly used for the carrying out of individual or collective punitive measures, in which case they sometimes act independently of the *go-master,* thus forcing him to bring one of his highest ranking masks into action in order to maintain his authority. In the higher categories we also find masks which appear at the *initiation* in various functions, such as e.g.: purifying the village, both from evil influences and material filth; entertaining those who have remained behind in the village; exercising supervision over those who are to be initiated and imparting a little elementary schooling in spiritual and practical matters. Finally, in the area where the forest yields place to the savanna, this category includes the so-called *sagbwe* masks or running masks, who have their own hierarchy. Their general task is to supervise, guard and protect the village. In particular they are vigilant against fire, which constitutes a real danger in certain times of the year when strong squalls occur.

The lower categories include masks which may be distinguished according to their specific activities as *dancing masks, singers, palaver masks* and *begging masks*. Their function is mainly that of providing the community with entertainment and amusement, in which a didactic element is often discernible, though the fear and awe inspired by the supernatural being manifest in the mask are not entirely lacking. (For a full discussion of the separate categories of masks see 1945, pp. 132–514. Synopsis in Vandenhoute 1952; mainly 182–187).

An essential characteristic of the hierarchic system is the passing of masks from one category to another. A new mask begins its career in one of the lower categories; in which one, often depends on accidental circumstances at the time of its first appearance in public. If the owner is held in general esteem when he dies, then his mask moves into one of the higher categories. There is no general rule about this: a begging mask can suddenly be promoted to the highest rank of ancestor masks if its owner held a prominent position in the community. The dead man's relations profit by this at once, as in future they are counted among the notable families.

We see, then, that there is no correlation between the form and the function of a mask, though there are few exceptions, which can be left out of account here. Generally speaking, it is only possible to discuss the function of a Dan or Gere mask seen in a museum if we are acquainted with the history of that particular mask.

Just as a mask can gain in importance, it can also lose rank. This happens when it no longer proves able to gain the favour of the ancestors, or when it is accidentally damaged or attacked by termites. Formerly such masks were thrown away deep in the bush, or left to moulder in the hut. Nowadays they are sometimes sold to whites, and what we find in European collections are mainly such masks which are "no good" any more.

This brings us to a point where the aesthetic factor of the work of art comes into play. For not only does a damaged mask lose its functional value, but for a new mask to please the ancestors *it has to be as beautiful as possible.* This idea is emphasized again and again by the leaders of the community. The mask has to be *"as beautiful as possible":* the aesthetic quality finally depends on the capability of the artist, and not every village or area has an artist of real prominence to work for them. The artist is very much aware of his responsibility for carving a fine mask. While working on it, he is continually anxious to succeed in making a beautiful mask, "for that pleases the ancestors".

Just as Himmelheber did, Vandenhoute also tried to seek out the criteria for a "beautiful mask" by comparing the judgment of leading men among the Dan as to the aesthetic qualities of certain masks with his own opinion. It was repeatedly found that about masks he considered decidedly poor or particularly fine he was in agreement with the connoisseurs among the Dan, whereas about the intermediate ones opinion was very much divided, as one might expect.

By means of these experiments, and especially by carefully observing the working-method of some of the artists, Vandenhoute was able to formulate a few criteria of beauty.

In the first place *symmetry* according to the vertical axis is consciously sought and strictly maintained. But symmetry alone is not sufficient, there must also be *balance, rhythm* and *harmony* between the various masses, surfaces and lines which constitute the mask. (See Plate 32.) In introducing these concepts we certainly enter upon a difficult, even a dangerous terrain. Balance, rhythm and harmony are matters which may be more readily perceived by intuition than concretely and exactly measured. Yet the Dan sculptor does indeed work according to these concepts, though he cannot formulate them. For when he is working on a mask he gradually shapes it by taking off a bit now here, then there, continually pausing to feel and measure the work; every now and again he spends some time regarding it critically, sometimes holding it upside down or back to front, screwing up his eyes and bending his head back while holding it at arm's length and scrutinizing it intently. The sculptors are unanimous in saying that thinking is the hardest part of the work here. This thinking indicates the severe tension which accompanies the process of creation for the sculptor, the struggle with his material, the struggle also to clarify the form he has envisaged in his mind and find its adequate material expression.

Besides these *criteria of form* account is also taken of the *finishing* (polishing and colouring), while finally *criteria of use* are also important, i.e. whether the wearer can see and breathe properly in it, and whether it fits the face well.

Though it would certainly be desirable to continue these experiments, yet for the present we can already draw the conclusion that our criteria of beauty are to a certain extent in agreement with those of the Dan. And in any case we can draw the important conclusion that the Dan too apply purely aesthetic criteria. Here we must bear in mind that beauty is far more a vital necessity to the Dan than to the European, for the mask must be beautiful in order to induce the favour of the ancestors. And without a mask no contact is possible with them, so that the community would be doomed.

One might say, then, that the wooden mask (together with its costume, or alone, appearing in public or remaining unseen) is the materialization of a supernatural being (the Being of the mask: *ge*) with the object of bringing supernatural powers into action for the benefit of life upon earth, and thus ensuring the continued existence of individuals and community.

At the same time the mask complex has been consciously used by political and religious leaders to ward off outside influences. In the North to prevent the intrusion of Islam, without much success. In the South, and in the North also, to counter-balance the secret societies thrusting in from all sides (the *poro* organisation).

The masks from the Upper Cavally area fall into two big groups as to *style,* which coincide with the two most important groups of the population, the Dan and the Gere-Wobe. Within each of these groups we find differences in style connected with the various sub-tribes, and these differences sometimes show as local variations of style. In general the masks from the stylistic area of the Dan have more of an idealized naturalism than those of the Gere-Wobe. The latter are fond of duplicating features such as the eyes, the cheek-bones, or even the nose. Also there is a certain preference for a geometrical, "cubistic" looking, scheme of forms.

Within these two stylistic areas Vandenhoute was able to demonstrate several *stylistic centres* after a careful analysis of a great number of locally collected masks. Each of these is the radiating centre of a particular *sub-style*. On these grounds it is possible to determine the provenance of a mask with a fair amount of certainty from its stylistic traits. An excellent summary of this stylistic investigation was published in the *Mededelingen* of the National Museum of Ethnology, Leiden (Vandenhoute 1948), where further particulars are to be found.

INTRODUCTION, NEW ZEALAND,
SEPIK RIVER, AND NEW IRELAND
FROM *ARTS OF THE SOUTH SEAS*

Ralph Linton and Paul S. Wingert

IN TRYING to gain an understanding of Oceanic cultures and the development of their many contrasting components, a survey of the factors that produced them is necessary. The native populations of the entire region are composed of descendants of successive waves of migrants from the Asiatic mainland who belonged to many different racial types and represented various phases of cultural progress. It is generally believed that the ancestors of the aborigines of Australia were very early settlers who remained relatively undisturbed by later migrations. The Papuans of central and western New Guinea may also have come at a very early date but were followed by the ancestors of the Micronesians and Polynesians. The Melanesians originated probably from an early intermixture of Papuans with the later migrants.

In certain sections racially well defined groups have lived next to each other for generations without losing their cultural identity, while in others they have merged to form new homogeneous groups. In the case of successive migrations of people of the same ancestry, the newcomers were either completely absorbed by the early settlers or formed an aristocracy within a racially uniform people.

Selected and reprinted from *Arts of the South Seas,* by Ralph Linton and Paul S. Wingert in collaboration with René d'Harnoncourt, copyright 1946 by The Museum of Modern Art, with the permission of Mrs. Ralph Linton and Paul Wingert, and The Museum of Modern Art.

The great variety of inherited aptitudes and cultural characteristics the immigrants brought with them was further diversified by the climatic conditions and natural resources of the islands on which they settled. In central Australia they found vast deserts and steppes; in the mountains of New Zealand cool pine forests; on the coast of New Guinea dense tropical jungle, and in Micronesia small wind-swept coral atolls with just enough soil to support a few palm trees and patches of scrub. Once the influx of Asiatic migrants ceased, innumerable regional cultures grew out of the adjustment of many distinct groups of people to a great diversity of physical surroundings. These cultures developed undisturbed by influences from outside Oceania, but the constant traffic from island to island made for a wide distribution of regional ideas and art forms.

The division of Oceania into four major regions comprising twenty cultural areas is a convenient device to organize the exceedingly complex material into more or less homogeneous units, and has been adopted as such in this book. A similar organization of the material can be found in many anthropological publications, except that Fiji, usually considered as part of Melanesia, is here included among the island groups of Polynesia. This was done because the art of the Fijians is very closely related to Polynesian work although their languages, cultural characteristics and physical appearance are predominantly Melanesian.

As has been said, there is little uniformity in the scope and content of the various cultural areas. Some of them, like the Huon Gulf, cover only a small section of an island while others, like Central Polynesia, include several archipelagoes. The arts of Easter Island, New Zealand, the Marquesas and the Admiralties show few stylistic variations while those of the Solomons and the Sepik River area of New Guinea can be subdivided into many distinct local styles. In the case of both Australia and Micronesia the entire region was treated as a unit because the available material, in spite of its often considerable esthetic merit, is too limited in its variety to make subdivision practicable.

A careful examination of a representative collection of the

Introduction from Arts of the South Seas

arts of the South Seas reveals the existence of a number of basic trends that often extend through many cultural areas and sometimes even cross regional borders. The extreme economy of means, for example, that produces such elegant simplicity in the sculpture and useful objects from Micronesia can also be clearly recognized in some of the Fijian and Central Polynesian work and may even be traced to the islands of northern Melanesia. (See Plate 35.) This trend may well have originated in the scarcity of raw materials on the Micronesian coral atolls which made wasteful elaboration impractical. Its appearance in island groups such as Fiji and Samoa, where natural resources are abundant, suggests that it eventually turned into a style accepted mainly for its esthetic appeal. This is further borne out by the application of its formal characteristics to ceremonial figures that served no utilitarian purpose.

Very pronounced in the arts of Central Polynesia is a preoccupation with geometric order which may well reflect the intricate, systematic structure of social and religious concepts. Many objects are decorated with angular patterns that often cover their entire surface. (See Plate 34.) In some cases, as in the adzes from the Hervey Islands, these patterns are so deeply incised that the adzes can no longer be used as tools and serve only ritual purposes. Such geometric designs have evidently a ritual significance of their own and occasionally become so elaborate that they change the basic shape of an object until it becomes an abstract form. The emphasis on geometric order is less evident but still noticeable in the arts of New Zealand and other marginal regions of Polynesia, where it survives in decorative surface patterns superimposed on organic forms. In Melanesia still another dominant tendency appears. The art of the Sepik River area and the Papuan Gulf of New Guinea, as well as that of some of the other nearby islands, has a strong almost violent emotional quality. This is most apparent in the carved images of ancestor and nature spirits produced in this region. (See Plate 37.) Organic interplay of curved surfaces lends these sculptures life and motion. Distortions and exaggerations and the use of strongly contrasting colors give them an aggressive dramatic intensity. Many of the figures are the work of men initiated into the secrets of ceremonial life and are purposely made to awe the uninitiated members of the tribe. Even if the means employed by the artist to impress his audience are often spectacular, one cannot speak of intentional deception, for the artist believes his work to be filled with the power of the spirits and considers himself their agent and instrument. A combination of showmanship and deep conviction makes this art an ideal vehicle for its magic content.

To what extent this trend has spread outside Melanesia is difficult to ascertain. It is evident, however, that the dramatic intensity of the Easter Island carvings is similar to that of Melanesian sculpture and that the basic forms of Maori carvings resemble in dynamic quality the work from certain sections of New Guinea.

Far too little research has been done up to now to make possible a systematic analysis of Oceanic art based on considerations of content and form, but even a preliminary survey provides many stimulating points of departure. There is no doubt that the great variety of styles and the outstanding quality of individual works of art from the South Seas would make such a study a major contribution to our knowledge of the primitive arts of the world.

POLYNESIA

NEW ZEALAND

The history of the New Zealand natives, commonly called Maori, is better known than that of any other people who were ignorant of the art of writing. All Polynesians had a keen interest in genealogies and in the deeds of ancient chiefs, but in most regions the knowledge of these things was confined to a small group of learned men with semi-sacred functions. Among the Maori the same sort of knowledge was widely disseminated. Each tribe had a sort of college in which the ancient lore was taught to all young men of any social position. The chants in which this lore was embodied had to be learned verbatim and students who failed to

Introduction from Arts of the South Seas

pass the final examinations lost heavily in prestige. While the historical records were, quite naturally, designed to show the tribe in a good light, they were as accurate as much of the American history taught in our own schools fifty years ago.

According to these traditions, the first Polynesian explorers to leave a record reached New Zealand about the year 900 A.D. Some of the legends say that they found there a few people who could speak their language, but most of the great island seems to have been uninhabited at that time. The explorers brought back to Central Polynesia tales of a great wingless bird, the moa, and samples of New Zealand jade, an unsurpassed material for ornaments and implements. A number of other Polynesian voyagers visited the island during the next three hundred years and a few local settlements were made. Finally, in the thirteen hundreds, there was a great migration from eastern Central Polynesia: mainly the Cook, Austral and Society groups. The names of the canoes in which these migrants came have been preserved as carefully as we preserve the name of the Mayflower and most of the modern Maori trace descent from the crew of one or another of them.

The settlement of New Zealand was something new in Polynesian experience. After many generations spent in small islands with strictly limited resources, the immigrants found themselves in a rich, wide land where there was room for all. However, the new land was much colder than anything they had encountered before. Most of their familiar crops would not grow and many of their familiar materials were lacking. In the course of time they developed a new and distinctive culture with arts and crafts differing markedly from those of the other Polynesians.

Traditions tell that the voyagers of the great migration came in double canoes or canoes with outriggers. Both were abandoned by the later Maori who did most of their water travel on rivers or close to shore. The native kauri pine provided gigantic logs and the Maori replaced the plank canoes of their ancestors by huge dugouts sometimes as much as eighty feet long and wide enough to seat two paddlers abreast. These canoes were provided with projecting figure-heads and a high, upward-curved stern piece intricately carved.

The airy thatched houses of Central Polynesia were unsuited to the damp and cold climate of New Zealand. Ordinary dwellings became little more than hastily constructed hovels, but each village had one great house on the building of which the skill and wealth of the villagers were concentrated. This house was used for all sorts of ceremonies and also served as a dormitory in which all the villagers slept in cold weather. It was oblong with a projecting porch at one end and, under the porch, a single door and window. The gable door and window frames and sometimes the entire house front were decorated with elaborate carvings. The walls inside were made with alternate carved panels and thick, rigid mats woven in bold red, black and white designs. The posts supporting the ridge pole were also carved and the rafters were painted with elaborate scroll designs. At the bottom of the central house post there was usually a naturalistic human figure, but the figures on the carved panels were highly conventionalized with a wealth of surface decoration in fluid, curvilinear style. All figures were supposed to represent ancestors.

Since the paper-mulberry could not be grown in New Zealand, the bark-cloth garments of other parts of Polynesia were replaced by heavy cloaks made from New Zealand flax. Skeins of this soft, strong fiber were placed side by side and fastened together with pairs of slender cords which were given a half turn between each pair of skeins. This technique, which is known as twined weaving, was widely used in Polynesia in the making of fish traps but only here was it applied to fabrics. Cloaks were shaped so that they would hang smoothly on the wearers' shoulders and the better ones were often covered on the outside with feathers or provided with closely woven borders decorated with simple angular geometric designs.

New Zealand jade was prized both for its utility and for its beauty. It was exceedingly tough and hard so that cutting implements made from it were little inferior to those of metal. Small implements of finely colored jade were often worn as ornaments.

Introduction from Arts of the South Seas

The most prized of all native decorations was the *hei tiki,* a small grotesque human figure carved from fine green jade. The making of such an ornament required months of labor and *hei tiki* were handed down in chiefly families as heirlooms. In some cases they were worn only in alternate generations, being buried with the owner, then dug up and worn again by a grandchild. There was also a regulation that the wife of a captured chief had to send her *hei tiki* to the wife of his captor.

The art of tattooing was highly developed, but this sort of decoration was practically limited to men. Women were marked only upon the lips, but men had the entire face tattooed, and also the thighs. Maori tattooing was really flesh carving. The designs were cut into the skin with a small, chisel-like blade. Pigment was made from the dung of dogs which had been fed on very fat meat until over-secretion of bile colored their dung black. This was rubbed into the cuts so that they healed as a series of grooves. Since the grooves became obliterated in time, a man who was careful of his appearance would have his tattooing gone over and deepened from time to time. No two face tattooings were identical, and in early days chiefs drew details of their face tattoo on treaties with the whites by way of signature.

Although the ancestors of most of the Maori came from a part of Polynesia in which religion and government were both highly organized, the historic Maori lacked such organization. They had no sacred structures, no images toward which worship was directed and no distinct class of priests. Their only sacred objects were small carved pegs upon which the spirits were summoned to alight so that they could receive offerings and hear prayers. In government, each tribe stood alone under the rule of its hereditary chief who was bound to all the tribesmen by ties of blood. Slavery was fairly common, the slaves being prisoners of war who had been temporarily reprieved from being eaten, but defeated tribes were usually wiped out. Conquest kingdoms of the Central Polynesian sort were unknown in New Zealand.

The Maori were the most warlike of the Polynesians and their courage and determination won the respect of Europeans. Villages were built on hill tops or ridges for defense and were elaborately fortified with ditches and palisades. Attacking parties carried on regular siege operations. Chivalrous behavior was admired and in some cases a besieging force would draw off the night before a final assault and even send supplies to the besieged so that the defenders would be well rested and fed and able to put up a good final battle. Cannibalism was regular. The flesh of slain enemies was an important part of the spoil after a successful battle, and captives, irrespective of age or sex, were usually eaten. Just as in the Marquesas, the relatives of a man who had been eaten were under a revenge obligation until the account could be squared, but the ultimate insult was to cook an enemy and then discard him as unfit for food.

As with most really determined fighters, the Maori warrior's equipment was comparatively simple. Staves pointed at one end so that they could be used as either clubs or spears were made in two standardized forms, but the favorite weapon was a short club, never more than two feet long. This was made from stone, preferably jade, or whalebone, or hard wood. The end of the weapon was ground to a sharp edge and it was used for stabbing rather than striking. The favorite thrusts were those delivered at the temple or just below the ribs. Apparently this weapon was developed from a stone adze blade or chisel held in the hand.

The Maori, like many other primitive groups, had two quite distinct art styles. Robes, baskets and mats, all of which were made by women, were decorated with simple angular geometric designs. This held even for such articles as feather robes, where there were no technical limitations on the sort of designs which might have been used. In wood carving, rafter painting and tattooing, which were men's arts, only curvilinear designs were employed. Highly conventionalized human faces and figures were extensively used in wood carving for decorative effect but never appeared in painting or tattooing. A few simple, semi-naturalistic images were carved to commemorate men and women of high rank. In these the poses are static, in sharp contrast to the vigorous action portrayed in many of the conventionalized figures.

Introduction from Arts of the South Seas

The Maori regarded such commemorative figures as portraits, but the portraiture consisted in an accurate reproduction of the individual's facial tattooing.

Maori decorative carving finds no close parallel elsewhere in Oceania. Its vigorous, sweeping curvilinear style and organization of design in terms of the entire surface to be decorated contrast sharply with the art of other Polynesians. These tended to use small angular geometric motifs and to divide the area to be decorated into numerous zones or sections. These differences have led many writers to seek the origins of Maori art in some sort of Melanesian influence, perhaps the presence of a Melanesian substratum in the New Zealand population. However, there are no indications of such a substratum and the few art objects which have been found in archaeological work in New Zealand differ sharply from the work of the historic Maori. Moreover, the historic Maori style has little in common with any Melanesian style as regards either its designs or its techniques of execution.

A careful analysis of the motifs which the Maori used as design elements and especially of the conventions employed for depicting human beings reveals many similarities between Maori art and that of the Marquesas Islands. Marquesan culture seems to have been a survival of the type of culture which existed in Central Polynesia prior to the arrival of the second wave of Polynesian immigrants. Since the ancestors of the Maori came from eastern Central Polynesia, they probably brought these design elements and conventions to New Zealand with them, then developed their distinctive art on the spot. While Maori art evolved in the direction of all-over design and sweeping curvilinear composition, Central Polynesian art, under the influence of the migrants of the second wave, evolved in the direction of increased angularity and the division of the surface to be decorated into zones or sections.

The Maori master carver trained himself to visualize his design in its entirety before he began to carve, then worked without the aid of sketches or guide marks. This ability to visualize designs and carry them in the mind was reflected in certain forms of virtuosity. In some objects it is clear that the design was conceived in terms of a field larger than the object to be decorated and even different in shape. The object was superimposed upon the imaginary design field and only those parts of the total design which fell within the area covered by the object were reproduced upon it. Other objects are decorated with two or more designs, each complete and coherent in itself, which have been superimposed upon each other. The artist's audience, who understood the skill required for compositions of this sort, were able to draw esthetic satisfaction from designs which seem, to the European, incomplete or confused. This appreciation of technique for its own sake resulted in the production of some exceedingly rococo pieces, especially after the introduction of steel tools. However, many Maori carvings deserve to rank among the art masterpieces of the world.

MELANESIA
INTRODUCTION

. . . A hot humid climate produces dense jungles, fetid swamps and a luxuriant flora, but the big mammals of Indonesia and the Asiatic mainland are not found here. The crocodile is the largest animal and a variety of other reptiles and brilliantly feathered birds exists. Volcanic eruptions, tidal waves and storms give to many parts of this region a melodramatic, violent quality that has strongly affected the lives and beliefs of its inhabitants.

In discussing the cultural characteristics of Melanesia as a whole, it must be remembered that local accents and interpretations often make for great variations from one island to another and sometimes even within the limits of a single small island. Generally speaking, religious practices center in the belief in two kinds of very powerful spirits: spirits of the dead, who are the subject of a wide-spread ancestor cult, and spirits that represent natural forces or mythological and legendary beings. The latter are frequently of totemic nature and are often the "property" of the clan claiming to be their dependents. In some areas com-

Introduction from Arts of the South Seas

munal rites, prolonged, elaborate, dramatic spectacles, were performed to venerate and to gain the favor of these spirits while in other places similar ceremonies were conducted by restricted secret societies. Many of these performances were staged when a new member was initiated into the practices and secrets of the society. These ceremonies played an important role in the social as well as the religious life of the people and each one of them called for the making of objects such as clubs, paddles, drums, shields, figures, staffs, personal ornaments and masks. In many regions, elaborate men's clubhouses were built on the open spaces used for dances and dramatic spectacles.

A number of carvings and personal ornaments were made for use in secular dancing. Among the most lavishly decorated objects were the utensils used in betel-nut chewing, a wide-spread habit producing a mild stimulation. The areca (betel) nut was ground and mixed with slacked lime, placed in the mouth on a pepper leaf and chewed. Carved and sometimes painted containers were made to hold the lime, mortars and pestles to grind the nut, and a great variety of spatulae to transfer the lime from the container to the mouth. . . .

At least two major traditions can be discerned in Melanesian art. One of these achieves dramatic effects through distortion, strong color contrasts and sometimes huge dimensions. A bold interplay of curved lines and surfaces gives a violent driving force to most ceremonial sculpture. Its sensuous organic forms seem imbued with a powerful magic. This trend is most evident in the central regions of Melanesia, in sections of the Sepik River area and the Gulf of Papua in New Guinea, in the New Hebrides and in parts of New Britain.

The other tradition seems strongest in the outlying archipelagoes such as the Solomons and Admiralties, but it is also found in the Massim area of New Guinea. The sculptures of these latter regions are usually of moderate or small size. In the Massim area and in most of the Solomons polychromy is rare and in the Admiralties the use of color is purely decorative. Dignity and elegance distinguish the figures which are frequently quite life-like in their proportions. Wherever emotion is expressed, it seems controlled by the restrictions of formal treatment. . . .

THE SEPIK RIVER AREA

The art of the Sepik River region has more variety and is richer than that of any other section of Oceania. This area includes the coast north and south of the mouth of the river and the areas bordering on both banks for a considerable distance up the large and meandering stream and its tributaries. Vast swamps are found along the coast and in many places along the shores of the Sepik. Grassy plains, high plateaus and high mountains make up the terrain along its length. Seasonal floods inundate parts of both banks along the middle and lower reaches. At these times great hard-wood logs are swept downstream and provide material from which houses and carvings are made, while up and down the Sepik the river itself provides a broad avenue for the distribution of objects from one region to another.

A number of Papuan tribes, each speaking a language unintelligible to the others, make up a rather extensive population. Village or group cultivation of crops forms the basis of their economy. Intermittent warfare is waged between many of the tribes and some of them, such as the Kwoma, are fairly isolated. Tribes from which important collections of objects have been obtained include the Iatmül, Arapesh, Mundugumor, Tchambuli and the Abelam.

All the cultures of the Sepik River region have certain basic elements in common that appear in many local variations. These are: the men's secret society, the men's clubhouse and the performance of spectacular ceremonies. The rites involve everywhere the use of a vast number of carved and decorated objects. These objects are of two kinds—sacred hidden ones which may be seen only by a particular group of persons, and others that are used and seen by everyone. In both categories, representations of supernatural spirits are frequent and the sense of the dramatic is very strong. There is a sharp division among the people mark-

Introduction from Arts of the South Seas

ing off the initiates—those who can participate actively in the rites—from the uninitiates, usually women and children, who compose the audience. To impress this audience, the men will make great efforts and go to extraordinary trouble. This segregation is a fundamental factor in the social and ceremonial life of the entire region, but its enforcement varies considerably in degree from tribe to tribe.

The number of objects produced in the Sepik area is enormous. Among them are figures ranging from eight inches to eight feet and masks measuring from a few inches to several feet. Stools, neck rests, slit-gongs and shields are decorated with human or animal design motifs. Elaborate wooden hooks of all sizes, used to hang belongings out of reach of the rats, are made in many villages. On the coast and along the rivers canoes are built, some with prows shaped realistically in the form of large crocodiles. In some sections human skulls are painted and covered with clay modeling to represent heads. Even pottery, a craft that is but little developed in Oceania, is found here in great variety including painted and incised vessels, bowls, large jars and roof ornaments.

Every tribe produces a number of wood carvings of ceremonial and artistic importance and makes use of leaves, feathers, shells, furs, etc., for their decoration. The dominant color is red in all shades from pink to maroon. It is often combined with black, white, yellow and purplish gray. Many of the carvings are made of a heavy, close-grained wood and every time they are to figure in a ceremony they are decorated and painted anew.

Sepik River art is for the most part the work of professional artists, or at least men of recognized skill, and in some places tradition provides opportunities for the display of connoisseurship by tribal members. For instance, when cult figures are set up in the Kwoma men's house, they are formally appraised and words of appreciation are addressed to the successful artist. All kinds of objects are constantly traded. Sometimes they are acquired from a distant tribe together with the ceremonial dances, rhythms and songs for which they were made. Often the new owners do not understand the original meaning of the pieces or even the words of the songs pertaining to them. Such purchases seem to be motivated by a desire to enrich local ceremonies with new objects and forms. A ceremony whether religious or social remains, in fact, fashionable for a limited time only and is then superseded by a new one. It is therefore impossible for us to classify objects by function and meaning since an object may be considered sacred in one village while in the next village it may be used only for amusement.

The constant trading of objects among the tribes produces an often bewildering intermingling and diffusion of style elements. In some cases, as with the Iatmül tribe of the central Sepik region, this trading results in an eclecticism that incorporates alien form elements into the local traditions. With others it leads to large-scale importation of alien cultural elements and objects, reducing the local products to the status of mere copies. A good example of such a parasitic art is that of the Arapesh. Further inland are a group of small tribes, the Tchambuli, Abelam, Mundugumor, Kwoma and the Aibom, who have very distinctive styles of their own, although they too participate extensively in the inter-tribal trade of designs and objects. In the region around the mouth of the river a number of very fine woodcarvings are found that belong to still another culture which has long since disintegrated under European contacts.

Many ceremonial carvings are made specifically for secret rites attended only by men. The importance of these rites along the Sepik River is well indicated by the large size of many of the men's clubhouses. These houses are commonly used as storerooms for ceremonial objects and as meeting places for the male members of the clan or village. They also serve as a focal point in the ceremonial life of the village where the most important rites of initiation are performed.

The most common type of men's house along the main river is rectangular in plan, with very high spire-like front and back gables between which the sagging roof forms a deep saddle. It resembles the roof types found in Sumatra. Other Sepik men's

Introduction from Arts of the South Seas

houses have an asymmetrical arrangement of gables, the front one being often very high, the back one comparatively low.

In some areas a special house was built to store secret objects. Among the Abelam this type of house has a very high triangular front covered with painted strips of bark. Access to any building housing secret objects is restricted to those who have undergone the proper initiation, and in some regions every object has its individual initiation rites.

Among the Kwoma carved and painted figures are set up in the men's house during these rites, and novices are at first led to believe that these figures are powerful supernatural spirits. Later they are told that the objects are but man-made symbols, a secret which must be kept from the uninitiated women and children who never cease to believe that the spirits actually dwell in the house. Carved figures play a somewhat similar role among other tribes. In some instances, they represent the totemic ancestors of the clan. In the coastal regions near the mouth of the river they were made to commemorate recently deceased members of the tribe. Sometimes carved figures were also used as house posts or kept near burial grounds.

Many other objects from the Sepik region—neck rests, lime containers, mortars, pestles, spatulae, shields, drums, hooks, canoe prows and flute stops—show a richness and variety of style comparable to that of the figures and masks, and in many cases the figures, birds or other animal forms which served as the principal decorative motifs had a significance beyond that of mere decoration. The flute stops, for instance, sometimes represented supernatural spirits, and with some tribes, like the Mundugumor they are among the most secret and sacred objects in their possession. Sound-making instruments, such as the flute, drum and bull-roarer, are closely associated with the supernatural since they represent the voices of spirits, and are thus an important part of the initiates' secret paraphernalia.

The variety of Sepik River art is one of its chief characteristics. Since the elaborate religious and social ceremonies required a great display of carved and painted objects there was an ever-present need for new paraphernalia, and this gave rise to a technical proficiency and creative interpretation of traditional forms unsurpassed in any other area of Oceania.

The diversity of conventions used in the representation of facial features and parts of the human body is truly bewildering. Eyes, for example, appear as pin-points or as huge circles, as narrow slits or as wide ovals. Heads may be round, oval or diamond-shaped and arms and legs vary from long thin stems to massive stumps. These stylizations appear on figures in countless combinations and make it very difficult in some cases to ascribe specific styles to specific groups.

Future study of the distribution of the most typical renderings of some characteristic feature such as the nose may help in tracing styles to their place of origin. The nose is by far the most prominent of all individual features in Sepik sculpture. (See Plate 7.) No matter what its size or shape, it is always accentuated by plastic or color treatment and its various forms are clearly enough defined to make several basic types recognizable. The most spectacular type resembles a long trunk often touching the chin or even the breast, genitals or feet of the figure. Another type often extending way below the chin turns into the neck and head of a bird. Still others are short and broad with flaring nostrils, or straight, pointed and beak-like. The only element that all of these nose types have in common is the hole in the septum for the insertion of ornaments similar to those worn by the people themselves.

With the exception of the composite noses ending in birds' heads which are found in a restricted region of the Upper Sepik, all these other types appear in more or less pronounced form in many sections of the Sepik area. However it seems likely that a detailed study of these nose types will eventually reveal their various places of origin and greatly contribute to the clarification of the involved style problem of the entire region.

It is extremely difficult to single out features common to all the different styles of the Sepik River area because they are made up

Introduction from Arts of the South Seas

of such a vast number of design elements and combinations of design elements, and have so little homogeneity of proportions. There are certain tendencies such as the emphasis on noses and heads and the frequent use of organically curved surfaces, that appear in almost all Sepik carvings, but these are shared by other Melanesian styles. Sepik River art derives its unique character from its remarkable ability to make plastic forms the carrier of strong emotions. It lacks to a great extent the traditional, formal restraints that give uniformity to other regional styles. Based on human and animal shapes that are often distorted or combined to produce grotesque and fantastic effects, this intense, sensual, magic art depends for its plastic impact almost entirely on the bold integration of its design elements. Imagination ordered but not restricted by feeling for form makes the art of the Sepik River an ideal instrument for its main purpose—the release of magic power.

NEW IRELAND

A wealth of fantastic and elaborate carvings make New Ireland one of the most interesting sources of Oceanic art. Single figures, superimposed figures forming high poles, a vast variety of masks, and long planks carved into frieze-like reliefs were produced in great numbers. They are all richly painted in red, yellow, white, blue and black and decorated with various materials such as shell, bark-cloth and fiber and have a remarkable and often astounding degree of intricacy. Many of the forms, including the human figure, birds, pigs and snakes, appear in their entirety or in part, singly or in combination, always surrounded by complicated geometric shapes. Typical of New Ireland art was the extensive use of the opercula (valves) of marine snails for eyes.

Each object was unique in composition or in the elements of its composition and almost every one had its own particular meaning. For this was a mortuary art devoted to the commemoration of specific physical and mythological ancestors. The content of dances and ceremonies, and the basic forms of the objects used in them were rigidly prescribed by tradition, but enough freedom was given the artist in matters of composition and detail to allow for considerable variation.

New Ireland, together with New Britain, forms part of the Bismarck Archipelago. Its inhabitants are mainly Melanesians. The island is about two hundred miles long by twenty miles wide. It was discovered in 1616 by Lemaire and Schouten and was named by Carteret in 1767. When the Germans took possession of it they renamed it New Mecklenburg. The old material culture has been almost completely swept away and only a few objects are now made for sale to Europeans. The island is very similar to the majority of the islands of Melanesia: a high mountainous interior covered with a dense jungle, and a surrounding coastal plain. Although mainly agriculturists, the coastal peoples were also fishermen.

Ancestor rites were the dominating feature of New Ireland culture. Ceremonies or cycles of ceremonies were staged in commemoration of dead ancestors, all of whom, legendary as well as recently dead, were represented or symbolized by a great number of extremely elaborate carvings which were made for use in these rites. Dancing, feasting and the exhibition of the carved and painted objects were the main features of the most spectacular of New Ireland ceremonies, the *Malagan,* which consisted of memorial festivals held from one to five years after the death of a person. Tradition decreed so strongly that these be performed that the survivors of the deceased would lose caste if they did not conform, while their prestige would be enhanced in proportion to the magnificence of the ceremonies held. This attitude served as a powerful incentive to provide the maximum of food for the feasts and the richest possible carvings. These carvings were called *Malagan* like the ceremonies in which they were used. The greater proportion of New Ireland art was made for use in the *Malagan.*

Clan organization was basic to the social system of New Ireland and had great influence on its ceremonial art, since each clan had the right to use particular designs in its carvings. The prep-

Introduction from Arts of the South Seas

aration for and the supervision of the performance of the *Malagan* ceremonies were always in the hands of the influential elders of the clan. They knew the symbols and forms prescribed to represent clan totems and the exploits of their legendary and recent dead. They also knew the secret rites which had to accompany the making of these objects. These men were, in fact, through their knowledge, the guardians of the future material and spiritual well-being of a clan, since this depended on the aid of the ancestral spirits honored by these ceremonies.

When the influential men of a clan wished to stage a *Malagan* ceremony, one or more sheds were built within a high-walled enclosure, usually adjacent to the cremation or burial ground of each clan. Here, it was believed, the power of the spirits of the clan dead was strongest. Expert carvers were employed who worked in secret within the enclosure. It often took the better part of a year to make the objects needed in great ceremonies. Paid well for their services, the artists worked under the direction of the clan elders who saw that the appropriate symbols and forms were used in their proper context. In the meantime a great quantity of food was being collected—taro, bananas, pigs—for certain parts of these ceremonies were communal and provision had to be made for much feasting. At last everything was in readiness. The frieze-like reliefs, single figures and some of the masks were arranged against the back wall of the enclosure in an open shed and the huge "poles" were set up nearby. Finally, the festival began when the front wall of the enclosure was dramatically pulled down, "unveiling" the carvings to the assembled crowd. There were shouts of amazement, recognition and delight. For two to four days, traditional processions and dances were performed in which the smaller carvings and masks were carried or worn. Between ceremonies, feasts were held. Although the *Malagan* was a memorial festival in honor of the dead, it was not mournful—it was rather an occasion for the expression of joy. With the exception of a few wooden masks and one type of frieze, the carvings were discarded after the ceremonies and allowed to rot away.

Large carved masks with perforated side-pieces were used in a ceremony (*dzafunfun*) associated with the *Malagan* cycle. (See Plate 40.) In these rites children were secluded within the clan enclosure for the length of time during which the food was assembled and paraphernalia prepared. At the appointed time big figures (*murua*) wearing masks and girdles of colored leaves emerged from the enclosure, each with a child in its arms. Each figure represented a particular ancestor spirit who became a guardian of the child it carried. A dance and a feast concluded the ceremony. As a result of these rites, children were made wards of specific ancestor spirits on whose aid and protection their future welfare depended.

Crested helmet-like masks were worn in other dances performed as part of the *Malagan* cycle. The crest, built up of yellow, blue, red and white fiber over a wooden frame, represented in monumental proportions the old method of wearing the hair during the mourning period when a crest from front to back was formed by shaving the head on each side. It is said that the dance in which they were worn represented the courting of the women by the men of the tribe. While the dance itself may have had a fertility theme, it is likely that the masks depicted specific clan ancestors. Other New Ireland masks were made of painted bark-cloth stretched over a wooden frame with carved parts such as eyes, nose or mouth, attached.

Most New Ireland sculpture has parts that are carved free of the background and others that project from a central core, thus producing an open-work effect characteristic of the art of the region. In the tall poles an open framework surrounds a central pillar built of a succession of strongly sculptured forms. Within the basic shape of the log, this framework defines and restricts the space around the central form elements, but its carved and painted surface designs often obscure the subtle relationship between the core and the openwork shell of the column. Many of the masks have attached parts such as elaborate side-pieces and fantastic nose constructions. The surfaces of these, too, are covered with painted designs.

Introduction from Arts of the South Seas

With few exceptions, the art of New Ireland is composed of two conflicting elements: the clearly organized, although frequently complex, carved parts and the profuse, elaborate surface designs. This combination gives the objects an appearance of nervous movement and tension. Although distinctive in style, the openwork and intricate character of the over-all pattern of the objects suggests Indonesian affinities, while the face types, dominated by enormous looped noses, compare with certain carvings from New Caledonia, the New Hebrides and the Sepik River area of New Guinea.

New Ireland *Malagans* commemorated mythological ancestors such as the sun and the moon, long-dead relatives and the recent dead who were the immediate reason for the ceremony. Innumerable sun and moon symbols occur on all of the objects. The moon is symbolized by a boar's head or tusks, by snake, fish and bird forms, by clam shells and by white striations about the eyes of a figure; the sun, by the head of a bird and by rayed disks, while a representation of the circular breast ornament (*kapkap*) was in some areas a symbol of the sun and in others of the moon. Carved human forms represented dead relatives, but these were frequently combined with other, often fantastic, forms and symbols in order to refer to a legend or event associated with the ancestor. Other elements in the designs are clan totems and badges and a number of design fill-ins, which seem to have been used for no other purpose than to balance and enrich a pattern. The desire to include in one sculpture representations of physical and mythological ancestors and symbols of their deeds resulted often in a conspicuous elaboration.

Related in style to the *Malagan* carvings, another type of ancestor figure (*uli*) was made in central New Ireland. (See Plate 39.) *Ulis* are powerfully proportioned, bearded, phallic figures with large protruding breasts that convey a feeling of strong sexual aggression. They are carved in the round and have large heads with ferocious expressions. Some have smaller figures attached to their bodies which illustrate a story or legend connected with the ancestor. *Ulis* were used in extremely sacred rites in which women could not participate. One series of such ceremonies lasted sometimes over a year. The figures were never discarded, but were carefully preserved for future use.

In the south of New Ireland, small chalk figures were carved at the death of a person, set up in a special house for a certain time and then destroyed. Although women were permitted to stand in front of the house and mourn the deceased, they were not allowed to see the figures. Very simple but impressive, even monumental in style, they are similar to figures found in eastern New Britain. There is an underlying resemblance between their forms and some of those found in the more elaborate carvings to the north, suggesting that the latter style may have started from such simple but fundamentally strong sculptural beginnings.

Some of the finest breast ornaments of Melanesia come from this island. These are called *kapkaps* in pidgin English. A *kapkap* consists of a disk of tridacna (giant sea clam) shell to which is attached a wheel-shaped, perforated tortoise-shell ornament of extreme delicacy. That these breast ornaments may have had more than mere ornamental significance is obvious from their use in carvings to symbolize the sun or the moon.

In addition to its religious significance, New Ireland art served an important social function by integrating the various elements of a loosely organized society. It is characterized by multiplicity of detail, openness of design and rich use of color, and represents the apex of formal virtuosity in Oceania.

BIBLIOGRAPHY

ABELL, WALTER
1952 "Toward a Unified Field in Aesthetics." *Journal of Aesthetics and Art Criticism* 10 (3):191–216.
ANONYMOUS CONQUEROR
1917 *The Anonymous Conqueror.* New York. Cortes Society.
ARNDT, W.
1962 "The Nargorkun-Narlinji Cult." *Oceania* 32 (3):316–17.
ARNHEIM, RUDOLPH
1954 *Art and Visual Perception.* Stanford. University of California Press.
BALFOUR, HENRY
1893 *The Evolution of Decorative Art.* London. Percival and Co.
BARBA, LIC. ÁLVARO ALONSO
1640 *Arte de los Metales.* Madrid.
BARNETT, HOMER G.
1953 *Innovation: The Basis of Culture Change.* New York. McGraw-Hill.
BARRY, HERBERT, III
1957 "Relationships Between Child Training and the Pictorial Arts." *Journal of Abnormal and Social Psychology* 54:380–83.
BARRY, HERBERT, III, CHILD, I. L., and BACON, M. K.
1959 "Relation of Child Training to Subsistence Economy." *American Anthropologist* 61:51–63.
BASEDOW, HERBERT
1925 *The Australian Aboriginal.* Adelaide. F. W. Preece & Sons.
BAUMANN, HERMANN
1935 *Lunda.* Berlin. Würfel Verlag.
BEGOUEN, HENRI, COMTE
1928 "Empreintes de Doigts Préhistoriques et de Quelques Dessins." *Institut International d'Anthropologie. IIIe Session.* Amsterdam.
BEIER, ULLI
1960 *Art in Nigeria.* Cambridge. Cambridge University Press.

BENEDICT, RUTH
1935 *Zuni Mythology.* Columbia University Contributions to Anthropology, 21. New York. Columbia University Press.
BENNETT, W. C.
1943 "The Position of Chavín in Andean Sequences." *Proceedings of the American Philosophical Society* 86:323–27.
1944 *The North Highlands of Peru. Excavations in the Callejón and at Chavín de Huántar.* Anthropological Papers of The American Museum of Natural History, 39 (1).
1946 "The Archaeology of Colombia," in *Handbook of South American Indians,* Vol. 2, ed. J. H. Steward. Bureau of American Ethnology Bulletin 143. Washington, D.C.
BERGSÖE, PAUL
1937 *The Metallurgy and Technology of Gold and Platinum Among the Pre-Columbian Indians.* Trans. F. C. Reynolds. Copenhagen.
BERNAL, IGNACIO
1960 "Toynbee y Mesoamérica." *Estudios de Cultura Nahuatl* 2:43–58.
BOAS, FRANZ
1927 *Primitive Art.* Oslo. (Reprint 1955. New York. Dover.) Harvard University Press.
BOGGS, S. H.
1950 *"Olmec" Pictographs in the Las Victorias Group, Chalchuapa Archaeological Zone, El Salvador.* Notes of the Carnegie Institution of Washington, 4 (99).
BOHANNAN, PAUL
1961 "Artist and Critic in Tribal Society," in *The Artist in Tribal Society,* ed. Marian W. Smith. New York. Free Press of Glencoe.
BOXER, C. R.
1948 *Fidalgos in the Far East, 1550–1770.* The Hague. M Nijhoff.
BRAIDWOOD, R. J., and WILLEY, G. R.
1960 Ms "Conclusions" in *Courses Toward Urban Life.* Symposium to be published by the Wenner-Gren Foundation for Anthropological Research, New York. (Publ. 1962, Chicago. Aldine.)
BRAINERD, GEORGE W.
1942 "Symmetry in Primitive Conventional Design." *American Antiquity* 8:154–66.
BREUIL, H.
1952 *Quatre Certs Siècles d'Art Pariétal.* Montignac.

BRUNER, JEROME
  1963 "The Conditions of Creativity," in *Contemporary Approaches to Creative Thinking*, eds. H. E. Gruber, G. Terrell, and M. Wertheimer. New York. Atherton Press.
BULLOUGH, EDWARD
  1952 "'Psychical Distance' as a Factor in Art and an Esthetic Principle." *British Journal of Psychology*, V (1913). Reprinted in *A Modern Book of Esthetics; An Anthology*, ed. Melvin Rader. New York. Henry Holt and Co.
BUNZEL, RUTH
  1929 *The Pueblo Potter*. Columbia University Contributions to Anthropology 8. New York. Columbia University Press.
CAMERON, A. L. P.
  1885 "Notes on Some Tribes of New South Wales." *Journal of the Royal Anthropological Institute*, XIV:357.
CARPENTER, EDMUND
  1961 "Comments on Haselberger, the Study of Ethnological Art." *Current Anthropology* 2:361–62.
CARRIÓN CACHOT, REBECCA
  1948 "La Cultura Chavín. Dos Nuevas Colonias: Kuntur Wasi y Ancon." *Revista del Museo Nacional de Antropología y Arqueología* 2 (1):99–172. Lima.
CASO, ALFONSO
  1938 *Exploraciones en Oaxaca; quinta y sexta temporadas, 1936–37*. Instituto Panamericano de Geografía e Historia, Publicación 34. Mexico, D.F.
  1942 "Definición y Extensión del Complejo 'Olmeca'," in *Mayas y Olmecas, Segunda Reunion de Mesa Redonda Sobre Problemes Antropologicas de Mexico y Centro America*. Sociedad Mexicana de Antropología. Chiapas. Tuxtla Gutierrez.
CASO, ALFONSO, and BERNAL, IGNACIO
  1952 *Urnas de Oaxaca*. Memorias del Instituto Nacional de Antropología e Historia, Vol. 2. Mexico, D.F.
CASSIRER, ERNST
  1923 *Philosophie der Symbolischen Formen, I: Die Sprache*. Berlin. Bruno Cassirer.
  1944 *An Essay on Man*. New Haven. Yale University Press.
  1946 *Language and Myth*. Trans. S. K. Langer. New York. Harper & Bros.
CHERRY, COLIN
  1957 *On Human Communication*. Cambridge. Massachusetts Institute of Technology.

CHILDE, V. G.
   1950 "The Urban Revolution." *Town Planning Review* 21 (1:) 3–17.

Codice Xolotl 1951, ed. C. E. Dibble. Mexico.

COE, MICHAEL D.
   1954 *Chavín: its Nature and Space-time Position.* Seminar Paper, Peabody Library. Harvard University.
   1957 "Cycle 7 Monuments in Middle America: a reconsideration." *American Anthropologist* 59:597–611.
   1960 "Archaeological Linkages with North and South America at La Victoria, Guatemala." *American Anthropologist* 62:363–93.
   1960 Ms "The Olmec Style and Its Distributions." Ms. prepared for the *Handbook of Middle American Indians*. (Publ. 1964, ed. Robert Wauchope. Austin. University of Texas Press.)
   1961 Ms "Social Typology and the Tropical Forest Civilizations." To be published in *Comparative Studies in Society and History*.

COE, MICHAEL D., and BAUDEZ, C. F.
   1961 "The Zoned Bichrome Period in Northwestern Costa Rica." *American Antiquity* 26:505–15.

COLLIER, DONALD
   1959 *Agriculture and Civilization on the Coast of Peru.* Paper presented at the meeting of the American Anthropological Association, December 1959, Mexico, D.F.
   1960 Ms "The Central Andes," in *Courses Toward Urban Life*. Symposium to be published by the Wenner-Gren Foundation for Anthropological Research, New York. (Publ. 1962, Chicago. Aldine.)

CONRAD, JOSEPH
   1947 *The Portable Conrad,* ed. Morton Dauwen Zabel. New York. Viking Press.

CORTÉS, HERNANDO
   1519–26 *Five Letters, 1519–1526.* Trans. J. B. Morris. New York. McBride & Co. 1929.

COURLANDER, H.
   1939 *Haiti Singing.* Chapel Hill. University of North Carolina Press.

COVARRUBIAS, MIGUEL
   1942 "Origen y Desarollo del Estilo Artístico 'Olmeca'," in *Mayas y Olmecas, Segunda Reunion de Mesa Redonda Sobre Problemas Antropologicas de Mexico y Centro America.* Sociedad Mexicana de Antropología. Chiapas. Tuxtla Gutierrez.
   1946 "El Arte 'Olmeca' o de La Venta." *Cuadernos Americanos* 5 (4:) 153–79.

1957 *Indian Art of Mexico and Central America.* New York. Alfred A. Knopf.
DAPPER, OLFERT
1676 *Naukeurige Beschrijuinge der Afrikanische Gewesten.* Amsterdam. Meurs.
D'AZEVEDO, WARREN L.
1958 "A Structural Approach to Esthetics: Towards a Definition of Art in Anthropology." *American Anthropologist* 60:702–14.
DEACON, BERNARD A.
1934 *Malekula.* London. G. Routledge & Sons Ltd.
DELLA SANTA, ELIZABETH
1959 "Les Cupisniques et l'origine des Olméques." *Revue de l'Université de Bruxelles* 5:340–63.
DENNETT, R. E.
1906 *At the Back of the Black Man's Mind.* London. Macmillan.
DEVEREUX, GEORGE
1961 "Art and Mythology, Part I: a General Theory," in *Studying Personality Cross-Culturally,* ed. Bert Kaplan. New York. Harper & Row. 361–86.
DEWEY, JOHN
1934 *Art as Experience.* New York, Minton, Balch & Co.
DRUCKER, PHILIP
1943 *Ceramic Sequences at Tres Zapotes, Veracruz, Mexico.* Bureau of American Ethnology Bulletin 140. Washington, D.C.
1952 *La Venta, Tabasco, a Study of Olmec Ceramics and Art.* Bureau of American Ethnology Bulletin 153. Washington, D.C.
DRUCKER, PHILIP, HEIZER, R. F., and SQUIER, R. J.
1959 *Excavations at La Venta, Tabasco, 1955.* Bureau of American Ethnology Bulletin 170. Washington, D.C.
DUYVENDAK, J. PH.
1940 *Inleiding tot de Ethnologie van de Indische Archipel.* Gröningen. J. B. Wolter.
EAST, RUPERT
1939 *Akiga's Story.* London. Oxford University Press.
ELKIN, A. P.
1954 *The Australian Aborigines.* Sydney. Angus & Robertson.
ELKIN, A. P., BERNDT, RONALD and CATHERINE
1950 *Art in Arnhem Land.* Chicago. University of Chicago Press.
EMRICH, DUNCAN
1946 "Folklore: William John Thomas." *California Folklore Quarterly* 5:355–72.

ENGEL, FREDERIC
　1956　"Curayacu-a Chavinoid Site." *Archaeology* 9 (2:) 98–105.
ESTRADA, EMILIO
　1958　*Las Culturas Pre-Clasicas, Formativas, o Arcaicas del Ecuador.* Publicacíon 5, Museo Victor Emilio Estrada, Guayaquil.
ESTRADA, EMILIO, and MEGGERS, B. J.
　1961　"A Complex of Traits of Probable Transpacific Origin on the Coast of Ecuador." *American Anthropologist* 63:913–39.
EVANS, CLIFFORD, and MEGGERS, B. J.
　1957　"Formative Period Cultures in the Guayas Basin, Coastal Ecuador." *American Antiquity* 22:235–46.
　1958　"Valdivia—an Early Formative Culture on the Coast of Ecuador." *Archaeology* 11:175–82.
FAGG, WILLIAM
　1955–56　"The Study of African Art." Allen Memorial Art Museum, Oberlin College, *Bulletin* 12 (Winter), 44–61.
FENTON, WILLIAM N.
　1941　"Masked Medicine Societies of the Iroquois." *Annual Report of the Smithsonian Institution for 1940.* Bureau of American Ethnology. Washington, D.C. 397–430.
FENTON, WILLIAM N., and KURATH, GERTRUDE P.
　1953　*The Iroquois Eagle Dance.* Bureau of American Ethnology Bulletin 156. Washington, D.C.
FERDON, E. N.
　1953　*Tonala, Mexico, an Archaeological Survey.* School of American Research Monograph 16. Santa Fe.
FIRTH, RAYMOND
　1925　"The Maori Woodcarver." *Journal of the Polynesian Society* 44:277.
　1956　"The Social Framework of Primitive Art," in *Elements of Social Organization.* London. Watts & Co., Ltd. 155–82.
FRANCK, KATE
　1946　"Preferences for Sex Symbols and Their Personality Correlates." *Genetic Psychology Monographs* 33:73–123.
FRASER, DOUGLAS
　1962　*Primitive Art.* New York. Doubleday.
　1966　"The Heraldic Woman: a Study in Diffusion," in *The Many Faces of Primitive Art.* Englewood Cliffs, N.J. Prentice-Hall. 36–99.
FRAZER, SIR J. G.
　1911　*The Golden Bough.* Vol. I. (3rd edition.) London. Macmillan.

FREUD, SIGMUND
 1922 *Introductory Lectures on Psychoanalysis.* Trans. Joan Rivière. London.
 1938 "The Interpretation of Dreams," in *The Basic Writings of Sigmund Freud,* ed. A. A. Brill. New York.
 1947 *Leonardo da Vinci: a Study in Pyschosexuality.* Trans. A. A. Brill. New York. Random House.

GARCÍA GRANADOS, R.
 1940 "Reminiscencias Idolátricas en Monumentos Coloniales." *Instituto de Investigaciones Estéticas, Anales.* Mexico.

GEERTZ, CLIFFORD
 1957 "Ethos, World View, and the Analysis of Sacred Symbols." *Antioch Review,* Winter 1957–58:421–37.

GESELL, A.
 1925 *The Mental Growth of the Preschool Child.* New York. Macmillan.

GÓMEZ DE OROZCO, F.
 1939 "La Decoración en los Manuscritos Dispanomexicanos Primitivos." *Instituto de Investigaciones Estéticas, Anales* 1 (3).

GOODALE, JANE C.
 1959a *The Tiwi Women of Melville Island.* Ph.D. Dissertation. Ann Arbor, Michigan. Microfilms.
 1959b "The Tiwi Dance for the Dead." *Expedition* 2:3–14.

GORBEA, V.
 1958 *Culhuacan.* Mexico.

GRAJALES RAMOS, GLORIA
 1953 "Influencia Indígena en las Artes Plásticas del México Colonial." *Instituto de Arte Americano e Investigaciones Estéticas, Anales* 6.

GREENBERG, JOSEPH H.
 1957 *Essays in Linguistics.* Chicago. University of Chicago Press.

GREENGO, R. E.
 1952 "The Olmec Phase of Eastern Mexico." *Bulletin of the Texas Archeological and Paleontological Society* 23:260–92.

GRIAULE, MARCEL
 1947 *Arts de L'Afrique Noire.* Paris.
 1948 *Dieu d'eau: Entretiens avec Ogotemmêli.* Paris. Éditions du Chêne.

GRIAULE, MARCEL, and DIETERLEN, GERMAINE
 1953 "The Dogon," in *African Worlds,* ed. Daryll Forde. London. Oxford University Press.

GROSSE, ERNST
 1894 *Die Anfänge der Kunst.* Freiburg/Leipzig (American edition: *The Beginnings of Art,* Appleton, New York, 1898).

GUAMAN POMA DE AYALA, FELIPE
 1936 *Nueva Coronica y Buen Gobierno* (c.1616). Paris. Institut d'Ethnologie.

GUERRERO LOVILLO, JOSÉ
 1949 "Las Musallas o Sarias Hispanomusulmanas y las Capillas Abiertas de Nueva España." *Arte en America y Filipinas.* Sevilla.

GUILLAUME, PAUL, and MUNRO, THOMAS
 1926 *Primitive Negro Sculpture.* New York. Harcourt, Brace.

HABERLAND, WOLFGANG
 1953 "Die regionale Verteilung von Schmuckelementen in Bereiche der klassischen Maya-Kultur." *Beiträge zur Mittelamerikanischen Völkerkunde,* II. Hamburgischen Museum für Völkerkunde und Vorgeschiehte. Hamburg.

HADDON, A. C.
 1895 *Evolution in Art.* London. Walter Scott, Ltd.

HALLOWELL, A. I.
 1947 "Myth, Culture, and Personality." *American Anthropologist* 49:544–56.

HARLEY, GEORGE
 1950 *Masks as Agents of Social Control in Northeast Liberia.* Papers of the Peabody Museum of American Archaeology and Ethnology, Harvard University 32 (2).

HART, C. W., and PILLING, ARNOLD
 1960 *The Tiwi of Northwest Australia.* New York. Holt, Rinehart & Winston, Inc.

HASELBERGER, HERTA
 1961 "Methods of Studying Ethnological Art." *Current Anthropology* 2:351–84.

HAWTHORNE, AUDREY
 1967 *The Art of the Kwakiutl Indians.* Seattle. University of Washington Press.

HEINE-GELDERN, ROBERT
 1959 "Representation of the Asiatic Tiger in the Art of the Chavín Culture: a Proof of Early Contacts Between China and Peru," in *Actas del 33 Congreso Internacional de Americanistas,* I. San José, Costa Rica.

HEINE-GELDERN, ROBERT, and EKHOLM, GORDON F.
 1951 "Significant Parallels in the Symbolic Arts of Southern Asia and Middle America," in *Selected Papers of the 29th International Congress of Americanists,* I., ed. Sol Tax. University of Chicago Press. 299–309.

HEIZER, R. F.
  1960 "Agriculture and the Theocratic State in Lowland Southeastern Mexico." *American Antiquity* 26:215–22.
HENLE, MARY
  1963 "The Birth and Death of Ideas," in *Contemporary Approaches to Creative Thinking*, eds. H. E. Gruber, G. Terrell, and M. Wertheimer. New York. Atherton Press.
HERSKOVITS, MELVILLE J.
  1937 *Life in a Haitian Village.* New York. Alfred A. Knopf.
  1941 *The Myth of the Negro Past.* New York. Harper & Bros.
  1944 "Dramatic Expression Among Primitive Peoples." *Yale Review* 33:683–98.
  1948 "The Aesthetic Drive: Graphic and Plastic Arts," in *Man and His Works.* New York. Alfred A. Knopf. 378–413.
  1950 "Music in West Africa." Pamphlet accompanying *Tribal, Folk, and Cafe Music of West Africa.* New York. Field Recordings, Inc.
HERSKOVITS, MELVILLE J., and HERSKOVITS, FRANCES S.
  1934 *Rebel Destiny.* New York. McGraw-Hill.
  1936 *Suriname Folklore.* New York. Columbia University Press.
  1947 *Trinidad Village.* New York. Alfred A. Knopf.
HERSKOVITS, MELVILLE J., and WATERMAN, R. A.
  1949 "Musica de Culto Afro-Bahiana." *Revista de Estudios Musicalos*, I:65–127. Mendoza.
HIMMELHEBER, HANS
  1935 *Negerkünstler.* Stuttgart. Strecker und Schröder.
  1938 *Eskimokünstler.* Stuttgart. Strecker und Schröder.
  1967 "The Present Status of Sculptural Art Among the Tribes of the Ivory Coast," in *Essays on the Verbal and Visual Arts.* Proceedings of the 1966 Annual Spring Meeting of the American Ethnological Society, ed. June Helm. Seattle. University of Washington Press. 192–99.
HOLM, BILL
  1965 *Northwest Coast Indian Art: an Analysis of Form.* Seattle. University of Washington Press.
HOLMES, WILLIAM H.
  1887 *The Use of Gold and Other Metals Among the Ancient Inhabitants of Chiriqui.* Bureau of American Ethnology Bulletin 3. Washington, D.C.
  1890 "On the Evolution of Ornament—an American Lesson." *American Anthropologist* (old series) 3:137–46.
HONIGSHEIM, P.
  1928 "Gesellschaftbeddingtheit der sogenannten primitiven Kunst." *Verhanlungen des Deutschen Soziologentages*, 6.

HORTON, R.
  1963 "The Kalabari Ekine Society; a Borderland of Religion and Art." *Africa* 33:94–113. London.
IDOWU, E. B.
  1962 Olódùmarè, God in Yoruba Belief. New York. Longman's.
ISHIDA, EUCHIRO, and others
  1960 *Andes, the Report of the University of Tokyo Scientific Expedition to the Andes in 1958.* University of Tokyo.
JACOBSEN, C. F., JACOBSEN, M. M., and YOSHIOKA, J. G.
  1932 "Development of an Infant Chimpanzee During Her First Year." *Comparative Psychology Monograph* 9 (1).
JENSEN, E.
  1933 *Beschneidung und Reifezeremonien bei Naturvölkern.* Stuttgart. Strecker und Schroeder.
JIMÉNEZ MORENO, WIGBERTO
  1959 "Sintesis de la Historia Pretolteca de Mesoamerica," in *Esplendor del Mexico Antiguo,* Vol. 2. Mexico, D.F. Centro de Investigaciones Antropológicas de México.
JONES, A. M.
  1949 *African Music.* Livingstone. Rhodes-Livingstone Museum.
JOYCE, T. A.
  1923 "Pakcha." *Inca* Vol. I:761–78. Lima.
KELEMEN, P.
  1951 *Baroque and Rococo in Latin America.* New York. Macmillan.
KLEIN, MELANIE
  1949 *The Psycho-analysis of Children.* London.
KLÜVER, H.
  1933 *Behavior Mechanisms in Monkeys.* Chicago. University of Chicago Press.
KOCHNITZKY, LEON
  1949 *Negro Art in Belgian Congo,* 2nd ed. New York. Belgian Government Information Center.
KOFFKA, K.
  1925 *The Growth of the Mind.* New York. Harcourt, Brace.
KOLINSKI, M.
  1936 "Suriname Music," in *Suriname Folklore,* eds. M. J. Herskovits and F. S. Herskovits. New York. Columbia University Press.
KRIS, ERNST
  1934 "Zur Psychologie der Karikatur." *Imago* XX:458.
KROEBER, A. L.
  1927 "Coast and Highland in Prehistoric Peru." *American Anthropologist.* 29:625–53.

1944a *Peruvian Archaeology in 1942.* Viking Fund Publications in Anthropology No. 4. New York. Viking Fund, Inc.
1944b *Configurations of Culture Growth.* University of California Press.
1951 "Great Art Styles of Ancient South America," in *The Civilizations of Ancient America*, ed. S. Tax. Selected Papers of the 29th International Congress of Americanists, Vol. I. University of Chicago Press.
1957 *Style and Civilizations.* Ithaca. Cornell University Press.

KRUIJT, ALBERT C.
1906 *Het Animisme in den Indischen Archipel.* 's-Gravenhage.

KUBLER, G.
1943 "Two Modes of Franciscan Architecture." *Gazette des Beaux-Arts* XXIII.
1946 "The Quechua in the Colonial World," in *Handbook of South American Indians*, Vol. 2, ed. J. H. Steward. Bureau of American Ethnology Bulletin 143. Washington, D.C.
1948 *Mexican Architecture of the Sixteenth Century.* New Haven.
1952 *The Indian Caste of Peru, 1795–1940.* Washington, D.C.

KUBLER, G., and GIBSON, C.
1951 *The Tovar Calendar.* New Haven. Connecticut Academy of Arts and Sciences.

KURATH, GERTRUDE P.
1960 "Panorama of Dance Ethnology." *Current Anthropology* 1: 233–54.

LAMING, A.
1959 *Lascaux.* London. Penguin.

LAMING-EMPERAIRE, A.
1962 *La Signification de l'Art Rupestre Paléolithique.* Paris. A. J. Picard.

LANGER, SUSANNE K.
1942 *Philosophy in a New Key.* Cambridge. Harvard University Press.
1953 *Feeling and Form.* New York. Charles Scribner's Sons, Inc.

LANNING, E. P.
1959 *Early Ceramic Chronologies of the Peruvian Coast.* Mimeographed. Berkeley.

LARCO HOYLE, RAFAEL
1941 Los Cupisniques. Lima. "La Crónica" y "Variedades."

LASSWELL, HAROLD D.
1954 "Key Symbols, Signs, and Icons," in *Symbols and Values: an Initial Study*, eds. Lyman Bryson, L. Finkelstein, R. M. MacIver, and R. McKeon. New York. Harper & Bros. 199–204.

1959 "The Social Setting of Creativity," in *Creativity and Its Cultivation*, ed. H. H. Anderson. New York. Harper & Bros.

LEACH, E. R.
1954 "Aesthetics," in *The Institutions of Primitive Society, a Series of Broadcast Talks* by E. E. Evans-Pritchard and others. Chicago. Free Press of Glencoe.

LEASON, P. A.
1939 "A New View of the Western European Group of Quaternary Cave Art." *Prehistoric Society Proceedings* 5.

LENZ, HANS
1948 *El Papel Indígena Mexicano*. Mexico. Editorial Cultura.

LEON Y GAMA, N. DE
1832 *Descripción Histórica y Cronológica de las Dos Piedras*. Mexico.

LEROI-GOURHAN, A.
1958 "Le Symbolisme des Grands Signes dans l'Art Pariétal Paléolithique." *Bulletin de la Societé Préhistorique Française* 55.
1963 *Art et Religion au Paléolithique Supérieur*. Paris.
1964 *Les Réligions de la Préhistoire*. Paris.
1965a *Le Geste et la Parole*. Paris. Albin Michel.
1965b *Préhistoire de l'Art Occidental*. Paris. Editions d'Art Lucien Mazenod.

LESSER, ALEXANDER
1961 "Social Fields and the Evolution of Society." *Southwestern Journal of Anthropology* 17:40–48.

LEWIS, PHILIP
1961 "The Artist in New Ireland Society," in *The Artist in Tribal Society*, ed. Marian W. Smith. New York. Free Press of Glencoe.

LINTON, RALPH
1941 "Primitive Art." *Kenyon Review* 3:34–51.
1949 "Marquesan Culture," in *The Individual and His Society*, ed. Abram Kardiner. 5th printing. New York.

LOMAX, ALAN
1959 "Folk Song Style." *American Anthropologist* 61:927–54.

LOTHROP, S. K.
1956 "Peruvian Pacchas and Keros." *American Antiquity* 21.

LOWIE, ROBERT
1956 *The Crow Indians* (reprinted). New York. Holt, Rinehart & Winston.

LOWINSKY, EDWARD E.
1946 *Secret Chromatic Art in the Netherland Motet*. New York. Columbia University Press.

LUQUET, G. H.
 1930 *The Art and Religion of Fossil Man.* Trans. J. Townsend Russell, Jr. New Haven. Yale University Press.
MCALLESTER, DAVID P.
 1954 *Enemy Way Music: A Study of Social and Esthetic Values as Seen in Navaho Music.* Cambridge. Peabody Museum of American Archaeology and Ethnology, Papers 41 (3).
MCCARTHY, F. D.
 1958 *Australian Aboriginal Rock Art.* Sydney. Trustees of the Australian Museum.
 1960 "The Cave Painting of Groote Eylandt and Chasm Island." *Records of the American-Australian Scientific Expedition to Arnhem Land* 2, ed. Mountford. London.
 1965 "The Aboriginal Past: Archaeology and Material Equipment," in *Aboriginal Man in Australia,* eds. R. M. and C. H. Berndt. London.
MCCARTHY, F. D., and MCARTHUR, M.
 1960 "The Food Quest and the Time Factor in Aboriginal Economic Life," in *Records of the American-Australian Scientific Expedition to Arnhem Land,* ed. Mountford. London.
MACCURDY, GEORGE GRANT
 1911 *A Study of Chiriquian Antiquities.* New Haven.
MCELROY, W. A.
 1954 "A Sex Difference in Preferences for Shapes." *British Journal of Psychology* 45:209–16.
MACINTOSH, N. W. G.
 1952 "Paintings in Beswick Creek Cave, Northern Territory." *Oceania* 22 (4):266.
MACNEISH, R. S.
 1958 "Preliminary Archaeological Investigation in the Sierra de Tamaulipas, Mexico." *Transactions of the American Philosophical Society* 48 (6).
MALRAUX, ANDRÉ
 1953 *The Voices of Silence.* New York. Doubleday.
MANGELSDORF, P. C., MACNEISH, R. S., and WILLEY, G. R.
 1960 Ms "Origins of Agriculture in Mesoamerica." Ms prepared for the *Handbook of Middle American Indians.* (Publ. 1964, ed. Robert Wauchope.) Austin. University of Texas Press.
MARQUINA, I.
 1951 *Arquitectura Prehispánica.* Mexico. Instituto Nacional de Antropología e Historia, Secretariade de Educación Publica.
MARYON, HERBERT
 1954 *Metalwork and Enamelling,* 3rd edition. London. Clarendon Press.

MAZA, FRANCISCA DE LA
  1959 *Cholula.* Mexico.
MEAD, MARGARET
  1945 *The Maoris and Their Art.* New York. The American Museum of Natural History.
  1959 "Creativity in Cross-Cultural Perspective," in *Creativity and Its Cultivation,* ed. H. H. Anderson. New York. Harper & Bros.
MEGGITT, M. J.
  1962 *A Study of the Walbiri Aborigines of Central Australia.* Melbourne.
MERRIAM, ALAN P.
  1962 *A Prologue to the Study of African Arts.* Yellow Springs. Antioch Press.
  1964 *The Anthropology of Music.* Evanston. Northwestern University Press.
MILLS, GEORGE
  1953 *Navaho Art and Culture: A Study of the Relations Among Cultural Premises, Art Styles and Art Values.* Ph.D. Thesis. Harvard University.
  1957 "Art: an Introduction to Qualitative Anthropology." *Journal of Aesthetics and Art Criticism* 16:6.
MONTGOMERY, R. G., SMITH, W., and BREW, J. O.
  1949 *Franciscan Awatovi.* Peabody Museum Papers 36. Cambridge. Harvard University.
MORRIS, CHARLES
  1938 "Foundation of the Theory of Signs," in *International Encyclopedia of Unified Science* I (2). Chicago. University of Chicago Press.
  1946 *Signs, Language, and Behaviour.* Englewood Cliffs, N.J. Prentice-Hall (reprinted 1955).
MORRIS, DESMOND
  1961 *The Biology of Art.* London. Cox and Wyman.
MOUNTFORD, C.
  1958 *The Tiwi, Their Art, Myth and Ceremony.* London. Phoenix House.
  1961 "The Artist in Australian Aboriginal Society," in *The Artist in Tribal Society,* ed. Marian W. Smith. New York. Free Press of Glencoe.
  1965 *Ayer's Rock: its People, their Beliefs, and their Art.* East-West Center Press. Honolulu.
MOYSSÉN, XAVIER
  1958 "Las Cruces de Toluca." *Instituto de Investigaciones Estéticas, Anales* 27.

MUENSTERBERGER, W.
1939 "Die Ornamente an Dayak-Tanzchilden und ihre Bedeutung für Religion und Mythologie." *Cultureel Indië* I:337–43.
1940 *Bataks, Dajaks, en Toradja's.* Arnhem.
1945 "Over Primitieve Kunst en over den Korwar-Stijl in Indonesië en Oceanië." *Cultureel Indië* VII:63.
1950 "Some Elements of Artistic Creativity Among Primitive Peoples." *Beiträge zur Gesellungs- und Völkerwissenschaft* (Thurnwald-Festschrift) :313 ff. Berlin.

MUNN, NANCY L.
1962 "Walbiri Graphic Signs: an Analysis." *American Anthropologist* 64:972–84.

MUNRO, THEODORE
1963 *Evolution in the Arts.* Cleveland. Cleveland Museum of Art.

MUNRO, THOMAS
1949 *The Arts and Their Interrelations.* New York. Liberal Arts Press.

MURDOCK, G. P.
1949 *Social Structure.* New York. Macmillan.
1957 "World Ethnographic Sample." *American Anthropologist* 59:664–87.

MURRAY, K. C.
1949 "Tiv Pattern Dyeing." *Nigeria* 32:42–47.

NEUMEYER, A.
1947 "The Indian Contribution to Architectural Decoration in Spanish Colonial America." *Art Bulletin* XXX. New York.

NEVERMANN, HANS
1933 *Masken und Geheimbünde in Melanesien.* Berlin.

NORDENSKIÖLD, E.
1931 "Origin of the Indian Civilization in South America." *Comparative Ethnological Studies* IX. Göteborg.

NOÜY, LECOMTE DU
1936 *Biological Time.* London. Macmillan, New York.

OGDEN, C. K., and RICHARDS, I. A.
1923 *The Meaning of Meaning.* London. Routledge & Kegan Paul.

OLBRECHTS, F. M.
1933 "Notre Mission Ethnographique en Afrique Occidentale Française." *Bulletin des Musées d'Arts et d'Histoire* 5:98–107.
1939 "Ivoorkunst-expeditie der Rijksuniversiteit te Gent en van het Vleehuis-museum te Antwerpen. Voorlopig verslag over de

werkzaamheden: November 1938–Januari 1939." *Kongo-Overzee* 5:177–87.

1946 *Plastick van Kongo*. Antwerp. Uitgeversm i.j. N.U.

ORTEGA Y GASSET, JOSÉ
1956 *The Dehumanization of Art and Other Writings on Art and Culture*. Trans. Willard T. Trask. New York. Doubleday.

PALM, E. W.
1953 "Las Capillas Abiertas Americanas y sus Antecedentes en el Occidente Cristiano." *Instituto de Arte Americano e Investigaciones Estéticas, Anales*, 6. Buenos Aires.

PARKINSON, R.
1907 *Dreissig Jahre in der Südsee*. Stuttgart. Strecker and Schröder.

PEIRCE, CHARLES S.
1885 "On the Algebra of Logic: a Contribution to the Philosophy of Notation." *American Journal of Mathematics* 8:181.
1931 *Collected Papers*, eds. Charles Hartshorne and Paul Weiss. Cambridge. Harvard University Press.

PÉREZ DE BARRADAS, JOSÉ
1954 *Orfebrería Prehispánica de Colombia: Estilo Calima*, Vol. I. Madrid.

PHILLIPS, WILLIAM
1957 "Introduction: Art and Neurosis," in *Art and Psychoanalysis*, ed. William Phillips. New York. Meridian Books. xiii–xxiv.

PIETTE, E.
1907 *L'Art Pendant l'Age du Renne*. Paris. Masson et Cie.

PIÑA CHAN, ROMAN
1955 *Chalcatzingo, Morelos*. Direccion de Monumentos Pre-Hispanicos, Instituto Nacional de Antropologia e Historia, Informes 4. Mexico, D.F.

PORRAS, R.
1948 *El Cronista Indio Felipe Auaman Poma de Ayala*. Lima.

PORTER, A. K.
1928 *Spanish Romanesque Sculpture*. Florence.

PORTER, M. N.
1953 *Tlatilco and the Pre-Classic Cultures of the New World*. Viking Fund Publications in Anthropology 19. New York Wenner-Gren Foundation for Anthropological Research, Inc.

POWDERMAKER, HORTENSE
1933 *Life in Lesu*. New York. W. W. Norton.

PREUSS, K. TH.
1931 *Arte Monumental Prehistorico*, 2 vols., 2nd ed. Bogotá. Escuelas Salesianas.

PROSKOURIAKOFF, TATIANA
- 1950 *A Study of Classic Maya Sculpture.* Carnegie Institution of Washington, Publication 593. Washington, D.C.
- 1954 *Varieties of Classic Central Veracruz Sculpture.* Contributions to American Anthropology and History 58. Carnegie Institution of Washington, Publication 606. Washington, D.C.
- 1961 "Portraits of Women in Maya Art," in *Essays in Pre-Columbian Art and Archaeology,* eds. S. K. Lothrop and others. Cambridge. Harvard University. 81–99.
- 1962 "The Lords of the Maya Realm." *Expedition* 4 (1):14–21.

RADCLIFFE-BROWN, A. R.
- 1948 *The Andaman Islanders* (reprint). Chicago. Free Press.

RAINEY, FROELICH
- 1959 "The Vanishing Art of the Arctic." *Expedition* 1.

RANDS, ROBERT L.
- 1955 *Some Manifestations of Water in Mesoamerican Art.* Bureau of American Ethnology Bulletin 157, Anthropological Paper 48. Smithsonian Institution. Washington, D.C.

RATTRAY, R. S.
- 1927 *Religion and Art in Ashanti.* London. Clarendon Press.

RAY, DOROTHY JEAN
- 1967 *Eskimo Masks: Art and Ceremony.* Seattle. University of Washington Press.

REICHEL-DOLMATOFF, GERARDO
- 1959 "The Formative State, an Appraisal from the Colombian Perspective," in *Actas del 33 Congreso Internacional de Americanistas,* I. San José, Costa Rica.

REIK, THEODORE
- 1919 "Die Pubertätsriten der Wilden," in *Probleme der Religionspsychologie.* Vienna.

REINACH, S.
- 1903 "L'Art et la Magie. À Propos des Peintures et des Gravures de l'Age de Renne." *L'Anthropologie* 14.

RICARD, R.
- 1933 *La "Conquête Spirituelle" du Mexique.* Paris.

RIESMAN, PAUL
- 1960 *Freedom, Being, and Necessity.* M.S. Thesis. Harvard (unpublished).

ROBERTSON, DONALD
- 1959 *Early Colonial Mexican Manuscript Painting.* New Haven. Yale University Press.

ROGERS, CARL R.
- 1959 "Towards a Theory of Creativity," in *Creativity and Its Cultivation,* ed. H. H. Anderson. New York. Harper & Bros.

RÓHEIM, GÉZA
1930 *Animism, Magic and the Divine Kingdom.* London.
1941 "Myth and Folk-tale." *American Imago* 2:266–79.
1951 "Mythology of Arnhem Land." *American Imago* 8:181–87.
ROMERO DE TERREROS, M.
1923 *El Arte de México, las Artes Industriales en la Nueva España.* Mexico.
ROSTOVTZEFF, M. I.
1927 *A History of the Ancient World.* Oxford.
ROWE, JOHN H.
1961 "The Chronology of Inca Wooden Cups," in *Essays in Pre-Columbian Art and Archaeology,* ed. S. K. Lothrop and others. Cambridge. Harvard University Press. 317–41.
RUPPERT, KARL, THOMPSON, J. E. S., and PROSKOURIAKOFF, TATIANA
1955 *Bonampak, Chiapas, Mexico.* Carnegie Institution of Washington Publication 602.
SACHS, CURT
1937 *World History of the Dance.* New York. W. W. Norton.
1940 *The History of Musical Instruments.* New York. W. W. Norton.
SACHS, HANS
1951 *The Creative Unconscious,* 2nd ed. Cambridge, Mass.
SAHAGÚN, FRAY BERNARDINO DE
1959 *Book 9.* Trans. C. E. Dibble and A. J. O. Anderson. Santa Fe.
SANDERS, W. T.
1956 "The Central Mexican Symbiotic Region: a Study in Prehistoric Settlement Patterns," in *Prehistoric Settlement Patterns in the New World,* ed. G. R. Willey. Viking Fund Publications in Anthropology 23. New York. Wenner-Gren Foundation for Anthropological Research, Inc.
1957 *Tierra y Agua (Soil and Water). A Study of the Ecological Factors in the Development of Meso-American Civilizations.* Doctoral Dissertation. Harvard University.
SAPIR, EDWARD
1949 *Selected Writings of Edward Sapir in Language, Culture, and Personality,* ed. David G. Mandelbaum. University of California Press.
SCHAEDEL, MARY
1949 "Peruvian Keros." *Magazine of Art* XLII. New York.
SCHAEFFER-SIMMERN, HENRY
1958 *Eskimo Plastik aus Kanada.* Kassel. F. Lometsch, Verlag.

SCHAPIRO, MEYER
　1953　"Style," in *Anthropology Today*, ed. A. L. Kroeber. Chicago. University of Chicago Press.
SCHÄRER, HANS
　1946　*Die Gottesidee der Ngadju-Dajak in Süd-Borneo*. Leiden. E. J. Brill.
SCHUSTER, CARL
　1952　"A Survival of the Eurasiatic Animal Style in Modern Alaskan Eskimo Art," in *Selected Papers of the 29th International Congress of Americanists* III, ed. Sol Tax. Chicago. University of Chicago Press. 35–45.
SEMPER, G.
　1860　*Der Stil Die Stie in den technischen und tektomischen Künsten, oder praktische Ästhetik*. Frankfurt a.M./Stuttgart.
SHARPE, ELLA FREEMAN
　1950　"Certain Aspects of Sublimation and Delusion," in *Collected Papers on Psycho-Analysis*. London.
SHEPARD, A. O.
　1948　*The Symmetry of Abstract Design with Special Reference to Ceramic Decoration*. Carnegie Institution of Washington, Contributions to American Anthropology and History 47.
　1956　*Ceramics for the Archaeologist*. Carnegie Institution of Washington, Publication 609.
SHOOK, E. M., and KIDDER, A. V.
　1952　*Mound E-III-3, Kaminaljuyu, Guatemala*. Contributions to American Anthropology and History 11 (53).
SIEBER, R.
　1959　"The Aesthetic of Traditional African Art," in *7 Metals of Africa*. Catalogue of an Exhibition. Philadelphia. University of Pennsylvania Museum. 9–13.
　1964　Class notes; lectures given at the University of Wisconsin.
SIEGEL, SIDNEY
　1956　*Nonparametric Statistics for the Behavioral Sciences*. New York. McGraw-Hill.
SIMÓN, FRAY PEDRO
　1953　*Noticias Historiales*. Vol. II. Bogotá. Ministerio de Educación Nacional.
SMITH, M. W. (ed.)
　1953　*Asia and North America; Transpacific Contacts*. Society for American Archaeology, Memoir 9.
SPEISER, FELIX
　1924　*Südsee, Urwald, Kannibalen*. Stuttgart.
　1941　*Kunststile in der Südsee Führer durch das Museum für Völkerkunde*. Basel.

SPENCER, B.
1914 *Native Tribes of the Northern Territory of Australia.* London. Macmillan.

SPINDEN, H. J.
1913 *A Study of Maya Art, Its Subject Matter and Historical Development.* Peabody Museum Memoirs 6. Cambridge. Harvard University Press.

SPRATLING, W.
1955 "25 Años de Platería Moderna." *Artes de México* III. Mexico.

STEINMANN, ALFRED
1939 "Indonesische Textilien und ihre Ornamente," in *Ausstellung Indonesische Textilien.* Kunst gewerbemuseum Zürich.

STIRLING, M. W.
1943 *Stone Monuments of Southern Mexico.* Bureau of American Ethnology Bulletin 138. Washington, D.C.

STREHLOW, T. G. H.
1964 "The Art of the Circle, Line and Square," in *Australian Aboriginal Art,* ed. R. Berndt. New York. Macmillan.

SYDOW, ECKART VON
1928 *Primitive Kunst und Psychoanalyse.* Vienna.
1930 *Handbuch der Afrikanischen Plastik* I. Berlin.

TELLO, J. C.
1942 "Origin y Desarrollo de las Civilizaciones Prehistoricas Andinas," in *Actas y Trabajos Cientificos del XXVII Congreso Internacional de Americanistas, Lima, 1939* I. 589–720.
1943 "Discovery of the Chavín Culture in Peru." *American Antiquity* 9:135–60.
1960 *Chavín, Cultura Matriz de la Civilización Andina. Primera Parte.* Revised by T. Mejia Xesspe. Publicacion Anthropologica del Archivo "Julio C. Tello," Vol. 2. Lima. Universidad Nacional Mayor de San Marcos.

THAUSING, MORIZ
1884 *Dürer, Geschichte seines Lebens und seiner Kunst* II. Leipzig.

THOMPSON, J. E. S.
1948 *An Archaeological Reconnaissance in the Cotzumalhuapa Region, Escuintla, Guatemala.* Carnegie Institution of Washington, Contributions to American Anthropology and History 9 (44).

TILLMANN, GEORG
1940 "De Motieven der Batakweefsels." *Cultureel Indië* II:7–15.

TOZZER, A. M.
1930 "Maya and Toltec Figures at Chichen Itza," in *23rd International Congress of Americanists.* New York. 155–64.

TRILLING, LIONEL
1945 "Art and Neurosis," in *The Liberal Imagination*. New York. Viking Press.

TURNER, VICTOR
1964 "Betwixt and Between: the Liminal Period in *Rites de Passage*," in *Symposium on New Approaches to the Study of Religion*, ed. June Helm. Proceedings of the 1964 Annual Spring Meetings of the American Ethnological Society.

UCKO, P. J.
1965 *Anthropomorphic Figurines from Predynastic Egypt and Neolithic Crete*. London.

UHLE, MAX
1887 *Über die ethnologische Bedeutung der malaiischen Zahnfeilung*. Berlin.

VALCÁRCEL, L.
1932 "Vasos de Madera del Cuzco." *Museo Nacional de Lima, Revista* I. Lima.

VALENTINE, CHARLES A.
1961 *Masks and Men in a Melanesian Society; the Valuku or Tabuan of the Lakalai of New Britain*. University of Kansas Publications (Social Science Studies). Lawrence.

VANDENHOUTE, P. J. (L.)
1945 *Het Masker in de Cultuur en Kunst van het Boven-Cavallygebied*. Ms. Thesis. University of Ghent.
1948 *Classification Stylistique du Masque Dan et Guéré de la Côte d'Ivoire Occidentale (A.O.F.)*. Mededelingen van het Rijksmuseum voor Volkenkunde 4. Leiden.
1952 "Poro en Masker. Enkele beschouwingen over 'Masks as Agents of Social Control in Northeast Liberia' door Dr. G. W. Harley." *Kongo Overzee* 18:153-98.

VASTOKAS, JOAN M.
1967 "The Relation of Form to Iconography in Eskimo Masks." *The Beaver*. Autumn:26-31.

VISSER, R.
1906 *Jahresberichte des natürwissenschaftlichen Vereins zu Krefeld*.

VIVAS, ELISEO
1955 *Creation and Discovery, Essays in Criticism and Aesthetics*. New York. Noonday Press.

VON HAGEN, W. V.
1945 *La Fabricación del Papel entre los Aztecas y los Mayas*. Mexico.

WARBURG, A.
 1938-39 "A Lecture on Serpent Ritual." *Journal of the Warburg and Courtauld Institute* II. London.

WATERMAN, RICHARD A.
 1943 *African Patterns in Trinidad Music.* Doctoral Dissertation. Northwestern University (unpublished).
 1948 "'Hot' Rhythm in Negro Music." *Journal of the American Musicological Society* I:3-16.
 1951 "The Role of Spirituals and Gospel Hymns in a Chicago Negro Church." *Journal of the International Folk Music Conference* (London) III.

WAUCHOPE, ROBERT
 1954 "Implications of Radiocarbon Dates from Middle and South America." *Middle American Research Records* 2 (2). Middle American Research Institute, Tulane University. New Orleans.

WEIANT, C. W.
 1943 *An Introduction to the Ceramics of Tres Zapotes.* Bureau of American Ethnology Bulletin 139. Washington, D.C.

WEISMANN, ELIZABETH WILDER
 1951 *Mexico in Sculpture.* Cambridge.

WESTHEIM, PAUL
 1950 *Arte Antiguo de México.* Mexico. Fondo de cultura economica.

WETHEY, H.
 1949 *Colonial Architecture and Sculpture in Peru.* Cambridge. Harvard University Press.

WHITE, LESLIE A.
 1949 *The Science of Culture.* New York. Grove Press.

WHITING, J. W. M.
 1954 "The Cross-Cultural Method," in *Handbook of Social Psychology,* ed. G. Lindzey. Cambridge, Mass. Addison-Wesley.

WHITING, J. W. M., and CHILD, I. L.
 1953 *Child Training and Personality.* New Haven. Yale University Press.

WILLEY, G. R.
 1951 "The Chavín Problem, a Review and Critique." *Southwestern Journal of Anthropology* 7:103-44.
 1955 "The Prehistoric Civilizations of Nuclear America." *American Anthropologist* 57:571-93.
 1959 "The 'Intermediate' Area of Nuclear America; its Prehistoric Relationships to Middle America and Peru," in *Actas del 33 Congresco Internacional de Americanists* I. San José, Costa Rica.
 1960 "New World Prehistory." *Science* 131:73-83.

WILLIAMS, F. E.
1930 *Orokaiva Society.* London.
1940 *The Drama of Orokolo.* New York. Oxford University Press.

WILSON, JOHN
1947 "The Artist of the Egyptian Old Kingdom." *Journal of Near Eastern Studies* 6:231–49.

WINGERT, PAUL
1962 *Primitive Art.* New York. Oxford University Press.

WIRZ, PAUL
1950 "Der Ersatz für die Kopfjägerei und die Trophäen-Imitation." *Beiträge zur Gesellungs-und Völkswissenschaft* (Thurnwald-Festschrift). Berlin.

WOLF, E. R.
1959 *Sons of the Shaking Earth.* Chicago. University of Chicago Press.
1964 *Anthropology.* Englewood Cliffs, N.J. Prentice-Hall.

WOLFE, ALVIN W.
1969 "Social Structural Bases of Art." *Current Anthropology* 10:3–44.

INDEX

Abelam tribe, 394, 396, 397
Abstract art, xiii, 33; -primitive art, differences, 47–48
Acceptance, 107–8 and n
Acculturation, xv; African influence on music of the Americas, 227–44; arts, and their changing social function, 203–11; Pre-Columbian art motifs, colonial extinction, 212–26; subliminal culture patterns, 234
Acculturation in the Americas, 227n
Admiralties, arts, 384, 393–94
Adouma, 117
Aesthetic(s), xiii, 64, 92, 207; -anthropology, convergence, 67; comparative, 173–74; defined, 173; experience, 43–46, 66, 74–75, 77, 78; form, 40, 42, 49, 72, 91, 173; judgment, 59, 61, 172; of primitive art, 174; theory, 43, 77; Western, 204
Africa, 24, 124, 127, 249, 251; art, 35, 359, changes in, 209, cultural values, 205–7, 366–82, imperialism, 28, interpretations, 36, social change, 210–11, study of, 365, styles, 34, tools, 368–69; artists, 172–81, 251; British influence, 206; carving, 48, 368; "fetishes," 377–78; Ife art (see Ife); influence on music of the Americas, 227–44; Ivory Coast, 30–31; music, 93, 235, 240, 242 (see Afro-American music); sculpture, 30–31, 33, 39, 175, 354, 356, 367–70; self-image, 211. See under tribe and type of art
African Arts/Arts d'Afrique, 354n
African Worlds, 52
Afro-American music, 227n, 239; characteristics, 228–30, 233–38, 239n, 240, 242, 243–44; development, 230–32; Latin America, 239–40; Negro populations, 239–41; North America, 239, 240–41, 244; reasons for African influence, 227, 231–32, 238, 241; rhythm, 233, 238
Ahuitotl, 218
Aibom tribe, 396

Alaska, 318, 329, 342; Eskimo masks, 170; -Siberia link, 347
Alice in Wonderland, 168
Altamira, 166
America(n), 25; antiquity, extinction, 212, 223–25; art styles, 282; Indian societies, 324, end, 224–25, -Roman Empire, 223–24; native culture survivals, 216–17; Negro, cultural characteristics, 227, music, 231–33, 239, 241, 244, spirituals, 232, 240
American Anthropological Association, 140n, 282n
American Anthropologist, 140n, 282n
American Ethnological Society, 182n
American Museum of Natural History, 303
American Psychoanalytic Association, 106n
American Psychological Association, 3n
American Society of Aesthetics, 66n
Americas, 124; music, African influence, 227–44; primitive art, 106 (*see also* Oceania)
"Anaturalism," 106
Ancestors: -art, relationship, 113, 118; cult, 124, 266, 360, 392, 400; images, 121 and n, 124–25, 126 (*see* Masks)
Andamans, 104, 160, 161
Andes, 223
Animals, 3–19, 134, 137, 264, 265, 333–35; -man, relationship, 265, 266; Palaeolithic parietal art, 259, 260–62
Anthropologists, 160, 313, 356; art interpretation, 35–36
Anthropology: -aesthetics, convergence, 67; -arts, relationship, 61, 93–105, 182–83 (*see also* Arts-in-culture); development lines, 66–67, 77; limits, 297; methodology, 67, 98; new interest in behavior, 67; qualitative, art as introduction to, 66–92; "science," xi
Anthropomorphism, 114, 263
Apollinaire, Guillaume, 29, 30
Arabic music, 228
Arapesh, 161, 394, 396

Archaeologists, 137, 312, 313, 342
Archaeology, 160, 213; aims, 139; art, 129–30; chronology refinement, 139; grave looting, 311–12, 313, 314; Maya sites, 311, 312, 316
Architecture, 70, 87, 94, 96
Arctic, 163; art, vanishing, 341–53; burial cult, 346; culture change, 343; Ipiutak, 344, 345–47, 348, 350; man's conquest of, 341–42; Okvik style, 344, 349, 350–51; Old Bering Sea style, 344, 348, 349, 350, 351; Punuk style, 344, 348, 349, 350–51; shamanism, 346–47; skeletons, 346; Thule period, 351. *See* Eskimo
Arctic Sea, 341
Argentina, 242
Aristotle, 169
Arnhem Land, 119, 183n
Art: aesthetic-iconic, 63; ancient, 283; anthropological approach, xii; appreciation, 24–25, 56, 60–61, 74; aspects of, 66, 89–90, 203; characteristics, 55, 72, 77, 83–84; "communal," 176–77; conception, breadth of, 73–74; content, 143; criterion, 69; criticism (*see* Criticism); critics (*see* Critics); -culture, relationship, xi–xii; definitions, 71, 76–81, 90, 203; "enemy," 213; evaluation, 173; -experience, 46; folk or "community," 176; -for-art's-sake, 204, 248, 252–55; forms, 22, 24–25, 184, 345; function, 73, 104; historians, 62–63, 77, 129, 208; history, 92, 204; horizons, 25; icon and, 39–65; identification-understanding relationship, 108; imitation-of-reality, concept, 79; interpretation, 35–36; -life, interdependence, 110–11, 113; meanings, 26, 45, 46, 143; as mirror, 62, 63; -national policy, 27; *nouveau*, 22; objects, 190; origins, 22, 23, 78, 92; pan-human implications, 160; product, 183, 203; qualitative mode, 81–92; -society, relationship, 76, 147n, 183 *and* n; souvenir, 166, 210, 222, 329; "stages," 86–87; style, xii, 106–7; "survival," 222; symbolism, xiii–xiv, 213; theories, 21, 36, 76; in translation, 167; utility, 73; value, 79, 211; variables, 160–61; viewer, 45, 46; wish-fulfillment aspect, 159
Artifacts, 63
Artist, 69, 364–65; aboriginal, 122–28; aesthetic principles, 172; African, 366, 369–72; behavior, 97, 100; creativity, conditions, 185–87; critic, 172–81; expatriate, 222–23; -patron relationship, 206; personality, 144; primitive, 161ff., 173, 174–200; "primitives," 48; product, 69, 73, 100; role, 89–90, 100, 113; -society, relationship, 143–44
Artistic activity, 68–69, 76, 185; scope, 247; social, correlation, xi–xii; prestige, 192
Artist in Tribal Society, 172n
Arts: anthropology, relationship, 93–105 (*see* Arts-in-culture); characteristics, 96–97, 98; product-behavior, distinction, 97; reflection of cultural change, 208; social functions, 203–11; symbolism, 101–4; tribal, 210
"Arts and crafts." *See* Crafts
Arts-in-culture, 66, 68–69, 71–78, 92, 172; development, 93–94; influence, 90n; materiality, 70–71; Middle America, 135; studies, 81n, 93–94; universality, 76
Arts Magazine (The Art Digest), 20n
Arts of the South Seas, 383n
Ashanti, 125, 160, 161, 229–30
Asia, 216, 345, 346, 347, 392; migrants from, 383, 384
Aspects of Primitive Art, 39n
Atlantis, 357
Atomic theory, 84
Aubin tonalamatl, 220
Audience, 89, 90, 204
Australia, 20, 25, 112, 120, 122, 124, 125, 127, 384; aborigines, 42, 111, ancestors, 383, art, 252, 275, rock art, 248–51, 256, 257, 276, sacred art, 118–19, totemism, 279; artist, 251; initiation ceremonies, 251
Azcapotzalco, 299
Aztecs, 218, 222, 298; goldworkers, 51, 302, 306; style, 133, 134

Babira, 230n
BaFioti, 115–16, 120
Baga of French Guinea, 39
Bali, 67, 147n, 161
Bambara, 123, 183n, 367
Banks Islands, 113
Baoulé culture (Ivory Coast), 30–31
Barnes Collection, 40
Barren Grounds, 342
Barry, Herbert, III, 141n, 142, 147n, 154, 156–57, 160–61
Basongye people, 99–100
Batak (Sumatra), 119–20, 123
Baumann, Hermann, 121 *and* n
Bear cult, 347
Behavioralism, 97–99; -arts, 104
Belgian Congo, 99–100, 114–15
Bella Coola, 323
Benedict, Ruth, 100
Benin, 31, 52, 360, 361, 362–63
Bering Strait, 342, 343, 344; culture, 347–48
Bini art, 358
Birds, 114–15, 261, 327–28
Bismarck Archipelago, 400
"Black arts," 69
Black Sea, 345
Boas, Franz, 35–36, 66
Borneo, 111–12, 113, 115
Brass casting, 174
Brazil, music, 239, 241, 243–44
Britain, 28, 93; Africa, 206, 209; rock music, 243
British Museum, 303, 357
British New Guinea, 22
Buddhism, 84, 89
Bunzel, Ruth, 58–59, 60, 66
Burial cult, 187–90, 346
Bushmen, 248, 279

California, 321
Cambodia, 122
Cambridge University, 20
Cameroons, 174
Canada, 342; Department of Northern Affairs and National Resources, 166; National Museum, 347
Cannibalism, 390
Canoe building, 321
Cape Prince of Wales, 344, 348
Cape Spencer, 346, 347

Carnegie Corporation of New York, 227n
Carvings, 167, 207–8, 327–32; scrimshaw, 330. See *under* area *or* tribe
Cascade Mountains, 329
Casma Valley, 287
Cave paintings, 51; Franco-Cantabrian, xii; palaeolithic, 247–81; prehistoric, 213; totemism, 266. *See* Palaeolithic cave art
Caves, 278; use of, 274–76. See *under* name of cave
Cellini, Benvenuto, 298
Central America, 301
Central Asia, xv
Central Australia, 183n
Central Polynesia, 384, 387, 388; art, 385, 391; conquest kingdom, 389
Ceremonialism—art, 337–38
Chan-Chán, 300
Chaos, deliberate, 71
Chavín art style, 282–87, 291, 292, 296; causality, 292ff.; in cultural historical perspective, 287–90; dating, 287; -Olnec linkage, 288–90; as precursor to civilization, 290–92
Chavín de Huántar, 285–86, 287, 290–91
Chenchu, 160–61
Chiapas, 285, 292
Chibchachun (deity), 300
Chibchas, 300
Chichén Itzá, 130, 299, 316
Children, 275, 281
Chimpanzee, drawings, figural preferences, xiii, 3–19
Chimus, 299–300
China, 26, 296; clay sculpture, 315; music, 228; Ordos region, 345
Chinook, 321
Chiricahua, 160–61
Chiriqui, 304
Cholula, 214, 222
Christ, 341; dove, an analogy, 42
Christianity, 175; acculturation, 217; crucifixion, 221; cultural succession, 214; Eskimos, 353; symbolism, 71, 223–24
Churches, 111, 205, 340
Civilization, 60; criteria, 293
Classical imagery, 29

Index

Clay sculpture. *See* Jaina
Cobo, Father, 304
Codex Borbonicus, 220
Coe, Michael D., 282n, 284, 285, 286, 288, 290, 291, 295
Cognition, 82, 83
Collectors, 69; "approach," 182
Colombia, 289; goldwork, 300, 301, 302, 303, 309
Colonialization, 214 *and* n; cultural survivors, 225–26
Columbia River, 318, 321
Columbus, Christopher, 28
Comanche, 161
Commarque, 254
Communal art, 176–78
Communication, xiv; art, relationship, 90 *and* n
"Community" art, 176
Conceptualization, 97–98; music, 99–100
Congo art, "discovery," 28
Connoisseurs, 69
Contemporary art, 91, 173; native, 352
Cooking, as an art, 89
Copador, 136
Cortes, Hernando, 299
Costa Rica, 299
Covarrubias, 129, 284, 285, 292
"Crafts," 96
"Creations," 184n
Creativity: comparative, 173; conditions of, 185–97; cultural context, 182–200; expectation-evaluation norms, 198; incubation period, 186; "passion and decorum," 185, 194; primitive societies, 181; problem of, 173; process and artistic act, 184–85; Western, 173, 175, 177
Criticism (art): -art, relationship, 81; contemporary, 173; defined, 173; primitive societies, 174, 179
Critics (art), 59–60, 129, 137, 173, 175; -artist, interaction, 176, in African Society, 172–81
Croce, 76, 172, 175
Crow Indians, 102
Cuba, 227n; music, 241, 243–44
Cubism, 29, 32, 33, 122
Culhuacán Augustinian cloister, 222
Cultural change, 205–6, 208
Cultural conflicts-arts, xv, 213

Cultural patterns, 66–67, 72
Culture(s): art, 92; aspects of, 94, 95, 140; change (introgression), 293–94; development, regional differentiation as precondition, 296; explants, 216, 219–21; fragmentation, 216, 222; human value-systems, xi; interplay, 167, 171, 216–19; intra-areal heterogeneity, 294–95; juxtaposition, 216–17; native, survival modes, 216; oral, 170; termination (*see* Eschatology); transplants, 216, 221–22. *See* Arts-in-culture
Current Anthropology, 163n
Cuzco, 300

Dadaism, 71
Dahomey, 160; music, 229
Dan (people), 366, 367, 371–72, 373; concepts of beauty, 380–81; masks, xii, 376ff.; religion, 373–76
Dance, 89, 93, 94, 96; African, 233, 235; literature, xv; masks, 34–35; medium, 70; music, 241–42; primitive, function, 110; ritual, 118–19, 121, 125; symbolism, 101, 102
Danish National Museum, 352
Danzantes (Monte Alban), 133–35
Darwin, Charles, 21, 85
Darwinism, 21
Datu, 119, 120
Da Vinci, Leonardo, 68
Dayaks, 111–12, 115
De Anda, Luis A. A., 311, 313
Decoration, 27, 110
Decorative Art of British New Guinea, 20
Decorative arts, 75, 86, 87
Denmark Strait, 344
Design, 145, 146–48 *and* n, 151, 153
Dewey, John, 76, 78–79
Dieu d'Eau ("God of Water"), 41
Diomede Islands, 344, 348
Dogon (people), 40–42; art, understanding, 50; twin figures, 40, 41, 45, 46, 49, 50, 55, 56, 63
Don Juanism, 153n
Dorset carvings, 167
Drama, 94, 96

Drawings: chimp-child relationship, 18–19; primitive people, 26
Dublin, Ireland, 20
Dürer, Albrecht, 24–25, 298
Dutch Guiana, 239
Dutch interiors, 53

Early Christian art, 218
East Africa, 248n
East Cape, Siberia, 342, 343, 344, 347, 348
Easter Island, 114, 122, 384, 386; stone sculptures, 23, 350
Ecuador, 289, 300; Chorrera phase, 290; goldwork, 302, 304
Egypt, 289, 301, 354, 357, 359; arts, 26, 315
Einstein, Albert, 82
El Greco, 47
Encyclopedia Britannica, 172
Engraving, 247, 251; rock, 251
Enlightenment, 26, 212, 213
Environment, 164; art, relationship, 252, 326
Epigraphy, 130
Eschatology, 213, 223
Eskimos, 67, 124, 163–71, 322, 328, 343; art, 163–71, aboriginal, 166–67, ancient classic, 344, souvenir, 166–67, styles, 344–45; artifacts, 165–66; carvings, 51, 163, 165, 166, 170, 183n; characteristics, 168, 170; culture, 342, 351, neo-, 343, 349, paleo-, 343, 345; design, 329; environment, 164–65, 168; "fossil ivory," 349; history, 342–43; language, 164; masks, xii, 352–53; oral tradition, 168, 169; origin, 342, 344; Polar, 341; religion, 353; sites, 342, 345, 349, 350
Ethiopians, 24
Ethnography, xv, 66, 174, 256, 323; parietal art, 247–51
Ethnology, 50, 51, 61; -art, 61
Ethnomusicology, 93, 98, 227n, 229, 230
Ethos, of an epoch, 172
Euro-African musical syncretism, 230
Euro-American culture pattern, 227
Europe, 141, 208, 209, 212, 223–24, 301, 331, 342, 389; art, 26, 215, 332, 357, 20th century, 106; artist, 364–65; calendar, 219; Central, 215; folk music, 228, 230, 232, 235; heraldry, 218; metallurgy, 302, 303; music, 234–35, 243, -African differences, 233–38; Paleolithic, 62; traders, 321; Western, 260–61
Exhibitions, 27
Experience, 78, 81; Iconic, 44; as origin of art, 92
Explorers, 25, 26, 312, 400; 18th century, 320–31, 329, 331; Polynesian, 387
Extinct cultures, reconstructing, 160

Fairy tales, art, 167, 168
Fertility cult, 31, 255–66, 279
"Fetishes," 110, 115–16, 377–78
Figures, primitive, 106; function, 110; Western reaction to, 109–10
Figurine art. *See* Jaina
Fiji, 384, 385
"Fine arts," 283
Flaubert, Gustave, 22–23
Folk music, 176, 228, 230, 232, 235
Form: art definition, 203; quality linkages, 90
France, 312; 20th century artists, 31. *See* Paris
Franciscans, 216, 217
Franco-Cantabrian cave painting, xii
Franco-Flemish Renaissance, 25
Freedom, Being, and Necessity, 163
French Congo, 117
French Equatorial Africa, 33
French Guinea, 39
French Sudan, Bambara sculpture, 31
French West Africa, 366
Freud, Sigmund, xiii, 68, 103, 114; dream censorship, 109
Function (art), 27, 73, 75
Funerary figures, 40, 41

Gabun, 29
Gauguin, 23–24, 27, 106; eclecticism, 23, *Self-Portrait,* 23
Gba, 175 *and* n
Geist, Otto, 347, 349, 350
George III, King of England, 25

Index

Gere (people), 366, 367, 372, 373, 377, 378, 379, 381–82
Germany, 29, 93, 356, 400; Bronze and Iron Age remains, 29; vitalist art theory, 36
Glyphs, 218–19
Goemai, 208
Gold, 298, 301
Gold Coast, 229
Goldsmiths: ancient American, 298–310; annealing, 302–3, 304, categories, 298–99, techniques, 301–2, 309, tools, 309–10, volume and value, 301; esteem, 300; Renaissance, 298
Göttingen University, 25
Graphic art, 183n, 185
Grave looting, 311–12, 313, 314
Greco-Roman civilization, ending, 224
Greece, 24, 304, 357; ethos-art relationship, 62; European sculpture, 354, 357, 359; Orthodox Church, ikons, 42; Tanagra figurines, 315
Greenland, 342, 343
Grove, Richard, 66n
Guardian spirit cult, 324–25
Guatemala, 285; Lake Atitlán, 316; marimba, 342; Ocos pottery, 290
Guerrero, 285
Guianas, 302
Guillaume and Monroe, 40, 42, 44, 45, 49, 56–57
Guinea, 29; Coast, 357
Gunther, Erna, 318

Haddon, Alfred C., 20–23, 24, 35, 66
Haida Indian, 43, 51, 322, 323, 329, 331
Haiti, 239, 243–44
Hampatong, 111–12
Harvard University, 142, 212n
Haselberger, Herta, 93, 163n, 166
Hausa, 207, 209, 210
Hawaii, 25, 26
Head-hunting, 115
"Heathen figures," 110
Herbalism, 208
Herodotus, 24, 341
Hervey Islands, 385
Heye Research Center, 170
Hidalgo, 221
Hindu music, 234

Hopi Indians, 51, 161, 216; *kachina*, 51
Huarmey collar, 303
Huastec style, 133
Humanities, 94, 95–96, 105; models, 170
Humanity, new concept of, 36
Humboldt Bay, 121
Huon Gulf, 384

Iatmül tribe, 394, 396
Iberian sculpture, 32
Ibo, 178, 206, 364
Ica Valley, 287
Icon: analogy, 42; art and, 39–65, opposing claims, 47, 49, works, 46, 47; defined, 42; experience, 44; meanings, 43
Iconography, 208; Olmec, 284
Ife: art, 354–65: discovery, 356, origin, 359, sculptures, 354, 356, 357, Yoruba, 364, twin-figures, 357
Ifo masks, 183n
Ifugao, 161
Igala: carvings, 207–8; changes in arts, 209–10; mask, 208–9
Imperialism, 28; -art, relationship, 27
Impressionism, 106
Incas, 221, 291, 299, 300, 304
India, xv, 113, 216
Indian arts, 26; Northwest Coast, 35–36; Southwest, 51
Indigenismo, 224
Indo-Arabic area, 228
Indonesia, xv, 34, 110, 392, 403
Infanticide, 279
Information storage, media, xiv
Initiation rites, 114, 251
"Innovations," 184n
Interior decoration, 87–88
International Institute of Africanists, 52
Introgression, 293–94
Intuition, 70, 76
"Inventions," 184n
Ireland, 20
Iroquois Indians, 102
Isla de los Sacrificios (Veracruz), 316
Islam, 218, 378, 381
Italy, 25; Renaissance, 215

Itumba mask, 33
Ivory Coast, 30, 366

Jaina: archaeological remains, interpreting, 316; expeditions, 312, 313; figurines, 311, 314–15, 317; graves, 313–14, 315; inaccessibility of site, 312; Maya ceremonial center, 315–16; occupation dates, 316–17
Jamaica, 240
Japan, 216, 351; art, 147n, 209; current, 331; medieval, 60
Javanese culture—symbolic activities, xiv
Joyce, James, 170
Judeo-Christian concepts, 26

Kama Sutra, 89
Kamchatka, 318
Kaminaljuyu, 135, 292
Klee, Paul, 35, 167–68, 170
Kluckhohn, Clyde, 140n, 147n
Kodiak Island, 318
Koran, 378; law, 209
Korvar (ancestor figures), 34, 121–22
Kramer, Hilton, 20n
Kroeber, A. L., 72, 282, 283, 286, 289
Kubler, George, xv, 212, 214n, 215n, 217, 218
Kulab, 124
Kulu ("soul"), 116
Kuntur Wasi, 287
Kurath, Gertrude, xv, 93, 102
Kuskokwim Eskimos, 124
Kwakiutl, 160–61, 324–25, 332, 334, 338
Kwoma tribe, 394, 395, 396, 397

Labastide cave, 274–75
Lake Atitlán (Guatemala), 316
Landscape painting, 87
Langer, Susanne, xiii, xiv, 101
Language, symbolic nature, xiii
Lapps, 342
Larsen, Helge, 345, 346, 352
Las Aldas, 288
Lascaux, 166; animals, 265, 278
Latin America: African influence on music, 239–44; Euro-African musical syncretization, 231; "Mestizo art," 215; suppression of artistic expressions, 213–14
La Tuc D'Audoubert cave, 275
La Venta, 131, 285, 288, 290
Law, 209
Leroi-Gourhan, 254, 258, 259, 260n, 264, 266–74, 276, 280; parietal art, interpretation, 266–74
Liberian masks, 39
Lima, 223
Lime, 34
Linton, Ralph, 123–24, 184n, 383 *and* n
Literacy, 147n, 170
Literature, 87; aesthetic experience, 75; anthropological, 94; "folklore," 93; oral, 93, 94, 96, 97, function, 104, symbolism, 102
London: Exhibitions, 27
Lower Central America, 289
Lower Congo, carvings, 31–32
"Lower sense arts," 89

McAllester, David P., 67, 102–3; *Enemy Way Music,* 102
Magdalenian period, 260, 342; caves, 51
Magic, 113, 119–20, 256; aboriginal rock art, 248; classic division, 256; sympathetic, 248–49, 255. *See* Totemism
Malanggan (images), 118
Malay: *kabasaran,* 113
Malraux, André, 40, 52; *Voices of Silence,* 40
Mammoth, 260, 261
Man-animals, distinctions, xii–xiii
Mangareva (Central Polynesia), 35
Maori, 112, 125, 161, 386; art, 27, 386. *See* New Zealand
Maps, 218
Marquesas, 123, 161, 350, 390; arts, 384; -Maori, similarities, 391
Marriage, form of—art style, relationship, 152–56, *Table 3,* 154
Marshalls, 161
Masai, 160–61
Masks: African, 366, 367, 369–70, Dan, 376ff., types, 378–79; ancestral, 121 *and* n, 126, 378; begging, 379; Belgian Congo, 114; carved after death, 118; Dan, xii, 376ff.; dance, 34–35,

Index 435

379; Eskimo, xii, 170, 352; "face," xii; Ibo, 206; Ifo, 183n; Itumba, 33; Liberian, 39; Melanesian, 39; Mende, xii; New Ireland, 402; Northwest Coast Indian, 324, 337–39; palaver, 379; primitive, 106–7, function, 110, Western reaction to, 109–10; sacrificial, 378; Sepik, 114; skulls, function, 112–13; "spirit," xii; symbolism, 115; Upper Cavally, 381
Materiality, 70–71
Mathematics, 78–79, 91
Matisse, Henri, 29
Matriliny, xi, xii
Mayas, 130, 131, 299, 314; archaeological sites, 311, 312, 317; art, 129, 314–15; Jaina, 315–16, 317; *Study of Classic Maya Sculpture*, 131; style, 133, 134, 135
Mbouéti, 117
Mead, Margaret, 125, 183n
Medieval Ages: Cathedral, 205, -arts relationship, 340
Mediterranean, 358; antiquity, 214, 218; music, 228
Medium, selecting, 70–71
Melanesia, 34, 63, 117, 127, 349, 383, 384, 392–94, 400; art, 385–86, 393, 404; cultural characteristics, 392; Maori, 391; masks, 39, 47
Melville Island, 185
Mendoza Codex, 309n
Merriam, Alan P., xiii, xv, 93, 94, 95, 96, 100
Mesoamerica, 133, 287–88, 290–96; art style, 282, 283, 291 (*see* Olmec, Classic Period), 311, pre-Classic, 285; sites, 316; water cult, 316. *See* Middle American Art
Mesolithic culture, 343
Mesopotamia, 26, 289
"Mestizo art," 215
Metallurgy, 301, 302, 304, 331–32, 358. *See* Goldsmiths
Mexico, 25, 215, 218, 311, 312; art: ancient, 27, motif survivals, 214; calendar, 219; Enlightenment, 213; excavations, 212; folk music, 242; goldwork, 298ff., 301, 309n; "open chapels," 217–18;

pre-Columbian themes, 213 *and* n; Tenochtitlan, 219; Toltecs, 299
Mexico City, 212, 312; National Museum of Anthropology, 312, 313
Michelangelo, 47
Michoacán, 221
Micronesia, 383, 384, 385
Middle Ages, 111, 141, 223–24
Middle American Anthropology, 129n
Middle American Art: Aztec, 133, 134; Classic, 133–35, 138, 139; Copan, 136; -crafts, interaction, 134–35; -culture, relationship, 135; Danzantes, 133–34; data, 130; design data, 130ff.; Esperanza Phase, 131; ethnographic details, 130; form analysis, 131–33; grotesque, 134; Huastec, 133; jaguar, 134, 139; Kaminaljuyu, 131; Maya, 133, 134, 135; Mixtec, 133, 134, 135; motifs, 138; Olmec, 131, 133, 134; Santa Lucia Cotzumalhuapa, 134; schools, 131–32; studies, 129–39; styles, 133–34, 137–38; symbolism, 130, 134, 139, Tajin, 131; Teotihuacan, 133, 136; time-space reconstructions, 139; Toltec, 133, 134; Totonac, 133; unity, clue to, 139; Yucatan, 132; Zapotec, 133
Missionaries, 26, 28, 217
Mixtec style, 134
Modern, art, 46, 47, 48; industrial, 223; -primitive, relationship, 32–33, 36, 46–48 (*see* Picasso)
Modigliani, 35
Moluccas, 113
Monogamy—art style, 153–56
Monte Alban, 291–92
Montespan cave, 274
Montezuma, 299
Montol, 208
Moore, Henry, 39
Morelos, 285
Mortuary art, 399–400
Moslem arts, 26–27
Motifs, 138–40, 213ff., 284
"Movement," 48
Mozart, Wolfgang A., 168
Muensterberger, Warner, xiv, 106 *and* n, 110, 111, 113, 122

Mundugumor tribe, 34, 394, 396, 397
Munn, Dr. Nancy, 182n, 183n
Munro, Thomas, 71, 76
Murdock, George P., 141n, 142 *and* n, 149, 154, 160; "World Ethnographic Sample," 142, 157
Murngin, 161
Musée de l'Homme (Paris), 331
Museo Nacional, 218
Museum of Natural History, 49
Museum of Primitive Art, 39 *and* n, 49, 52, 53, 54, 61
Museums, 26, 331, 347, 348, 349, 357, 365, 382; art-ethnological, rivalries, 63–64; colonial, 33; ethnographical, 39; exhibition techniques, 27–28; experiences of viewers, 45; as sanctuary for artistic role-playing, 69
Music, 70, 87, 94, 96, 101, 239; African, 93, 228–30, Europe, 230–31, influences on Americas, 227–44 (*see* Afro-American music); Americas: African influence on, 227–44; anthropology of, xv; Basongye, 99–100; "blues" scale, 238; calypso, 239, 240; China, 228; Europe, 230–31, 234, 238, 239n; folk, 176; "folk-rock," 243; Freudian conceptions, 103; handclapping, 234; Hindu, 234; jazz, 232, 235, 242–43; Latin America, 239; Northwest Coast Indians, 339; "rhythm and blues," 241; "rock-and-roll," 243; "soul," 241, 243; studies, 97; symbolism, 101–3; syncretization, 230–31, 232; West African, 238–39
Muslim art, 62
Mythology, 100, 140

National Geographic Expedition, 182n
National Museum of Canada (Ottawa), 331
National Museum of Ethnology (Leiden), 382
Native art, power of belief, 353
Native cultures, survival modes, 216
Natural History, 298n, 311n
Naturalism, 106; aesthetic of, 176
Natural sciences, models, 170
Natural selection theory, art, 21

Nature-art, relationship, 79
Navahos, 67, 72, 75, 102, 160, 161, 247; culture, 68; dry painting, 183n; form-quality linkages, 81n; music, symbolism of, 102
Nazca, 215n, 292
Nazca Valley, 287
Near East, xv; Ancient, 304
"Negro Africa," music, 229–30
Negro sculpture, 28, 29, 32, 40
Neo-Classicism, 26
Nepeña Valley, 287
New Britain, 112–13, 400, 404; art, 393
New Caledonia, 403
Newcomb College, Art Department, 156
New England whalers, 329–30
New Guinea, 20, 113, 114, 121, 384, 386; Massim area, 393–94; Orokaiva, 118; Papuans, 383, 385, 393; sculpture (*korvar* figures), 183n; Sepik (*see* Sepik River area); South, 34
New Hebrides, 35, 112, 113, 124–25, 393, 403
New Ireland, 112, 117, 124, 183n, 399–404; art, 399, 400, 403, 404; culture, 400; *kapkap*, 404; Lesu, 117–18; *Malagan*, 400, 401–2, 403; masks, 402
New Mecklenburg, 400
New South Wales, 114
New World civilization: factors influencing, 296–97; Golden Axis, 299
New York Academy of Science, 203n; *Annals*, 203n
New Zealand, 25, 27, 384; arts, 384, 385, 390–92; Maori, 112, 125, 386, 387, 389, 390–92, cannibalism, 390, jade, 387–89, tatooing, 389
Nigeria, 28, 207, 360; artists, contemporary, 364–65; arts, 364, changes in, 209–10; central, 174; Ife sculptures (*see* Ife); Nok sculptures, 354–56; Northern, 208; Southern, 360
Nigerian Museum in Lagos, 174
Niger River, 40
Noa Noa, 23
Nok culture, 354, 355, 356, 358; sculptures, 355–56

Index

Non-literate peoples: arts-late civilizations, relationship, xi, xiv
Non-objective art, 46, 47, 87, 91
Nootka-Kwakiutl, 323, 324, 328, 329, 331, 338; Wolf Ritual, 338
Nootka Sound, 331
Norsemen, 342
North Africa, 27, 209, 215
North America, 247, 256, 301
North Pacific Coast, 322
North Pole, 342
Northwest Coast Indian Art (catalogue), 318n
Northwest Coast Indians, 170, 318–40; animals, 333; art: anatomy, 326–32, basis, 324–26, relation of environment, 333–36, sculpture, 327, -social patterns, relationship, 323–24, 336–40, styles, 322, 329, 332, uses, 336–40; Cannibal Society, 325, 334, 338; climax of society, 32; cultural development, 322, 324; dance, 337, 339–40; European contact, 331; "Grease Trails," 321; masks, 337–39; music, 339; religion, 324; totem poles, 319, 322, 323; "tribes," 322, 323, 328, 338–39
Northwestern University, 227n
Nuclear America, 290, 292, 293

Oaxaca, 130
Ob River, 345
Oceania, 112, 113, 114, 121, 122, 391, 394; art, 33–34, 35, 384–86, 395, 404, sources, 399, styles, 34, Western reaction to, 109; cultures, 383ff.; major regions, 384
Oedipus situation, 153
Okvik-Ipiutak art, 167
"Okvik Madonna," 166
Old Bering Sea culture, 347
Olmec art style, 129, 133, 134, 282, 284–87; causality, 292ff.; Chavín linkage, 288–90; climax region, 285, 287; in cultural historical perspective, 287–90; dating, 285; derivative influences, 292; iconography, 284; monuments, 291; motifs, 284; precursor to civilization, 290–92; religion, 296; theme, 284
Omaha, 160–61

Onitsha, 360
On the Music of the North American Savages, 93
"Open chapels," 217–18
Order, primitive understanding of, 52
Organization of American States, 129n
Oriental civilizations, 141
Ornaments, 112, 114; analysis of, 27
Orokaiva, 118
Ortega y Gasset, José, 45, 46, 47, 50, 53–54
Ottawa, Canada, 331
Owo, 360

Pacific, 331, 350
Pahouin (West Africa), 122
Painting, 44, 70, 71, 106, 247
Paiute, 161
Paleolithic art, xii, 166
Palaeolithic cave (parietal) art: animals, 259–64, 270–71, 277, 278; anthropomorphism, 263; art-for-art's-sake, 252–55; art galleries, 254, -Australian aborigines, 248–50; characteristics, 257–58, 260n, 263–64, 272, 276, 280–81; children, 281; classification, 253; conclusion and problems, 274–81; content, 260–61, 263, 269, 276, 277, 278; context, 252–53, 254, 256, 274; critical analysis, 247–81; ethnographic parietal art, 247–51; intent, 259; Leroi-Gourhan, 266–74; localities, 276–77; magic, 256, 277, 278; meaning, 274; purpose, 278–79, 281; religious importance, 258, 273; signs, analysis, 266ff.; superpositioning, 254–55, 258–59, 269, 276–77; symbolism, 268 *and* n, 271–74, 280; techniques, 254–55; "theatre," 278; "themes," 270–71, 280; totemism, 255–66
Palaeolithic man, 252, 274–76; environment, 278
Palaeolithic period, 260–61
Panama, 299, 301, 302; Chiriqui, 302, 304
Pan American Union, 129n
Pan-human implication of art, 160
Papago, 161

Papuan Gulf, 34–35
Papuans, 22, 383
Parietal art: ethnographic, 247–51; -mobile, differences, 274. *See* Palaeolithic cave art
Paris, 28, 331; Expositions, 27
Parsons, Talcott, 76
Patios de Indios, 300
Patron-artist relationship, 210
Pax Britannica, 206
Peary, Admiral, 342
Peru, 214, 215n, 222n, 288, 290–92, 296; art, 214, 282, 283 (*see* Chavín); colonialization, 214n; culture area, 287; environment, 294–95; excavations, 285–86, 289n; goldsmiths, 299–300, 301, 302, 304; Incaic Period, 299; *keros* and *pakchas,* 220–21; mochica art, 292; prehistory, 287; religion, 296
Philosophy, 78, 86; -arts, function of, 100–1
Photography, 87
Picasso, Pablo, 29, 48, 49, 109; primitive art, 32–33; self-portrait, 32
Plains Indians, 63, 325
Plastic art, 183n
Platinum, 300–1
Plato, 24; *Laws,* 24
Platonic Idealism, 205
Poetry, 87, 108n, 163, 165
Point Hope, Alaska, 343, 344, 345, 347, 352–53
Polar Eskimo, 341
Polygamy, 153–56
Polygyny, 154–55, 156, 159
Polynesia(ns), 23, 34, 52, 113, 321, 383, 384, 386–92; art, 24, 35
"Poro Society mask," 39
Portraiture, 87
Portugal, 216, 231
Post-Impressionists, 60
Pottery, 135–36, 288, 395
Pound, Ezra, 170
"Powder metallurgy," 301
Pre-Columbian art motifs, colonial extinction, 212–26; convergence, 216, 217–19; destruction, 224–25; eschatology, 223; explants, 216, 219–21; fragmentation, 216, 222; heraldic and commemorative records, 218; interest in, 312; juxtaposition, 216–17; language, 214; manuscripts, 219–20, 221; murals, 222; native survivals, 222–23; picture-writing, 218; pre-Conquest: construction, 217, peoples, 24, themes, 214–15; provincial or folk art, 215; religion, 226; survivals, 214–16; symbolism, 214, 219, 221–22; transplants, 216, 221–22; utility, 214; values, 221; *Xicalcoliuhqui,* 222
Pre-Columbian civilization, 290, 301; and early great styles, 282–97. *See* Chavín *and* Olmec
Pre-Conquest, 217, 218, 298ff. *See* Pre-Columbian art motifs
Pre-literate culture, xiv
Prestige-cultural change, 207
Primates, non-human, aesthetics of, xii–xiii
Primitive art: aesthetics, 174; aggression, 117; ambivalent attitudes toward, 23–24; ancestral cult, 118, 121 *and* n, 124–25, 126; appreciation, 24–25, 26, 27, 35, 108; "art," 110; artist, 122–25, 127–28; characteristics, 33, 36, 38, 113–15, 118; collections, 25–26; colonialism, 33–34; death, 119–21; discovery, 20–36, 106–7; evaluating, 172–73; exploration, 26; fertility rites, 118; fetishes, 115–16; function, 110; Haddon's evolutionary theory, 22, 23; as icon, 49; images, 118; initiation rites, 118; interpretations, 29–32, 122; killing, 117, 127; magic, 110, 119–21; man's aims, 124; meanings, 43, 51, 53, 61–62; missionaries, 26; modern affinity for, 32; modern art, comparison, 46–48; 19th century, 26; Picasso, 32–33; precepts, 172–73; preconditions, 127–28; primitive life, parallels, 52–53; processual approach to, 183 *and* n; psychic force, 110; roots, 106–28; sacred, 118–19; sailors, 26; sculpture, 122; skulls, 115, 117, 118, 122; "spookiness," 35; styles, 48, 121–22; symbolism, 114, 115, 118–19; 20th century, 28–29, 32; universal patterns, 126; viewing, 27–

30, 46, 47, 48–55; Western critics, 59–60, 109; women, 123–25, 127
Primitive Negro Sculpture, 40
Primitive societies, 60, 110, 114, 118, 123, 250, 256, 278; aesthetics, 58, 59, 181; artist, 113, 122–25, 161ff., 174–200; art-life interdependence, 110–11, 113; criticism, 174; ethnological accounts, 51; "living," 276, 279, 281; man-animal relationship, 265, 266; oldest views of, 29–30; parallel patterns, 126; style, 58, 62; world view, 52, 63
Primitivism: "hard" and "soft" concepts, 30
Product (art), significance, 104–5
Proskouriakoff, Tatiana, 129, 292
Proto-literate culture, xiv
"Pseudo-ethnographic" art objects, xv
Psychical distance, 72, 74
Psychoanalysis, 108
Psychology of art, 77, 81n, 92
Public object, 71–72, 75, 76
Pucara culture, 292
Pueblo Indians, 58, 59, 60, 216–17 *and* n; revolt, 319
Puerto Rico, 240
Puget Sound, 337, 339
Purist-relationist paradox, 90–91

Qualitative experience, 83–86, 88, 92
Qualitative mode, art and, 81–92
Quatsino, 338
Queen Charlotte Islands, 329

Radiocarbon dating, 285, 287, 343, 344, 354, 362
Raleigh, Sir Walter, 302
Rangga, 118, 119, 125
Reality-art, relationship, 87
Recuay culture, 292
Reindeer, 260 *and* n, 261, 280, 342
Relationism, in arts, 91–92
Religion, 88, 89, 114, 141, 214, 296; as prime causal force, 293
Renaissance, 24, 39, 219, 223, 224, 298
Riesman, David, 140n
Rock art, 248–50. *See* **Caves** *and* **Palaeolithic cave art**

Rockefeller Institute, 219
Roheim, Géza, xiv, 106n, 119, 120
Romanticism, 27, 141
Rome, Ancient, 223, 344, 359; American Indian, comparison, 223–24
Rouffignac cave, 260, 261
Royal Anthropological Institute, 172n
Russia, 345, 349. *See* Soviet Union

Sahagún, Friar, 220, 298, 301, 306
St. Lawrence Island, 347, 348, 349–50
Salish, 322, 323, 324–25, 339
Salvador, 285
Samoa, 25, 161, 385
Samoyeds, 342
San Agustín sculptures, 289
Sandawe, 248n
Sand paintings, 247
Santa Lucia Cotzumalhuapa, 134
Science, 84–85, 86, 90n, 91
Sculpture, 70; development, 122; primitive mass production, 110; 20th century, 106. *See under* Africa, Jaina, Ife *and* Nok
Senegal, 29
Senoufo, 367
Senses, interplay, 168–71
Sepik River area, 34, 112, 122, 403; art, 114, 384, 385, 393–99
Sex: as an art, 89; differences-design preferences, 153. *See* Symbolism
Siberia, 342, 345, 346, 350, 351, 353; Alaska, link, 347; Animal Style, 345
Slavery, 33–34, 231, 242, 389
Social science, 66–67, 70, 80, 105, 170; art, 67, 92; humanities, 94–96; methodology, 66–67; Research Council, 227n
Societies: artist, relationship, 142–43; social conditions-art style, 140–60, 203–11; wish fulfillment, 159–60
Solomons, 112, 113, 114; arts, 384, 393–94
Southampton Island, 351
Southeast Asia, 34, 113
South Pacific, 33, 349
South Seas, 23, 25, 114; art, 384–

85, 386, primitive, 106, 109; idyllic vision of life, 33
Souvenir art, 166, 210, 222, 329
Soviet Union, 93, 167, 342; West, 225. *See* Russia
Space, 168, 169, 170
Spain, 215, 221n, 231, 240, 247, 248; Conquest, 301, 316, 319; American confrontation, 224–25
Spiritualized violence, concept, 29
Styles, 48, 55–56, 72, 106–7, 208, 344; acceptance-rejection, 107–8; characteristics, 81, 137; as cultural maps, 140–60; determinants, 158; diffusion, 158–59; early great, 282–97; evolution, 66; great art as criteria of civilization, 293; modern art, 48; new success determinants, 109; 19th century, 22–23; primitive art, 48–49, 58, 121; reality, 72; social conditions, 140–60; standards, 210, 283; technique, 66; traditional, and social change, 210–11; vs. motif, 138–40
Sumatra, 123, 396; Batak, 119–20
Surrealists, 35
"Survival art," 222
Swaixwe mask, 324, 325
Symbolism, 82–83, 89, 91, 101–4, 114–15, 193n, 213–14, 225, 247; calendrical, 219; feline, 292; Freud, xiii–xiv; Middle American art, 130, 134; Pre-Conquest, 221–22; primitive art, 115; rock art, 250, 268 *and* n, 271–74; sex, 155
Syrian *kalybe,* 218

Tabasco, 284, 285, 288
Tahiti, 25, 26
Tanagra figurines, 315
Tchambuli tribe, 394, 396
Teotihuacan style, 133, 136, 292
Thonga, 142, 161
Tiahuanaco art, 222, 292
Tiv, 174, 176–78, 181
Tiwi; creativity, 182–200; *pukamani,* 188, 190, 193n, 198; values, 190–93
Tlatilco, 288–89, 292
Tlingit, 322, 323, 331, 332, 339
Toltec, 130, 133, 134; Period, 299

Totemism, 43, 248, 251, 255–66, 319, 322, 323, 336
Toulouse-Lautrec, 106
Tourism-art deterioration, xv
Tourist art, 210, 329. *See* Souvenir art
Trinidad, 239, 240
Tsimshian, 51, 322, 323, 331

Universality, 76, 90n
University of Alaska, 349, 353; Museum, 348
University of Leipzig, 93
University of Pennsylvania Museum, 182n
University of Tokyo, 289n
U. S. National Museum, 348, 349
Utility, 73–74, 75; survival, 214

Values, xv, 190, 205, 210
Vancouver, 322, 324
Van Gogh, 27, 106
Veracruz, 131, 134, 242, 284, 285, 316; Classic style, 292; Tabasco region, 287
Visual arts, 94, 96, 97; social meaning, 141–43
Vodun cult, 239

Water cult, 316
West Africa, 56, 121, 127, 238–39, 241, 244, 358; art, 106, 109, 110, 127, 355; Ashanti, 125; Ba-Fioti, 115–16; Pahouin heads, 122
Western civilization, 60–61, 173, 175, 204, 228; art, xiv–xv, 28, 110; Classical concepts, 26; literacy, xiv
Wobe (people), 366, 367, 372, 373, 378, 381–82

Xipe Totec, 222, 298, 299

Yakut, 160–61
Yoruba, 174, 210, 358; art, 357, 363; Ife, 364
Yucatan, 132, 217–18, 299, 311, 317

Zapotec, 51, 133
Zuñi, 58, 63, 100, 161